Boeing 727

TRIUMPH

IN THE SKIES

Dan Dornseif

SCHIFFER MILITARY

4880 Lower Valley Road · Atglen, PA 19310

Copyright © 2020 by Dan Dornseif

Library of Congress Control Number: 2020930872

"Schiffer Military" and the arrow logo are trademarks of Schiffer Publishing, Ltd.

Designed by Jack Chappell
Cover design by Molly Shields
Type set in Compacta/Geo Slab/Akzidenz Grotesk/ Minion

ISBN: 978-0-7643-6051-0
Printed in China.

Published by Schiffer Publishing, Ltd.
4880 Lower Valley Road
Atglen, PA 19310
Phone: (610) 593-1777; Fax: (610) 593-2002
E-mail: Info@schifferbooks.com
Web: www.schifferbooks.com

For our complete selection of fine books on this and related subjects, please visit our website at www.schifferbooks.com. You may also write for a free catalog.

Schiffer Publishing's titles are available at special discounts for bulk purchases for sales promotions or premiums. Special editions, including personalized covers, corporate imprints, and excerpts, can be created in large quantities for special needs. For more information, contact the publisher.

We are always looking for people to write books on new and related subjects. If you have an idea for a book, please contact us at proposals@schifferbooks.com.

To Miriam, Alex, Daniel, and Sarah

Contents

Foreword

The business of creating our beautiful commercial jets is unlike any other in the world. It is a highly competitive business that demands perfection. Airplanes must be built to last, and the return on the considerable investment made on the development of a new commercial jet can take decades. It requires strategic patience, a willingness to play the long game, and leadership that has vision and a high tolerance for risk—sometimes the "bet the company" kind of risk. This is what it takes to design and build an airplane that is going to be a winner, an airplane that will define how humanity will travel well into the future.

The 727 is one of the best examples of what it takes to build a winner. Three decades after the last one was delivered, the 727 remains one of the top-selling commercial jets in history, surpassed only by the 777, 737, and A320 family.

Even before the 707 made its first flight in the last days of 1957, it became apparent that only the world's major airports could handle the big jets and that Boeing would need to develop a smaller plane that could bring jet service to smaller fields.

Today there is fierce competition between Boeing and Airbus, but back in the beginning of the jet age the field was much wider. Boeing's competition included US companies Lockheed, Convair, and later Douglas, which jumped in with what would become the DC-9. At the same time, Boeing also faced multiple overseas competitors, including the de Havilland Trident, the Sud Aviation Caravelle, and the BAC 111, all of which had the potential of shutting Boeing out of the European and other international markets.

Adding to Boeing's challenges were the myriad conflicting demands from customers: some wanted four engines, another wanted a twin, still others were very satisfied with prop planes and not interested in a jet. The harshest reality was that the commercial jet business was still in its infancy and that Boeing was still grappling with the considerable start-up and production cost of the 707. The decision to go forward on a new commercial plane, the 727, was seen as a tremendous financial risk that many at Boeing advised against.

It was one of the most formidable environments ever faced by a new airplane program; fortunately, the company had outstanding leadership. CEO William Allen, arguably the pioneer of the "jet age," as well as legendary chief engineer Ed Wells, worked closely with the point man bringing the 727 to life, the brilliant and dedicated Transport Division (forerunner of Boeing Commercial Airplanes) chief engineer John E. "Jack" Steiner.

The challenge was to design a fast, quiet, reliable jet that could serve smaller airfields. Steiner clearly understood the challenge: "Bring out an airplane that was needed, to extend jet travel into smaller cities. We want to get more people traveling, not just those who think they can afford it, but those who thought they couldn't afford it." His strategy for winning was also simple: "Build the best possible airplane."

To meet that challenge, the team from the technical staff, including its head, Bill Cook, and chief aerodynamicist Joe Sutter, invented a new wing design that pioneered the innovative triple-slotted flap and included leading edge lift devices that together enabled the 727 to take off and land at airfields shorter than 5,000 feet. The clean swept-back wing also kept the plane fast, allowing the 727 to outpace its competition. Other technological firsts included an onboard APU (auxiliary power unit), single-point refueling, and onboard air stairs.

On December 5, 1960, after nearly five years of intense study that looked at over 150 different designs, Boeing announced the three-engine 727, with forty orders each from launch customers United Air Lines and Eastern Air Lines.

The first 727 rolled off the line in Renton, Washington, on November 27, 1962, and then on February 9, 1963, Boeing test pilot Lew Wallick, copilot R. L. "Dix" Loesch, and engineer M. K. Shulenberger took the 727 up for its first flight. After a year of testing, the 727 went into service, and much to the surprise of airline operators, the 727's actual performance was 10 percent greater than originally projected.

On December 11, 1967, an all-new stretched 727-200 was delivered, and two weeks later, Boeing celebrated the 500th delivery—well over the 400 planes Boeing had hoped to sell when the program started.

The early success of the 727 was noted colorfully by Boeing president William Allen: "I've had a few dreams in my life . . one was to have a large airline customer call me up and, instead of giving me hell, tell me he is delighted with an outstanding airplane, better than he bargained for. This happened with the 727. We have done an outstanding job on that airplane."

In September 1984, after a twenty-two-year production run, the last of 1,832 727s was delivered (a 727-200F to Federal Express)—the once "very risky" 727 had become one of the greatest-selling commercial jets in history.

Over the years I have talked to a lot of 727 pilots who loved their airplane; it was fast, fun to fly, and a lot like flying a fighter plane. I have enjoyed tremendously their stories and enthusiasm for the 727. Storytelling is as much a part of being a pilot as is actually flying; as all of you who love airplanes know, if you can't be up flying, the next best thing is to talk about flying.

Dan Dornseif is one of those great pilot/storytellers who is the real deal, a pilot who loves flying and loves airplanes. When he is not flying, he is talking about flying, and even better, he is writing about flying, and when he needs a break he turns to building beautifully detailed model airplanes. He is also an incredible researcher who spends hours either listening with great excitement to former employees as they recount their time at Boeing, or going through flight test data with an eagle eye to find that one exciting nugget that binds together a part of this story. With those excellent qualities, it is no wonder that Dan created the best book ever on the 737, and it is without a doubt that you are holding in your hands the best and final word on one of history's most beautiful and successful airplanes—the 727.

Michael Lombardi
Boeing corporate historian
April 2019

Acknowledgments

The creation of this book would not have been possible without the outstanding people who have contributed to my work. Many of these people designed, built, flew, or marketed the Boeing 727 or were on the scene as history was made by this special airplane. Several contributed their images and artwork to help tell the story, while others spent hours editing and assisting me with research. Additionally, Boeing, the Dee Howard Foundation, the Federal Aviation Administration, the Museum of Flight, NASA Langley, Pratt & Whitney, Southwest Airlines, and Quiet Wing generously shared company resources to make this book possible. I am grateful to the following people for their support and assistance: Capt. Les Abend, Capt. Andy Allen (United Airlines), Dave Anderson, D. Paul Angel, Harry Arnold, Ernie Austin, Chuck Ballard, Bob Bogash, Murray Booth, Dr. Phil Condit, Don Cumming, Jenny Dervin, Alex Dornseif, Miriam Dornseif, Wayne Fagan, Brenda Fernandez, Bruce Florsheim, Clifford Forester, John Fredrickson, Capt. John Fredenhagen, Ernie Gee, Russ Gold, Richard Goolsby, Jennings Heilig, William Hernandez, John Hindmarch, Terry "TC" Howard, Capt. Tom Imrich, Duane Jackson, Dennis Jenkins, Jonathan Jenkins, George Kanellis, Ron King, Phil Kirk, Kenneth Kirkland, Scott LaLonde, Jake Lamb, Robin K. Little, Michael Lombardi, Tom Lubbesmeyer, Barbara McCormick, Capt. Jim McRoberts, Bill McIntosh, Fred Mitchell, Capt. John Moktadier, Terry L. Morgan, Peter Morton, Vic Page, James Patterson, Petr Popelar, James Raisbeck, Chris Salley, Rob Sherry, Shane Stewart, Marlene Taylor-Houtchens, Capt. Steve Taylor, Peter Swift, Larry Timmons, Daryl Wall, Rebecca Wallick, Bucky Walter, Richard West, Carissa Wheeler, Jack Wimpress, Flip Wingrove, Capt. Brien Wygle, and Francis Zera

Interviews

Anderson, Dave (Boeing, retired): Museum of Flight, Seattle, Washington, November 18, 2017, and January 20, 2018

Arnold, Harry (Boeing, retired): Lake Carillon, Washington, April 25, 2018

Ballard, Chuck (Boeing retired): Museum of Flight, Seattle, Washington, January 20, 2018; Bellevue, Washington, April 24, 2018

Bogash, Bob (Boeing, retired): Museum of Flight, Seattle, Washington, November 18, 2017

Booth, Murray (Boeing, retired): Museum of Flight, Seattle, Washington, January 20, 2018

Condit, Phil (Boeing, retired): via teleconference, June 21, 2018

Cumming, Don (Boeing, retired): Museum of Flight, Seattle, Washington, January 20, 2018

Fagan, Wayne (Dee Howard): via teleconference, October 1, 2018

Florsheim, Bruce (Boeing, retired): Museum of Flight, Seattle, Washington, January 20, 2018

Forester, Clifford (Boeing, retired): Museum of Flight, Seattle, Washington, January 20, 2018

Fredenhagen, Capt. John (Reeve Aleutian Airways, retired): via teleconference, October 23, 2018

Hindmarch, John (Boeing, retired): Museum of Flight, Seattle, Washington, November 18, 2017, and January 20, 2018; Rainier Golf and Country Club, Seattle, Washington, April 21, 2018

Howard, Terris "TC" (Boeing, retired): Rainier Golf and Country Club, Seattle, Washington, April 21, 2018; via teleconference, October 13, 2018

Imrich, Capt. Thomas (USAF, FAA, Boeing, retired): Museum of Flight, Seattle, Washington, November 18, 2017; January 20, 2018; Arlington, Washington, October 9, 2018

Jackson, Duane (Boeing, retired): Museum of Flight, Seattle, Washington, November 15, 2018

Johnson, Jim (Boeing, retired): via teleconference, June 21, 2018

Kanellis, George (Boeing, retired): Rainier Golf and Country Club, Seattle, Washington, April 21, 2018; via teleconference, May 8, 2018

King, Ron (Boeing, retired): Rainier Golf and Country Club, Seattle, Washington, April 21, 2018

Little, Robin (Boeing, retired): Rainier Golf and Country Club, Seattle, Washington, April 21, 2018

Lombardi, Michael (Boeing): Museum of Flight, Seattle, Washington, January 20, 2018

McCormick, Barbara (Northeast Airlines, retired): via teleconference, May 19, 2018

McIntosh, Bill (Boeing, retired): Museum of Flight, Seattle, Washington, January 20, 2018

McRoberts, Capt. Jim (Boeing, retired): Bellevue, Washington, April 24, 2018

Mitchell, Fred (Boeing, retired): Museum of Flight, Seattle, Washington, January 20, 2018

Morton, Peter (Boeing, retired): Museum of Flight, Seattle, Washington, November 18, 2017, and January 20, 2018; via teleconference, June 21, 2018

Neir, Robert (Boeing, retired): Rainier Golf and Country Club, Seattle, Washington, April 21, 2018

Page, Victor (Boeing, retired): Museum of Flight, Seattle, Washington, January 20, 2018

Raisbeck, James (Raisbeck Engineering): Museum of Flight, Seattle, Washington, November 18, 2017; Rainier Golf and Country Club, Seattle, Washington, April 21, 2018

Taylor, Capt. Steve (Boeing, retired): Museum of Flight, Seattle, Washington, January 20, 2018

Taylor-Houtchens, Marlene (Boeing, retired): Museum of Flight, Seattle, Washington, November 18, 2017, and January 20, 2018; Rainier Golf and Country Club, Seattle, Washington, April 21, 2018

Timmons, Larry (Boeing, retired): Rainier Golf and Country Club, Seattle, Washington, April 21, 2018

Wallick, Rebecca: via teleconference, January 27, 2018

Walter, Bucky (Boeing, retired): Rainier Golf and Country Club, Seattle, Washington, April 21, 2018

Wimpress, Jack (Boeing, retired): Museum of Flight, Seattle, Washington, November 18, 2017; Rainier Golf and Country Club, Seattle, Washington, April 21, 2018, and January 20, 2018; via teleconference, June 21, 2018

Wingrove, Flip (Boeing, retired): Museum of Flight, Seattle, Washington, January 20, 2018

Wygle, Capt. Brien (Boeing, retired): Bellevue, Washington, January 22, 2018

Introduction

This book commenced with the intention to write the most complete, accurate, and up-to-date volume on the Boeing 727 jetliner. This airplane has always held a special place in my heart, since I was a young child. In 1978, my first airplane flight was aboard a Pacific Southwest Airlines 727, adorned with its unique smiling paint scheme. That event began my passion for airplanes and flying, a drive that led to a career as a Boeing 737 captain for a major airline in the United States. Further, it also sparked a keen interest in understanding the history of aviation and a desire to share it with fellow professionals and enthusiasts.

Preparation for this project included the acquisition of many books and resources on the Boeing 727. I studied the history of the airplane, along with technical and systems data. Further information still needed to be sought, which led me to the Boeing Archives in Bellevue, Washington. With the assistance of Boeing corporate historians Michael Lombardi and Tom Lubbesmeyer, I was able to truly dig into the history of the 727. Jack Steiner, the man who spearheaded the design of the 727, kept meticulous records, to which I was given access. Research into the development and test-flying of the 727 was provided through reading the actual flight test documentation for the aircraft. Company leaders, test pilots, and engineers were interviewed, which allowed me to learn firsthand the inside story of this most significant aircraft.

The Boeing 727 was a pioneering jetliner in that it brought advances in technology that led to greater fuel efficiency, lower noise levels, and lower crew workload than previous jet transports. It soon outsold all other jetliner models of the time, with a total of 1,832 airframes completed, and became the most numerous jetliner in operation until the later successes of the Boeing 737 and Airbus A320 airliners. The service life of the 727 has spanned fifty-six years and continues today, with a limited number of aircraft fulfilling corporate transport and cargo roles worldwide.

While this is certainly a book about an aircraft, it is just as much about the people who worked and took risks to build a better, safer airplane. We will explore the bold personalities involved who often took personal ownership of the project and were willing to take carefully assessed risks. This mindset was encouraged by Boeing management, with the company's respected leader, William Allen, who often led by example in this regard, doing what was necessary to build the best jetliners in the world. The culture at Boeing was and is quite rare, where people at all levels take immense pride in the amazing products that they produce. Throughout the story, this shines through repeatedly and is the reason that the 727 became a bestselling airliner.

Boeing's slogan, "Bringing People Together," was exemplified by the 727. It was designed to bring jet transport to communities that, up to that point, had never experienced jet service. In a time when jetliners were largely the domain of the wealthy, the efficient design of the 727 brought jet comfort and speed to people around the world. The exclusiveness of the "jet set" became a thing of the past, largely due to the company's vision and the creation of a truly superior machine. This is the story of Boeing's magnificent Model 727.

The world says the Boeing 727 is its favorite trijet.

Thank you, world.

Over one billion people have flown Boeing 727s all over the world. No other jetliner has carried so many passengers. We asked 80,000 people in 90 countries why they preferred the 727s. Among the reasons given: more room for carryons, pleasant interiors, not too big and easy on-easy off. More than 70 airlines now fly Boeing 727s to nearly every major city in the world. Next time take off on the No. 1 trijet.

BOEING
Getting people together

The Dawn of the Jet Age

In the late 1950s and early 1960s, jet airliners were relatively new and highly publicized. Unlike today, jet transportation was almost exclusively a luxury for the well-to-do and powerful businessmen. Trans World Airlines capitalized on this by introducing their "StarStream" livery and made it a lavish occasion when movie stars were onboard. Photos were taken as famous people deplaned the aircraft for publicity purposes, and National Airlines even took up the slogan "Airline of the Stars" to create a high-class persona. Jetliners, along with many of the propliners of the period, featured elegant lounges to allow a relaxed, enjoyable, and social environment while onboard.

In the following pages, we will look at key aircraft that existed at the time, and analyze their strengths and weaknesses to gain an understanding of the engineering challenges involved with building jetliners. Aircraft must be designed with the correct mixture of compromises; otherwise, the machine, no matter how technically competent it might be, is destined to fail. Many designs fell short of turning even a small profit for their manufacturers, sometimes even driving these companies out of the airliner business entirely. The financial risks were enormous, and since it was often a "winner takes it all" scenario, it was not an endeavor for the faint of heart.

The Alpha: de Havilland's Comet

On May 2, 1952, the jet age dawned for commercial purposes with the service introduction of the de Havilland DH.106 Comet. The bullet-like aircraft, with four de Havilland "Ghost" engines buried in the wing roots, was one of the single largest technological advancements in the history of aviation. With the Comet in operation, it appeared that Great Britain would continue to be a powerful force in aviation. This first jetliner was operated by British Overseas Airways Corporation (BOAC), Air France, and Union Aeromaritime de Transport. With an additional pending sale to Canadian Pacific Airlines, the Comet gained worldwide acceptance and recognition for de Havilland.

Instead of the expected success, however, the Comet's fortune was about to turn in a most tragic and dramatic way. Over a short period of time, two Comets, BOAC's G-ALYZ (c/n 6012) and Canadian Pacific's CF-CUN (c/n 6014), failed to climb away from the runway on takeoff. It was quickly found in the aftermath that if the nose of the aircraft was raised too early, at too high of an angle, or both, the significant increase in induced drag would inhibit further acceleration. This led to the wing being unable to create enough usable lift for takeoff, with devastating consequences. De Havilland redesigned the leading edge of the wing to prevent this issue, but it was too late, and the sale to Canadian Pacific was lost.

The Comet's safety record sustained a further blow on May 2, 1953, when G-ALYV (c/n 6008) was witnessed wingless, in an uncontrolled descent, shortly after departing Calcutta, India. It had taken off during a severe thunderstorm, and the ensuing crash claimed the lives of all forty-three people onboard. The investigation concluded that the aircraft had sustained a structural failure of the portside horizontal stabilizer due to gust loads or aggressive pilot control inputs (or both), leading to a wing failure and subsequent crash. The accident occurred exactly one year, to the day, since the Comet had entered service, and it led to the questioning of its structural integrity, bringing the Comet's design under greater scrutiny.

Shortly thereafter, two even more mysterious accidents occurred. The first production Comet 1 (G-ALYP, c/n 6003), operating as BOAC 781, plummeted into the Mediterranean Sea from 27,000 feet on January 10, 1954, shortly after departing Rome, Italy. The event

A de Havilland DH.106 Comet 1 rests on the ramp between flights. This example, F-BGSB (c/n 6016), was delivered to UAT on February 19, 1953. Following the Comet 1 accidents, it was withdrawn from service in April 1954 and subsequently broken up at Le Bourget Airport in Paris, France. *Clinton H. Groves Collection via Wikimedia Commons*

was so sudden that a transmission from the Comet crew to a company Argonaut was abruptly ended in midsentence. BOAC grounded their Comet fleet until the British government cleared the aircraft back into service following the Abell Committee's findings, on March 23, 1954, that there was no detectable fault with the aircraft. Not two weeks later, G-ALYY (c/n 6011), also having just departed from Rome, crashed under suspiciously similar circumstances at the cost of a further twenty-one lives.

Less than two years after entering service, the remaining Comet 1 aircraft were permanently grounded, and an exhaustive investigation into the phantom cause of these crashes ensued. Focused on the possibility of the fuselage's structural failure, one of the remaining airframes, G-ALYU (c/n 6007), was placed in a specially constructed water tank and subjected to repeated pressurization cycles. These tests simulated the pressure changes experienced in flight, but at an accelerated rate. Since water was used as the pressurizing medium, only a very small quantity of liquid needed to escape to equalize pressure after a failure. Thus, a failure of the fuselage pressure hull would be obvious, without tearing the entire structure apart. Throughout the testing, the water pressure inside the fuselage plunged to zero on several occasions. Each time, the failure was repaired and testing continued to discover the next weak link. After an equivalent of 9,000 hours of flight on the airframe (both actually accrued and simulated), weaknesses were discovered around the automatic direction finder (ADF) antennas on the upper surface of the fuselage. Additional cracks formed around the square window and escape hatch frames, as well as on the aft face of the main wheel well bays. The cause of the losses of 'YP and 'YY was deemed to most assuredly be from the violent and sudden destruction of the pressure hull due to explosive decompression.

Further investigation was conducted when additional wreckage from 'YP was pulled from the sea and brought to Farnborough for analysis. It was concluded that the failure on 'YP began in the vicinity of the cutout around the ADF antennas and propagated down the fuselage on the port side toward the window line before continuing aft. This caused a large portion of the fuselage to break from the rest of the aircraft suddenly enough to leave paint marks on the tail as the entire aircraft literally unraveled. It was a stark reminder of what jetliners had to endure during their service life, and of the extreme conditions that engineers had to account for in their designs.

Although extremely tragic, these accidents led to a greater understanding of the nature of metal fatigue. The forces involved, along with the effects of thousands of pressurization cycles and corrosion, were studied in minute detail. The advancement of knowledge gained from the Comet fatigue issues has since been incorporated into every jetliner in the skies today.

This was not the end of the Comet story, however. Once the root cause of the accident was established, de Havilland set about to create new versions of the aircraft. Available engine thrust from the early Ghost engines was anemic at best, which drove the construction of the lightest airframe possible. This, combined with the lack of applied knowledge of metal fatigue at the time, led to the construction of an airframe that proved not to be strong enough for the extreme forces waged upon its structure in high-altitude flight. The advent of the Rolls-Royce Avon engine provided enough thrust to breathe new life into the Comet design. Several follow-on versions were built, including the Comet 2, which was similar to the Comet 1 in size but had enhanced structural strength and could be easily differentiated from its predecessor by its oval-shaped windows. Only one Comet 3 was ever flown, and it featured a fuselage stretched to 111 feet. It was soon widely outnumbered by the similarly stretched Comet 4 series, which arrived in service in 1958.

The Comet 4 was a greatly improved version that had a transatlantic capable range of 3,225 statute miles and could accommodate eighty-one passengers. G-APDC conducted the first-ever nonstop jetliner flight across the Atlantic on October 4, 1958, under the command of Capt. Roy Millichap. Although this was an incredible accomplishment, unfortunately for de Havilland and the British aircraft industry, it was too little, too late. The Americans and the Soviets were already well under way with developing airplanes that were faster and more refined. Future jetliners, including the Boeing 727, owed many of their design innovations to the learnings from the trailblazing and daring de Havilland Comet program.

The Boeing 707 and Douglas DC-8

The Boeing 707-320-series airplanes featured an enlarged wing that provided additional lift and increased range. The introduction of the Pratt & Whitney JT3D turbofan brought somewhat quieter operation and additional thrust. This aircraft (N322F, c/n 18975, l/n 445) was a 707-349C model and first flew on September 11, 1965. This aircraft took part in an around-the-world journey, flying over both poles in November 1965. Because of this feat, the airplane was nicknamed "Pole Cat." *Courtesy of the Boeing Company*

The DC-8 was the primary competitor for the Boeing 707. This DC-8-32 (N801PA, c/n 45254, l/n 6) is seen in Prague, Czechoslovakia, during the early 1960s. Pan American operated this aircraft until 1969. *Courtesy of Petr Popelar*

Prior to entering the jetliner arena, Douglas was well respected for building safe and efficient propliners. This DC-6B (I-DIME, c/n 44252, l/n 442) was being operated by Societa Aerea Mediterranea during the late 1950s and early 1960s, before entering service with Alitalia. *Courtesy of Petr Popelar*

Having learned from the tragedies of the de Havilland Comet 1 design, Boeing set out to also make use of the design knowledge acquired during the development of the B-47 strategic jet bomber program. The high-speed drag reduction reaped from the use of sharply swept wings was discovered by Boeing early on, when designer George S. Schairer studied German airframe technology shortly after the Third Reich's defeat in World War II. Schairer, a fluent German speaker, was able to communicate and comprehend the studies that the German aerodynamicists were willing to share with the Boeing delegation during a visit to postwar Germany. This technology was the basis for the wing design of the B-47, with which all Boeing jetliners share a common heritage.

Boeing began studies for a large jet-powered transport as early as 1948. Over the next six years, many different design possibilities were explored until the eightieth permutation, the model 367-80 (commonly known as the "Dash 80"), was flown for the first time

on July 15, 1954. It was a one-of-a-kind aircraft built to be a technology demonstrator, and ultimately proved the viability of a jet transport both for military and commercial applications. From this aircraft, the Boeing 707 and the military C-135/KC-135 were developed and proved to be successful designs both for Boeing and the operating customers alike.

The first variant of the 707, the 707-120 series, was pressed into development by an order for twenty aircraft from Pan American World Airways on October 13, 1955. With the Dash 80 being considered the "prototype" aircraft, the first flight of a "production" 707 occurred on December 20, 1957, with N708PA (c/n 17586, l/n 1). The first American jet passenger service was conducted by Pan American on transatlantic routing from New York to Paris on October 26, 1958. The ship, N711PA (a Boeing 707-121, c/n 17590, l/n 5), was flown under the command of Capt. Samuel Miller, assisted by First Officer Waldo Lynch, Flight Engineer James Etchison, and Navigator A. Powell.

Nearly six months prior to the first 707 service, the Douglas Aircraft Company flew its first jetliner, the DC-8. It was designed for the exact same mission as the 707 and was quickly poised to be a head-on competitor. At this time, Douglas was enjoying a near monopoly as a builder of highly regarded airline aircraft and was not about to lose that position to Boeing or any other competitor without a fight. As recounted in Rebecca Wallick's excellent book *Growing Up Boeing*, Lew Wallick's daughter shared an interesting and amusing story regarding the rivalry between Boeing

Boeing's George Schairer (*right*) meets with the famous rocket designer Wernher von Braun during the early years of the jet age. Many of the advances in high-speed aerodynamics, such as the swept wing, were developed from German research during World War II. *Courtesy of the Boeing Company*

and Douglas. The story goes that on May 30, 1958, the DC-8 prototype, N8008D (c/n 45252, l/n 1), awaited its first flight, looking smart in its red, white, and blue paint scheme. Douglas was naturally keen to gather as much publicity as possible for the aircraft, and many representatives from the news media eagerly waited for the promised photo-taking opportunity. At the same time, Boeing test pilot Lew Wallick and CAA pilot Walt Haldeman were conducting low-altitude testing just offshore from the Los Angeles basin with N707PA. Once the tasks were complete, Wallick guided the jet back toward the airfield at Edwards Air Force Base, when he began to hear the chatter about the DC-8's first flight on the common flight test frequency. Wallick decided that it might be interesting to take a closer look at the 707's nemesis and soon made contact with the control tower at Long Beach Airport. When he requested permission for a flyby, the tower controller eventually cleared him to fly past with no altitude limit. The 707 flight display was accomplished with gear and flaps extended at 500 feet along the airport's diagonal runway and completely upstaged Douglas's festivities. It was said that Donald Douglas Sr. was so hopping mad about the whole incident that he threatened retribution. Nothing could be done, however, because the 707 flight was completely legal. All is fair in love and war!

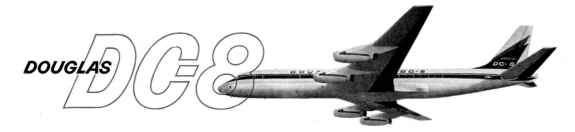

DOUGLAS DC-8

Pilots call it…*(and so will you!)* "The world's most <u>advanced</u> jetliner!"

Already, more than 500 pilots have flown the Douglas DC-8 Jetliner, which goes into regular airline service next month. To a man these pilots voice their enthusiasm about the world's most modern jetliner.

"It's in the DC tradition, and that's good enough for me" . . . "Remarkable approach and stability

More airlines have chosen the DC-8 than any other jetliner!

characteristics" . . . "I've flown them all and this is *it!*" . . . these are the kind of reports these experts are giving.

As a passenger, you'll share their enthusiasm—for reasons of your own—when you take your first flight in the DC-8. You'll appreciate the many innovations Douglas has de-

signed to give you the world's most comfortable jet journey. And you'll rely on the DC heritage of experience, research and testing that has made Douglas airplanes the most popular aircraft in aviation.

Make a date with the DC-8! You'll agree with pilots who call it the world's most advanced jetliner.

These world-famous airlines will fly you almost anywhere on earth by DC-8! Alitalia-Linee Aeree Italiane • Delta Air Lines • Eastern Air Lines • Japan Air Lines • KLM Royal Dutch Air Lines • National Airlines • Northwest Orient Airlines • Olympic Airways Panagra • Panair Do Brasil • Pan American World Airways • SAS—Scandinavian Airlines System • Swissair Trans-Canada Air Lines • Transports Aeriens Intercontinentaux • Union Aeromaritime De Transport • United Air Lines

The Douglas DC-8 went on to be a competent jetliner and a solid competitor, although it did have a disadvantage of being ten months behind the Boeing 707's head start. On September 18, 1959, first Delta Air Lines, then shortly thereafter United Airlines, inaugurated DC-8 service. In an ongoing effort to continually improve the new Douglas jet, modifications to the wing leading edges added an additional 4 percent chord to create a significant drag reduction. While testing this new modification, a Rolls-Royce Conway–powered DC-8-43 (N9604Z, c/n 45623, l/n 130) maintained a speed of Mach 1.012 for sixteen seconds during a controlled dive, thus becoming the first jetliner to successfully attain supersonic velocities. One of the chase aircraft during this historic feat was a Lockheed F-104 reportedly flown by none other than Col. Chuck Yeager, the first pilot to officially break the sound barrier in 1947.

The DC-8, like the 707, gained a reputation for dependable service. While the 707 met with greater sales success by ultimately selling 856 examples, the DC-8 still sold a solidly respectable 556 airplanes. Still, many airlines such as National, United, and Delta chose the DC-8 over the 707. Others, such as Pan American, operated both of these long-range airplanes in a mixed fleet. Boeing's willingness to create new versions of the 707, tailored to the needs of individual airlines, certainly had a sizable role in the 707's success. This flexibility came with a price, however, since each deviation from the original design increased costs and moved the break-even production number to a higher value and further delayed true profitability for the design. The economics of the 707 sales led Boeing's Jack Steiner to look for ways to create airplanes that appealed to all airlines, without the high production costs associated with the logistical complications of offering too many variants.

By the late 1950s and early 1960s, with the jet age in full swing, manufacturers began to see a need for modern, fast, short-range airliners to tap into new and emerging markets.

The Lockheed L-188 Electra II

The Lockheed L-188 Electra was seen as the primary competitor for the Boeing 727 during its development and early operational years. *Courtesy of Petr Popelar*

The Lockheed company had significant experience designing and successfully marketing innovative aircraft for years, both in the military and civilian worlds. Famed aircraft such as the Lockheed Model 12 became legendary through the pioneering efforts of Amelia Earhart. Additionally, the fork-tailed P-38 Lightning fighter aircraft

from World War II was one of the most impressively engineered fighter/interceptors of the conflict.

In the airline world, Lockheed developed the L-049 Constellation, which first took to the air on January 9, 1943, and gave the impression that it was sculpted by an artist. It had sweeping lines, four powerful engines, a distinct triple-tailed design, and was a hit with the world's airlines. Soon, as reciprocating turbocompound engine technology reached ever closer to its pinnacle, the aircraft was developed into progressively more-advanced versions. These included the iconic L-1049 "Super G" Constellation, and finally the L-1649 "Starliner" with its high-aspect-ratio wings and enormous four-row turbocompound radial engines. While the Constellation was loved by the public and airlines alike, its days were already numbered due to the emergence of jet technology.

Lockheed, being the forward-thinking company that it was, had noticed that turbine engine technology was becoming ever more reliable and desirable. Jet engines were designed to create brute thrust, but also, this power could be harnessed to turn a large-diameter propeller. This engine type, which eventually became known as a "turboprop," offered higher speeds than existing reciprocating-engine-powered airliners, while using less fuel than pure jet engines. Lockheed soon took particular notice of the British Vickers Viscount, a turboprop that became popular by promising quiet, efficient operation. Powered by four Rolls-Royce Dart turboprop engines, the aircraft was soon noticed by US airlines too, with Capital Airlines ordering sixty of them in May 1954. The British machine was perfect for their short-stage-length route structure.

It rapidly became apparent that there was a new airplane market emerging that could be tapped by Lockheed. American Airlines approached Boeing, Convair, Douglas, and Lockheed to create a four-engine turboprop-powered airliner. Both Boeing and Convair dropped out of the competition early, but Douglas proposed a turboprop-powered DC-7 derivative, dubbed the DC-7D. Lockheed offered an aircraft concept known as the CL-303, which unsurprisingly bore some resemblance to the C-130 Hercules airlifter, which was also under development. American rejected both proposals but reapproached the manufacturers the following year, looking for a larger aircraft with a 2,000-mile range and high cruising speeds. Eastern Airlines also gave some input, which resulted in a larger design initially known as the CL-310. This design became the Lockheed L-188 Electra and commanded orders both from American and Eastern for thirty-five and forty aircraft, respectively.

The resultant aircraft first flew on December 6, 1957, and quickly proved to be an able and versatile machine. Powered by four Allison 501 turboprop engines, the L-188 had increased capacity for up to ninety passengers in a spacious 128-inch-wide cabin. Featuring a maximum speed of 448 miles per hour, the Electra entered airline service with Eastern Airlines on January 12, 1959. The honeymoon was short, however, as mysterious accidents began to occur. It was discovered that a phenomenon known as "whirl mode" resulted in two aircraft disintegrating in midair. While the cause was identified and promptly remedied, a measure of public trust in the aircraft had been forever compromised. Even with this being the case, any short-to-medium-range aircraft entering the market would surely need to compete favorably with the Electra's performance and economics.

The Convair CV-880

Convair had development experience both in commercial piston airliners and cutting-edge, supersonic military aircraft such as the delta-winged "Century Series" F-102 and F-106, along with the blindingly fast Convair B-58 strategic nuclear bomber. Having vast knowledge of both businesses, it was only natural for Convair to capitalize upon these strengths and produce a jetliner with nimble handling and exceptionally high subsonic cruise speeds.

Convair was known as a world-class builder of high-performance military jets during the late 1950s and early 1960s. The XB-58 shown here (55-0660) was one of two B-58 prototype aircraft constructed for flight testing. A total of 116 of the Mach 2–capable nuclear bombers were built. *Courtesy of the United States government*

As early as 1953, Convair explored the commercial possibilities of a jet-powered transport, while both Boeing and Douglas conducted development programs of their own with the 707 and DC-8, respectively. The famed aviator and eccentric businessman Howard Hughes was involved in secretive talks with Convair brass and designers in a series of meetings that often occurred with intense security, late at night, and in undisclosed venues. At the time, Hughes held controlling interest in Trans World Airlines and owned Toolco, which purchased aircraft and leased them to TWA in order to gain a tax advantage while benefiting both organizations. The first concept considered was an airliner version of their enormous Convair XB-60, but it was soon deemed impractical.

This series of secret discussions, known by those who attended as "Project Southern Comfort," continued into 1956, when a new design emerged. To highlight its anticipated cruise speed of 600 miles per hour, the concept was initially named the Skylark 600. The aircraft featured four wing-mounted engines, similar to the Boeing 707 and Douglas DC-8 designs, but with a cruciform-type horizontal stabilizer, midway up the vertical stabilizer. The size of the Skylark design varied as talks continued through 1956, and settled on an airplane with a typical capacity for eighty passengers, and medium-to-long-range capability. The nonafterburning version of the military J-79 engine, which powered both the McDonnell F-4 Phantom II and Convair's own B-58, was being released for use on civilian applications as the General Electric CJ-805. After considering the possibility of using the Pratt & Whitney JT3 employed on the 707, Convair selected the CJ-805 for its new jetliner. To enable a high speed of 600 miles per hour (or 880 feet per second, as the aircraft's eventual name reflected), the fuselage was kept narrow and allowed only five-abreast seating.

Wings of a narrower chord than those of the 707 and DC-8 were integrated into the design for further speed capability.

On June 7, 1956, Convair made a deal with Hughes for the first thirty delivery slots, with an additional ten awarded to Delta Air Lines, which could be intermixed into the first deliveries at Hughes's discretion. This decision to essentially give the first thirty slots to one customer (Toolco/TWA) was a previously unheard-of practice, for reasons that would become all too obvious over the following decade.

The XB-60 was a pure jet derivative of the B-36 strategic bomber. The pictured aircraft (49-2676) was the only example built, and it first flew in 1952. *Courtesy of the United States government*

The first flight of the Convair CV-880 took place at San Diego's Lindbergh Airport on January 27, 1959. *Author's collection*

Cathay Pacific Airways received this CV-880M (VR-HGG, c/n 22-7-8-60) from Japan Airlines in 1970. The CV-880 was powered by four General Electric CJ-805-3 turbojet engines, derived from the military J-79 engine used on high-performance tactical aircraft. *Courtesy of Christian Volpati via Wikimedia Commons*

On January 27, 1959, the rebranded Convair CV-880 (N801TW, c/n 22-1-1, l/n 1) made its first flight from Lindbergh Field, in San Diego, California. The aircraft was certainly fast, with a true airspeed cruise of 615 mph, and after entering service gained a reputation for being mechanically bulletproof, as relayed by veteran TWA mechanic Clinton Groves. Delta Air Lines gave the 880 the nickname "Delta Queen" in keeping with Delta's Royal Crown DC-7. In Jon Proctor's book *Convair 880 and 990*, one Delta Airlines pilot, Paul W. Bennett, described the aircraft thus: "Queen signifies haughty, aloof, possessing a feminine mystique. The 880 isn't and doesn't. It is . . . deliberate, brawny, certainly very rapid, and thoroughly masculine in all of its movements. Some have said it is noisy and dirty. But, feminine, it isn't." The CV-880 had a reputation for having fighter-like handling, but also for being somewhat difficult to handle during a low-speed failure of one of the outboard engines, and had a propensity to experience a coupled yawing and rolling motion known as Dutch roll.

Several factors contributed to the design falling short of a commercial success, with the first being the decision to make the CV-880 a medium-to-long-range airplane. There was a good possibility that the aircraft would have been better suited as a lighter, short-range airliner. Even then, the fuel consumption and operating economics were not ideal, though the aircraft was very swift indeed. The body, narrower than those offered by both Boeing and Douglas, negatively affected passenger comfort, particularly on longer flights for which the aircraft was designed. Additionally, the advance deliveries agreed to by Hughes and Toolco are believed to have cost untold sales, with both Boeing and Douglas more than willing to expedite aircraft deliveries to perspective customers. In the end, Convair sold only sixty-five 880s, a situation that caused substantial losses for the revered airplane manufacturer. More than anything else, it is believed by many that the Convair 880 simply had the wrong economics for the time period.

Delta Air Lines was an early customer for the CV-880. Luxurious lounges were installed to increase passenger appeal, and the Convair jetliner was known for providing a smoother ride than most airliners during turbulence. *Author's collection*

The Boeing 720

Early in 1956, Boeing began looking into the viability of a short-range version of the Boeing 707-120 long-range jetliner to expand jet service on regional routes. The goal from the outset was to maintain as much commonality with the 707 as possible to minimize the need for retooling, research, and development. Initially, twin- and four-engine configurations with shortened wings were explored for the new design, known as the Boeing 707-020. Airline interest in such an aircraft was growing quickly. While Boeing assessed the possibilities with the 707-020, most of the company's resources were occupied in the furtherance of the Intercontinental 707-320 project, which was in late development during 1956 and early 1957.

By mid-1957, Boeing saw a lucrative opportunity to invest in the short-range jet market. Other manufacturers, such as Vickers and Lockheed, were already providing turboprop Viscounts and Electras to the short-range sectors. Boeing had considered this course of action as well, but Boeing's leader, William M. "Bill" Allen, wisely saw jet airliners as the future of the industry. With interest primarily from United Airlines, Boeing announced the intention to proceed with a short-range jetliner. Back in late 1955, United had issued an order for the Douglas DC-8, a head-to-head competitor for Boeing's long-range 707. Seemingly, United's leadership was concerned that a decision to buy the 707-020 would be construed by industry analysts as a reversal, or that the DC-8 purchase was being seen as a mistake. To preclude this, he urged Boeing to change the name of the new aircraft. Initially, Boeing announced that the new design would be designated as the Boeing 717 in July 1957. Patterson, reportedly not liking the sound of the new name, insisted on another change, and the aircraft became forever known as the Boeing 720. From a marketing standpoint, the new Boeing 720 name created an appearance of being completely distinct from the 707.

In reality, the Boeing 720 was every bit a 707 derivative, merely optimized for short-haul flying from shorter runways. Since the 720's mission required far less fuel than her long-range sister, the aircraft could be significantly lightened by using thinner metal gauges and lighter-weight components, such as the landing gear assemblies. The airlines wanted the wide 707 fuselage cross section, though, which was common to the 720. The body was shortened to 136 feet, 2 inches, a reduction of 8 feet, 4 inches compared to the 707-120. Aside from the gauge of the wing skin and structure, the 720 retained a wing design that was essentially the same as the 707-120, but engineers felt that it needed to be slightly tuned for the short-range, high-speed mission. To reduce drag and increase cruise speeds, Boeing designed a composite overlay (known widely as "the glove") that was installed inboard of engines #2 and #3. The glove changed the chord of the inboard wing, while also increasing the sweep. Since this portion of the wing is the thickest part, particularly near the fuselage, the increase in sweepback caused a sizable decrease in high-speed drag. This naturally translated into a higher operational cruising speed, which was already well in excess of any other short-range aircraft flying at the time. To further improve takeoff and landing performance, the 720 made use of Krueger-type leading edge flaps, which deployed automatically in conjunction with the trailing edge flaps. These, combined with the added glove and reduced weights, made the 720 available to many airports that did not possess the runway facilities required by the heavier 707-120.

The proven lightweight version of the Pratt & Whitney JT3C (the -7) was offered without water injection, alongside the slightly heavier and uprated -12, which provided for even better airfield and climb performance, albeit with a bit of an aircraft weight penalty. With certification flight testing complete, the Boeing 720 was certified by the Federal Aviation Agency on June 30, 1960. Initially, the aircraft had a maximum takeoff weight of 213,000 pounds, with later versions approved up to 229,000 pounds and maximum indicated speeds of 399 knots below 23,400 feet, and Mach 0.906 at and above 23,400-foot pressure altitude.

Boeing capitalized on the smooth, quiet comfort of their new jetliners.
Courtesy of the Boeing Company

The coin, the watch and the flower...

Within a few weeks you'll be able to board a luxurious Boeing 707. Your first flight in this jet-age airliner will be one of the travel highlights of your life. You'll cruise serenely through high, weatherless skies, so completely free from vibration you'll be able to stand a half-dollar on edge.

The 707 cabin, the most spacious aloft, will be so quiet you will be able to hear the ticking of a

watch. The flower you bought when you left will be fresh when you arrive, for the 600-mile-an-hour Boeing jet will carry you across a continent or an ocean in half the time required by a conventional airliner. Flight in the 707, even veteran airline travelers will find, is new and exciting—and secure. This superb luxury liner is by Boeing, the most experienced builder of multi-jet aircraft in the world.

These airlines already have ordered Boeing jetliners:
AIR FRANCE • AIR-INDIA INTERNATIONAL • AMERICAN AIRLINES
BRANIFF INTERNATIONAL AIRWAYS • BRITISH OVERSEAS
AIRWAYS CORPORATION • CONTINENTAL AIR LINES
CUBANA DE AVIACION • LUFTHANSA GERMAN AIRLINES
PAN AMERICAN WORLD AIRWAYS • QANTAS EMPIRE AIRWAYS
SABENA BELGIAN WORLD AIRLINES • SOUTH AFRICAN AIRWAYS
TRANS WORLD AIRLINES • UNITED AIR LINES • VARIG AIRLINES
OF BRAZIL • *Also the* MILITARY AIR TRANSPORT SERVICE

BOEING 707 and 720

The Boeing 720B

In 1959, Pratt & Whitney made a new version of the JT3 available, known as the JT3D-1. This power plant was a "fan jet" version of the previous engine that differed largely by the inclusion of an additional, oversized first compressor stage, often referred to as "the fan." On this engine, a percentage of the air propelled by the fan was bypassed around the turbojet core, resulting in increased thrust and reduced noise and fuel burn metrics. These engines could be easily recognizable by the larger inlet and additional fan shroud extended aft of the fan section. Available thrust was increased to 17,000 pounds, with the follow-on JT3D-3 capable of generating 18,000 pounds of thrust. This allowed increased gross weights up to a maximum "flaps-up" flight weight of 233,000 pounds. It is an interesting note that the late-model 720B was approved for a maximum takeoff weight of 234,000 pounds. So, in operation at maximum takeoff weight, it would have to burn through 1,000 pounds of fuel before retracting the wing flaps after takeoff. While the 720B brought a substantial improvement in performance and fuel economy, advances in aircraft and engine design continued to be incredibly fast paced during this period. The Boeing model 727, which would come on to the airline scene in February 1964, rapidly consigned these older-technology jetliners into obsolescence.

In total, sixty-five pure turbojet (JT3C-powered) Boeing 720s were produced (interestingly, the same number of sales as the competing Convair 880), with an additional eighty-nine 720B turbofan-powered airplanes delivered from the factory. Some carriers, such as American Airlines, elected to modify their earlier "straight" 720s to 720B standards in order to extend the useful life of the aircraft. Others, such as United and Eastern, retired their 720 fleets unmodified. Many of these aircraft went on to serve for years with air carriers around the globe and were even occasionally chartered for high-profile rock-and-roll artists such as the Bee Gees, Elton John, and Led Zeppelin.

The de Havilland DH.121 Trident

De Havilland of Great Britain was a pioneering company led by Sir Geoffrey de Havilland, whose organization was intimately involved in the early chapters of aviation history and was still at the forefront when the jet age dawned. The company produced the Vampire and Venom jet fighters for the Royal Air Force and Royal Navy, prior to bringing to reality the world's first operational jetliner, the ill-fated DH.106 Comet 1.

Following the Comet accidents, de Havilland made good use of those difficult lessons in designing a new short-to-medium-range aircraft. In 1956, British European Airways (BEA) put forth a specification for a new advanced-technology jetliner that was larger and faster than the Sud Caravelle. The aircraft was to have a capacity for eighty to one hundred coach-class passengers and a maximum takeoff gross weight in the neighborhood of 126,000 pounds. The de Havilland company was optimistic about this size category and projected a market for 500 machines. The 13,500-pound-thrust-class Rolls-Royce Medway and the 12,130-pound-thrust Rolls-Royce RA29 Avon turbojet engines were considered to be the best power plant choices, and the design process began.

In May 1959, BEA laid a major design specification change onto the table. The airline management's criteria focused on a smaller airframe than was previously sought. The revised specification called for a maximum capacity of eighty passengers and a 100,000-pound maximum takeoff weight. BEA absorbed much of the expense of the change while de Havilland set to work on the altered design. On August 12, 1959, BEA signed a £28 million purchase order for twenty-four jets, with deliveries to be complete by the fourth quarter of 1965. The decision to downsize the design was based on what turned out to be a temporary wobble in passenger-boarding numbers. While de Havilland publicly went along with the wishes of BEA, many analysts within the organization vehemently disagreed with the change. Some still refused to sign the change orders, even under threat of termination. History proved that these individuals were correct. This decision to make the Trident a smaller aircraft, in hindsight, is regarded by most experts as being a regrettable long-term mistake.

The Boeing 720B featured the Pratt & Whitney JT3D turbofan engine, which brought greater thrust with less fuel usage and noise. *Courtesy of the Boeing Company*

The de Havilland Trident 1 was similar in design and concept to the Boeing 727. G-ARPP (a Trident 1C) carried construction number 2121. It was involved in a nonfatal landing accident that damaged two parked Tridents, one of which (G-ARPI, c/n 2109) was repaired and later crashed in 1972, due, in part, to the T-tail deep stall characteristic. *Courtesy of Petr Popelar*

The aircraft developed into a much more compact aircraft than originally conceived by de Havilland, and was designed around the use of the smaller 10,100-pound-thrust-class Mk. 1 Rolls-Royce RB.163 turbofan (later marketed as the Rolls-Royce Spey). The RB.163 was advertised to provide the best fuel efficiency at the time for an engine of this thrust class. The aircraft retained the same fuselage cross section as the original de Havilland design but was shortened by roughly 13 feet. Commensurate with the weight reduction, the wing design was scaled down to reduce wing area by roughly 30 percent. Soon after these decisions were made on the Trident in 1959, Boeing completed its design specification for the new Boeing Model 727, a larger-capacity design with a high-lift wing.

Soon thereafter, on December 17, 1959, another well-known British airplane manufacturer, Hawker Siddeley, merged with de Havilland. Though de Havilland maintained some autonomy for a short period, by the time the first Trident was delivered, it had become the Hawker Siddeley Trident, with no reverence given to its true origins. On January 9, 1962, after delays due to poor weather, the first flight of the Hawker Siddeley Trident was conducted with G-ARPA (c/n 2101) under the command of the esteemed de Havilland test pilot John Cunningham. The flight was not without

The Trident 1C pictured here (G-ARPP, c/n 2117) served with BEA and later British Airways until early 1983. *Courtesy of Petr Popelar*

Iraqi Airways operated the Trident 1E, sporting this attractive livery. YI-AEB (c/n 2127) flew for the carrier until 1977 and is seen here with leading edge droops in the extended position. *Courtesy of Petr Popelar*

a glitch, however, as one of the swiveling main landing gears jammed against the inboard landing gear door assembly, due to a malfunctioning sequence valve. The fast-thinking crew depressurized one of the ship's hydraulic systems, allowing the main gear to extend via gravity and air loads. This problem aside, Cunningham indicated that he was content with the aircraft's handling and performance. After a lengthy flight test program involving over 1,600 hours of flight time, the Trident received its Certificate of Airworthiness on February 18, 1964.

The Trident 1C entered revenue service with BEA on March 11, 1964, with routing from London Heathrow to Copenhagen, Denmark. As the aircraft began day-to-day airline operations, it became apparent that the center engines on the Trident fleet, being fed air through its S-shaped duct, were beginning to experience difficulties with compressor stalls. This was due to disturbed air entering the inlet and causing too great of a pressure differential across the compressor inlet to the engine, leading to a momentary reversal of airflow through the engine. To remedy this, four small vortex generators were installed in the inlet, similar to the corrective action taken by Boeing on the 727 months earlier, during its flight testing. With the compressor stall issue mitigated, larger problems loomed on the horizon for the Trident. While BEA reported that the Trident 1C was well received by passengers, industry experts recognized that the Trident was, in fact, too small. This led to designs being implemented to increase passenger capacity. The Trident 1E was introduced with a cabin volume similar to the earlier model, but with increased gross weight gained by installing upgraded Spey 163-2W engines, which utilized water injection to increase takeoff thrust to 10,680 pounds each. To aid in short-field operations required by many potential customers, the leading edge "droop" system was replaced by slats to maximize lift while still minimizing drag. The maximum takeoff weight was increased to 134,000 pounds, which allowed for seven-abreast seating for a maximum of 149 passengers. Given that the aircraft had a fairly narrow fuselage, the use of a seven-abreast layout was certainly at the expense of passenger comfort.

The Trident was also susceptible to a condition that is known as a "deep stall," which is sometimes referred to as a "super stall." This characteristic is commonly a trait of T-tailed aircraft designs, where the wake of the wing and engine nacelles diminishes the effectiveness of the high-mounted horizontal stabilizers and elevators during times when the aircraft travels at extremely high angles through the passing air (for more information, see "The Deep stall Incident" on page 69). The danger of this condition was well understood, and redundant safety devices known as stick pushers were installed on the Trident to automatically force the yoke forward before a deep stall situation could become critical. Even so, two accidents with the Trident still occurred due to deep stalls after certification. The first was on a preproduction test flight with a Trident 1C (G-ARPY, c/n 2126) on March 6, 1966, during which stalls were conducted with the safety devices inhibited. The aircraft entered a condition that resulted in inadequate control authority to effect a recovery. The second occurred on June 18, 1972, when a BEA Trident 1C (G-ARPI, c/n 2109), operating as "Beeline 548," seemingly dropped from the sky near the Staines River in Middlesex, England, just after takeoff. The investigation revealed that the airplane entered a deep stall after an inadvertent retraction of the leading edge "droops" at a speed nearly 60 knots below the minimum droops-up speed of 225 knots. This put the airplane immediately into an aerodynamic stall situation, which progressed quickly into a deep stall, leaving the crew without

This cover was flown aboard the first flight of the stretched Trident 3 on November 8, 1971. *Author's collection*

Conclusion

While this "golden age" of aviation is often looked back upon with reverence and nostalgia, the truth of the matter is that jet aviation was well outside the reach of most of the world's population. Boeing and other purveyors of fine jet aircraft saw this as an incredible opportunity to sell thousands of jets, bringing the jet age to people who otherwise would have never had the opportunity to enjoy such freedom and convenience. The challenge was to create an aircraft that was cost effective to build and operate, while giving it the performance and capabilities needed to access regional airports around the world.

The following is the story of Boeing's beautiful Model 727.

the control authority or the altitude to recover successfully. The accident, which claimed 118 lives, was attributed to pilot error, with additive factors being a possible heart problem experienced by the captain. These accidents, along with two losses experienced by another T-tail design, the BAC One-Eleven, illustrated the intolerance of the high-tail designs to extreme angles of attack.

Even with the challenges of the Trident design, Hawker Siddeley made admirable attempts to compete with the 727, which was developed during the same time period. The longer-range Trident 2E was developed, while the need for greater passenger capacity brought forth the Trident Super 3B, which featured a fuselage stretched 16 feet, 7 inches to gain comfortable passenger accommodation. In order to obtain the required power, the late-model Spey Mk. 512, capable of producing 11,960 pounds of thrust, was employed. This ultimate Spey version still left the aircraft underpowered, though, which necessitated the inclusion of an additional Rolls-Royce RB.162 "booster" engine, rated for a thrust output of 5,250 pounds, to be installed above the center engine at the base of the rudder. Even with this addition, the limits of both the selected engine and airframe size for the Trident had simply reached absolute design limits. Operating at the higher weights, particularly with the later, heavier models, gave the aircraft a reputation for being a "runway hog." Crews, painfully aware of the aircraft's limitations, affectionately referred to the Trident as the "Gripper" because of its reluctance to leave the ground.

Despite its limitations, the Trident still served as the backbone of BEA's fleet at London Heathrow for nearly two decades, providing reliable service. The Trident was also on the leading edge of avionics technology, designed from the beginning to employ an automatic landing system for use during low-visibility approaches common to BEA's route structure.

The sad truth is that while the Trident was a competent design, it was far too small for future requirements. With the size reduction exacted by BEA and accepted in 1959, de Havilland essentially ceded the short-to-medium-range market to Boeing's Model 727 before either was even in production. Ultimately, only 117 Tridents were sold, but had the originally sized de Havilland concept been built, equipped with high-lift enhancements and more-powerful engines, its story may have been quite different.

2

Designing an Industry-Leading Jetliner

The Boeing 707 wasn't just a quantum leap forward for Boeing, but for the entire airline industry. A close military relative of the sleek jetliner, the KC-135, had likewise revolutionized the capabilities of the United States Air Force's Strategic Air Command, allowing faster, more efficient support of the United States' nuclear countermeasure forces at the height of the Cold War. By 1958, the 707 was widely recognized as the airliner of the future; an icon of advancement and technology. At that time, Boeing's competition was primarily the Douglas DC-8, an airplane designed with similar goals in mind and contending for many of the same contracts. It was an eminently competent jetliner; a worthy opponent that proved popular with the airline customers. There were even a few airlines, such as Braniff, Lufthansa, and Pan American World Airways, that operated both types concurrently.

The 707 was selling well, but the investments that Boeing made into the development of this extraordinary airplane ran very deep, with the firm having truly "bet the farm" on the program. There were also several different permutations of the 707 that offered different engines, fuselage lengths, wing designs, and performance parameters. During the late 1950s, two more derivatives were on the way; namely, the Boeing 720 and the Boeing 707-320 Intercontinental. The 720 was intended to be a shorter-range airplane with a slightly curtailed fuselage and a highly modified inboard wing section optimized for its role. The 707 Intercontinental series featured a larger wing, which increased both fuel capacity and lift to allow for true intercontinental range. The advent of the turbofan Pratt & Whitney JT3D engine increased the capabilities of these aircraft further and could also be retrofitted to earlier 707 versions. These engines were quieter and more fuel efficient than the previous pure turbojet engines.

The JT3D turbofan-powered Boeing 720B was more powerful and fuel efficient while producing less noise than the standard 720. Clearly visible is the leading edge glove added to the section of the wing between the inboard engine and the fuselage, which increased lift and reduced drag. This was standard on all 720s and was added to many 707-100B-series aircraft. *Courtesy of the Boeing Company*

StarStream...powerful reason to fly TWA

It looks like many others. But when it takes off, you know the StarStream* is no ordinary jet. Four huge DynaFan* engines get this beautiful giant off the ground and on up above the weather faster than any other transcontinental jet. You'll cruise so silently, so smoothly, it's hard to believe you're putting ten miles behind you every minute. And if there's a headwind, your pilot can tap a tremendous reserve of power to keep you right on schedule. Next time you fly, in the U.S. or overseas, be a name-dropper. Ask for the StarStream.

Nationwide
Worldwide
depend on

*StarStream and DynaFan are service marks owned exclusively by Trans World Airlines, Inc.

Author's collection

Competition was intense with Douglas for the lion's share of the blossoming jetliner market. This, combined with the significant number of differing 707 versions occupying the Renton, Washington, assembly line, eventually led to expensive inefficiencies and logistical issues for Boeing. By the late 1950s, Boeing was struggling financially and still a long way from a break-even point with the 707 because of these factors.

In 1958, Maynard Pennell was the chief designer of Boeing's Transport Division. He had worked extensively on the 707 program and was also instrumental in convincing management to move forward with the long-range Intercontinental 707. Boeing engineer Jack Wimpress described Pennell:

> He had a very calm personality. He was very thorough and gentlemanly. If you wanted to talk about a problem and have the right people in there to discuss it, he would listen to them all and then make a decision. There was never any table pounding, and I don't think that anyone felt that if the decision didn't go their way, that they didn't get a fair hearing.

Pennell had a vision for the future and strongly felt that Boeing needed to develop a smaller short-to-medium-range jet to tap into the markets currently being served by propeller-driven airliners. He knew that the market would eventually demand jets for such routes, and wanted Boeing to seize the opportunity. He was not the only one.

John E. "Jack" Steiner

John E. "Jack" Steiner, the mastermind behind the Boeing 727.
Courtesy of the Boeing Company

Jack E. Steiner was first hired as an engineer with Boeing in 1941 and eventually became regarded as one of the most gifted aircraft designers of all time. Although he considered the professional path of becoming a lawyer, instead Steiner attended the Massachusetts Institute of Technology, where he earned an MS in aeronautical engineering. By 1958, Steiner had assembled an impressive résumé that went all the way back to the advancement of the Boeing B-377 Stratocruiser, an airliner development of the venerable Boeing B-29 Stratofortress. Working under Pennell, Steiner was the project engineer for the Boeing 707's preliminary design effort and shared Pennell's excitement about a new, specialized airliner that could bring the jet age to smaller communities around the world.

Jack Steiner was noted to have a "throttles to the radar screen" mentality in all that he did. He was known to set very high standards for himself and likewise expected those around him to do the same. Boeing engineer Bruce Florsheim recalled:

> I worked directly for Jack Steiner. Jack was the consummate product development person. He understood that product development was not just simply coming up with good designs. To get a new airplane program launched, the key was marketing, and by marketing, I don't mean taking your product to the customer and selling it. Marketing is the art of understanding what the customer really wants and transforming that into a product that meets those needs. Jack knew that product development meant doing the design over, and over, and over again; doing all of the trade studies, doing competing configurations until it finally met what the customers wanted. He was a great boss. He cared for the people who worked for him. He was easy to talk with, but he was very, very intense. He would try to get a lot of things done in a very short period of time. He would do things on a very short time frame that you couldn't do today.

> He was a tireless boss. I can remember many late nights, bringing presentation material to him at his home so that he could go out early in the morning to catch an airplane and talk to the customers. I also remember bringing him more stuff before takeoff. You can't do the same thing today, but Jack always worked until the very last moment and would arrive for his flight with ten minutes or less before his scheduled departure time. The Boeing drivers all knew this, and they planned accordingly.

Jack Wimpress remembered:

> Jack was very difficult to work for if you had any other interests in your life. Over and over again, he would call us into his office on a Friday afternoon and say, "Here's what I want to see Monday morning."

Boeing's Peter Morton observed:

> My desk was right on this aisle way, and he would be walking past towards his office in the other corner of the

building. I used to say to myself, because he would lean forward, "He is leaning forward and walking fast enough that the aerodynamic drag keeps him from falling down!" He never looked at anybody; he would just focus. He was on a mission! Steiner's secretary was Marcie Burkhart, and my impression was that when Jack was traveling, which was a lot, Marcie would come to work very early, and her dictating machine would be filled with phone calls from Jack, over the night. Of course, she would transcribe and relay his assignments. When Marcie called, you knew Jack was calling, so you hustled to do whatever was requested.

Steiner was considered an incredibly gifted engineer but also carried a reputation with many as an unrelenting taskmaster because of his unshakable drive. This drive, however, was instrumental in creating one of the most successful jetliners in history.

The Boeing 707 was well into production and selling well, but the expenditures on the program were creating red ink in the accountants' ledgers. Because of this, many felt the financial timing was not ideal for a new aircraft program. This was likely true, but the company possessed a large cadre of talented and experienced engineers who would soon need a new project to challenge them as the 707 development efforts wound down. An abundance of different concept ideas had already been devised for a short-range jetliner, dubbed "the Boeing Model 727," with thirty-seven studies having already been completed by February 1956. On May 6, 1958, Bruce Connelly, vice president and general manager of Boeing's Transport Division, appointed Steiner to lead the planning group for the new

Bruce Connelly, vice president and general manager of Boeing's Transport Division, is seen during one of Boeing's sales tours. *Courtesy of the Boeing Company*

short-range jet. Fred Maxam, the preliminary design engineer on the scene, was working on the latest rendition. This concept featured two engines on long forward-swept pylons, adapted from the 707 and 720, attached to a highly swept wing. It was soon realized that while a four-engine jet was naturally balanced because of the wing's sweep, placing the outboard engines farther back, on a twin-engine jet it would leave the engine weight very far forward. Ultimately, this would force most of the fuselage to be behind the wings to counterbalance the engine weight. This dynamic would lead to issues with a lack of space for cockpit electronics and the nose landing gear well. New ideas needed to be explored. Jack Steiner was famous for saying, "If we don't have a few problems, we will die of comfort!"

Of more concern to Steiner was the market and how many airplanes it could actually support. Additionally, how could Boeing get there before Douglas, which would certainly have its own offering for the airlines? Lockheed was also testing their L-188 "Electra," due to enter service in 1959 with Eastern Airlines. While the Electra was not a pure jet, it did have a spritely cruise speed of 400 miles per hour while burning a fairly economical amount of fuel. Meanwhile, the Europeans were also hard at work. In France, SUD had been developing the graceful Caravelle jetliner, which first flew in 1955 and was preparing to enter service in 1959. De Havilland, of Great Britain, was looking to introduce a new short-to-medium-range jet as well. First and foremost, Boeing desired to beat Douglas to the market, but to have a chance at gaining a foothold, they needed to develop an airplane that was technically superior to any other offering.

While Steiner truly believed that the future was bright for a smaller, short-to-medium-range jetliner, there were many among the ranks at Boeing who were skeptical about if not completely against the new development. Some felt that an additional aircraft program, especially one that was forecast to have development and production costs that might approach one billion dollars, could sink the entire company should it fail to sell successfully. This mindset was understandable when considering Boeing's less-than-stellar track record at selling commercial aircraft up to this point. The 1930s saw Boeing build the Model 247, an all-metal, twin-engine monoplane that was soon overrun by Douglas's DC-2 and DC-3 airliners. The late 1940s and early 1950s brought about the Boeing 377 Stratocruiser. Only fifty-six of these airliners were built, with the airframe's success occurring mainly on the military side as the KC-97 aerial tanker. Neither of these aircraft were considered a commercial success, but Boeing remained stable due to profits coming from military sales. The red ink garnered by the early 707 program solidified the feelings among many that the commercial business was very risky to Boeing's future. Others were concerned that the 727 might compete with the newly developed medium-range Boeing 720 they were currently marketing. Both viewpoints had some merit at that particular juncture, but Pennell and Steiner also saw that the current financial, product, and marketing situations were not static. Decisions had to be made that would benefit Boeing in future decades. Steiner wrote of his philosophy regarding interference of a new airplane with existing Boeing products:

> I believe that one must constantly try to obsolete one's own product and that major airlines or government agencies are sophisticated enough to carry on a dialog on this subject without killing near-term sales. It is only through such a continued dialog that the really correct derivatives will make their appearance.

Early Boeing 727 Concepts

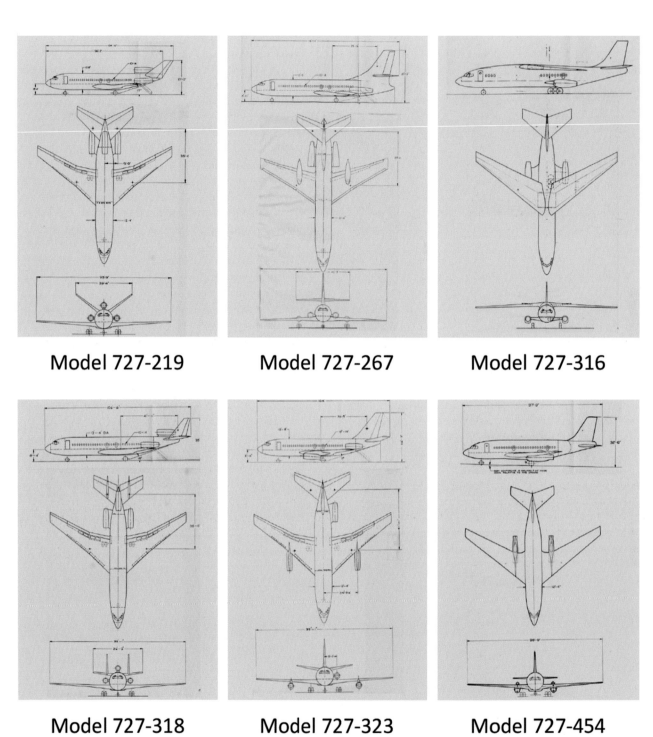

Model 727-219   Model 727-267   Model 727-316

Model 727-318   Model 727-323   Model 727-454

Boeing engineers explored many "outside the box" ideas for the new aircraft. *Courtesy of the Boeing Company*

Steiner was motivated to prove the feasibility of the 727 jetliner and did not waiver under the pressure from naysayers wanting to kill the program. His job was to build the best airplane his team could create, but the timing had to be just right.

By March 1958, Steiner was feeling the need to move quickly on the 727 feasibility studies. There were rumblings from Douglas in Long Beach that a new airplane, designed for the shorter-range markets, was on the horizon. Boeing needed to devise a solid plan expeditiously. With the agreement of Bob Murphy, assistant to sales director George Sanborn, Steiner brought together representatives from each department to submit a reliable estimate of the development and manufacturing costs of the proposed 727 program.

The Sud Caravelle featured a ventral airstair, similar to the eventual installation on the Boeing 727. The "cruciform" tail and triangular cabin windows are noteworthy characteristics of the Caravelle. *Courtesy of Petr Popelar*

Two or Four Engines?

Within Boeing, the fight for the 727 was concurrently waged on multiple fronts. While the cost analysis was being prepared by the involved parties, Steiner worked on acquiring more information to help direct the final configuration of the 727. In the company of sales engineer Art Curren and chief of preliminary design Don Finlay, Steiner set out for San Francisco to visit United Airlines. The delegation shared design ideas with United's vice president of engineering, Bill Meltzer, who made it clear that United was in favor of a design that had more than two engines. First and foremost, public perception was a key factor. United believed that until the traveling public became comfortable with jet airplanes, there would be a strong preference

for a machine with four engines. At the time, twin-engine aircraft had more-restrictive takeoff weather minima than aircraft with three or four power plants. This was a significant factor for United, with its large operation in San Francisco, a city commonly plagued by fog in the summer months, along with Denver, whose high-altitude operations were also perceived as a challenge for twin-jet performance. The issue came from the necessity for an airliner to be able to climb away, meeting obstacle clearance requirements, after suffering an engine failure just prior to liftoff. A four-engine aircraft, for example, would lose only 25 percent of the thrust available if such an event were to occur. The twin, on the other hand, would lose 50 percent of its power. This, combined with the warm, thin air on a summer day in Denver, would most certainly create some performance challenges.

Boeing also approached Eastern Airlines, which had already put forth an order for forty Lockheed L-188 Electra turboprops but was still interested in a pure jet airplane in the same size class. Eastern's management believed that the most economical airplane for their operation was a two-engine machine, and were thus seemingly unconcerned about the issues deemed significant by United. Some of this was surely due to the differing route structures of the two carriers, which presented different challenges. Steiner and the others on his team found themselves at a crossroads, where two extremely significant airlines were wanting completely opposite design parameters. The team was essentially painted into a corner, with neither a two-engine nor a four-engine design making everyone content, regardless of how good the airplane might be.

Trans World Airlines was also actively resisting the turboprop options offered by Lockheed and Vickers, and were willing to wait for a turbojet aircraft to meet their short-to-medium-range needs. Jack Steiner telephoned TWA's headquarters in Kansas City and spoke with Bob Rummel, their vice president of engineering, who knew Steiner well from past projects. He confirmed that TWA needed a smaller jet to complement its fleet of 707s currently on order. The two men were speaking of the controversy regarding two- versus four-engine configurations when Rummel, hitting the proverbial nail on the head, asked Steiner, "Why don't you compromise on three

While Jack Steiner was a very serious and intense engineer, many of the cartoon drawings distributed during the 727 program showed a distinct sense of humor about the design process. *Courtesy of the Boeing Company*

Different teams were set up to explore and draw conclusions on the best-possible configurations for the 727. *Courtesy of the Boeing Company*

engines and make a GOOD airplane?" Although the preliminary design team had considered the three-engine concept, it had not been completely explored as a viable option, with the majority of the serious efforts thus far concentrating on either two or four engines.

Rising Costs

Back in Seattle, various departmental representatives met in an attempt to keep the 727 cost objectives under control. Joe Sutter, the engineering representative, was of the opinion that if the 727 was to be significantly different in design from the 707, there should be a dedicated "prototype" aircraft. Conversely, the finance people felt that the expense of a nonsalable prototype would be unacceptable. The compromise was to have the first aircraft be a "preproduction" airplane, which could be sold for revenue service at a later date. The engineers involved recognized the thinly veiled issue, though, since major flaws in many past aircraft designs weren't discovered until being built and flight-tested. Without a prototype airplane to act as a buffer between a potential design error and the stream of production airplanes, an overlooked issue could prove costly. The staff knew that they would have to get it right the first time out.

It was also evident that the 727 would have to share as much parts commonality as possible with the 707 to help control development and logistical costs. Steiner learned from the 707 program that conducting thorough research beforehand could narrow down the number of options offered to airlines, which also helped in cutting

production expenses. Even with these cost control measures in hand, it was beginning to appear that the price point on the 727 would be quite high. It was estimated that the price per aircraft would have to be in the neighborhood of $3.5 million to break even at the 200-aircraft delivery target. On the other side, the sales staff projected that they could sell roughly 180 airplanes by 1965 at a price of $2.5 million each. The difference between the cost of building the new jet and the price that Boeing could successfully sell them for was seemingly too great. The numbers were not adding up in a favorable way, and the future of the 727 project was looking bleak. This sent the engineers back to the least expensive development option: a scaled-down four-engine aircraft, similar to the 707, that risked the possibly of alienating Eastern Airlines. There were no good options.

Jack Steiner realized that the most effective way to market a $3.5 million airplane was to ensure that it offered operational efficiencies that no other jetliner could match. By building an incredibly good product, the high price tag could be justified. With these ideals in mind, Connelly approached Boeing's president, Bill Allen, on behalf of the 727 project. Allen and Connelly were of the mindset that a go/no-go decision needed to be reached quickly, since Douglas was romancing United with a proposal for a small four-engine jetliner, marketed as the Douglas DC-9. Pratt & Whitney appeared to be investing considerable effort on the four-engine DC-9 proposal, too, and was working with the Long Beach manufacturer to produce a suitable engine. How serious was United about the Douglas jet, and how much time did Boeing have to present a superior product before it was too late? There were many questions and few answers.

On June 2, 1959, the Model 727 Product Evaluation Study was formed with Steiner as the director. Due to the compact timeline required, the results from the study were due just two months later, on August 1. Steiner's plan was to have the data ready for presentation to Boeing management early, after only six weeks, to allow proposals to be sent to the airline customers as expeditiously as possible. An optimum configuration, one that would meet the combined needs of American Airlines, Eastern, TWA, and United, would have to be established as soon as possible. The best strategy required working closely with each carrier and drawing them into the design process. While Steiner's attitude was to make sure the 727 program flew with

Boeing's well-respected leader, William M. "Bill" Allen, climbs the boarding ladder on a newly built B-47 strategic bomber. *Courtesy of the Boeing Company*

An artist's conception of the four-engine DC-9 concept that was pitched to United Airlines in 1959. *Courtesy of the Boeing Company*

a "do whatever it takes" mentality, the question still loomed: How many engines, and how would they interface with the airframe?

The airframe design was not the only obstacle to overcome. Regardless of the number of engines the 727 would eventually utilize, there were no truly compatible engines readily available with suitable classes of thrust. Rolls-Royce was developing the new RB.163 (later known as the "Spey") for de Havilland's jetliner project, but these engines were too thrust limited for what Boeing's designers envisioned for a two- or three-engine airplane. Bill Allen and Jack Steiner met with leaders from General Motors' Allison aero engine division about the possibility of an agreement to build a larger Rolls-Royce engine, the RB.141 Medway, under license in the United States to SAE standards. This engine development could be appropriate for a twin-engine 727, should that configuration be selected. Allison was willing to work with Boeing to supply engines with favorable payment and financing arrangements, but this was not the only valuable takeaway for the Boeing executives. Allison's vice president of engineering, Cy Osborn, had his finger on the pulse both of American and Eastern Airlines because of their respective purchases of the Allison 501–powered Electras. Osborn shared his knowledge that American was agreeable to a twin-engine small jet, while Eastern was looking at either a two- or three-engine platform as ideal. This gave Boeing some valuable information and also signaled a bit of a shift on Eastern's preferences. Over the course of this meeting, it became apparent to Steiner that Bill Allen was beginning to show excitement for the 727 program.

Pennell had spoken with representatives from the Rohr Company, which specialized in designing and manufacturing engine cowlings and thrust reverser systems for jetliners. They indicated that Douglas had procured an order for thirty-nine DC-9s to an undisclosed customer. The fear was that Boeing had just lost a possible order from United. Bill Allen had developed a good rapport with United's president, W. A. "Pat" Patterson, and decided to take the direct approach on the topic. He telephoned Patterson and found that United was not yet married to the DC-9. Douglas had yet to officially launch the DC-9 because they required at least one more order before committing to production of the new, four-engine jet concept. This left United willing to wait until August to investigate Boeing's conclusions and proposal for a short-range jetliner. A brief stay of execution had been obtained!

After weeks of burning the midnight oil and weekends spent trying to solve the seemingly unsolvable, the 727 research team, now totaling 106 people from different departments within Boeing, brought their research to the meeting with senior Boeing management. Jack Steiner made the case for both the four-engine and twin-jet concepts.

The four-engine aircraft was desirable to United Airlines because of the demands of their specialized route structure and would be less expensive for Boeing to build because of their experience with four-engine airplanes. This would essentially be a scaled-down 707 derivative and was the path of least resistance with regard to engineering, but it would also harbor operating expenses estimated at 6 percent higher than a twin jet. Would this be the best product for the customer in the long run? The twin jet would offer better economics than the four-engine platform, but mounting the engines out in front of the wings would cause issues with the balance of the aircraft. Given their desires, United would likely buy the four-engine DC-9 concept over a twin, creating a problem regarding market share with Douglas. Either option would also require the development of new engines of appropriate thrust classes. Costs were still too high, which, combined with the red ink still prevailing from the 707/720 program, was difficult for Bill Allen and the other leaders to accept. Could the lessons from the 707 program lead to efficiencies capable of counterbalancing the 727's high development costs?

The meeting ended on less than a positive note, since costs, aircraft configurations, and the possibility of the new Boeing jet stepping on sales for the 720 raised deep concerns for everyone present. Jack Steiner was disappointed with the outcome of the meeting but was also galvanized more than ever. More input was needed both from the airlines and the engine manufacturers to bring the situation into sharper focus. Up to this point, a three-engine possibility was not seriously analyzed, with nearly all of the effort going into the two- versus four-engine competition.

Jack Steiner reviews the 727 concept studies with his engineering staff. Joe Sutter, who was responsible for much of the wing design on the 727, stands next to him with arms crossed. Joe Sutter later became the driving force behind both the 737 and the 747 designs. *Courtesy of the Boeing Company*

Bill Allen (*left*) and United Airlines' W. A. "Pat" Patterson discuss the Boeing 727. *Courtesy of the Boeing Company*

Why Not Three?

In Great Britain, de Havilland had been working tirelessly on their DH.121 Trident jetliner project, which was being designed to the specifications of British European Airways (BEA). Throughout the process, the size point of the aircraft had been changed, progressively shrinking from de Havilland's original concept. Designed around the use of three RB.163 engines rated to 9,850 pounds of thrust, the modified design could accommodate eighty passengers. The Trident design featured three aft-mounted engines: one podded engine on either side of the rear fuselage, and the third buried in the tail cone, which would be fed air from an intake above the body. On August 12, 1959, de Havilland received an order for twenty-four airplanes of this design, which effectively launched the Trident program.

News of the Trident order was quickly noticed by Boeing, generating great interest. Up to this point, in late August 1959, the trijet idea had not been thoroughly explored by the team, but as investigation continued, it began to materialize as a good possibility. Talks with TWA's Bob Rummel suggested that the three-engine airplane would be ideal because of the near-centerline thrust making controllability after an engine failure much easier for the pilot. The wing would provide greater efficiency too, since it would be free of pylons and engines. Rummel had Steiner's attention, and the three-engine platform was beginning to appear viable.

According to the book *Billion Dollar Battle*, a visit to Eastern Airlines yielded the same response from Froesch, who went straight to the point. "The trijet is the airplane that you should build," he told Steiner. "There is no doubt about it, as far as Eastern is concerned." A paradigm shift had occurred at Eastern headquarters largely because the company's president, Eddie Rickenbacker, was intent on using the new aircraft for the long overwater flight from New York to Puerto Rico. Not only was a twin jet no longer seen as ideal, it was no longer desirable at all. American was of the stance that the airline would prefer a twin, but had no serious misgivings with a three-engine configuration. There was some mention, however, that they would like to use an existing engine type; namely, the Pratt & Whitney JT3D. Meltzer, at United, began to put more weight in the economic issues associated with the four-engine jet, and showed a large amount of interest in the trijet configuration. The die had been cast!

In 1978, Jack Steiner wrote about the three-engine decision:

> Thus, to launch the 727 program, we had to some way find a middle ground between United's desire for four engines and Eastern's desire for two. The middle ground proved to be a three-engine airplane, and this, more than any other one factor, led to the three engines on the 727.

The Pratt & Whitney "Turbo Wasp"

As the old saying goes, "Good things take time, but great things happen all at once." Before these latest developments almost instantly came to fruition, Boeing's Don Finlay had set off for Derby, England, to meet with Rolls-Royce. His goal was to hammer out a plan to create an engine that would be appropriate for the four-engine 727

concept. Rolls was agreeable, and the preliminary details were being worked out on the development of such an engine when he received an urgent correspondence from Seattle. Finlay was quickly brought up to speed that the four-engine airplane was yesterday's news, and the trijet was now looking to be the answer to Boeing's dilemma. Steiner arrived in Britain expeditiously to sit at the table with Rolls-Royce. Because of the configuration change, he was now asking for a completely different engine. Steiner's idea was for Rolls-Royce to create an enlarged version of the RB.163 for use on the new 727, which might be built under license by Allison in the United States as the ARB.963. The perception was that Rolls-Royce was lukewarm, while not directly rejecting the idea.

Further correspondence with Eastern's Eddie Rickenbacker yielded that he had experienced problems with Allison and was not satisfied with their handling of issues with the Allison 501 engines on their Electra fleet. He was also concerned about using the Rolls engine because of the great distance between his maintenance facilities and Derby, England. He felt that this could lead to unacceptable delays in dealing with technical issues in service. Consequently, Steiner was motivated to approach Denny Pearson (later to become Sir Denny Pearson) of Rolls-Royce about manufacturing the ARB.963-9, rated to 13,000 pounds of thrust, in the United States as an exclusive Rolls-Royce product. The choice, dictated by Eastern, was to either build the engine in the US or lose the sale. For reasons unknown to Steiner, Pearson was unable to commit.

Boeing found itself on the doorstep at Pratt & Whitney, looking for a new engine at the eleventh hour. The J52 engine was already in service with the US Air Force on the AGM-28 Hound Dog missile

Eddie Rickenbacker, a famous World War I pilot, led Eastern Airlines during the development of the 727. *Courtesy of the Boeing Company*

ROLLS-ROYCE
SPEY
BY-PASS JETS

powering short and medium haul airliners

The Spey family of by-pass jets has been chosen to power the de Havilland Trident, BAC One-Eleven and the Fokker F.28. The Spey's economy of operation is an inherent factor in the low operating costs of these aircraft.

DE HAVILLAND TRIDENT

BAC ONE-ELEVEN

AERO ENGINES · MOTOR CARS · DIESEL AND PETROL ENGINES · ROCKET MOTORS · NUCLEAR PROPULSION

This was one of the first times in history that a jet engine was designed for a specific aircraft, when Pratt & Whitney purpose-built the JT8D engine for the Boeing 727. This engine went on to become one of the most prolific aero engines of all time, powering the highly successful Douglas DC-9 series and the later Boeing 737 Original series jetliners. *Courtesy of Pratt & Whitney*

and would serve as the basis for the new engine. A newly designed compressor section was added, from which roughly half the output was consumed by the engine's core for combustion, while the remaining high-velocity air propelled through this stage was bypassed around the core. This bypassed air, mixed with the core's exhaust prior to exiting the jet pipe, allowed additional thrust and efficiency to be gained, with a significant reduction in environmental noise.

The new engine, initially called the "Turbo Wasp," was later redesignated as the JT8D. It featured two counterrotating axial compressor spools, employing a total of thirteen compressor stages. At full power, the compressor squeezed the air up to 14.6 times atmospheric pressure prior to delivering it to the nine annular combustion chambers. Here, fuel was introduced to this highly pressurized hot air, and the ignition process, once the engine was up to idle speed, became self-sustained until fuel supply was shut off. With the fuel energy added, the gas flow proceeded to the twin-spool turbine stages, where energy was extracted to turn the compressor sections via counterrotating shafts in the center of the engine. In this way, the JT8D provided the intake, compression, combustion, and exhaust cycles, like any other combustion engine.

A cutaway model of the Pratt & Whitney JT8D engine. *Courtesy of Chadi Akkari*

The Cost-Effective Solution

Back in Seattle, the operating-cost analysis looked favorably upon the trijet configuration. While operating-cost estimates showed a marked difference between two and four engines, the difference between two and three was minimal, at just 0.3 percent more. Although Steiner and others at Boeing were sensitive to the appearance of "following" de Havilland with the three-engine configuration, it was quickly realized that this was the configuration that would work for each of the customers' needs. In this regard, it was ideal, but the development and production costs were a different story. It would simply cost more to build the very best product possible. Serious efforts would have to be put forth to make the development and manufacturing processes more cost effective.

John Yeasting was Boeing's vice president of finance and was the man that Jack Steiner needed on his side for any chance of a 727 program being born. With this in mind, Steiner called a meeting on the financial status of the program. Yeasting was generally agreeable and wisely saw the red ink on the 707 program as the cost of learning a new business. That being said, he indicated what Steiner had known all along—that this program would have to be run using the 707 "investment" as a learning tool versus an impediment.

Steiner came up with a plan to keep costs under control. Naturally, the 727 would incorporate as much parts commonality as possible

with her older sisters; that was a given. Special attention would be cast upon minimizing tooling changes and streamlining the manufacturing process. The 727 was planned as a purely commercial venture, which effectively eliminated many of the documentation requirements that Boeing had on the 707 for the military. Most importantly, the number of options available to the airlines would be very limited and based on market analysis from the start. Once underway, changes would be made only with great discretion. In these ways, the additional development costs could be offset and the optimal airplane built.

Steiner's team pressed on with the design of the new trijet. Steiner had a list of objectives for the 727. They were as follows:

- Maximum passenger appeal
- Low direct operating costs
- Short-field capability
- Low noise impact
- All-weather operation
- Operational flexibility and self-sufficiency
- High profit potential

With these goals in mind, the team set out to design the 727 in such a way as to meet and exceed expectations in all of these categories.

The problem of fitting three engines onto the tail of the aircraft caused engineers to come up with several different possibilities. Initially, a V-tail design, similar to the popular Beechcraft Bonanza private aircraft, was considered, with the center engine mounted in the crux of the V-tail. This idea was quickly ruled out, since Joe Sutter and other aerodynamicists found that the configuration was unfavorable for the 727. Additionally, it was ill advised to mount an engine above a structure that would carry electric conduits, because of fire hazards caused by the inevitable fluid leaks from the engine. A concept with two wing-mounted engines and one mounted asymmetrically on the side of the aft fuselage was even, albeit briefly, entertained. Most of the designs included a center engine buried in the aft fuselage with

Many designs were wind tunnel tested to determine the best overall configuration for the 727. This cruciform-tail concept was not pushed forward due to complications with the stabilizer jackscrew assembly interfering with the center-engine S-duct. *Courtesy of the Boeing Company*

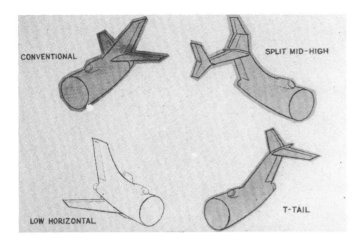

These are the four primary tail configurations considered during the early development of the 727. *Courtesy of the Boeing Company*

an over-the-fuselage S-shaped duct feeding air to it. Conventional, mid-fuselage-mounted horizontal stabilizers were tried in the wind tunnel but were not deemed satisfactory, as was one with the stabilizers mounted near the bottom of the body. Painting outside the lines, so to speak, a horizontal stabilizer, mounted atop a short vertical surface with twin vertical stabilizers on the tips, was also explored. A Caravellesque "cruciform" configuration with the horizontal stabilizers mounted midway up the vertical stabilizer showed some promise and looked appealing to boot but caused technical problems interfacing the stabilizer in close proximity to the S-duct for the center engine.

After reviewing all the possible configurations, two were selected, one as the primary design and the other as an alternate. Both entries incorporated a T-tail configuration with one engine buried in the rear fuselage, fed by an S-duct drawing air from above the fuselage, ahead of the stabilizer. On both concepts, the vertical stabilizer was sharply swept at a 55-degree angle. These ideas differed mainly in the placement of the other two engines. The primary design featured the other two (engines #1 and #3) mounted to the sides of the rear fuselage with a pod and pylon arrangement. The alternate design moved these engines to their respective wing, on long, forward-swept pylons.

The Launch of the 727 Program

> I think we can build a better plane.
> —William Boeing, 1914

In 1960, Boeing identified four major customers for the 727 in the United States. These carriers were American, Eastern, TWA, and United. At least two of these would have to submit substantial orders for the 727 program to move forward. American had recently committed to the Lockheed Electra for their short-haul requirements and thus was seen as a possibility, though not a strong one. TWA was strapped financially and was unlikely to be able to assume a launch customer role with the 727. That left Eastern and United, which made preventing Douglas's DC-9 concept sale to United of paramount importance. The hesitation that Douglas had in launching the four-engine DC-9 concept with only one order allowed United to play the field. This gave Boeing just enough time to devise a plan, address the internal financial struggles that were ensuing, and commit to producing the 727.

William Boeing (*right*), with his pilot Eddie Hubbard, stand in front of Boeing's first aircraft, the Model B&W. *Courtesy of the Boeing Company*

On December 5, 1960, both Eastern Airlines and United Airlines put forth orders for forty jets each, thus launching the Boeing 727 program. This order, totaling $350,000,000, was, according to the Boeing press release of the same date, "believed to constitute the largest transaction in the history of the transportation industry." This deal was announced to the world at a press conference by Boeing's president Bill Allen, United's vice president of engineering and maintenance, J. A. Herlihy, and Eastern's president, Malcolm A. MacIntyre. During the event, Bill Allen stated that the 727 program was based on "the definite need for such an aircraft and the enthusiastic acceptance of jet transportation by the airlines and the traveling public." Allen then continued, "These initial orders for the 727, totaling eighty aircraft, plus intense interest by many other domestic and overseas airlines, resulted in our decision to proceed, at full speed, with this new and promising product."

This celebration marked Boeing's whole-hearted commitment to build the new 727 jetliner.

Creating the Jetliner of Tomorrow

Choosing the Optimum Three-Engine Configuration

Courtesy of the Boeing Company

Jack Steiner set up two design teams to study and make a final decision on an ideal configuration for the new trijet 727. Both the primary concept (featuring a T-tail and aft-mounted engines) and the alternate concept (retaining the T-tail and S-ducted center engine, but with podded engines attached beneath each wing) were assigned to separate teams. At the conclusion of these studies, strong opinions existed supporting each design.

Jack Steiner wrote of the findings:

In the end, we found that there were advantages and disadvantages to each. The loadability of the aft engine airplane was definitely harder, particularly as future stretch models were envisioned. However, there was some evidence of a drag improvement, particularly when the short field and very high lift plus wing area trades were considered. Wing area, of course, affected economics. There were even some indications that the aft engine airplane was slightly cheaper to build because its systems were more concentrated. None of the effects were decisive, but we opted for the aft engine configuration. A minor additional defense of this configuration is that it results in a very quiet front half of the passenger cabin during takeoff and landing, an advantage which becomes more or less lost as cruise speed is gained.

After the primary, aft-mounted engine option was selected, another interesting permutation emerged that, as Jack Steiner said, had the engineers "enamored." The idea was to cluster all three engines together in the aft fuselage, sharing a common low-profile intake that would be largely contained in the aircraft's boundary layer. This boundary layer is a thin "skin" of air that an airplane carries with it in flight. The thought was that if the common intake, which would encircle the fuselage, operated in this region, parasite drag could be reduced. This concept was looked at carefully, but the issue arose that all three engines would have to be mounted in line with one another in a cluster. This could lead to serious consequences in the event of an uncontained failure of one of the engines, damaging one or both of the remaining power plants. Because of this concern, this variation was soon abandoned for the original S-ducted and pod-mounted configuration, which had the center (#2) engine staggered behind the side-mounted units.

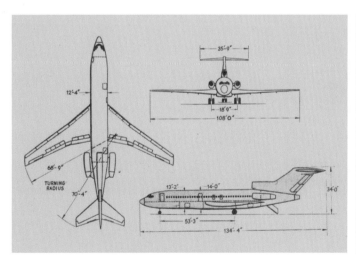

Primary Configuration

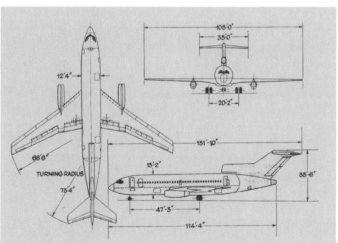

Alternate Configuration

Courtesy of the Boeing Company

Now, from the world's most experienced builder of jetliners

BOEING 707   BOEING 707 INTERCONTINENTAL   BOEING 720

The new short-to-medium range Boeing

The superb new Boeing 727 is a high-performance jetliner for service over short-to-medium routes. With it, airlines will be able to extend jet service to many more cities. Eastern Air Lines and United Air Lines have already ordered eighty 727s for delivery in 1963.

The three-engine 727 incorporates many of the structural and systems components that have been proved in the Boeing 707 and 720. It also has the same cabin width, permitting 4- 5- or 6-abreast seating.

The 727 is designed to operate from 5,000-foot runways with full payload, and to serve economically on routes from 150 to 1,700 miles. It offers 850 cubic feet of cargo space. Speed is 550 to 600 mph.

Of equal importance, the 727 is backed by the outstanding performance and reliability demonstrated in more than 238,000,000 miles of Boeing jetliner operations . . . good reasons why *more* airlines have ordered *more* jetliners from Boeing than from any other manufacturer.

These 20 airlines (plus MATS) *have ordered 337 Boeing jetliners:* AIR FRANCE • AIR-INDIA • AMERICAN • AVIANCA • B.O.A.C. • BRANIFF • CONTINENTAL • EASTERN • EL AL • ETHIOPIAN • IRISH LUFTHANSA • PAN AMERICAN • QANTAS • SABENA • SOUTH AFRICAN • TWA • UNITED • VARIG • *and* WESTERN. *In addition,* NORTHEAST, PERSIAN *and* PAKISTAN *operate Boeing jetliners under lease.*

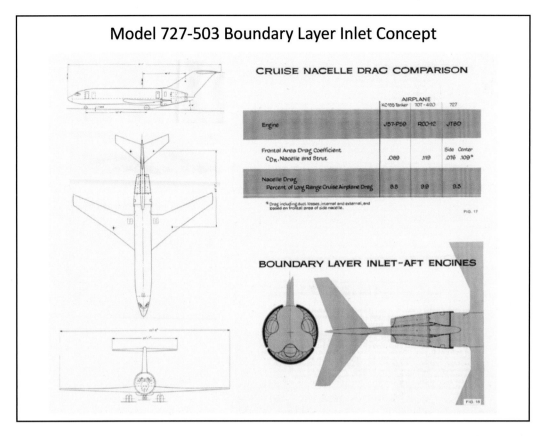

Model 727-503 Boundary Layer Inlet Concept

CRUISE NACELLE DRAG COMPARISON

	AIRPLANE		
	KC-135 Tanker	707-420	727
Engine	J57-P59	RCO-12	JT8D
Frontal Area Drag Coefficient C_{D_N}, Nacelle and Strut	.089	.119	Side .076 Center .309*
Nacelle Drag Percent of Long Range Cruise Airplane Drag	8.8	9.9	9.3

* Drag including duct losses, internal and external, and based on frontal area of side nacelle.

FIG. 17

BOUNDARY LAYER INLET-AFT ENGINES

FIG. 18

The concept of the boundary layer inlet was intended to reduce drag by placing the whole inlet within, or close to, the fuselage boundary layer. Although it was an ingenious idea, it was believed that placing all three engines in alignment with and in proximity to one another would increase the risk of one uncontained engine failure that could damage the remaining engines. Thus, the idea was eventually shelved. *Courtesy of the Boeing Company*

The Gauntlet

Once all the needs and desires of the airlines were taken into account, the following list of design requirements was determined and implemented. The 727 airplane needed to be able to

- carry a full payload 1,500 nautical miles from a 6,000-foot-long runway (sea level, 90°F), cruising at 30,000 feet at a speed of Mach 0.80, and land on a runway no longer than 4,900 feet in length
- carry a useful payload (seventy-five passengers) from Denver to Chicago, with a takeoff temperature of 90°F
- certify to a 35-knot crosswind for takeoff, and
- meet wet-runway landing-distance requirements under operational airline conditions

The world's finest minds in aircraft design had their work cut out for them. Next, we will look at the evolution of the design in greater detail.

The Fuselage

Moving forward with the rear-mounted, three-engine primary configuration, the decision was made early on to retain the wide 707 upper fuselage cross section to create a roomy, comfortable cabin. This was also cost effective because it increased commonality with the 707/720 aircraft and featured the same robust semimonocoque design made from 2024 aluminum alloy. Additionally, this was an advantage over the Trident, which was being designed with a narrower fuselage. Boeing was confident that a cramped cabin would not sell well, particularly in the United States. Therefore, accommodations for a seventy-passenger first-class layout or a 114-seat all-tourist-class

This illustration shows the final concept configuration. Note the Tridentesque center engine inlet and the dihedral applied to the horizontal stabilizers. On the final design, these featured a 2-degree anhedral (angled downward toward the stabilizer tips) to reduce the likelihood of aerodynamic flutter. *Courtesy of the Boeing Company*

configuration could be provided, with a midship galley located just forward of the wing, on the starboard side of the cabin.

A lower fuselage lobe of smaller cross section was selected, for the portion forward of the wing, in order to reduce frontal area drag. This reduced the cargo-carrying capacity somewhat but was a necessary compromise to meet the 727's high-speed/low-drag requirements. A shorter baggage compartment was also to be placed behind the wings. To increase capacity and aid in balancing the aircraft for proper center of gravity (CG) loading, the aft lower fuselage lobe was made deeper than the forward section, yet still slightly shallower than the 707 cross section.

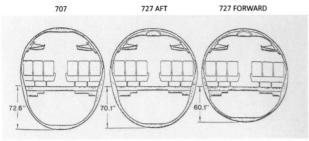

707   727 AFT   727 FORWARD

72.6"   70.1"   60.1"

LOWER FUSELAGE LOBE COMPARISON

Both the forward and aft lower-lobe sections on the 727 differed from those of the 707. Later, the Boeing 737's fuselage would share the dimensions of the 727's forward section. Courtesy of the Boeing Company

The 727 was designed for shorter-stage lengths than the 707, requiring more takeoffs and landings (per flight hour) on average. Although each takeoff and landing added some measure of wear and tear to the airframe, this was not the most significant issue. Each time the aircraft climbed to altitude, the 727's fuselage was pressurized up to 8.6 psi and subsequently depressurized for landing. Each cycle increased the possibility of metal fatigue, which required mitigation during the design stage (see "The Alpha: de Havilland's Comet" on page 10). Additional structure and improved body skin splices were incorporated to meet these design challenges and to increase service life. As a safeguard against fatigue cracks, the use of steel rivets was kept to a minimum. Anticorrosion measures were equally important, since Skydrol, the standard hydraulic fluid used on Boeing jets, is somewhat corrosive to aluminum structures. Therefore, a Skydrol-resistant coating was applied to the internal surfaces of the fuselage structure to prevent such damage.

The Cockpit

Due to the requirement to take maximum advantage of the 707/720 components already engineered and developed, the 727 was designed using the nose and cockpit fuselage section from her older sisters. This gave the 727 a "familiar" appearance when compared to the older Boeing jetliners, while maintaining a high level of similarity for crews transitioning from one type of Boeing jet to another. Naturally, there were significant systems differences with the 727 that required many changes, to the overhead and flight engineer panels in particular. Accommodation for two pilots, a flight engineer, and two observers was provided, along with ample stowage space for the crew's flight kits. Entry and exit was accomplished through the cockpit door, into the cabin. In an emergency, either pilot side window could be translated aft, and with use of the supplied escape ropes, expeditious egress was possible.

CONTROL CABIN

The 727-200 control cabin (fig. 1) is a highly efficient, workable arrangement. Stations are provided for the captain, first officer, third crewman, and an observer. A station for a second observer is optional. Each station is provided with a diluter-demand oxygen regulator, a demand-type mask assembly, ashtray, coffee cupholder, reading light, headset, and microphone holder. Individual air-conditioning outlets are provided for each crew member, as well as several outlets for general air distribution. The interior is surfaced with an attractive, durable molded plastic material. Most of the cabin walls are insulated with fiberglass blankets for sound suppression. Insulated drip pans above the circuit breaker panels and the overhead panels protect the instruments, switches, and circuitry against moisture condensation and large temperature variations. Any condensate in this area is collected by the drip pans and drained overboard through the airplane body drain system. Miscellaneous equipment including fire extinguishers, crash axe, escape straps, emergency landing gear crank handle, spare bulb box, coat hanger rod, and hat clips is installed. Stowage space is provided for a log book, smoke goggles, and life vests. Structural provisions for a periscopic sextant mount are made in the control cabin ceiling.

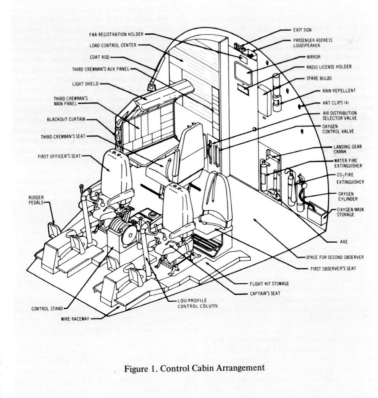

FAA REGISTRATION HOLDER
LOAD CONTROL CENTER
COAT ROD
THIRD CREWMAN'S AUX PANEL
LIGHT SHIELD
THIRD CREWMAN'S MAIN PANEL
BLACKOUT CURTAIN
THIRD CREWMAN'S SEAT
FIRST OFFICER'S SEAT
RUDDER PEDALS
CONTROL STAND
WIRE RACEWAY
LOW PROFILE CONTROL COLUMN
CAPTAIN'S SEAT
FLIGHT KIT STOWAGE
FIRST OBSERVER'S SEAT
SPACE FOR SECOND OBSERVER
AXE
OXYGEN MASK STORAGE
OXYGEN CYLINDER
CO₂ FIRE EXTINGUISHER
WATER FIRE EXTINGUISHER
LANDING GEAR CRANK
OXYGEN CONTROL VALVE
AIR DISTRIBUTION SELECTOR VALVE
HAT CLIPS (4)
RAIN REPELLENT
SPARE BULBS
RADIO LICENSE HOLDER
MIRROR
PASSENGER ADDRESS LOUDSPEAKER
EXIT SIGN

Figure 1. Control Cabin Arrangement

Courtesy of the Boeing Company

The focus of the wing design on the 727 began with the Boeing 720 airfoil as a starting point, but it needed to be tailored to the specific mission of the new jetliner. Concurrent with the quest to develop the ideal wing, the engineers kept a close eye on the desired control qualities of the new airplane. The goal was to meet the performance objectives while having favorable stability and handling characteristics, with a minimum amount of artificial feel and stability augmentation. The eventual 727 wing design was optimized to have lower drag numbers for a given amount of lift than the 720 wing. While less drag meant less fuel burn and improved operating costs for the airlines, as with almost every situation in aircraft design, it was not without compromises. In this instance, the potential top speed (or Mach number, given the atmospheric environment) of the wing would be slightly reduced, compared with its predecessor.

Joe Sutter and his team worked diligently on the wing design for the 727. It needed to be small enough to allow high cruise speeds, while not leading to an unacceptable drag increase. A smaller, highly loaded wing was also advantageous, in that it allowed for a more comfortable ride through turbulent air for the passengers and crew. To help effect both the comfort and low drag requirements, Boeing engineers wanted to use a highly swept wing that would accomplish both objectives. Initially, a sweep of 35 degrees was thought to be ideal, due to its similarity to the sweepback used on the 707, which had yielded good performance characteristics. Boeing kept a close working relationship with its customers, which led to valuable input from the technical staff at United Airlines. United was already flying the DC-8, which featured a wing swept at 30 degrees. United, due to their positive experiences with the Douglas machine, wanted the proposed sweep reduced on the 727 to match the DC-8. When the final configuration of the 727 wing was brought forth, a compromised sweep of 32½ degrees (at quarter span) was selected to aid in suiting the jet to United's needs. Also, attendant to United's high-altitude takeoff performance requirements in Denver, the wingspan for the 727 was increased 6 feet to meet the required climb performance goals.

The wing design featured a dual spar structure with wing ribs stationed every 27 inches and a stressed skin structure to provide

high strength. Upper wing surfaces were constructed with 7178S aluminum skin and stringers, while the lower surfaces were made from 2024 aluminum. Fatigue risk was mitigated for the wings by reducing the number of chordwise skin splices to two on each airplane, where each wing met the fuselage. The sealed portion between the wing spars provided the required volume for fuel storage. This area in the left wing was fuel tank #1, with the same area in the right wing being tank #3. The forward and aft spar structures carried through the body, below the cabin floor. This volume within the fuselage and inboardmost wing sections comprised the #2 (center) tank. Realizing the possibility of marketing the 727 to the military, provisions for additional range were provided by incorporating a slight bend on the inboard portion of the forward wing spar, thus increasing the volume of the thickest portion of the tank. Likewise, the fuel venting of the wing and center tanks was designed to military standards.

High Lift

The requirement for high-speed cruise would dictate a relatively small, highly swept airfoil design. This type of wing has excellent characteristics at high speed but typically requires unacceptably high takeoff and landing speeds. Eastern Airlines required the 727 to operate safely (with required FAA takeoff distance buffer additives) from the short runway at New York's La Guardia Airport, while climbing steeply enough to also meet the noise limits imposed there. This desire created a most restrictive set of requirements for the 727. Furthermore, Eastern wanted the ability to operate the 727 on the route from Boston to La Guardia, then to Washington, DC; Atlanta; and eventually terminating at Miami, WITHOUT refueling! This dictated a landing and subsequent departure from La Guardia at very high weights due to the trip fuel onboard. Boeing engineers had to pioneer new ideas and technology to meet these equally important but conflicting customer requirements. Fortunately for the 727 program, high-lift research was already occurring in the background at Boeing, conducted by the esteemed aerodynamics engineer Bill Cook.

It was found that the use of a Fowler-type trailing edge flap system would be required. Fowler flaps extend aft and then down to increase the camber (curvature) of the top of the wing, while simultaneously increasing wing area. The wing depends on relatively low pressure above the wing, caused by the air accelerating over the curved upper surface, with comparatively high pressure below, so an increase in the velocity of the air flowing above the wing causes more lift to be generated. Particularly with the Fowler flap system, a slot between the wing and the extended flap panel is commonly used to allow the high-pressure air beneath the wing to spill through to energize and accelerate the airflow above the flap. The aerodynamics staff felt that the use of a slot between the wing and the trailing edge flaps would be helpful, but why not provide additional airfoil-shaped flap panels with two additional slots to compound this desirable effect? This idea gave birth to the triple-slotted Fowler flap, but it required a complex assembly of tracks and jackscrews to move the flap structure into and out of the extended positions. Many hours of engineering work were spent to design a strong actuating system that could also be accommodated by small fairings to allow for maximum aerodynamic efficiency.

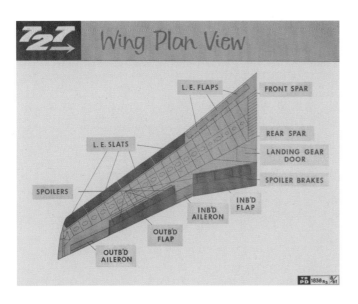

Courtesy of the Boeing Company

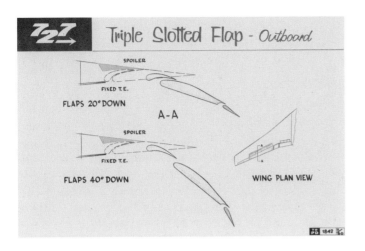

727 Triple Slotted Flap - *Outboard*

SPOILER
FIXED T.E.
FLAPS 20° DOWN
A-A
SPOILER
FIXED T.E.
FLAPS 40° DOWN
WING PLAN VIEW

727 Triple Slotted Flap - *Inboard*

AIR BRAKE
WCP
FIXED T.E.
TAKE-OFF CONDITION: 20° FLAP
10° FLAP (REF)
A-A
WCP
FIXED T.E.
LANDING CONDITION: 40° FLAP
A-A

The triple-slotted Fowler flap design was extremely effective at generating lift at relatively low airspeeds. The slots between the flap panels allowed high-pressure air beneath the wing to transition to the top side of the flap assemblies, energizing airflow to create additional lift. *Courtesy of the Boeing Company*

An excellent set of trailing edge flaps, however, was not going to be enough to meet the challenging La Guardia performance gauntlet. Boeing used an experimental leading edge "slat" system on the XB-47, B-47A, and early B-47Bs, which showed a fair amount of promise with increasing lift at low speeds. This concept was also used on the Convair 880M jetliner just a few years prior and showed moderate success. These were panels that, when retracted, were faired into the leading edge of the wing. During extension at low speeds, these panels slide forward and down, creating an even-greater curvature to the upper surface of the wing. On the 727, the aluminum slat panels articulated forward and down at a 55-degree angle on steel tracks.

The Boeing 707/720 airplanes employed cast-magnesium Krueger-type flaps on the leading edges of each wing to reduce takeoff and approach speeds. These devices, normally stored in compartments on the lower surface of the wing, deploy down and forward to create more wing camber during takeoff, approach, and landing operations. The 727 design called for the use of three Krueger-style leading edge flaps for the relatively thick, inboard wing sections of each wing.

Positioned outboard of the Krueger flaps, four slat panels were installed to complete the high-lift package. The leading edge devices were automatically extended and deployed, with reference to the trailing edge flap position, by means of hydraulic sequence valves.

Takeoffs on the 727 were typically made with the trailing edge flaps set to position 5. At this setting, all the leading edge slats and Krueger flaps were extended to provide maximum lift at low speeds. This worked well for liftoff and initial climb from the runway, but as the aircraft reached 1,000 feet, there was the need to accelerate and eventually retract all the high-lift devices completely. This required the aircraft speed to increase well beyond the optimum lift/drag speed for flaps 5, prior to arriving at a safe airspeed to achieve a "clean" wing configuration. This speed transition caused a loss of performance, especially critical during engine-out operations. Due to the need for excellent climb performance with an engine failure under the most-demanding atmospheric circumstances, an intermediate

727 Flap Support Structure

WING UPPER SURFACE
FOREFLAP
A-A
WING LOWER SURFACE
TRACK
FAIRING (FIXED TO FLAP)
CARRIAGE OPEN POSITION
B-B
C-C

One of the major challenges in designing the triple-slotted flap system involved developing the actuator design, which had to be very strong, yet compact enough to allow the use of small aerodynamic "canoe fairings."

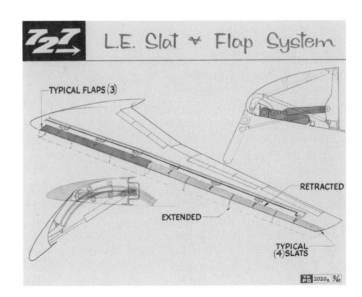

727 L.E. Slat & Flap System

TYPICAL FLAPS (3)
RETRACTED
EXTENDED
TYPICAL (4) SLATS

In addition to the trailing edge flap system, leading edge slats and Krueger flaps were installed on the wing's leading edge to create additional camber, thereby significantly enhancing low-speed handling and performance. *Courtesy of the Boeing Company*

This photo was taken as the trailing edge flaps transitioned from position 2 to position 5. At position 2, slat panels 2 and 3 (the middle pair of slats) are already extended. When flaps 5 is selected, on the leading edge the remainder of the slats (seen in transit) extend along with the Krueger flaps. *Courtesy of the Boeing Company*

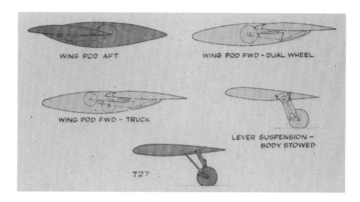

Due to the wing sweep and the large trailing edge flaps employed on the 727, engineers looked at several different methods of stowing the main landing gears while in flight. The aft-retracting solution was used in many designs produced by the Tupolev Design Bureau. *Courtesy of the Boeing Company*

flaps 2 setting was incorporated. At flaps 2, the trailing edge flaps retracted slightly while all the leading edge devices, except for the middle two slats on each wing, would retract completely. This created a good coefficient of lift while accelerating, and significantly improved engine-out climb performance.

Landing Gear

As designers incorporated the highly swept wing into the 727 design, complications with the main landing gear configuration soon emerged. Additionally, a decision had to be made regarding where to store the retracted main landing gears while in flight. Because of the wing sweep, much of the wing's lifting surface was behind the inboard, aft section of the wing. This tended to make the aircraft's typical balance point (center of gravity, or CG) fairly far back on the fuselage. Keep in mind also that the design required large trailing edge flap assemblies to adhere to the aircraft's mission capability from short runways. Similar to the Soviet Tupolev designs, Boeing engineers initially felt that the easy answer was to house the retracted landing gears in pods, one on each wing. While this may have been appealing from a purely mechanical standpoint, it would have also created an operational issue with aircraft cargo loading. The 727, due to its rear engine layout, had a fairly small space between the trailing edge of the wing and the pod-mounted engines—barely enough for the loading equipment. Adding a trailing edge pod to this area would curtail this space further, making the 727 far too difficult to load. There was even a design drafted to split the landing gear pod on the right wing, while at the gate to facilitate servicing, but this concept was eventually abandoned. This still left engineers asking how this landing gear issue could be solved.

Back to the drawing board, the engineers ultimately devised a landing gear that mounted forward of the trailing edge flap assemblies, close to the body. Using a dual-wheel landing gear with 49 × 17 tires (instead of a 707-style four-wheel arrangement) allowed for tighter taxi turns with minimal tire scrubbing. Hydraulic brakes were included for each main wheel, normally powered by the B hydraulic system. To further redundancy, an emergency pressurized-air system was added in case of a hydraulic failure. Jack Steiner wrote about the new main landing gear design:

We finally settled on a skewed axis, dog-legged oleo strut. . . . It enabled us to get rid of the external pod and still have a ground wheel position that was far aft, permitting loading flexibility.

Although eliminating the landing gear pods was an aerodynamically and operationally advantageous solution, the aft-swept main landing gear would need to retract sideways into a compartment located in the body of the aircraft, due to the thin chord of the wing. This compartment would be located just behind the rear wing spar carry-through and the center fuel tank, contained within the center section structure. This in itself was not necessarily a problem, but the use of this space would seriously limit the volume of the rear baggage compartment.

The nose landing gear was logically located underneath the aft portion of the cockpit and had hydraulically assisted steering capability with the captain's tiller, allowing for small-radius turns while taxiing and parking. The twin nosewheels were designed to include optional hydraulically powered brakes, complete with antiskid system management. The nose gear was designed to retract forward into its wheel well, with sequenced forward nose gear doors that would open while the landing gear was in transit, and would close thereafter to reduce drag.

The main landing gear well constraints on the volumetric space available for the aft baggage compartment caused a twofold challenge. The first issue was the required limitation of the overall cargo-carrying capability of the airplane. Equally important was the inherent weight and balance issue, which needed to be remedied. The aft volume might be required under some loading conditions, to permit flight within the certified center-of-gravity limits. In short, the stowage of the landing gear in the body would lead to some loss of the 727's operational flexibility. To mitigate this issue, the lower fuselage depth was increased from the 60.1-inch depth of the forward fuselage lower lobe to 70.1 inches for the aft body. It is a common misconception that the aft fuselage of the 727 is the same as the 707 series, but this is not completely true. Although it is close, the 707 was slightly deeper, at 72.6 inches. This increase of baggage capacity, combined with the larger and more spacious cabin, provided important advantages over the competing de Havilland Trident.

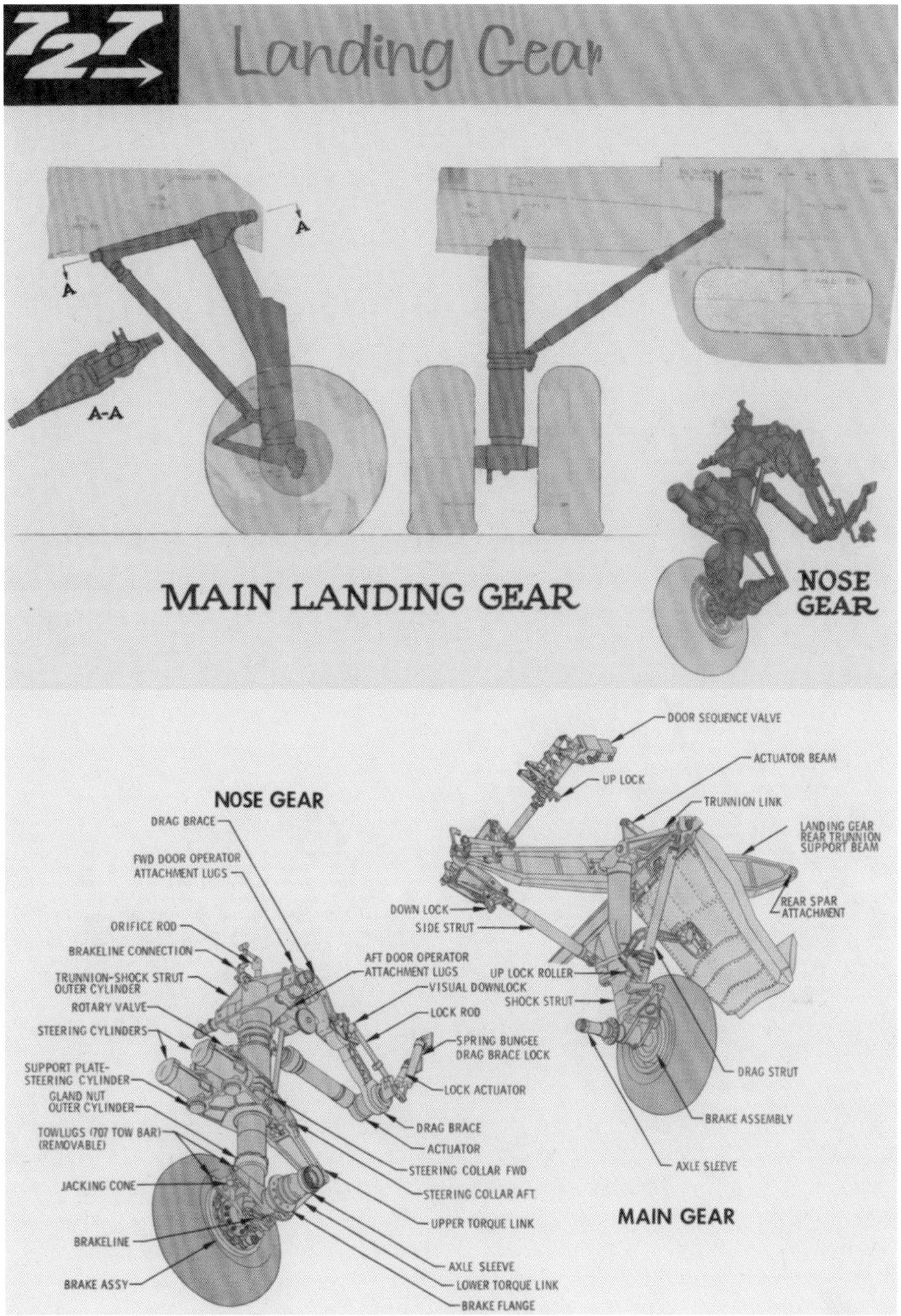

MAIN LANDING GEAR

NOSE GEAR

NOSE GEAR

- DRAG BRACE
- FWD DOOR OPERATOR ATTACHMENT LUGS
- ORIFICE ROD
- BRAKELINE CONNECTION
- TRUNNION-SHOCK STRUT OUTER CYLINDER
- ROTARY VALVE
- STEERING CYLINDERS
- SUPPORT PLATE-STEERING CYLINDER
- GLAND NUT OUTER CYLINDER
- TOWLUGS (707 TOW BAR) (REMOVABLE)
- JACKING CONE
- BRAKELINE
- BRAKE ASSY

- DOWN LOCK
- SIDE STRUT
- AFT DOOR OPERATOR ATTACHMENT LUGS
- UP LOCK ROLLER
- VISUAL DOWNLOCK
- LOCK ROD
- SPRING BUNGEE DRAG BRACE LOCK
- LOCK ACTUATOR
- DRAG BRACE
- ACTUATOR
- STEERING COLLAR FWD
- STEERING COLLAR AFT
- UPPER TORQUE LINK
- AXLE SLEEVE
- LOWER TORQUE LINK
- BRAKE FLANGE

- DOOR SEQUENCE VALVE
- ACTUATOR BEAM
- UP LOCK
- TRUNNION LINK
- LANDING GEAR REAR TRUNNION SUPPORT BEAM
- REAR SPAR ATTACHMENT
- SHOCK STRUT
- DRAG STRUT
- BRAKE ASSEMBLY
- AXLE SLEEVE

MAIN GEAR

The final solution was a main landing gear that was tilted aft from the mounts to allow room for the inboard trailing edge flaps. *Courtesy of the Boeing Company*

The Empennage Design

The empennage, or tail section, of the 727 was certainly the characteristic that made the aircraft instantly recognizable. To provide adequate strength, the vertical stabilizer featured a dual spar, rib, and stringer construction of 2024 and 7075 aluminum alloy. This structure was spliced integrally into the upper torque box on Section 48. The vertical stabilizer was swept at 55 degrees, which gave this beautiful jet much of its sleek, fast appearance. Good looks aside, this set the horizontal stabilizer farther aft on the airframe, which

increased the aerodynamic leverage of its control surfaces. This allowed for slightly smaller stabilizers and an attendant reduction in aerodynamic drag.

This T-tailed configuration was thoroughly wind-tunnel-tested both at low and transonic speeds to check for a condition called "flutter." Flutter is a high-frequency vibration that typically occurs at high speeds. Airframes, especially for aircraft such as the 727, which are designed to cruise at high indicated airspeeds at lower altitudes, and high Mach numbers at high altitudes, need to be designed to adequately dampen out this characteristic. This is

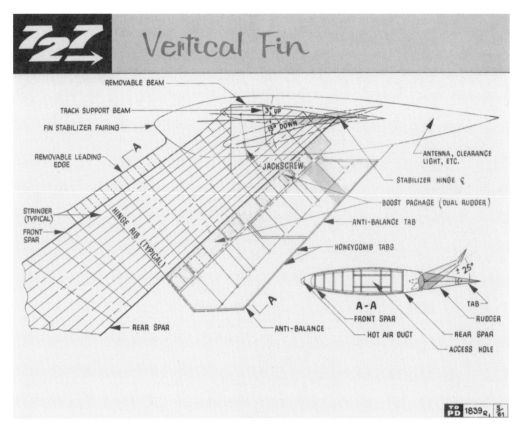

The vertical fin, known as Section 86 to the manufacturer, is seen here as a preliminary design. Note the Trident-style bullet fairing on the upper leading edge, which was recontoured on the actual aircraft. *Courtesy of the Boeing Company*

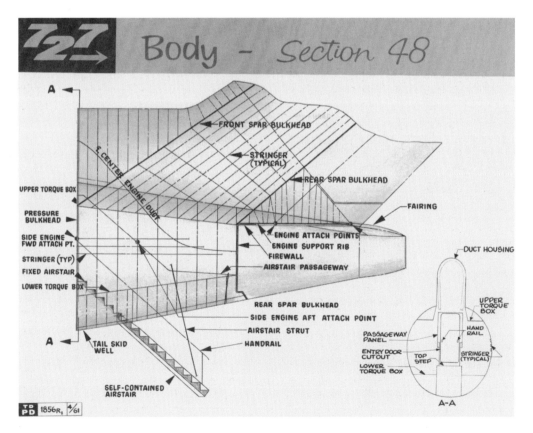

Section 48, which consists of the aft fuselage, incorporates upper and lower torque boxes to provide the rigidity necessary to support the flight loads of the T-tail design. *Courtesy of the Boeing Company*

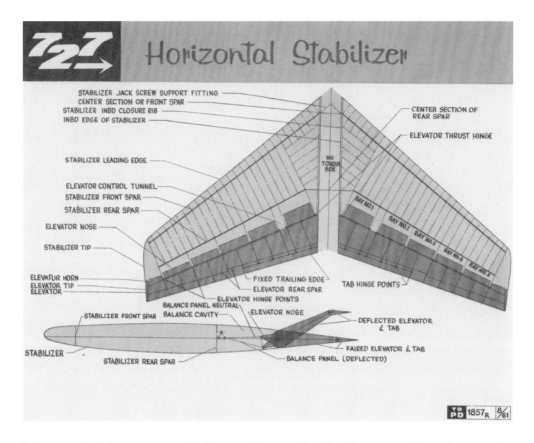

STABILIZER JACK SCREW SUPPORT FITTING
CENTER SECTION OR FRONT SPAR
STABILIZER INBD CLOSURE RIB
INBD EDGE OF STABILIZER

CENTER SECTION OF REAR SPAR

ELEVATOR THRUST HINGE

STABILIZER LEADING EDGE

NO TORQUE BOX

ELEVATOR CONTROL TUNNEL
STABILIZER FRONT SPAR
STABILIZER REAR SPAR

BAY NO.1

BAY NO.2

BAY NO.3

ELEVATOR NOSE

STABILIZER TIP

ELEVATOR HORN
ELEVATOR TIP
ELEVATOR

FIXED TRAILING EDGE
ELEVATOR REAR SPAR
ELEVATOR HINGE POINTS

TAB HINGE POINTS

BALANCE PANEL NEUTRAL
STABILIZER FRONT SPAR   BALANCE CAVITY

ELEVATOR NOSE

DEFLECTED ELEVATOR & TAB

STABILIZER

STABILIZER REAR SPAR

BALANCE PANEL (DEFLECTED)

FAIRED ELEVATOR & TAB

TD PD 1857R 8/61

The horizontal stabilizer incorporated balance panel bays to allow the pilot to control the surface manually in the absence of normal hydraulic pressure. *Courtesy of the Boeing Company*

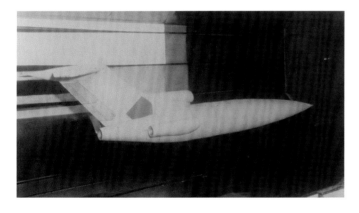

The high-cruise-speed aspect of the 727's mission led to the use of this transonic wind tunnel model. It was found that applying a 2-degree anhedral to the horizontal stabilizer gave optimum resistance to aerodynamic flutter. *Courtesy of the Boeing Company*

accomplished by giving the structure ideal rigidity and weight distribution, while also looking at the aerodynamics. Boeing aero engineers built a model called the Transonic Flutter Model to test for this, prior to the first aircraft even being constructed. It was a scale 727 aft body and tail section, with a rocket-like nose grafted into the front to allow undisturbed airflow over the stabilizer surfaces. With this model, engineers discovered that the ideal flutter resistance of the 727 empennage would occur with the horizontal stabilizers mounted with roughly 2 degrees of anhedral (see "Wind Tunnel Testing for the 727," in chapter 3, page 55). Flutter resistance would also be extensively tested during the upcoming flight test program.

What Is Flutter?

The phenomenon known as "flutter" is an extremely hazardous condition that involves the interrelations of the flexibility of a structure, the inertia of the mass attached, and the aerodynamic forces being acted upon the airframe. In keeping with the topic of aerodynamics, we will limit this discussion to aeronautics, but it is important to note that flutter also comes into play with the construction of tall buildings, suspension bridges, and suspended electric and telephone wires, even down to traffic signs. High winds, without adequate engineering provisions, can violently destroy any of these types of structures.

A typical aircraft scenario would occur when a bending force is enacted on a wing or stabilizer, which then causes the angle of attack for the involved airfoil to change. Let's take a wing, for example, that is subjected to a momentary increase in lift due to turbulence. As the wing bends up in response, in a swept wing, the leading edge of the airfoil near the tip will bend down slightly as the wing attempts to seek equilibrium. This, in turn, causes the wingtip to "unload" and bend back down, perhaps past its original position. Now, as the wing is flexed down, the airfoil leading edge tilts upward, thus increasing lift and bending the wing back up. If this cycle is dynamically unstable, due to aerodynamics or structure that is not properly engineered, the cycle becomes divergent and each flex becomes larger and amplified until structural failure occurs. This is an esoteric aspect of aeroelasticity involving many factors, including structural strength, stiffness, aerodynamics, weight distribution, and speed, among others. During flight test and certification, an aircraft must demonstrate that it does not have an undamped-flutter tendency. For the purpose of testing, a wingtip flutter vane is installed to deliberately excite the structure at different speeds and Mach numbers, ensuring that the structure does not have a divergent flutter mode.

Whirl Mode and the Lockheed Electra

While the 727 was being designed, a competing aircraft, the Lockheed L-188 Electra, began to experience a series of accidents that, at first, were unexplained. On September 29, 1959, Braniff Flight 542 was operating on routing from Houston, Texas, to Dallas, then was scheduled to continue on to Washington, DC, and New York. En route to Dallas, while level at 15,000 feet, the aircraft suddenly disappeared from radar. The culprit was found to be a catastrophic failure of the aircraft's port wing structure. Soon after, on March 17, 1960, an Electra operating as Northwest Airlines Flight 710 from Chicago's Midway Airport to Miami, Florida, crashed under similar circumstances. On the previous flight, the subject aircraft was witnessed to have experienced a "very hard" landing at Midway. The aircraft disappeared from radar screens without a single distress call.

The wreckage was studied and revealed that the entire right wing and the outboard portions of the left wing had separated from the fuselage. The fracture points showed a splintered failure that was indicative of an upward and downward type of flexing, causing the structure to exceed absolute limits.

After considering the grounding of the Electra fleet, on March 25, 1960, the Federal Aviation Agency (FAA) issued an emergency Airworthiness Directive, severely reducing the maximum airspeed limits on the Electra fleet from 324 to 275 knots. Still, the validity of the 275-knot limit was questioned, since both accidents had occurred when airspeeds were believed to be at or near this value. Five days later, the authorities further limited maximum cruise speed to 225 knots, with an absolute maximum airspeed of 245 knots. The FAA urged Lockheed to institute a complete study of the Electra design and possible causes for these accidents. The result was an industry-wide cooperation between Lockheed and the NASA Langley Research Center. In the furtherance of aviation safety, Boeing and Douglas, normally fierce competitors with Lockheed, worked side by side with the manufacturer, based in Burbank, California, and formed a program called the Lockheed Electra Action Program (LEAP) in mid-1960.

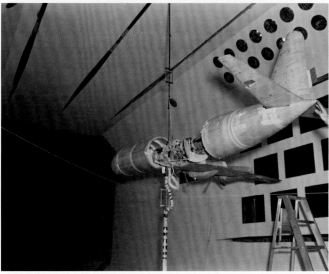

As part of the LEAP program, a scale structural model was assembled and placed in the wind tunnel at NASA Langley to discover the cause of two mysterious Lockheed Electra crashes. *Courtesy of NASA Langley*

The model revealed the phantom cause of the Electra accidents, a phenomenon known as whirl mode. *Courtesy of NASA Langley*

A one-to-eight scale model of the Electra was constructed, which included functional propellers and a scale representation of the aircraft structures. This was tested at NASA Langley's 19-foot wind tunnel. The model was subjected to representative flight loads, initially to no avail. Subsequent to this, the outboard engine/propeller mounts were weakened and the tests resumed. The result was the destruction of the model, with the failure point at the starboard wing root, similar to the wreckage patterns found at the Braniff and Northwest accident sites.

The results of the LEAP study led to a two-point conclusion on September 15, 1960. The first was that the Electra wing structure between the fuselage and the outboard engine nacelle was allowing excessive flex loads to be concentrated on the wing ribs, causing "shell distortion," which was complicit in the cause of the structural failures. The second was another cyclic phenomenon, known as "whirl mode." The Electra design included four very large and heavy Hamilton Standard propellers. Inclusive of the Allison 501 engine, the engine/propeller combination was mounted to the airframe with an extensive mounting structure to keep any wobbling of the propeller at bay. It was found that a series of hard landings, or for that matter one very hard landing, could compromise the rear mounting structure. This permitted just enough structural flex to allow this wobble, or whirl mode, to propagate at a higher amplitude and lower-than-normal cycle frequency of three cycles per second.

The whirl mode frequency was similar to the natural frequency of the wing structure on the L-188, which was just over three cycles per second. These two forces, acting together at frequencies that were in phase with one another, caused the sudden and catastrophic airframe failures. This was so sudden, in fact, that neither crew was allowed the time to even the begin a distress call.

Due to the LEAP findings and industry-wide cooperative efforts to find the cause of these accidents, the Electra design was modified, and the type lived on to provide dependable airline service for decades. This improved airframe design also became the basis for the prolific Lockheed P-3 antisubmarine aircraft, which is still in service today. These accidents, however, damaged the aircraft's reputation with the flying public, which almost certainly curtailed some airline orders for the Electra. It is an important point that this situation also brought increased scrutiny upon the FAA, which had approved the Electra for commercial operation. Because of these events, in part, the FAA began to operate with tougher and more-rigorous certification requirements, which would later have significant effects on the certification of the 727 (see "The Deep Stall Incident" on page 69).

The Flight Control System

The 727 required a state-of-the-art control system for good characteristics both in high-speed flight and at low approach speeds. Steiner was aware that a very talented flight control engineer, Bob Richold, had developed the flight control system for Lockheed's L-188 Electra, which was newly entering into service. Richold had previously worked with Boeing on the controls for its first jet, the B-47 strategic bomber. He learned that Richold, who had recently retired, had become wealthy from his invention of the electric-hydraulic transfer valve. Conveniently, he was living aboard a yacht on nearby Lake Union. In short order, Richold was asked to join Boeing's flight

control engineer, Ed Pfafman, in developing a system optimized for the 727's specific niche. Steiner wrote about this serendipitous situation:

> Those two individuals, plus the team that backed them, made the 727 control system a major state-of-the-art breakthrough—it really was. We built a flight controls test rig mockup and gave them all of the money they needed to work the bugs out before we built the airplane.

The design goals for the handling qualities were well defined from the beginning and were highly influenced by input from the airline pilot community. Handling was to be effective, even at low approach speeds, with the use of light pressures on the controls. These requirements called for the use of a completely irreversible flight control system that prevented external pressures on the flight control surfaces from being fed back through the flight control system to the pilot. This is an especially nice feature on the ground during high tailwinds, because it prevents the controls from slamming against their stops, and yokes from slamming against the pilot.

The lateral (roll) control of the aircraft utilized two ailerons on each wing, augmented by flight spoilers, to provide crisp and effective control. The inboard pair of ailerons was functional at all times, while the outboard ailerons were locked in the neutral position during high-speed flight (with flaps retracted). Pitch (nose up and down) control was provided by the elevators, mounted on the trailing edge of the horizontal stabilizers, high atop the swept vertical stabilizer. Elevator trim, used to set a neutral control condition over a wide range of speeds and configurations, was supplied through an electrically actuated jackscrew that adjusted the angle of incidence of the entire horizontal stabilizer. Yaw control (nose side to side) was provided by a dual rudder system, mounted to the trailing edge of the vertical stabilizer, which was normally powered through the redundant A and B hydraulic systems.

As a departure from the manual-control, tab-actuated 707 flight control design, the 727 employed a fully powered flight control system, more similar to that of the Lockheed Electra. The primary flight controls (ailerons, elevators, and rudders) were normally powered by the dual A and B hydraulic systems during normal operations. Through the use of a hydraulic-feel computer, this system allowed for a light and nimble control feel. In the very unlikely event of a dual A and B hydraulic-pressure loss, the ailerons and elevator surfaces could be actuated by the pilot through a cable backup utilizing servo tabs and balance panels to displace the controls. This mode, called "manual reversion," left the aircraft still easily controllable by the pilot, albeit with slightly higher control forces. The rudder control featured no manual reversion, but a triple-redundant backup was supplied hydraulically through the aircraft's standby hydraulic system. More information on these systems is provided in chapter 8.

Flight and Ground Spoilers

Many times, either because of Air Traffic Services (ATS) or terrain restrictions, higher altitudes and speeds are required when on approach close in to the destination airport. To allow a high level of flexibility for the 727, the wing was designed with five panels, called flight spoilers, on the upper surface of each wing, just forward of the trailing edge flaps. The flight spoilers were operated in conjunction with the aircraft's speed brake system, which was manually selectable by the pilot via a SPEED BRAKE handle in the center pedestal, just to the left of the thrust levers. When this handle was pulled aft by the pilot, the flight spoilers extended up, variable and proportionate to the distance the handle was pulled aft. This disrupted the airflow over the wing, increasing aerodynamic drag and decreasing lift, thereby allowing the 727 to rapidly descend and decelerate. The flight spoilers, as previously mentioned, were also used in conjunction with the ailerons to optimize roll control. This action, controlled by the mechanical spoiler mixer, was completely automatic.

In addition to the flight spoilers, each wing featured two ground spoiler panels, located just forward of the inboard trailing edge flaps. After landing, it was of paramount importance that the aircraft's weight was immediately transferred to the main landing gear wheels so that effective braking could begin. The ground spoilers were actuated after landing, along with the flight spoilers, to destroy the wing's remaining lift while creating a significant amount of drag to slow the aircraft.

Engine Installation

Once the three-engine concept was established, Pratt & Whitney expeditiously began to design a suitable engine for the 727. This new engine, the JT8D, was one of the first commercial engines developed for a specific airframe. In most instances up to this point, aircraft builders would select an existing engine and tailor the airframe accordingly. This adverse dynamic was centric with both the BAC One-Eleven and the Hawker Siddeley Trident, since they were built around an engine that lacked the growth potential they would later require, thus ultimately limiting their success.

On airliners with either two or four wing-mounted, podded engines, it is reasonably easy to make the engines, mountings, plumbing, wiring, and nacelles interchangeable. The 727 differed in that regard because each of the three engines had a unique interface with the airframe. The number 1 (port) engine was secured to the airframe on the engine's right side, the number 2 (center) engine mounted from above, and the number 3 (starboard) engine mounted on its left side. To mitigate this challenge, Pratt & Whitney designed the JT8D with this in mind and provided mountings for each position on every engine. During an engine change, the mechanic would simply install the appropriate mounting hardware, using only the mountings applicable for the required position. That meant that any JT8D could be mounted on any position on the 727 with a minimum amount of labor. It is noteworthy, however, that because of accessibility for maintenance, the nacelles were mirror images and thus not interchangeable.

Being mindful of the need for minimum spares inventory and expedited maintenance action, Boeing designed the Quick Engine Change (QEC) kit for the 727. The QEC included the engine itself, along with required plumbing, electrical-wiring harnesses, and accessories. These were engineered to be common to all three installations, with only the routing of the wires and hoses being adjusted for left, right, or center mounting positions.

Each engine was equipped with a provision for reverse thrust. The term "reverse thrust" sometimes leads people to believe that the rotation of the engine is somehow reversed; however, this is not the case. Instead, a set of blocker doors were located in the tailpipe of each engine. After landing, these would move into position to block the egress of exhaust gases and deflect them forward at a 45-degree angle through two ports that interacted with the passing slipstream.

After touchdown, or during a rejected takeoff, the pilot can activate the thrust reversers with handles mounted forward of each thrust lever. When the thrust reversers are selected, high-pressure pneumatics actuate the system to move the components into position. Once the blocker doors are in place, the engines are accelerated to a high-thrust setting, creating an enormous amount of drag and assisting the wheel brakes and spoilers in safely stopping the aircraft.

The engine inlets were another part of the power plant installation that drew considerable attention from the designers, since jet engine noise was becoming a major issue for neighborhoods located near large airports around the world. That, combined with the minimum noise requirements at La Guardia, caused a need for the 727 to be as quiet as possible. Much of the noise generated by a jet engine, particularly at high thrust, is projected forward from the engine inlets. To mitigate this to the maximum extent possible, a new technology was introduced on the 727. Inside the inlet, forward of the engine stators and first-stage compressor, the duct was lined with an acoustically tuned, perforated liner. This surface, featuring twenty-four small holes per square inch, was installed on top of a screen mesh. This trapped much of the transmitted high-pitch noise produced by the engine. This feature, pioneered on the 727, remains commonplace on jet engine installations today.

With the inclusion of the auxiliary power unit late in the design process, the 727 gained the ability to operate in the absence of most airport support equipment. *Courtesy of the Boeing Company*

Efficient Ground Operations

The Auxiliary Power Unit

To support the requirement from Eastern Airlines, the 727 needed to be as self-sufficient as possible and was accordingly designed to require only a limited amount of support equipment. The need to add an auxiliary power unit (APU) became a high priority for the designers of the 727. The APU consisted of small turbine engine that supplied electrical power through an incorporated 115-volt AC generator to operate aircraft systems at times when the engines were not running. The APU, weighing 820 pounds, was also a source for high-pressure bleed air to operate the air-conditioning systems and the engines' pneumatic starters.

The designers were challenged with determining a placement for the APU, since it required a significant amount of volume within the aircraft. Jack Steiner was working late one night, reviewing the work progression completed by his engineers. The main landing gear, which featured a dog-legged design, was required to retract into a rectangular compartment just aft of the wing center section. Because of this unique landing gear arrangement, there was some unused volume within the forward portion of the compartment, even with the main landing gears retracted. Upon viewing this, Steiner realized that this was essentially the only location in the airplane with adequate unused volume. Soon after, work commenced to install the APU into the main wheel well, which extended across the keel beam structure separating the left and right main landing gear wells. It was a tight fit, but the idea was successful and became the standard installation, with the APU exhaust being expelled next to the fuselage on the upper-right wing surface. One limitation to this configuration, however, was due to the completely enclosed main wheel well. Operation of the APU was limited to ground use only and thus was not useful for in-flight redundancy.

Incorporated Airstairs

To minimize the complement of ground equipment, the 727 was designed with a ventral airstair, which, using hydraulic power, deployed from the aft fuselage just forward of the number 2 (center) engine. A pressurized cabin door, located at the top of the stairs,

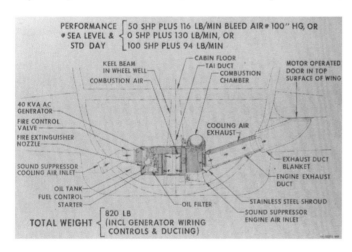

The auxiliary power unit was a late requirement for the 727 program. The only internal volume available for its inclusion was in the forward portion of the main landing gear well, across the keel beam. *Courtesy of the Boeing Company*

allowed the large airstair assembly to be free from pressurization loads. The airstairs served a dual purpose when the aircraft was not underway, since it was normally left in the deployed position to act as a tail stand. This prevented the aircraft from rotating onto the aft fuselage since the 727 (especially the later 727-200 model) was quite tail heavy when empty.

Boeing also offered an optional forward airstair for the 727. Normally folded and stored under the forward cabin floor, it would deploy and unfold when needed to provide the option of dual boarding and deplaning.

A mockup of the 727 aft body, ventral airstair, and aft cabin was constructed at Boeing's headquarters to drive home the operational convenience of the design. *Courtesy of the Boeing Company*

Forward Airstair Operation

Boeing also offered an optional forward airstair for the 727, adding greater flexibility and faster turn times. *Courtesy of the Boeing Company*

The Fuel System

The fuel system designed for the 727 utilized the volume between the forward and aft wing spars in both wings, as well as the volume between the wings in the fuselage, below the cabin floor. The standard fuel capacity was 7,680 US gallons, with the fuel being fed to the engines via electric pumps. In an emergency, fuel could be jettisoned from the aircraft to reduce landing weight and allow an expedited landing. Two pressure-fueling ports (located on the lower leading edge of the right wing) were provided to allow expeditious aircraft servicing. This eliminated the need to climb on top of the wing to fuel each tank, as was commonplace on older airliners. The fuel system will be covered in more depth in chapter 8.

Electrical Innovations

The electrical system developed for the 727 was designed to be rugged and more reliable than on previous airplanes. Modular instrument panels and electrical centers in the aircraft were designed to be easily removable to complete repairs away from the aircraft, thus reducing

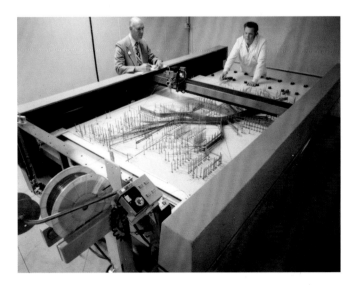

The electrical system of the 727 was designed to be robust and durable. Wiring looms were used to ensure that each harness was assembled correctly and consistently. *Courtesy of the Boeing Company*

maintenance hours and increasing access for technicians. One major innovation on the 727 involved the manufacturing process for the miles of wire incorporated into each jet. Prior to the 727, soldered wire joins had proven to be disadvantageous for long-term reliability. Boeing instituted an initiative to redesign these interfaces, using completely solderless, sealed connections. Although they were nearly four times the cost of traditional soldered connections, Boeing felt that the higher-quality electrical connections were well worth the investment. This system was so effective that many subsequent Boeing jetliners have utilized the same system.

Mitigating cost was also a significant goal for the 727. Eighty thousand wiring segments, organized into bundles, ran the length and width of the aircraft. These conduits were complex to manufacture, which was traditionally done by hand. On the 727, a major movement to computerize the manufacturing process to the highest extent possible led to these incredibly complex wire runs being marked and sorted in advance for the installers. Knowing that there were always unforeseen technological and avionic advances just beyond the horizon, additional dormant wiring runs were also installed to ease the later installation of new equipment.

There were also instances where new technology was rejected in favor of more-conventional "known quantity" systems. Most jetliners use alternating-current generators, which must turn at a specific rate to produce the requisite 400-cycle power. While APUs can be operated at a constantly governed speed, engine speeds, unfortunately, vary by necessity all the way from idle to maximum. Conventional systems used a constant-speed drive (CSD), which employed a liquid drive to maintain a constant generator speed, regardless of the engine's rotational speed. Technology had developed to the point that Boeing engineers were considering the possibility of a variable-speed, constant-frequency generator system (VSCF). This would have been brand-new technology, though, and engineers were concerned about taking such a large risk for such an integral system. The Sundstrand company felt that an improved CSD design could be produced with an overhaul period of 2,500 hours (five times that of the units on the 707), but at nearly half the cost. Ultimately, the engineers decided to work with Sunstrand on known, safe technology rather than run the risk of development problems with the VSCF.

Sundstrand manufactured the constant-speed generator drives for the early 727 aircraft. *Author's collection*

This diagram summarizes the progression of the early 727 design as of March 1962. Note the main landing gear pods, which were deleted soon thereafter. *Courtesy of the Boeing Company*

Into Production

During 1962 the basic design of the 727 became solidified, and development progress was quickly moving forward, with the eventual building of the first aircraft, E001, drawing near. One of the benchmarks of the 727 program was the extreme attention given to building an aircraft of the absolute highest quality, but with mindfulness of the costs involved for each decision. In a report titled "Managing the Development of the 727," dated April 1962, Jack Steiner wrote the following:

> Another interesting feature of the 727 development has been the attention to product cost. A separate staff-type organization with a direct tie to the Divisional Finance Department was set up to service the design groups with cost studies for alternate configurations. Hundreds of these studies were conducted, which enabled the design groups to select the best configuration considering both technical and cost aspects. The objective was not so much to select the lowest cost configuration as to have the relative cost considerations available when we did have to make a decision.

Effective and timely communication was exceedingly significant to program success, which led to the formation of the Customer Engineering Group. This allowed a direct line of communication between the customer airlines and the 727 engineering staff. Similarly, a group of handpicked manufacturing and tooling personnel were given desk space in the center of the 727 design workshop. This allowed for manufacturing input to be timed appropriately, so that needed changes could be requested, quickly received by the engineering staff, and easily executed.

The Boeing Company looked extensively for new avenues to communicate, design, and build the 727 in innovative and efficient ways. This open mindset, combined with the outstanding leadership demonstrated by President Bill Allen, along with the genius of men such as Maynard Pennell, Jack Steiner, Joe Sutter, and thousands of others, was centric in making the 727 an exceptional, world-class aircraft, the likes of which the industry had never seen before.

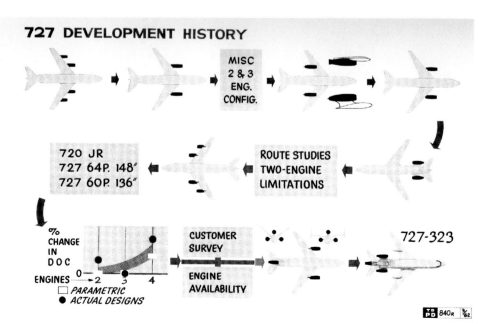

727 DEVELOPMENT HISTORY

MISC 2 & 3 ENG. CONFIG.

720 JR
727 64P. 148"
727 60P. 136"

ROUTE STUDIES
TWO-ENGINE
LIMITATIONS

% CHANGE IN DOC
ENGINES 0 2 3 4
☐ *PARAMETRIC*
● *ACTUAL DESIGNS*

CUSTOMER SURVEY

ENGINE AVAILABILITY

727-323

3

Building, Test-Flying, and Operating the 727-100

Preliminary Flight Testing for the 727-100 Program

New Technology and the Dash 80

The Boeing 367-80, widely known as the "Dash 80," was the first aircraft in the direct lineage of all future Boeing jetliners. It was a test-bed prototype that drew on the technology developed for the XB-47 program during the early years of the Cold War. This aircraft design led to the development of two family lines; namely, the Boeing 707 jetliner and the Boeing KC-135 military tanker.

The Dash 80 continued to test new technologies well after the first 707s and KC-135s became operational. Two of these technologies, specifically high-lift systems and aft fuselage-mounted engine configurations, were carefully tested with this machine in furtherance of the Boeing 727 program, which was still in the design stage during 1961.

The airline customers for the 727 required exceptional lifting ability from the short runways at New York's La Guardia Airport, while carrying a full load of passengers, bags, and enough fuel to comfortably fly to Washington, Atlanta, and then on to Miami. All of this needed to be accomplished while climbing smartly enough to minimize noise impact on adjacent neighborhoods too. Normally

The Dash 80 was used to test many aerodynamic advancements over the years, one of which was the aft-mounted engine position for the 727. This was installed on the port side of the aircraft for evaluation. Prior to the availability of the JT8D-1 engine, Boeing used a JT3P power plant, as seen here. Note the redirected exhaust nozzle, installed to protect the horizontal stabilizer. *Courtesy of Boeing via Flip Wingrove*

this scenario would require a large wing with good low-speed characteristics, but the mission for the 727 was also to provide high-speed, fuel-efficient flight. This capability called for a relatively small, highly swept wing, which would typically not perform well at low speeds. New high-lift technology was needed to satisfy all these requirements in order for the 727 to be a successful venture. The new wing had to be in its element at very high cruise speeds, while having a higher coefficient of lift than any other jetliner in the low-speed regime. Since neither of these requirements could be compromised, Boeing's engineering staff set to work on their daunting task.

From this development work, a new concept for the trailing edge flap system was conceived, with each flap separated into three separate airfoil-shaped sections, with gaps spaced in between. These gaps were included to allow some measure of high-energy air to transition from the underside of the wing to energize lift above the flap panels. Additionally, a multitude of leading edge flap and slat designs needed to be evaluated in concert with the new triple-slotted trailing edge assemblies to determine the viability of such arrangements. The theory behind these concepts was certainly solid, but these configurations had never been tried in real-time flight conditions.

The Dash 80 had previously been used to test the recontoured inboard leading edge "glove," which became production standard for the Boeing 720 jetliner. In 1961, this modification was still present on the Dash 80 and was used for the basis of high-lift testing for the 727 program.

Triple-Slotted Trailing Edge Flaps

An important element of the 727 design was the triple-slotted trailing edge flap system. The system was tested extensively on the Dash 80. The inboard flap installations were adjustable only on the ground. *Courtesy of the Boeing Company*

In order for the new trailing edge flaps to be tested, the existing flap system was removed from the Dash 80. On each wing, two banks of flaps existed on this aircraft, with an inboard aileron separating them, similar to the 727 design. For the purposes of aerodynamic testing, the inboard trailing edge flaps were ground-adjustable only, with settings ranging from positions "zero" through "60." The outboard flap position was adjustable in flight, with just the very aft panel being ground-adjustable only.

Leading Edge Devices

Testing of the leading edge slat system was conducted using different extension angles and configurations to optimize low-speed lift and handling. *Courtesy of the Boeing Company*

The leading edge devices were equally important for generating high-lift coefficients and were intended to be tested concurrently with the triple-slotted trailing edge flaps. The slats were designed to be faired with the upper portion of the wings' leading edges during high-speed flight. However, for takeoff and landing approaches, these were to be deployed to extract as much lift as possible from the wing at the low speeds required for short-runway operations. Slats were not a particularly new technology at this point in history, since they had previously been used with success on the Messerschmitt Me 262 jet fighter in the early 1940s, as well as on modern jet designs, such as the Boeing XB-47 prototypes, as well as ten B-47As and the first thirty B-47B strategic bombers. The unknown was how they would interface with the newly designed trailing edge flaps, and what would be the optimum deployment angles and gap distances from the wing itself. To test this adequately, wooden leading edge devices were installed on the Dash 80 to allow definitive testing of the high-lift system as a whole. These devices were ground-adjustable or removable (or both) for the purposes of this testing.

Dash 80 Flight Testing

As we move on to the topic of low-speed flight testing, it is important to discuss the causes of an aerodynamic stall, and why this area of operation is so critical. An airplane wing creates lift because relatively low-pressure airflow adheres to the wing's upper surfaces. The angle at which the wing or, more specifically, the wing's chord line, encounters the passing airflow is known as the angle of attack (AOA). As the aircraft slows, or as g-loading is increased, the AOA increases. Every wing design has a point where the AOA increases to an angle where the airflow over the top of the wing can no longer "make the corner." This causes a rapid reduction of lift and an attendant increase in aerodynamic drag as the wing plows its way through the air. This is called an aerodynamic stall and should not to be confused with a jet engine's compressor stall, as mentioned later in this chapter. Stall behavior is repeatedly scrutinized during flight test programs to ensure that less-than-desirable habits are not exhibited by the aircraft.

The first test flight for the high-lift systems on the Dash 80 occurred on February 22, 1961. The flight crew included J. R. Gannett (pilot), Lew Wallick (copilot), and P. C. "Flip" Wingrove (flight engineer). The trailing edge flaps were set to position 40, and wooden partial-span, leading edge slat assemblies were installed. This configuration yielded stall speeds down to 76 knots (87.4 mph), which was incredibly low for a fast, swept-wing jet. Although this was a good characteristic, it came with a price. In a postflight conference, Gannett described the aircraft's handling: "You can feel things changing on the wings on this airplane, in drag and also in lift as you slow down." Drag was high, and when the airplane was accelerated above 100 knots, the airplane began to shake, with buffet levels described by the crew as "objectionable," which became "unacceptable" above 120 knots. Changing the landing gear's position and adjusting the engines' thrust levels seemingly had no effect. At this point in the testing, leading edge devices were installed on the inboard portions of the wing both between and inboard of the engine pylons. In this configuration, the aircraft yielded a sharp pitch down during stalls that resulted in a very uncomfortable 15-to-20-degree nose-down pitch attitude. Although an aircraft should ideally pitch down in a stall, this was considered too much of a good thing. More testing needed to be performed while also checking the viability of other 727-centric concepts.

The Aft-Mounted Engine

It is common for multiple new concepts to be tested concurrently during a flight test program, and the experiments with the Dash 80 were no exception. In April 1961, the Dash 80 was placed in layup for additional modifications. Paramount was the addition of a fifth Pratt & Whitney JT3P engine, mounted to the aft, portside fuselage. Since the proposed 727 configuration featured podded, aft-mounted engines, Boeing engineers wanted to test the effects of such a configuration. The concept had to be modified to make it workable with the Dash 80 test bed. The fifth engine was mounted directly in front of the left-side horizontal stabilizer, likely inflicting blast and heat damage onto the airframe. Boeing engineer Chuck Ballard remembered the situation:

> I was assigned to design that tailpipe to get the exhaust off that stabilizer and to get the exhaust to exit at the same angle as the engine exhaust. So, we welded up these Inconel sections. There were about nine sections, if I remember correctly, and I had to do it on one of those old Merchant Figurematics . . . like twenty-four keys up and down. It took me months to design that!

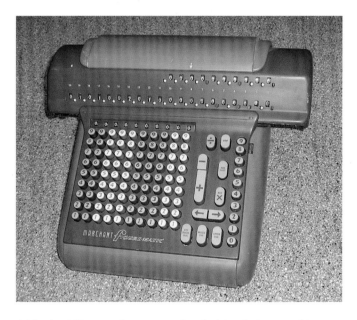

A Merchant Figurematic was an early calculator that was used to design the unique redirected-exhaust nozzle required for the side-mounted engine on the Dash 80. *Courtesy of Ancelli via Wikimedia Commons*

Technicians install the JT3P turbojet engine on the port side of the Dash 80 test-bed aircraft. This is the same type of engine used for the wing-mounted positions during this period. This view gives a good perspective on the redirected-exhaust nozzle. The JT3P was not fitted with a thrust reverser. *Courtesy of the Boeing Company*

On April 18, the first ground runs were performed on the aft-mounted engine, which was fed fuel from the aircraft's center fuel tank. For comparison, the number 3 engine (also a JT3P) was run at the same engine pressure ratios (EPRs). The number 3 engine exhibited a mismatch in rotor speeds compared to the aft-mounted engine, with its modified inlet and the special curved exhaust. This mismatch was found to be due to a restriction in the exhaust airflow and was quickly solved by simply removing the last 1.55 inches of the tapered jet pipe. In doing so, this increased the exhaust area by 5 percent and brought the engine back into specification.

Operation of the aft-mounted engine was unconventional, to say the least. The thrust lever for this power plant was not located in between the pilots in its customary place. Flip Wingrove, the flight engineer on many of these flights, explained:

I flew the flight engineer's position on the Dash 80 when they had the single aft-mounted engine on the fuselage. ... What we were doing was pretty limited because, among other things, aerodynamically it was not symmetric. All of the thrust and drag was off the centerline. After about the first two flights it became obvious. All of the engine controls were at the flight engineer's position. The pilot, Lew Wallick, had no throttle for that engine, and his head was 4 feet away from my head. Those first few flights he was turning around and saying things to me, such as "Don't touch the throttle without telling me first." We discovered that the asymmetry was kind of a limitation with the things we could do or fly on the airplane, but it was very, very interesting. Lew Wallick was a wonderful test pilot.

Although it was easy to control the asymmetry, it was imperative that the flying pilot have ample warning prior to a thrust change on the aft-mounted engine. Clear communication was the key to operating with this nonstandard configuration successfully and safely. As the flights were conducted in this configuration, the engine was subjected to a myriad of conditions to test the 727's aft-mounted engine concept. This included numerous in-flight engine shutdowns and restarts, which were executed without any issues across a wide range of altitudes and airspeeds.

Engine surges, also sometimes referred to as compressor stalls, occur when the steady running of a jet engine is interrupted. They can be caused either by a mechanical issue with the engine itself, or with airflow into the engine being turbulent or uneven in pressure. Many times, this presents a loud "bang" and, in severe circumstances, can even result in reverse flow through the engine, with still-burning

gases being expelled out through the engine's intake. Naturally, this situation is extremely hard on the engine, and a loss of thrust at a critical time creates additional safety issues. On earlier jetliners, the engine intakes were either buried in the wing root or located out in front of the wings on pylons, deliberately placing them in clean airflow. However, the necessity of the three-engine platform for the 727 resulted in its engines being placed simultaneously in the wake of the wings and near the fuselage's aerodynamic boundary layer. Because of this, during the Dash 80 testing, the susceptibility to compressor stalls became a key item of concern.

The aft-mounted engine was flown with different configurations of leading edge and trailing edge device deflection, with and without the use of speed brakes located on the upper surface of the wing,

The S-duct arrangement required by the 727's trijet configuration was one of the most significant challenges of the development process. A test rig was set up to evaluate engine performance with the duct installed. *Courtesy of the Boeing Company*

When the JT8D engine became available from Pratt & Whitney, it replaced the JT3P initially used. Seen here during thrust reverser testing, the redirected exhaust has been removed and the deployed reverser cover doors are evident. Temperature measurements on the side of the fuselage were conducted to ensure that the proximity of the engine to the body would not cause damage. *Courtesy of Boeing via Flip Wingrove*

directly in front of the engine. It was found that during stalls, the engine had a tendency to surge, particularly during slam engine accelerations. It is believed that this was due to the turbulent airflow on the top of the wing being ingested by the aft-mounted engine. Different combinations of open and closed auxiliary intake doors, nose domes, and airflow splitters were tried to determine the most advantageous configuration. The JT8D-1 engines were not yet available, so the preliminary testing with the JT3P engine was more theoretical in nature. Although the surge issue was never completely mitigated in this configuration, engineers still learned lessons for improving the 727's design. Later, testing with a preproduction JT8D-1 mounted on the aft fuselage position was also conducted with the Dash 80 test bed.

A closer look at the JT8D reverser installation on the Dash 80 test bed. *Courtesy of the Boeing Company*

During the ensuing three months, different combinations of leading edge devices (both slats and Krueger-type surfaces) and trailing edge flap panel sizes and gapping were systematically tested to achieve the best results. Wooden leading edge device panels were installed full span. The right wing was "tufted," whereby pieces of string were taped to the airfoil's upper and lower surfaces to observe its airflow and pinpoint the areas causing the buffet experienced by the flight crew. As viewed by the chase fighter, the airflow on the lower surfaces of the wing behind the leading edge devices was found to be turbulent, with an airflow reversal occurring on 30–50 percent of the surface. When the extension of the leading edge devices was reduced from 55 to 45 degrees, the speed of buffet onset was somewhat raised. While this was itself desirable, reducing this angle began to negatively affect the aircraft's stall behavior. The sharp nose-down

pitching noted before was eliminated, but instead the opposite effect was created, with a dangerous tendency for the nose to rise uncommanded during the stall.

When an airplane is stalled, ideally the pilot must continue to pull back on the control yoke, forcing the aircraft into the condition. A reduction of this aft control force should result in the aircraft recovering from the stall. In other words, the pilot should have to force the aircraft into a stall, and the aircraft should naturally seek a recovered state once the control input is removed. Reducing the slat angle too much was found to have the effect of "stick lightening," or the aircraft having a tendency to continue into a stalled condition without the deliberate aft yoke input. Continued testing was required to find just the right balance of high-lift coefficients, buffet margins, controllability, and aircraft stability. Modifications to the chord of the forwardmost inboard trailing edge flap segments were employed, along with sealing the gaps between the wing-mounted engine pylons and the leading edge devices, giving aerodynamicists valuable data for the 727 wing design.

The Dash 80, like the Boeing 707 and 720, had unpowered elevators and ailerons. The pilot's control inputs moved a small tab on the trailing edge of the control surfaces, which used the passing airflow to deflect the control surface accordingly. This required ample clean airflow to allow positive aircraft control. The addition of high-lift devices to the Dash 80, and the resultant low approach speeds, caused very limited lateral (roll) controllability. This was mentioned numerous times in the flight test documents, which dictated that it would be important for the 727 to have a fully powered flight control system. Although much was learned from these valuable tests on the Dash 80, the technology was certainly still in need of refinement. That being said, the test program proved that the slatted wing, combined with the triple-slotted trailing edge flaps, would make the required performance from La Guardia and Denver possible with the 727 configuration.

Another backup plan was also being considered in case the triple-slotted systems did not yield the desired results, or if developmental problems were encountered with the system's mechanical kinematics. The "Plan B" was a concept being developed for the military, known as the blown wing, and designers felt that it might be adaptable to the 727 design if needed. Engineer James Raisbeck was involved with the development and testing of this concept:

My understanding was that [the blown wing] was being considered as a backup system for the 727 if the [triple-slotted] flap turned out to be a nightmare. When you hang all of that stuff on the rear spar, there is a lot of bending moment there. There is a tremendous amount of stuff going on.

The blown-wing concept would use high-pressure air, most likely from the aircraft's engine compressors, injected into the airflow over the wing. This added lift energy to the wing, but at the cost of available engine power. If all else failed, it was an option, and incidentally, the Dash 80 workhorse continued on to test this technology for other applications, although it was soon deemed unnecessary for the 727 design due to the success of the new, robust flap systems.

Wind Tunnel Testing for the 727

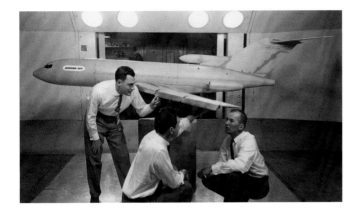

Aero engineers work on a wind tunnel model of the 727 as it neared its final configuration. The dihedral angle of the horizontal stabilizer and the low-set position of the pod-mounted engines were later changed, along with the shape of the bullet fairing located on top of the vertical stabilizer. *Courtesy of the Boeing Company*

The 727 was a unique airplane with several attributes that had heretofore never been used on a production jetliner, including the ducted center engine, T-tail, and high-lift systems. In July 1959, 727-specific wind tunnel testing began, even before the basic 727 configuration had been decided on during the autumn of 1959. In order to meet the design requirements for the new airplane, the design had to be equally well suited to very high cruise speeds, with exceptionally low takeoff and landing speeds. Most of the wind tunnel testing naturally focused on these two extreme corners of the flight envelope. At the higher end of the envelope, the 727 needed to be economical and safe at speeds approaching Mach 0.90 and indicated airspeed of 390 knots. While aerodynamic flutter was of key concern at these speeds, Boeing had already gained valuable experience with this phenomenon while testing their earlier jet designs. Prior to 1960, Boeing had conducted 2,925 hours of wind tunnel testing and 982 hours of flight testing on the B-47, B-52, 367-80, KC-135, and 707/720 to understand and mitigate the effects of high-speed flutter. Even with the carryover of this wealth of knowledge from previous experience, over 87,000 man-hours and fourteen weeks of wind tunnel time went toward testing the 727 design for flutter. Because of the thoroughness of these studies, it was discovered that providing a 2-degree anhedral (or downward slope toward the tips) to the horizontal stabilizers showed a remarkable reduction in the possibility of flutter onset. Later, during the 727 flight test program, an additional forty hours of actual 727 flight testing specific to high-speed flutter was conducted for aircraft certification.

Boeing's engineers also discovered an airflow separation over the upper, aft corner of the vertical stabilizer due to the 55-degree sweep angle of the surface. The addition of vortex generators on both sides of the stabilizer was utilized to aid in reattaching the airflow in this critical area. Because of the tail design of the aircraft, wind tunnel testing also pointed out the need for a significant aircraft system change due to higher-than-expected hinge loading on the 727's rudder assemblies. The primary flight controls on the 727 were intended to have a third mechanical "manual reversion" mode if

both of the redundant "A" and "B" hydraulic systems were lost. In such an instance, the pilot was able to move the control surfaces manually. This concept worked well for the ailerons and elevators, but wind tunnel data showed that the control forces were far too high to allow manual reversion for the rudder. Since rudder control also needed to be triple redundant, the addition of a third "center" (later renamed "standby") hydraulic system to power the rudder in an emergency was required.

The low-speed flight portion of the testing focused on the wing's lift coefficients with flaps and slats deployed, along with the reduction of aerodynamic drag as much as feasibly possible. Through careful analysis, the shape and positioning of the flap track fairings, sometimes referred to as "canoe fairings" because of their appearance, under the trailing edge of the wing, were optimized. This allowed the lowest-possible drag while promoting the free flow of air through the flap slots to maximize the system's aerodynamics. To accomplish this, these devices, and the machinery that they concealed, were kept out of high-velocity airflow areas.

The T-tail design of the 727 also created some challenges in calculating stress and side loads on the horizontal and vertical stabilizers throughout the flight envelope. They also needed to account for the downward wash from the wings, as well as the aerodynamic effects of air swirling around the fuselage and the pod-mounted engines. For these purposes, a wind tunnel model was fitted with stress sensors along the roots of the horizontal and vertical surfaces. Concurrently, airflow pressure distributions were measured to ensure that the tail structure of the 727 would be able to withstand the most-extreme flight conditions.

Just over 1,500 hours of wind tunnel testing time was completed prior to the first flight of the 727. During this period, analysis data were collected on flap and slat aerodynamic loads, aircraft stability and control, flap transition positions, and transit speeds. The extreme amount of care and preparation demonstrated by Boeing's 727 team led to a solid airplane design right out of the box.

Fatigue Testing

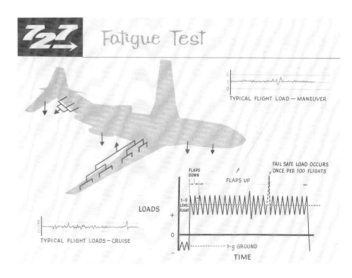

The 727 airframe was tested to higher loads than established operational limits, well in excess those experienced during normal airline operations. *Courtesy of the Boeing Company*

The structural testing of the 727 was the most detailed and rigorous program ever conducted at the time. As early as 1961, Boeing commenced fatigue testing of the basic 727 airframe, beginning with the joint structural components for the highly swept tail and empennage. This was soon followed by the wing and flap assemblies, which were tested for strength and operation under flight loads up to 110 percent of maximum, in temperatures ranging from −65°F to 160°F. These tests involved nearly 25,000 cycles (one complete extension and retraction) of the flaps and slats. During this same time period, from mid-1961 through early 1963, the landing gears were also tested in much the same manner. Simultaneously, approximately 336 ground-testing hours of the airframe for resistance to vibration damage was conducted on a dedicated test rig at an accelerated pace, with one "rig hour" being equivalent to eight flight hours. In total, the test airframe was subjected to an equivalent of 60,000 flight hours over a period of sixteen months. Boeing engineers had put the 727 through its paces and knew they had a very robust airplane, with most of this testing complete before Ship One ever took to the skies.

Extreme flight loads were repeatedly simulated with the test rig. *Courtesy of the Boeing Company*

Under a simulated load factor of 2.5 g, the operational, flaps-up limit for the 727, the wings of the 727 would deflect 5 feet. The photo on the left shows the unloaded condition, and the one on the right shows the wing under higher-than-operational load limits, deflecting nearly 8 feet. The 727 was later proven capable of enduring up to 6 g under extreme circumstances. *Courtesy of the Boeing Company*

Building and Flying the 727

Ship One

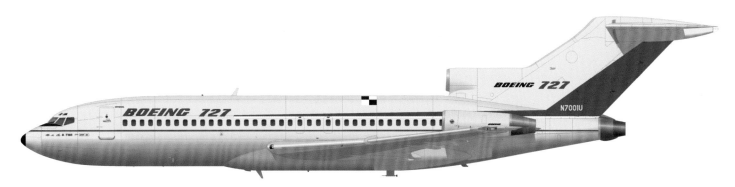

Courtesy of Jennings Heilig

Assembly of Ship One commenced with the station 870 bulkhead, which would later comprise the aft wall of the center fuel tank. Fuselage stations are named on the basis of their location in inches aft of the nose cone. Wing stations are similarly named in inches outboard from the aircraft's centerline. *Courtesy of the Boeing Company via T. C. Howard*

The vertical stabilizer, known on the factory floor as "Section 86," is readied for mating with the aircraft on May 10, 1962. The forward spar with the large opening for the number 2 engine S-duct is in good view. *Courtesy of the Boeing Company via T. C. Howard*

Section 86 being mounted to the aft fuselage (Section 48) in June 1962. *Courtesy of the Boeing Company via T. C. Howard*

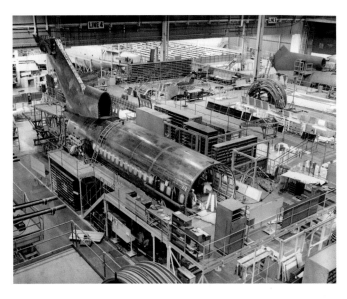

By August 17, 1962, Ship One takes shape, with the aft cabin structure (Section 46) attached to the partially assembled empennage. *Courtesy of the Boeing Company via T. C. Howard*

Ship One's left wing assembly is seen being completed on January 8, 1962. The combined left and right wing assemblies are known as Section 12. *Courtesy of the Boeing Company via T. C. Howard*

The left wing is being prepared for attachment to the fuselage in August 1963. Note the contour of the wing leading edge, with the slats not yet installed. *Courtesy of the Boeing Company via T. C. Howard*

The forward fuselage of Ship One is lowered into position for attachment to the aft body. *Courtesy of the Boeing Company*

Ship One is weight off wheels while undergoing final assembly. The external power cable is attached to the forward fuselage, just above the nose landing gear. Note the protective coating, which was green in color, applied to the upper fuselage. *Courtesy of the Boeing Company via T. C. Howard*

This view of a 727 in final assembly shows the center engine and pod engine mountings. *Courtesy of the Boeing Company*

The Renton Plant is seen here full of 727s. This facility is still in use today, building the Boeing 737 MAX-series jetliners. *Courtesy of the Boeing Company*

The cabin insulation for the 727 is seen being tailored by hand. *Courtesy of the Boeing Company*

The ducts that supply the passengers' overhead gasper vents are added prior to the sidewall insulation. *Courtesy of the Boeing Company*

Insulation not only keeps the cabin temperature more controllable but also attenuates aerodynamic noise, creating a much-nicer environment for passengers. *Courtesy of the Boeing Company*

MODEL 727 PRODUCTION BREAKDOWN

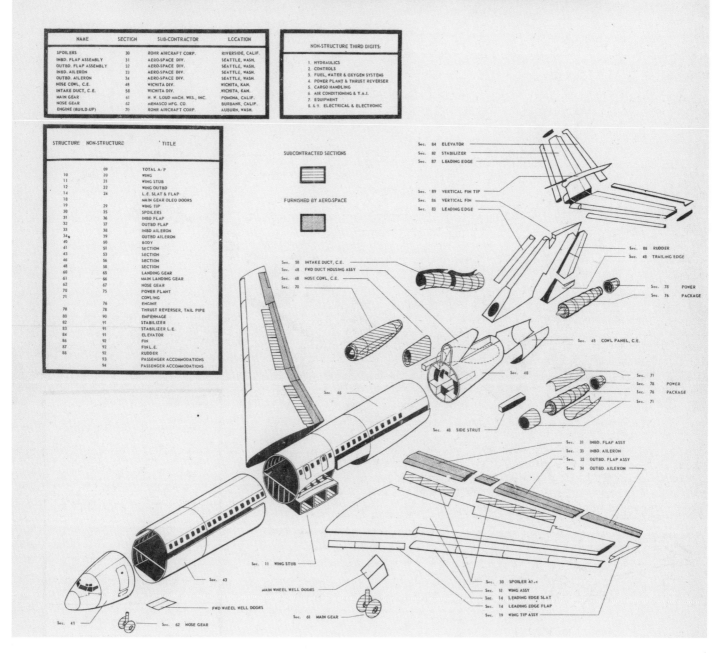

A breakdown of airframe components and major subcontractors involved with the production of the 727-100.
Courtesy of the Boeing Company

The 727 first flight crew stands in front of Ship One on November 11, 1962, during final assembly. Shown (*from left to right*) are Dix Loesch, Lew Wallick, and Shuly Schulenberger. *Courtesy of the Boeing Company via T. C. Howard*

The first 727 was presented to the world during a rollout ceremony at the Renton Municipal Airport on November 27, 1962. This airplane (c/n 18293, l/n 1) was given effectivity number E1, by which the aircraft was known internally at Boeing. Ship One was registered as N7001U, under an Experimental Airworthiness Certificate from the Federal Aviation Agency (which later became known as the Federal Aviation Administration in 1967). This aircraft was not technically considered a "prototype" as previously mentioned, but instead a "preproduction" airplane, built to the specifications set forth by United Airlines, its future owner.

Ship One is seen prior to the official rollout ceremony. The absence of airline logos on the nose of the aircraft indicates that this is a prerollout photo. *Courtesy of the Boeing Company*

Boeing personnel burn the midnight oil to prepare Ship One for rollout. *Courtesy of the Boeing Company*

UNITED STATES OF AMERICA
FEDERAL AVIATION AGENCY

CERTIFICATE OF AIRWORTHINESS

1. NATIONALITY AND REGISTRATION MARKS	2. AIRCRAFT AIRWORTHINESS CLASSIFICATION
N7001U	EXPERIMENTAL — Research and Development

3. This Certificate of Airworthiness is issued pursuant to the Federal Aviation Act of 1958. The aircraft identified hereon is considered airworthy when maintained and operated in accordance with the Civil Air Regulations and applicable aircraft Operation Limitations.

4. This Certificate will remain in effect as long as the aircraft is maintained in accordance with Part 43 of the Civil Air Regulations unless surrendered, suspended, revoked, or a termination date is otherwise established by the Administrator of the Federal Aviation Agency. Expiration date June 19, 1963.

5. DATE OF ISSUANCE	6. FAA REPRESENTATIVE	7. DESIGNATION NO.
2/8/63	W. C. Chin	WE-EMDO-46

8. Any alteration or misuse of this Certificate is punishable by a fine of not exceeding $1,000 or imprisonment not exceeding 3 years, or both.

GPO : 1959 OF—508835   Form FAA 134-38 (5—59)

The original "Experimental Certificate of Airworthiness" for Ship One, issued prior to its first flight. *Courtesy of the Federal Aviation Administration via Bruce Beadell*

Understanding the Numbers

The 727 was the first Boeing jetliner to be issued effectivity numbers, which is a practice still in use today with the latest models. Each individual airplane produced by Boeing has a unique Effectivity Number as well as a serial number (c/n), which never change and are carried by the airframe for its entire life.

In addition, until recently, Boeing jetliners used suffix customer codes to identify the airline for which an individual aircraft was constructed. For example, Ship One was a 727-22, which identified United Airlines (customer code 22) as the purchaser. A later 727-200-series aircraft, initially bought by Trans World Airlines, would be a 727-231, since "31" was that carrier's customer code. As customers became more abundant, these codes began to incorporate letters as well. For example, 727-200s originally delivered to Royal Air Moroc (customer code B6) were designated as 727-2B6s.

Registration numbers, however, do frequently change as airplanes are transferred from one airline to another. It is therefore not uncommon for an aircraft to wear several different registrations throughout its service life.

Although a close look at the forward fuselage shows the 727's family heritage with the earlier Boeing 707 and 720 models, this airplane was different . . . very different. Looking fast even with its wheels chocked on the ramp, this new aircraft featured strikingly sleek lines and a design that gave the airplane a naturally curvy, area-ruled appearance—an aggressive styling usually reserved for supersonic military jets. The famed French aircraft designer Marcel Dassault once said, "For an airplane to fly well, it must be beautiful." While his sentiment may not be literally true, the 727 certainly supported it.

Initially, the 727 Flight Test fleet was flown only by Boeing crews until the final production configuration of the aircraft was established and the aircraft performance was found to be within certification

specifications. Once this was accomplished, the FAA would grant a type inspection authorization (TIA). The TIA is used to authorize aircraft conformity, airworthiness inspections, and flight-testing demonstrations with evaluators from the FAA onboard. At the time, transport category aircraft were certified under a set of regulations known as CAR 4b. It is noteworthy that in 1967, this set of criteria was superseded by a revised regulation set called FAR Part 25, which remains the standard today. Subsequent to this FAA inspection opportunity, and once all requirements and concerns were satisfied, a type certificate for the 727 could be issued by the administrator.

Resplendent in the customary yellow and burgundy Boeing company colors, Ship One first took flight on February 9, 1963, under the command of Capt. Samuel Lewis "Lew" Wallick Jr., with Richard Llewellyn "Dix" Loesch in the first officer's seat, and Marvin Keith "Shuly" Shulenberger as the flight engineer for its historic first flight. This event began what Lew Wallick described as "the most intensive commercial certification program ever undertaken by Boeing." The

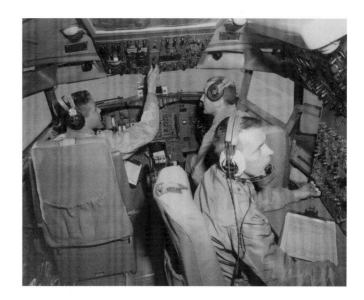

The 727 first flight crew prepares the aircraft for departure. *Courtesy of the Boeing Company*

This cover was flown onboard the first flight of Ship One on February 9, 1963. *Author's collection*

The first flight crew is congratulated by an exuberant William Allen after the aircraft's successful flight. *Courtesy of the Boeing Company*

airplane was reported to fly well, exhibiting excellent handling characteristics, but this first flight was not without a few minor glitches. As the airplane lifted off from the runway in Renton, Washington, the center (number 2) engine experienced a compressor stall, announced by a loud, reverberating bang, before promptly recovering to normal operation. Once up and away from the airport, it was found that the leading edge slats would not retract under air loads. These two issues needed to be resolved, but the flight was nonetheless deemed a resounding success. Wallick recorded, "This airplane is going to do what it was designed to do; there's no question about it," and further was quoted as saying, "It was much quieter in the cockpit than the 707. . . . The minor difficulties we encountered on this flight are less than you would expect. I'd say that this is a clean airplane."

E1 was the first of four machines used in the 727 certification flight test program. This aircraft was slated to conduct low-speed testing, high-speed evaluations including flutter tests, and FAA demonstrations following Boeing's initial company testing. For these purposes, this airplane logged 456 flight hours prior to delivery to United Airlines on October 6, 1964.

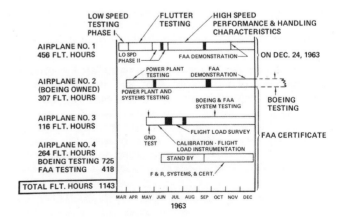

This chart details the certification task loading for each of the four flight test aircraft. *Courtesy of the Boeing Company*

Testing...
testing...

That busy airplane above is the brilliant new Boeing 727, America's first short-range jetliner. It's engaged in the most intensive test program in airliner history. During the rest of this year, four 727s will be put through exhaustive flight tests. You'll be able to fly aboard this magnificent new Boeing jet beginning early next year. You'll find the cabin roomy and luxurious; the ride, incredibly quiet and smooth. The 727 can operate from 5000-foot runways, bringing the advantages of jet travel to hundreds of smaller cities. These airlines have already ordered 131 Boeing 727s: American, Ansett-ANA, Eastern, Lufthansa, Trans-Australia, TWA and United. **BOEING 727**

Courtesy of the Boeing Company

Work began immediately on the initial issue with the center-engine compressor stalls. Compressor stalls can commonly occur when the airflow into the first-stage compressor is disturbed or not evenly distributed. Boeing's Jack Wimpress explained:

> The boundary layer is pretty thick back there anyway, and the thing is that taking in boundary layer air directly into the duct to the engine, it ends up having a very poor velocity profile. The engine gets a bunch of lousy air which could lead to compressor stalls.

When the nose of the 727 was rotated up for liftoff, the top of the fuselage modified the airflow into the oval-shaped center inlet, causing the problem. After reviewing the issue, aerodynamicists found that installing sets of small vortex generators (VGs) inside the throat of the S-shaped duct helped stabilize the airflow entering into the compressor to prevent the issue to the maximum extent possible. Mitigating compressor stalls was important because this was exceedingly undesirable for the longevity of the engine. Equally adverse was the momentary loss of thrust during critical flight stages, and loud unsavory noises emanating from the errant power plant. It was found that when a severe compressor stall occurred on these first preproduction JT8D engines, the reversal of airflow through the compressor would cause the spinning blades to contact the adjacent stator vanes, leading to rapid wear. Subsequent flight tests in the program were conducted with these VGs installed. This became the standard production configuration for the center engine inlet on the 727.

The requirement for high lift during takeoff and approach resulted in the installation of four large slat panels on each wing. Air loads were found to be higher than anticipated, resulting in the original slat actuators being underpowered for their retraction function. A sharp-eyed observer will note that all of the in-flight images from E1's first flight have the slats extended because of this issue. During Boeing's initial evaluation phase, these hydraulic actuators were replaced with more-powerful, redesigned units, and the issue was resolved. Shortly thereafter, the Krueger flaps were tested at various degrees of angular extension to find the ideal position for high lift and minimum drag.

As with all airplane designs, controlling the airflow over the wing in all phases of flight was set as a high priority for the 727. Aero engineers added small aerodynamic fences to the leading edge of the wing in differing locations and sizes for testing. Experiments were conducted with these installed at wing buttock lines 341, 410, and 486, with sizes ranging from 3 to 8 inches tall. While some of these test configurations employed multiple devices together, it was found that a single fiberglass fence, 5 inches tall and positioned at wing buttock line 341 on each wing, provided the best results. To aid in aircraft handling during stalls, small triangular stall strips were added on the inboardmost Krueger flaps. These were intended to cause the stalled airflow to propagate positively from the inboard portion of the wing, to cause a nose-down pitching moment. After testing, however, this method was found to provide negligible benefit in the handling of the aircraft. Vortex generators, similar to those used in the 727's unique center-engine S-duct, could also be used on other parts of the aircraft to stabilize airflow. While these were added to the wings and tested, they were found to be unnecessary.

During these early test flights, the slat scheduling was established to provide the best lift/drag performance while the aircraft was accelerating after takeoff or decelerating during approach to landing. This scheduling caused slat panels 2, 3, 6, and 7 to extend as the trailing edge flaps transited from the "up" position out to position 2, which was the least extended position for the trailing edge flaps. As the pilot selected the flaps to position 5, the remaining slats (1, 4, 5, and 8) would then extend along with all six inboard-mounted Krueger flaps.

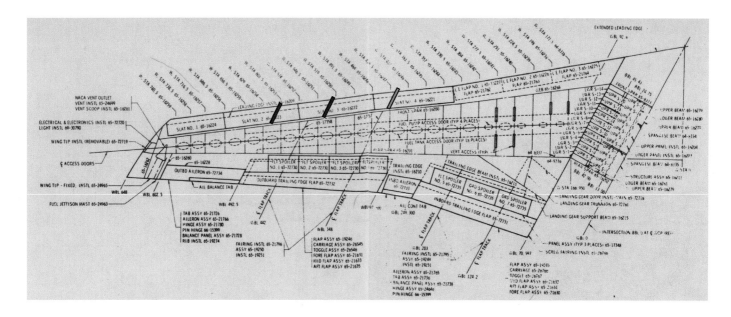

This diagram illustrates the three different stall fence locations that were tested during the 727 flight test program. The position of the production fence is shown in green. *Courtesy of the Boeing Company*

The "Bomb"

Courtesy of the Boeing Company

During many of the airborne tests, it was required to have accurate airspeed data for analysis purposes. Many times, the aircraft instrumentation became slightly inaccurate due to the extreme pitch and yaw angles required for flight testing. In order to achieve reliably accurate data, an aerodynamically shaped weight was lowered from the belly of the aircraft to collect flight data. Because of its bomb-like appearance, it carried the nickname "the Bomb," even on official flight test paperwork. This nickname was also further appropriate since this fixture had a propensity to becoming separated from the aircraft and cable during extreme maneuvers. Occasionally, a "bomb" would need to be transported on airline flights to replace a lost unit while away from base. It was often an interesting experience transiting security with this suspicious-looking device in hand.

When looking at flight test aircraft today, one might observe a small cone-shaped device trailing from the vertical stabilizer. This device trails in relatively undisturbed airflow and is used for the same purpose as the legacy "bomb" arrangement.

By early March, Boeing test pilots were already operating the airplane to speeds up to maximum structural design airspeed (Vd) and maximum design Mach number (Md). Vd and Md were established at 474 knots and Mach 0.95, respectively, well in excess of the normal operating redline values. The test pilots were keenly aware of the dangers of high-speed aerodynamic flutter, and the aircraft was evaluated for its ability to dampen out this tendency. Special vanes were installed on the tips of the wings and horizontal stabilizers to induce flutter, but the 727's design easily dampened out this potentially destructive phenomenon. Rigorous tests were conducted at 13,000 and 22,000 feet at Vd, and then subsequently at 22,000 feet and 35,000 feet at Md, testing the aircraft performance throughout the altitude spectrum. Early on in the test program, the elevator bias was set to 1 degree nose down to improve stability, and this was also tested and found satisfactory on these early flights.

Ship One departs for a flutter evaluation flight. On the right wingtip, temporary vanes were installed to excite any flutter tendency that the airframe might possess. Similar vanes were also attached to the starboard horizontal stabilizer, which is blocked in this view. The 727 proved to be inherently resistant to flutter. *Courtesy of the Boeing Company*

Excellent Performance

As the 727 flight test program proceeded, confidence was building that this aircraft was a sure winner. Not only was the aircraft handling excellent, but the data coming back from the aerodynamicists were even better. As previously mentioned, Boeing had some experience with the use of leading edge slats on the early B-47s. On these aircraft, because of aerodynamic "leakage" around the slats while retracted, cruising drag was higher than that of the later nonslatted B-47s. This was anticipated to be the same with the 727 design and was considered to be an acceptable compromise to fulfill the short-field mission requirements for the new aircraft. In actuality, the 727 proved not to have any significant leakage issues, producing drag numbers that were up to 7 percent less than estimated.

Low-Speed and Stall Testing

On April 3, 1963, E1 was placed in "layup" to prepare the aircraft for low-speed and stall testing, since this was the primary aircraft used for such evaluations. During these layup periods the aircraft's test instrumentation applicable to the next area of evaluation was installed, aircraft modifications were made, and general maintenance was performed.

One of the items to be tested was the production model Gianini/Safeflight stall-warning system, which was installed for thorough evaluation throughout the certification program. This system used angle-of-attack data, along with many other inputs, to sense an impending high-angle-of-attack/low-airspeed issue, which triggered a warning to the pilot. This warning was felt by the pilot as the system aggressively vibrated the yoke, giving the pilot tactile warning of a low-airspeed threat. Soon after these preparations had been made, stall testing began. For additional information on aerodynamic stalls, please see "Dash 80 Flight Testing" on page 51.

Center of gravity (CG), the loaded balance point of the aircraft, is a critically important factor in aircraft handling, so flight testing is used to establish their limits, on the basis of the demonstrated handling of the aircraft. This balance point is calculated with reference to the wing's average lifting-surface location, known as mean aerodynamic chord, more commonly referred to as MAC. Typically, on jet aircraft the location of the balance point is expressed as a percentage of MAC: 0 percent being the forwardmost point of MAC and 100 percent being the farthest aft. Generally, the acceptable range on most aircraft resides in the forward 40–50 percent of MAC for good stability characteristics. On flight test aircraft, a system of metal water barrels and associated plumbing were used, along with fuel usage or airborne fuel dumping, to change the aircraft weight and CG while still in flight. This often eliminated the need to return to base for reloading or redistribution.

Stalls were initially demonstrated at the forward end of the CG spectrum to establish the most-conservative stall speeds for given weights. This condition has the aircraft configured in a "nose heavy" state, which, during stalls, requires the most aerodynamic load on the tail to perform the stall maneuver. Raising the nose requires increasing downforce applied by the horizontal stabilizers and elevator surfaces. The wing must support not only the weight of the aircraft itself, but also the value of this downforce being generated. Simply stated, the more load the wing has to bear, for a given g-loading and flap configuration, the higher the stall speed will be. Because of this dynamic, with all else being equal, forward CG stalls occur at a higher indicated airspeed than aft CG stalls.

Although the forward CG stalls occur at higher airspeeds, this configuration generally offers good control stability. To recover from a stall, normally all that is required is to simply release back pressure on the yoke and allow the nose to fall, thereby effecting a positive recovery. Stalls during an aft CG condition generate lower stall speeds; however, the aircraft stability in this regime of flight often determines the aft CG limit for the aircraft. The aircraft's stability requirement would mandate that a stall is easily recovered by the pilot simply releasing back pressure on the yoke, which, in an extreme tail-heavy condition, may not be met. Here, the need for a wide range of allowable balance limits of the aircraft, especially important to any transport category aircraft, must also be tempered by proper aircraft behavior.

Thus, many tests were conducted with the aircraft in this aft CG condition, with much attention placed on aircraft handling and positive recovery. Testing occurred in all different aircraft configurations of landing gear, wing flap, and spoiler positions. Generally, the 727 did well in these tests, except for one condition in which the wing flaps were extended with the speed brakes deployed. Lew Wallick, along with copilot R. T. Johnson and flight engineer H. W. Sherman, conducted the stall at an extreme aft position of 40 percent MAC, when the maneuver became a bit interesting. As the airspeed bled off, with Wallick pulling the yoke back farther and farther to effect the stall, "stick lightening" occurred, where the aft stick forces were no longer required and the nose continued to rise at 156 knots. Recovery required an immediate full nose-down elevator input to recover the aircraft to stable flight. Clearly, the combination of flaps, speed brakes, and aft CG had the 727 flirting with the T-tail deep stall tendency, an unacceptable, if not fatal, characteristic. Without the use of speed brakes, however, the aircraft handling was docile. Because of this, the 727 was limited to speed brake use only with wing flaps retracted, except after landing or during a rejected takeoff. In fact, per modification FC 569-19-1, an aural warning horn was installed, which sounded if the speed brakes were selected with flaps extended while in flight, to ensure that distracted line pilots would never unwittingly find themselves in this situation.

Ballast was secured to the cabin floor to bring the aircraft up to the desired condition weight. The water barrels used pumps to move water forward and aft to adjust the aircraft's center of gravity, while in flight, to expedite testing. *Courtesy of the Boeing Company*

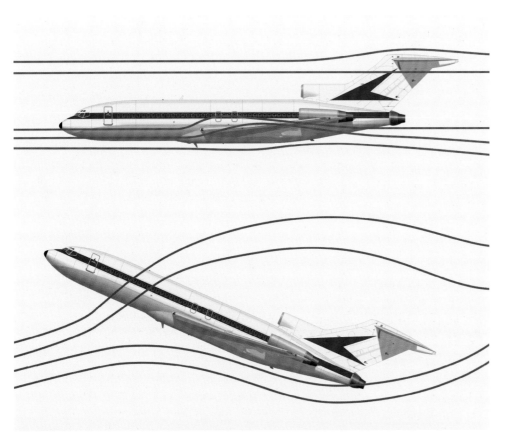

In normal flight, clean airflow flows over the horizontal stabilizer and elevator surfaces. Because of the elevated location of the horizontal stabilizers on a T-tailed airplane, when the aircraft is stalled and the pilot continues to pull farther aft on the yoke, it is possible for the angle of attack to become excessive. As the angle increases, the tail of the airplane flies into the wake of the wings and engine pods. This can blank out the airflow over the horizontal stabilizers, reducing the ability of the pilot to lower the nose to recover from the stall. *Courtesy of Jennings Heilig*

The Pratt & Whitney JT8D-1 engine shown installed on a 727. The accessory section, which includes the engine generator, hydraulic pump, and pneumatic starter, is clearly seen on the lower forward section of the engine. *Courtesy of Pratt & Whitney*

E1 once again went into layup on May 6, 1963, in order to replace its preproduction Pratt & Whitney JT8D engines with improved production models. With these production power plants installed, FAA flight evaluations commenced on September 5, 1963. By this point, E1 had already logged 278 hours, 21 minutes of preliminary testing prior to the commencement of FAA flight testing. These flights were flown by one Boeing test pilot (normally Lew Wallick) and one of three primary FAA pilots. During these evaluations, the function-and-reliability parameter was concurrently monitored as flight time was accrued, looking at the operation and maintainability of various aircraft systems.

With the FAA evaluators involved, the aircraft performance and handling behavior were systematically scrutinized. Additionally, various areas of interest, including non-normal aircraft system situations and simulated malfunctions, were observed. The stall series was methodically repeated with every imaginable configuration; with all available flap settings, and both with and without speed brake deployment.

The Deep Stall Incident

There is an abundance of evidence suggesting that a serious "deep stall" incident occurred at some point late in the 727 flight test program with FAA representatives onboard the aircraft. A deep stall occurs when the horizontal stabilizer flies into the turbulent wake of the stalled wing. This reduces the aircraft's natural tendency to nose down in order to properly recover from the stall. This phenomenon manifests itself most commonly with T-tailed airframes, as Boeing's Jack Wimpress explained:

Both the de Havilland 121 [Trident] and the BAC One-Eleven had fatal deep stall accidents, and the wind tunnel data on the 727 showed a pitch-up followed by a very strong pitch down. It looked very strong, so they stopped testing. After those accidents occurred, they tested it up higher and found that it would loop back again. There was a deep stall well above where they would normally fly the airplane.

Boeing aerodynamicist Dave Anderson also spoke of the 727's deep stall characteristic:

I think that some people thought that when you went through that nice recovery area, nobody in their right mind would get to that kind of angle of attack because they already had the nose down long before, and they would never even realize it was there.

Still, in flight test, many areas of the flight envelope are evaluated, such as aerodynamic stalls, which are unlikely to be seen during normal airline operations. According to several accounts while stall testing was being conducted by Lew Wallick and one of the FAA certification test pilots, an unexpected significant difference from any normal stall recovery occurred. The FAA pilot conducted the stall in a designated flight test configuration with partial flap and speed brakes extended. The configuration was similar to one in which Wallick experienced some "stick lightening," resulting in a "push" recovery earlier in the test program. Just after the aerodynamic stall

occurred, the FAA pilot continued the test for an "abuse condition" with an aggressive and prolonged pull on the yoke. The aircraft responded with an increased angle of attack, well past that of any earlier Boeing testing, with the flight path descending, but with the nose continuing to increase to a pitch attitude yielding nearly a 70-degree angle of attack. Don Cumming, a performance analyst who studied the test flight telemetry that day, shared his recollection:

Many of the parameters were off scale, but the elevator traces showed full down for seventeen seconds, and there was no airspeed data because the pitots were stalled, even though the pitots were a high-alpha design we used on flight test airplanes that did performance work. Bob Larson from Aero Staff and I reviewed flight test and wind tunnel data and noted a brief discontinuity in the pitching-moment data as the airplane reached very high angles of attack. We concluded it was caused by the T-tail passing out of the wing wake and entering a wake off the side engines. That was the basis of the 60-to-70-degree alpha [AOA] that has been quoted.

The 727 seemed to almost stop in midair and began to rapidly lose altitude. Lew Wallick, known to have quick reactions and outstanding stick-and-rudder skills, assumed control of the aircraft. While continuing to push full forward on the yoke, he retracted the speed brakes, selected flaps 5, and pushed the thrust levers as far forward as they would go. On jet engines without thrust limiters like the JT8D, this commands significant thrust above and beyond maximum rated power, potentially sacrificing the engines to save the aircraft. Jesse Wallick, Lew's brother and also a Boeing flight test engineer, was occupying the cockpit jump seat behind Lew and the FAA pilot. He reported that while in this nose-high attitude relative to the flight path, the aircraft was rolling back and forth while his brother aggressively attempted to regain control. Slowly, the 727's nose began to drop farther, exiting the stall as control was eventually regained, all without damage to the aircraft or its occupants.

It is important to be mindful that jet transports were still fairly new during this time period, and older certification requirements would have pilots hold an aircraft IN the stall to evaluate the aircraft behavior while being inappropriately controlled by the pilot.

Retired FAA air carrier inspector and later Boeing test pilot Capt. Tom Imrich explains:

As has happened in several eras over the course of aviation history, especially after the earlier-noted stall-related testing accidents with T-tail jets, there was great pressure on the FAA to ensure that any new jet aircraft would be approved only with the most thorough and comprehensive certification testing. In this spirit, the FAA test pilot was aware of the FAA's need to be viewed as thorough, independent, and conservative in using reasonably stressful tests when making a certification safety call. So, the FAA pilot flying the evaluation that day elected to explicitly examine a stall recovery "abuse case," by using what he considered to be a conservative technique to hold the full aft pitch input momentarily longer than normal, which in turn led to the deep stall. Today, with modern criteria and stall-warning systems, that "abuse" technique is no longer used, being considered as an excessively aggressive abuse test. However, at the time, it was still thought appropriate for assessment by that authority test pilot. He didn't expect it to almost lead to the loss of the test aircraft.

The desire for comprehensive certification testing in this case was undoubtedly underscored by the fact that other recent accidents were motivation to thoroughly investigate any new technologies or configurations. For example, it was only a few years earlier that the FAA learned two hard lessons with the highly technical "whirl mode" phenomenon, which led to the destruction of Braniff Flight 542 and Northwest Flight 710. Both these accident flights were operated with brand-new Lockheed L-188 Electras, each of which suffered a fatal in-flight breakup due to a then-unfamiliar structural engine-wing resonance that wasn't caught during original certification testing (see "Whirl Mode and the Lockheed Electra" on page 44).

As Capt. Imrich points out, these were the kinds of likely contributing factors leading the FAA certification pilot to inadvertently put the 727 into an unnecessarily high-risk, extreme stalled-flight condition that day. This 727 flight test's deep stall event was yet another painful lesson learned during our advancement into the jet age.

The FAA still left no stone unturned and was determined to ensure that the 727 was a truly safe airplane. Don Cumming explained the sequence of events:

This event caused a major FAA certification concern and a "Blue Ribbon" team to visit Boeing. I don't remember how many pilots descended on us, but in just a few days they performed several hundred stalls on our test airplanes. Slow entry rate, fast entry rate, turning, accelerated entry. No flaps-down, speed-brakes-extended stalls were performed, however. . . . The event was on E1, as was the bulk of the Blue Ribbon team['s] evaluation. This event also taxed our data-processing system, as it was coming very close to certification date and the FAA wanted every stall time history in a report. In those days, all our data plotting was done manually, so I had every person in the organization that could put a point in the right place plotting—including all the bosses and secretaries.

Other T-tailed aircraft—namely, the de Havilland (later Hawker Siddeley) Trident and the BAC One-Eleven—suffered from severe problems with the deep stall tendency. Both these aircraft mitigated the issue by installing a device called a "stick pusher." Onboard systems monitored aircraft angle of attack with other parameters and warned the pilot with a stall warning. If the pilot continued further into the stall and the angle of attack approached a limit value, the stick pusher would activate, mechanically and forcibly moving the yoke forward to reduce the angle of attack to a safe value. The 727, on the other hand, required a concerted effort to get the airplane into a deep stall, while giving the pilot plenty of warning of this trend. Boeing stability control engineer Murray Booth explained the difference:

By the way, the 727 had some forgiving characteristics in the stall. It was not like "My gosh, it's driving off a cliff." It had good buffet warning and initial pitch down. You would have to be asleep not to recognize this as a pilot. But, if you insisted on pulling it well through (we did because we wanted to understand it), you had to work at it to some degree. Once you got around that corner, well, you kind of lost it for a while. It wasn't like this deep stall was a cliff that it would fall off with no warning.

The flight test pilots are naturally expected to explore the entire flight envelope and thus discovered this tendency, though Boeing's engineers felt that no pilot would get anywhere near this corner of the envelope during normal operations. Murray Booth described why Sutter and the design team resisted the inclusion of a stick pusher as standard equipment on the 727:

I was drafted by Joe Sutter to do the best job we could on the deep stall and demonstrating first to ourselves what were the characteristics and what was the exposure. We were secondarily motivated by a couple of incidents on the BAC One-Eleven with the stick pusher. We were being asked by airline customers (American, United, and others), "Why don't you put a stick pusher in the 727?" All of us, especially Joe Sutter, knew the last thing we wanted to do was to put in a stick pusher, unless we were absolutely convinced [of] the risks associated with putting something like that in the airplane that can inadvertently take the controls when it wasn't needed (a failure). The cure was worse than the illness. My role at the time was to model and try to fully understand the extent to which the airplane contained some serious concerns. . . . In the end, we didn't put a stick pusher in the airplane. I think the service record over all of those years showed that it was the right thing to do. Back in those days, there was not a whole lot of confidence that artificial systems could be relied on. We had experience with runaway trim, yaw dampers, hard-overs, so you can see the mindset, which would be different today. The mindset was "Not a stick pusher!"

As a sidenote, much later when the British carrier Dan-Air London purchased the 727, the British certification authorities insisted that a stick pusher needed to be installed in all 727s operating under British registry. Boeing naturally complied and outfitted these few aircraft accordingly. The sensitive nature of the British authorities due to the loss of two BAC One-Elevens and a Trident during flight testing was, of course, understandable at the time.

Stability Testing
During the FAA evaluations of the 727 performance, high-speed testing was conducted. Once again, the aircraft was tested well in excess of the normal operating limits, sometimes even in reportedly rough air, showing that Wallick and the flight test engineers had a high level of confidence in their new machine. One issue was noted on E1 that required some further confirmation. At high Mach numbers and low indicated airspeeds, such as at high altitudes, this aircraft began to show a fairly strong tendency to roll to the left, requiring 30 degrees

of right yoke travel to null out the issue. This was confirmed both by the FAA and Boeing pilots on later evaluation flights as well but was occurring only at very high altitudes, while operating at high weights and Mach numbers. To conduct these tests, the engines had to be "overboosted" or operated at higher-than-certified thrust levels. While there was some conversation about limiting aircraft speed in this region to below Mach 0.90, Wallick pointed out that the aircraft would be capable only of Mach 0.87 with normal thrust limits and thus would not be operated in this corner of the envelope during normal operations. Because of this, the situation was ultimately agreed to be a nonissue, and no additional limitations were deemed necessary.

Operation with Flight Control Malfunctions

Extensive testing was conducted by Boeing and FAA pilots to explore the behavior of the 727 under different non-normal circumstances that might possibly, albeit rarely, be experienced during line operations. The 727 featured fully powered flight controls, with hydraulic power supplied both by A and B hydraulic systems for redundancy. In the extremely rare event that both of these sources were to fail, a backup "manual reversion" system was provided. This system was cable driven and allowed the pilot to still have adequate control of the aircraft in the absence of normal control power. The aircraft was checked throughout the range of its operating speeds with different combinations of flight control malfunctions.

Because jetliners were still quite new at many carriers, and even at the larger airlines, crews would transition from legacy propliners directly to the new Boeing 727. Many of the older airplanes, such as the Douglas DC-6, had flight control systems that were primarily manual by nature, with a fairly heavy control feel for the pilot—roughly akin to driving an automobile without power steering. Conversely, with normal hydraulic power the 727 had a light and nimble control feel. If the hydraulics were to fail or were turned off for demonstration purposes, the airplane would fall into the cable-and-tab-driven emergency mode: manual reversion. This mode was reportedly similar in feel to the primary control system on the Douglas propliners.

Boeing test pilot Capt. Brien Wygle recalls demonstrating flight in manual reversion to a team of United Airlines pilots:

ALPA sent a delegation of pilots to fly the airplane. In those days, ALPA was United's union . . . they ran the show, boy! So, I took them up and I was in the right seat. You could just see their faces just lit up. I remember demonstrating the hydraulic systems. I told the pilot, let's turn off one of the hydraulic systems and you can fly . . . the 727 flew nicely on one. It would slow down in response, but one was fine. Now, I will go one step further and turn them both off and you will be flying . . . mostly through the tabs. The United pilot was flying it manually now. You have to remember that these guys were flying props. He leaned over and said, "DC-6!" In other words, [it felt similar to] our most degraded system!

The distinctive highly swept vertical stabilizer on the 727 certainly made the airplane look fast, as well as setting the horizontal stabilizers as far aft as feasible to mitigate the deep stall tendency as much as possible. Additionally, this 55-degree sweepback was used to reduce aerodynamic drag, as Boeing's Bill McIntosh explained:

The reason that we put that much sweep on is because you have this huge S-duct. How do you fair that out? The way we could get around the pressure getting supersonic was to add sweep.

The S-duct also required the vertical stabilizer to be thicker in chord than would have normally been required. This thickness causes the airflow around the surface to accelerate, possibly even becoming supersonic, creating various problems, including a very sharp drag rise. Adding sweep delays this drag rise, effectively making the drag curve much more favorable. As with every compromise in aircraft design, though, the addition of sweep came with a price, as McIntosh continued:

One of the reasons that we added the vortex generators was that we had done a lot of flow visualization in the wind tunnel, and the top corner of the rudder was pretty murky, so we put on the vortex generators to try to avoid that, and it helped significantly. The sweep was so high that the boundary layer just wanted to creep out. Up in the corner, it was completely separated. We also got a rude awakening. They were measuring the hinge moments on the rudder. The project people would not let us do a nice streamlined cut. There would be a gap and you would have to seal that gap, so they insisted on this funny crooked thing, and we got a surprise that the hinge moments on one of the rudders was two or three times what we had anticipated. The original goal was to put some manual reversion in the airplane, and we left space in there for balance panels. Because of the way it was cut and the hinge moments being so high, we basically couldn't use it that way. We put on vortex generators and faired S-duct as carefully as we could. That was something that we did not anticipate, and that was no small effect; it was a huge effect. If you had done it streamwise, you would have ended up with large seals. This area up in here [pointing at upper aft vertical stabilizer] was seriously separated, and the vortex generators were put on to help.

Because an airplane is a fully integrated machine, one issue, in this case aerodynamic, can create the necessity of additional revisions to the airplane. All the primary flight controls (aileron, elevators, and rudders) were required to be triple redundant. Aside from the two independent hydraulic channels to the ailerons and elevators, the 727 was equipped with a cable-driven manual backup. This was not possible for the rudder, though, because of the higher-than-anticipated aerodynamic forces acting upon it. This was confirmed early on during wind tunnel testing and led to the inclusion of the third "standby" hydraulic system to give the pilots emergency control of the rudder in case of a dual system failure. Vortex generators, similar to the ones utilized in the center-engine S-duct, were used to reattach airflow tending to separate, by energizing the aerodynamic boundary layer. All 727s have a long row of vortex generators on both sides of the vertical stabilizer to reduce the airflow separation and improve stability about the yaw axis.

Even with these design features, one area of operation that did provide some level of handling difficulty on the 727 involved a situation when both yaw dampers were simulated to be inoperative.

Swept-wing aircraft commonly exhibit a tendency called "Dutch roll," which is an alternating rolling and yawing instability. To eliminate this, a device called a yaw damper is installed (the 727 has two redundant yaw dampers), stabilizing the aircraft's yaw (nose side to side) stability, which precludes the development of a coupled yaw/roll issue. The 727 was found to be somewhat prone to Dutch roll, particularly while at high airspeeds and at higher altitudes. Both FAA and Boeing pilots tested the aircraft at differing altitudes and airspeeds to establish the exact points, above which the aircraft became "divergent" or unstable. A direct result of this testing led to the following Airplane Flight Manual (AFM) airspeed limitations for the 100 series 727 while operating with both yaw dampers inoperative, which allowed the aircraft to operate within the certification criteria of CAR 4b:

280 knots at 26,000 feet
300 knots at 25,000 feet
320 knots at 24,000 feet
340 knots at 23,000 feet
350 knots at 22,000 feet and below

Additionally, if a dual yaw damper failure were to occur above these altitude and airspeed limits, it was found during flight test that the use of speed brakes not only would expedite the transition back into the envelope above but also aided in damping the Dutch roll on the 727 to a large extent. This procedure was also to be accomplished with the autopilot off and no use of rudder, in order to preclude any yaw/roll coupling issues.

The extremely unlikely possibility of an asymmetric slat extension malfunction, combined with an unusually low airspeed, was also explored. Because of the asymmetric lift-and-stall behavior caused by this condition, the aircraft began to exhibit a significant roll-off just as the aircraft's stall-warning system activated. This provided the pilot with little warning prior to the aircraft control becoming compromised. The FAA evaluators felt that this might catch the pilot off guard, possibly at low altitudes during an approach to landing. They found, though, that handling was vastly improved with a modest increase in airspeed of just 15 knots. This speed additive, incorporated into the Boeing 727 Non-Normal Checklist for approach and landing under this condition, was agreed on to provide a reasonable level of safety without unnecessarily increasing runway requirements.

The 727 utilized four large sets of Fowler-type, triple-slotted trailing edge flaps. Tests were conducted simulating a situation where an outboard flap panel became jammed. The aircraft's flap-monitoring system was designed to limit this somewhat, so that if an asymmetry of more than 5 to 6 degrees was detected, the system would automatically stop movement. Testing was conducted with the right outboard flap panel extended to position 25, while the panel on the left wing was positioned to the limits of this tolerance. Handling was found to still be acceptable even with the largest-possible asymmetry.

The 727 (like most jetliners) used a variable-incidence horizontal stabilizer to "trim" the aircraft, naturally stabilizing it at a desired airspeed. The stabilizer, adjusted by means of electric motors turning a large jackscrew, was adjustable through a large window of incidence angles to allow aircraft operation both at low and high speeds. Flight testing had to take into account the possibility of this system becoming jammed, so approaches and landings were conducted with the

stabilizer in various positions to ensure that the aircraft could still be landed safely. The use of a flaps 15 (intermediate setting) landing procedure, with 15 knots added to the normal approach airspeed, was found to be the most advantageous configuration for landing, since it minimized the pitch change control force required by the pilot. Lighter aircraft weights also were also found to ease handling under these circumstances, although no maximum weight limits were required in the final non-normal procedures.

The possibility of having an autopilot malfunction in which the stabilizer trim motors "run away" and continue to force the stabilizer out of trim was tested at high altitude during cruise flight to assess the aircraft's ability to recover after a reasonable reaction time on the part of an unsuspecting pilot. The test was conducted at maximum cruise engine thrust at 38,000 feet, with the trim running nose down for three seconds. This resulted in a dive angle of 8 degrees with speed exceeding Mach 0.935. Recovery was initiated with a 1.5 g pullout, during which the airplane exhibited some aerodynamic buffet, but overall handling was found to be very good. Additionally, similar tests with simulated roll control issues were conducted. These tests started with the aircraft operating at the maximum operating Mach number of 0.90. The test pilot rolled the aircraft into a 45-degree bank and let go of the controls for five seconds. The aircraft had a slight tendency to continue to roll into a steeper bank, but recovery was easily accomplished by the flying pilot.

Ship One was also used extensively for a test parameter called Vmu (velocity, minimum unstick), which determines the minimum speed at which an aircraft can become airborne at a given weight, flap configuration, and environmental condition. The Vmu maneuver tends to be spectacular, with the pilot carefully rotating the aircraft at very low speed to an extreme pitch attitude, which causes the tail skid to contact the runway surface prior to liftoff. In order to protect the number 2 engine tailpipe and reverser, an additional skid apparatus was installed.

An additional tail skid was installed during Vmu testing to protect the center engine tailpipe from contacting the runway. Note the position of the "huffer cart" air hose connection to the aircraft. In the absence of pressurized air from the APU or another running engine, the huffer cart could supply pressurized air to start the engines or run the air-conditioning packs. *Courtesy of the Boeing Company*

Vmu testing determined the lowest-possible liftoff speed for a variety of weight and flap configurations. Here the primary tail skid is dragging on the runway, while the secondary skid waits to protect the number 2 engine as the main landing gear wheels leave the surface. *Courtesy of the Boeing Company*

The flap selector handle incorporated detents for each usable flap setting. Note the raised gate for the flaps 2 position, which requires a deliberate effort by the pilot to go from position 5 to UP, preventing an inadvertent retraction of all the slats. *Author's collection*

In keeping with the short-field requirements for the 727 design, the airplane possessed a very powerful and capable high-lift flap system. Special attention went into ensuring that the flap and slat extension and retraction rates were ideal. If they were too slow, a tendency to exceed airspeed limits with flaps extended during climb-out would cause difficulty for the operating pilot. Too rapid, and the configuration change into and out of the high-lift configuration would be overly abrupt for the acceleration rate of the aircraft. Potential pilot error also had to be factored in to prevent accidental flap and slat retraction through a selection error, such as selecting flaps UP versus the intermediate position 2 setting. This type of error would cause the slats to retract, with grievous consequences at low airspeeds. While Boeing and FAA representatives discussed the possibility of installing an airspeed-activated lock to prevent such action, Boeing pilot Dix Loesch felt that passing the gate on the flap selector required a deliberate motion that would mitigate this risk. The pilot would move the handle forward to retract the flaps to position 2. Movement beyond position 2 would require a deliberate lowering of the handle in the detent, then continuing movement to the up position. Concluding the discussion, it was agreed that the already installed safety gate on the flap lever, combined with a fairly slow flap retraction rate, provided a good safety margin without a need for a lock at the flaps 2 selector handle position.

Another flight control malfunction possibility was explored, which involved the flight spoiler system. Each wing employs five flight spoilers, which are used for roll augmentation, in-flight speed brakes, and deceleration after landing. The possibility of one of these panels becoming jammed in the up position was plausible, so the aircraft's handling in this condition was evaluated. The most adverse scenario would be with the farthest outboard spoiler deployed. The #1 (left outboard) spoiler was blocked in the up position for the evaluation. The FAA pilot tested this condition, stalling the aircraft with the flaps set at position 40. In the postflight conference, this

pilot stated, "I did not carry the airplane into full initial [stall] buffet because both Lew and I were a little bit concerned over the possibility that this would change the stall characteristics to the point on causing some pitch-up with the airplane. So, I just went a little below stick shaker and then effected a normal recovery." This statement lends some credence to the idea that a stall with flaps and spoilers deployed on the 727 was to be approached with extreme caution; hence the operational prohibition of the use of flaps and spoilers (speed brakes) at the same time.

The 727, with its powered flight controls, required an artificial-feel system. Manually controlled airplanes give feedback to the pilot, similar to the feedback that a driver gets through an automobile's steering wheel. This tactile feedback is extremely important to the pilot of the aircraft, even more so than for the driver of a road vehicle. In fact, a skilled pilot can sense the condition and speed of the aircraft through the controls somewhat, even without reference to the normally available instrumentation. On a hydraulically powered control system, this "feel" feedback through the controls must be synthetically created through flight control feel systems. A failure of a feel channel, whether it be on the aileron, elevator, or rudder, can significantly change the controllability of the aircraft for the pilot. First the airplane was tested with the aileron feel disabled, which created no issues for the FAA or Boeing pilots, with the exception that the controls needed to be manually centered, since the normal "return to center" tendency was not present. When the rudder system feel was turned off, there was some level of difficulty, with a tendency to overcontrol the rudders. There was some discussion at the postflight briefing about perhaps using the feet of the nonflying pilot to dampen the controls as a procedure to deal with such a malfunction, but this was determined to be unnecessary.

Flap malfunctions on a high-speed airplane such as the 727 severely limit the pilot's landing options, often requiring very long runways due to the high speeds generated by a flaps-up landing. As a preventive measure, the 727 featured an alternate extension system both for the leading edge devices and the trailing edge flaps. If the normal A-system hydraulic power was lost, the third "standby" hydraulic system could be activated to extend the leading edge Krueger flaps and slats. Due to the lower pumping volume of the electric-pump-powered standby system, it took up to fifty-six seconds to complete the extension. It was also noted that there was a bit of asymmetric travel rate with the slats, but this caused no handling difficulties for the pilot. Multiple tests of the electric-motor-driven, alternate trailing edge flap system were also conducted, with no issues noted.

Normal landing gear extension and retraction were initially found to be slow and sluggish, particularly as the airspeed increased. The landing gear, among other utilities, used the engine-driven "A" hydraulic system for actuation power. Modifications to the system eventually resulted in acceptable retraction speeds and transit times. Like the flaps and slats, the landing gear system also featured an alternate extension system that could be operated in the absence of hydraulic power. This system was tested up to speeds of 270 knots and required four minutes, thirty-three seconds for the flight engineer to complete.

On every departure, jetliners must be able to accomplish a successful takeoff after suffering an engine failure just prior to liftoff, with enough remaining performance available to satisfactorily climb above all obstacles within defined margins. Every takeoff requires these critical calculations, which take into account the aircraft's weight and configuration, weather, runway conditions, and obstacles existing in the departure path. The 727 was tested and found to perform these tasks with ease, even from short runways. A prominent advantage of the 727 design was that little asymmetric thrust existed in the event of a pod-mounted engine failure, because the engines were mounted very near to the centerline of the aircraft. This feature made the aircraft handling relatively uncomplicated for the pilot. During postflight conferences, FAA pilots commented on the 727's straightforward handling with an engine failure experienced during takeoff.

Given this ease of handling, Boeing sought to reap all the operational benefits possible from the 727's three-engine layout. Although the Pratt & Whitney JT8D engine became one of the most durable and successful aero engines ever devised, there were occasions where one might be in need of repair in a remote location, far away from a proper maintenance facility. Boeing and the FAA tested the ability of the 727 to be ferried (flown without passengers, cargo, and nonessential crew) on two engines to return the aircraft to base for repairs. In-flight testing was conducted with an inoperative engine secured with an inlet plug on both the center and side-mounted engine positions. On one such test with the #3 engine secured, the thrust reverser on that engine inadvertently deployed, as evidenced by a REVERSER UNLOCKED light in the cockpit, which was visually confirmed by external personnel. This required the condition to be later repeated, since the performance numbers were slightly affected by the drag caused from the extended reverser doors. On flights with the center engine secured and plugged, a slight rumble was noted but not found to be of concern. Ultimately, the 727 was certified with this special two-engine ferry capability.

Later, when the 727 entered service, two-engine ferry flights were operated with several stipulations required by the FAA. Only specially trained pilots could fly such flights, and as a precaution the departure path of the aircraft needed to minimize flight over densely populated areas. Engine bleed air was required to be turned off to allow the two remaining engines to produce as much thrust as possible. Special two-engine performance charts were developed and used to ensure that takeoff and climb requirements could be met, and that proper airspeeds and thrust settings were utilized. With all these requirements met, the FAA deemed it safe to conduct such flights both with and without the engine inlet plug installed. Over the years, several airlines were granted FAA approval to conduct these unusual operations made possible by the flexibility of the 727 design.

All-Weather Operations

In keeping with the all-weather mission capability for which the 727 was designed, the aircraft needed to be able to handle and perform well, even with large amounts of ice accumulation on the airframe. Some portions of the aircraft (leading edge slats, engine inlets, windshields, upper VHF antenna, and probes) were heated either electrically or by hot bleed air from the engines' compressors. There were some areas on the airframe, however, where anti-icing was not deemed to be necessary. To test this, simulated ice shapes were temporarily installed on the inboard leading edges of the wings, the Krueger flaps, and the horizontal and vertical stabilizers on E1. Stalls showed no unusual handling, but the onset of stall buffet and stick shaker occurred at a higher airspeed than on a "clean" aircraft, which was to be expected. One FAA pilot commented on the 727's performance with ice accumulation: "So far as the general stall characteristics, I would say [they] met the requirements of the regulations. There was no tendency for the stick forces to reverse themselves, lateral control was good, and the stall itself was well defined, and there was good controllability to recover." Handling with ice accumulation was important, but aircraft drag performance was also evaluated, with many drag measurements being conducted with simulated icing to allow estimations of aircraft fuel burn and performance in these inclement conditions.

An engineer adds simulated ice shapes to the leading edge of a 727's horizontal stabilizer. The aircraft was test flown to confirm that a severe icing encounter would not cause adverse handling characteristics. *Courtesy of the Boeing Company*

In-flight visibility during takeoff, approach, and landing is critical for an all-weather jetliner. From early on in the test program, a rain-repellent system was installed and tested concurrently with the function and reliability testing. This system employed a pressurized bottle of Rainboe, a Boeing-formulated, spray-on rain repellent. This pilot controlled system connected the bottle to spray jets positioned forward of and directed onto the L1 and R1 windshields. In heavy precipitation the pilot could, with a push of a button, use this system to clear water from the windscreen. The system was effective enough that it became production standard on the 727 as well as later aircraft such as the Original and Classic series 737 airplanes. It is also noteworthy that the rain repellent fluid was "essentially non-toxic" according to Boeing maintenance manuals. However, as a precaution the fluid was given a strong citrus scent to alert pilots and maintenance personnel in the event of a leak inside the aircraft's pressure vessel.

Many hours of attention were devoted to ground operation and taxiing capabilities for the 727. One area of concern, given the aft-mounted locale of the engines, was the ingestion of water spray during takeoff, landing, or high-speed taxi operations through any deep puddles that might be on the runways and taxiways. Boeing engineers flooded a taxiway and brought the aircraft through at various speeds. It was discovered that the nosewheel tires tended to direct spray into the pod-mounted inlets. To eliminate this undesired effect, special "chined" nose landing gear tires were installed, with satisfactory results.

In addition to the standard main landing gear wheel brakes, the 727 featured optional nosewheel brakes to enhance landing and rejected takeoff performance, reducing stopping distances by 7 to 14 percent.

The nose tires were equipped with chines on the sidewalls, which deflected water away from the fuselage and the pod-mounted engines. *Author's collection*

Like the main wheel brakes, the nosewheel braking system employed an antiskid system to prevent wheel lockup. The antiskid system sensed wheel speed and reduced brake pressure if a wheel began to lock up, thereby increasing braking effectiveness and preventing tire damage. When an impending lockup was sensed, the antiskid metering valve would cycle several times a second, to release brake pressure in order to bring the offending wheel or wheels under control. It was noted that when heavy braking was applied, the nosewheel antiskid cycled more than the main wheel brakes. This was likely due to the much-lighter loading on the nose tires, but the system was found to be effective and was later installed on many production aircraft.

Ship One was retained by Boeing until October 6, 1964, when it was handed over to United Airlines. Here, it spent its entire operational life and conducted its last revenue flight on January 13, 1991, having accrued 64,492 hours and conducted 48,057 flights. After leaving the fleet at United, this historic aircraft was placed in storage for twenty-six years at Paine Field in Everett, Washington. After an extensive restoration to airworthiness, E1 was flown from Paine Field to Boeing Field on a ferry permit granted by the Federal Aviation Administration. Following this flight, this beautiful aircraft, wearing the original United Airlines delivery colors, has found a permanent home in the Museum of Flight Pavilion (see "The Restoration and Last Flight of Ship One with Bob Bogash" on page 108).

Ship Two

Ship Two (c/n 18464, l/n 2) was given Effectivity E2 and registered with the FAA as N72700. This airplane first flew on March 12, 1963, and played a significant part in the flight test program for the certification of the 727. For example, the fuel system for the 727 was largely tested using this aircraft. Modifications to the fuel-venting system were made. Baffling was also added to prevent fuel sloshing inside the fuel tanks, to eliminate transient balance issues during flight maneuvers. Additionally, fuel gauge calibration tests for the FAA were conducted at 20,000 feet for verification purposes.

In light of the compressor stall issues experienced with the center (number 2) engine, vortex generators were added to the S-duct, and testing for this modification was carried out at various altitudes. Air pressures were measured across the inlet face of the center engine, which showed significant improvement. The center engine inlet, along with the newly installed vortex generators, were thermally deiced using high-temperature bleed air, which also required evaluations to be conducted both with and without the use of inlet anti-ice systems.

The effectiveness of the dual air cycle machines, often referred to as "packs," was tested extensively on E2 while examining minimum engine power requirements for adequate air-conditioning and pressurization operation. This was an important metric because the air-conditioning packs use engine bleed air extracted from the eighth and thirteenth compressor stages of engine numbers 1 and 3 to operate the system and pressurize the cabin. Function of all system components, even down to the air-conditioning filter units, was thoroughly evaluated.

Boeing also sought to certify the 727 at higher gross weights, with a slightly expanded center-of-gravity window. After emerging from layup for the required modifications in August 1963, E2 flew eleven flights to support this engineering effort. Approaches and landings were made at the increased weights and with CGs as far forward as 13 percent MAC.

Ship Two in flight. In this photo, a Millekan camera was temporarily installed under the forward fuselage. This aircraft spent its entire life owned by Boeing, used as a flight test vehicle. *Courtesy of the Boeing Company*

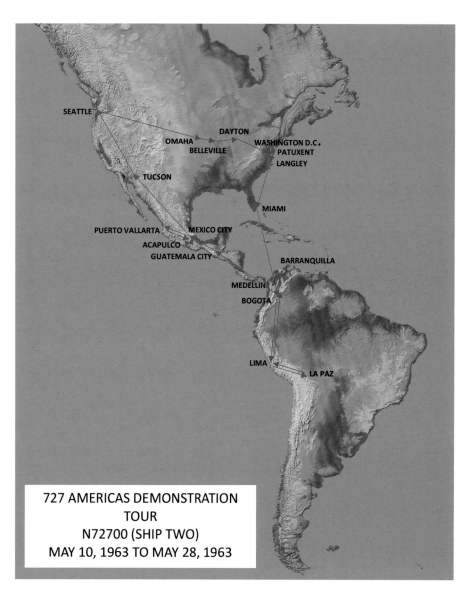

727 AMERICAS DEMONSTRATION TOUR
N72700 (SHIP TWO)
MAY 10, 1963 TO MAY 28, 1963

Author's collection

The Americas Tour

Throughout the test program, this airplane was also used to demonstrate the unique capabilities of the 727 to potential customers. In May 1963, Boeing showed great confidence in the 727 by using E2 for a tour of the Americas to generate both domestic and international interest in their new machine. The routing of the tour was as follows:

Date	From/To	Hours + Minutes
May 10	Seattle–Omaha	2 + 50
May 11	Omaha–Belleville	0 + 45
May 12	Belleville–Dayton	0 + 45
May 13	Dayton–Washington, DC	1 + 00
May 15	Washington, DC–Patuxent–Washington, DC	2 + 00
May 16	Washington, DC–Langley Field–Miami	2 + 15
May 17	Airplane maintenance was conducted in Miami	
May 18	Miami–Bogota	3 + 38
May 19	Bogotá–Barranquilla–Medellín–Bogotá	2 + 30
May 21	Bogotá–Lima	2 + 38
May 23	Lima–La Paz–Lima	3 + 40
May 24	Airplane maintenance was conducted in Lima	
May 25	Lima–Bogotá–Guatemala City–Mexico City	7 + 49
May 27	Mexico City–Puerto Vallarta–Mexico City–Acapulco–Mexico City	3 + 30
May 28	Mexico City–Tucson–Seattle	5 + 10

The 727 pauses briefly at Medellin during the Americas tour, drawing enormous crowds of well-wishers and enthusiasts. *Courtesy of the Boeing Company*

For the purposes of flight testing, along with function-and-reliability evaluations for Boeing 727 certification, Ship Two flew a total of 307 flight hours. After the 727 was certified by the FAA, it conducted an additional sales tour in late November 1964, when it was flown to Europe to generate foreign sales. The routing on this tour was as follows:

Date	From/To	Hours + Minutes
November 29	New York–Gander–Shannon	5 + 40
November 30	Shannon–Frankfurt	2 + 08
December 2	Frankfurt–West Berlin–Frankfurt	1 + 25
December 3	Frankfurt–Shannon	1 + 59
December 4	Shannon–Gander–New York	7 + 20
December 5	New York–Boeing Field, Washington	5 + 23

Ship Two remained under Boeing ownership for the rest of its service life and was used to test ideas and methods to improve operational reliability, efficiency, and utilization of the 727 airplane. Shortly after completion of FAA certification for the 727-100 program, testing was conducted with Ship Two to evaluate the capability of the 727 to use the ventral airstair to perform military airdrops for Civil Air Transport. The aft underside of the fuselage was tufted to allow observation of local airflows. The ventral airstair was equipped with a safety cable that prevented its full downward extension in case of an inability to fully retract it during the posttest landing. Amazingly, testing was conducted up to an indicated airspeed of 400 knots with little in the way of adverse effects, though it is noteworthy that some bouncing of the stairway was reported when the aircraft transited through approximately 340 knots. Throughout the testing, the pressure door to the cabin remained easily openable, the cabin was depressurized, and normal conversation was still possible at the doorway in the aft cabin. Additionally, the ventral airstair was removed from the aircraft, and a temporary plywood ramp was installed over the airframe-mounted portion of the stairway to permit the sliding of objects overboard. Sandbags of varying weights were dropped from the aircraft in the flaps 25 configuration at 125 knots. First, two 30-pound sandbags were dispatched, followed by an 8.5-pound bag of sawdust. To check the drop performance of items of differing densities, a

Items of different sizes and densities were dropped, confirming the 727's ability to conduct military-style drop operations for Civil Air Transport. *Courtesy of the Boeing Company*

200-pound box measuring 40 × 30 × 25 inches was also dropped. No tendency to get caught up in the aircraft wake was observed, thus demonstrating that airdrops were certainly possible from the 727.

In May 1964, the aircraft was taken to the high-altitude El Dorado Airport at Bogotá, Colombia. At 8,361 feet above sea level, the airport provided a good location to substantiate the 727's high-altitude performance and operation. To further demonstrate the capabilities of the aircraft, the Boeing crew traveled to the El Alto Airport at La Paz, Bolivia, at 13,323 feet above mean sea level, to create the ultimate climb performance evaluations. The FAA was also onboard to authenticate the 727's performance envelope. While engine starts had been performed well above this pressure altitude in flight, zero-airspeed ground starts were tested and found to pose no problems. Engine accessory cooling was also more than adequate under these extreme conditions, with one exception: the cooling of the generator drives created some issues during ground operations and required further study.

Boeing wished to expand the center of gravity and weight limits of the 727 in preparation for the new hybrid passenger/cargo 727QC, which was under development in 1964. Ship Two was structurally modified to allow an increase in maximum takeoff weight to 169,000 pounds while testing new CG limits as far forward as 9 percent of MAC. Boeing flew Ship Two to Edwards Air Force Base in California to conduct abuse takeoff tests, where early and aggressive rotation to takeoff attitudes were conducted and aircraft control authority was assessed. Vmu tests were also undertaken during this time period to establish the minimum liftoff speed for the high weight configuration.

Subsequent to testing for the 727QC program, Ship Two was equipped with long-range high frequency (HF) radio and LORAN navigation equipment and flown to Berlin to conduct suitability demonstrations for Pan American. This equipment was required because during this time of the Cold War, American airliners were allowed to travel to and from West Berlin only via narrow airway corridors through Soviet-occupied East Germany. Navigation therefore needed to be precise and redundant to avoid the planes' being shot down by Soviet interceptors. The demonstration was a success, and Boeing would go on to win the 727 sale to Pan American for operations on these technically difficult routes. Concurrent with these tests, Boeing also strived to improve on the original 727 brakes, which had experienced minor issues while in service. For these flights, the

Goodrich 2-872-3 brakes were installed per FC 1044-1-4 and paired with H-type steel rotors.

In May 1965, the slat actuator for the #4 slat (left wing, inboard panel) on Ship Two was modified to reduce the slat extension first by 15 and then later by 10 degrees. These tests were conducted using strain gauges on the slat structure to estimate slat loading for the 737, which was in early development by this time. By August of the same year, new brake combinations were tested in conjunction with CAT II low-visibility-approach certification trials conducted at Oakland, California. Toward the end of 1965, testing for the high-gross-weight 727QC continued, with simulated ice shapes added to aerodynamic surfaces to test the aircraft's handling in adverse weather. With the increased weight (170,000 pounds) and a new forward CG limit for landing of 11 percent MAC, autoland trials with the SP-50 autopilot presented no serious issues. It was determined that the airplane had ample elevator authority, even in this extreme nose-heavy, high-weight condition.

Although still being operated for flight test purposes by Boeing, in 1971 Ship Two's registration number was changed from N72700 to the less descript N1784B tail number. Under this registration, the aircraft was used to test wing configurations for the proposed 727-300, which was being studied in the 1975 time frame (see chapter 6, page 168).

Ship Three

Ship Three (N7002U, c/n 18294, l/n 3, Effectivity E3) also served in the flight test and certification for the 727. Many of the tests conducted with this aircraft occurred from June 1963 until the certification date of December 24, 1963. The area of focus for this airplane centered mainly on braking-performance parameters for rejected takeoffs (RTOs) and maximum-performance landings. The most extreme testing occurred in early October at Edwards Air Force Base in Southern California. Tests conducted here included RTOs with maximum brake energies recorded up to 25,570,000 foot-pounds on the main landing gear brakes and 5,350,000 foot-pounds absorbed by the nosewheel brakes. These RTO operations generated such a significant amount of heat from the heavy braking friction that, when it was safe to do so, many times the aircraft was flown with the landing gears down to effect brake cooling prior to further tests.

Ship Three wore a hybrid United Airlines paint scheme during the flight test program. *Courtesy of the Boeing Company*

Other flight tests saw special instrumentation installed to conduct flight load surveys for the wings and stabilizers. One structural area of great interest to the test engineers involved flight loads on the stabilizer trailing beam, which was carefully analyzed. In total, Ship Three flew 116 hours for the certification efforts—the lowest time logged of the four airplanes involved in the flight test program. Subsequent to the final FAA certification, Ship Three continued on with flight testing for a short period during which a slightly modified starboard horizontal stabilizer was installed, tested, and evaluated. Additionally, during this postcertification period, Boeing conducted testing of the air-conditioning system by measuring and studying in-flight temperature gradients both for the passenger cabin and cargo compartments.

United Airlines took delivery of this aircraft and flew it away on June 24, 1964. United continued to operate this aircraft until May 28, 1992. After providing long and dependable service with United, E3 was purchased by the City and County of San Francisco, where it spent many years visible on the ramp near the Superbay maintenance facility, also known as "the Ice Palace" because of the cold temperatures inside, at San Francisco International Airport (KSFO). It was here that this historic aircraft served as an emergency response trainer before meeting its fate at the hands of Aircraft Demolition, LLC, on January 23, 2014.

Ship Four

The last airplane to enter the 727 flight test and certification program was Ship Four (N7003U, c/n 18295, l/n 4, Effectivity E4), which served largely as a standby test ship but was also used to conduct continuous function-and-reliability testing in support of FAA certification. In order to generate further international interest and to provide "in-service"-type operational evaluations, Boeing management made a confident move to take Ship Four on a domestic circuit in the United States, followed by an around-the-world tour.

From a public-image point of view, this was a daring move because the aircraft was to be operated continuously over many flight hours away from base, carrying only required spare parts, while maintaining a tight demonstration schedule. Any lapse in reliability or any significant technical delay, such as waiting for parts, would be noticed on the international airline scene and widely publicized. The reality was that those who knew the 727 best, the people who designed and built it, knew it would perform. The routing of this unprecedented endeavor is shown below:

Ship Four was exposed to a wide variety of the climatic conditions that planet Earth has to offer. The routing took the aircraft to Canada; over the Atlantic; to Europe, the Middle East, India, Thailand, the Philippines, and Japan; and as far south as Australia. During one of these flights, on routing between Calcutta and Bangkok, this aircraft was subjected to substantial convective weather, which resulted in flying through turbulent conditions with heavy precipitation. Due in part to the highly swept and relatively small wings in the 727, the aircraft passed through the area with what was described as a "comfortable ride." During this flight, Ship Four endured a lightning strike of "moderate intensity," which the aircraft took in stride without any issues.

Air traffic controllers also took notice of the 727 and its special capabilities. The airport in Tokyo, Japan, is surrounded by terrain to the west, which typically results in a less-than-direct routing, while the eastbound arriving aircraft struggle to clear terrain, followed by a slam-dunk descent for landing. Although the 727 was an aerodynamically "clean" airplane, when required, the use of speed brakes (spoilers), combined with the deployment of the landing gear, could generate a very expeditious descent rate. Beginning at 37,000 feet, the Boeing crew requested an immediate descent, which was granted. In an internal publication titled *The Boeing 727 Story*, Jack Steiner described the scene:

The Japanese airport situation gives an unusual economic benefit to an airline that can normally use a high rate of descent. We averaged over 7,000 feet per minute (4 minutes, 50 seconds) from 37,000 feet to 3,000 feet and considerably confused the air traffic operator, who interrogated us repeatedly during the descent with considerable disbelief.

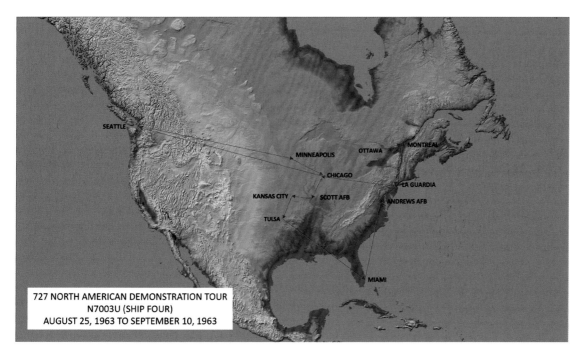

727 NORTH AMERICAN DEMONSTRATION TOUR
N7003U (SHIP FOUR)
AUGUST 25, 1963 TO SEPTEMBER 10, 1963

SEATTLE
MINNEAPOLIS
OTTAWA
MONTREAL
CHICAGO
LA GUARDIA
KANSAS CITY
SCOTT AFB
ANDREWS AFB
TULSA
MIAMI

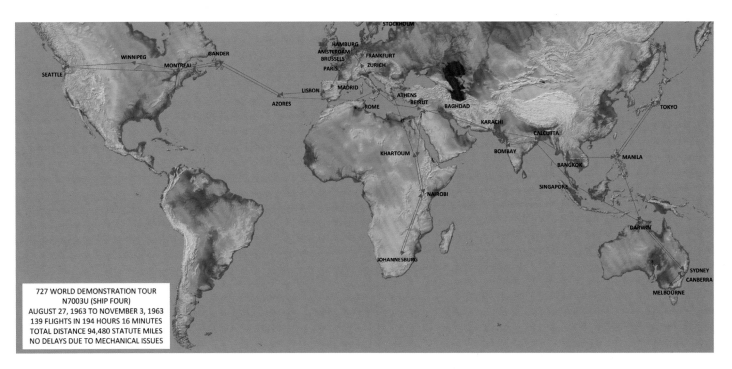

727 WORLD DEMONSTRATION TOUR
N7003U (SHIP FOUR)
AUGUST 27, 1963 TO NOVEMBER 3, 1963
139 FLIGHTS IN 194 HOURS 16 MINUTES
TOTAL DISTANCE 94,480 STATUTE MILES
NO DELAYS DUE TO MECHANICAL ISSUES

Author's collection

The Boeing flight crew is seen navigating during the world tour.
Courtesy of the Boeing Company

Ship Four remained overnight at Gander, Newfoundland, prior to completing the transatlantic crossing to Europe and points east.
Courtesy of the Boeing Company

The flight's navigator uses a temporarily installed port and a sextant to take celestial fixes to navigate during the world tour. *Courtesy of the Boeing Company*

Boeing's leader, Bill Allen (*right*), presents Italy's minister of transportation, Guido Corbellini, with a model of the Boeing 727. The Italian airline Alitalia did not immediately buy the 727 but later became a loyal 727-200 operator. *Courtesy of the Boeing Company*

For the 727, this was not difficult at all. Going back to the initial design of the airplane, the plus 2 degree angle of incidence at which the wings were mounted on the airframe was chosen in part, so that steep descents were still comfortable in the aircraft cabin. Boeing engineers noted that passengers typically are much more comfortable with a steep deck angle during a climb but would prefer not to feel the sensation of a high deck angle during descent. By choosing the ideal wing incidence angle, the body of the aircraft was relatively flat, even during an expedited arrival.

Apparently, according to Steiner, the Japanese controller still wouldn't let go of his skepticism over the event. Boeing headquarters was contacted by an airline's vice president, reporting that Ship Four had been recorded on radar in an "uncontrolled dive!" Soon enough, the special capabilities of the 727 would become realized the world over.

The 727 finally meets its nemesis, the Hawker Siddeley Trident, in Karachi, Pakistan. This was one of the few places where the 727 did not prevail, as Pakistan International Airways submitted an order for the Trident 1E instead of the Boeing jet. *Courtesy of the Boeing Company*

Bill Allen with Benigno Toda, president of Philippine Airlines, and his son. Although his airline never bought the 727, they were a good customer for Boeing, having later purchased 737, 747, and 777 aircraft for their fleet. *Courtesy of the Boeing Company*

Bill Allen enjoys the company of airline officials during Ship Four's stop in the Philippines. *Courtesy of the Boeing Company*

The changing of the guard. In Tokyo, Ship Four rests in company with a Boeing 720-030 (D-ABOQ, c/n 18250, l/n 263) that was less than two years old at the time. Note Ship Four's deployed thrust reverser doors. *Courtesy of the Boeing Company*

Ship Four occupying the ramp at Sydney, Australia, with a Qantas 707-138B (VH-EBI, c/n 18098, l/n 227). The 138B was a long-range version of the early 707 airframe, with a shorter fuselage. *Courtesy of the Boeing Company*

Ship Four receives much attention as it is readied for a flight to its next international destination. *Courtesy of the Boeing Company*

Boeing executives discuss the attributes of the 727 with airline officials prior to departure from Sydney. *Courtesy of the Boeing Company*

During its visit to Canberra, Australia, Ship Four was adorned with nose art while being shown to representatives from Trans Australia Airlines (TAA). *Courtesy of the Boeing Company*

Jack Steiner discusses the 727 with airline representatives during a demonstration flight to Melbourne, Australia. *Courtesy of the Boeing Company*

The welcoming committee was on hand for the 727's arrival in Melbourne. *Courtesy of the Boeing Company*

After heading back west to Europe, the aircraft visited Amsterdam, Netherlands. This photo shows the large size of the powerful triple-slotted Fowler flap system on the 727. *Courtesy of the Boeing Company*

The 727 received a warm welcome during its stay in Frankfurt, West Germany. Note the drooping Krueger flaps on the inboard wing section, which was normal for the 727 once hydraulic system A was depressurized. *Courtesy of the Boeing Company*

Ship Four keeps company with a piston-powered Convair 440 in Stockholm, Sweden. *Courtesy of the Boeing Company*

Representatives from Sabena Belgian World Airlines admire the high-lift systems of the 727 during a visit to the company's headquarters in Brussels, Belgium. *Courtesy of the Boeing Company*

On the ramp at Brussels, Ship Four sits with an SAS Caravelle III. SAS was a loyal Douglas customer and never purchased the 727. The company's fleet of Caravelles was later replaced with the DC-9 twinjet. *Courtesy of the Boeing Company*

Bill Allen and Bruce Connelly provide in-flight service to company personnel during the world tour. *Courtesy of the Boeing Company*

Joe Sutter (*left, seated*) participated in the world tour and played an important role in the development of the 727's high-lift systems. *Courtesy of the Boeing Company*

After leaving Boeing, Ship Four had a short tenure at All Nippon Airways. Here it is seen demonstrating its slow flight capabilities in formation with a Dornier 28 floatplane. *Courtesy of the Boeing Company*

After leaving All Nippon Airways, Ship Four served with Piedmont Airlines. This aircraft crashed due to a midair collision on July 19, 1967. *Courtesy of the Boeing Company*

The world tour was a resounding success, tallying 194 hours, 16 minutes of flight time across 139 separate flights. With mechanics and minimal spare parts carried onboard and no parts stores cached along the way, virtually no outside assistance was required during the trip. Amazingly, especially with a brand-new aircraft type, no mechanical delays of any kind were experienced during the 94,483-mile trip. Thus, the 727 had proven itself to be an extremely reliable jet, straight out of the box!

New Tri-Jet Acclaimed On All Sides

727 Completes World Tour Of Record-Breaking Flights

Latest Order:

BWIA Joins 727 List Of Customers

26 Countries Visited, 76,000 Miles Flown

Wherever It Flew, Crowds Hailed 727

Bell Keynotes:

727's Role Briefed At ASTA Meet

Ship Four logged a total of 264 flight hours in the furtherance of initial certification, largely filling the function-and-reliability testing role, while undertaking the world tour. Although this airplane was originally registered N7003U, it was never operated by United Airlines. After serving its role in the 727 flight test program, Ship Four was registered N68650 and was operated briefly by All Nippon Airways and Iran Air before being delivered to Piedmont Airlines on February 25, 1967.

Shortly thereafter, on July 19, 1967, Ship Four was lost in a midair collision over Hendersonville, North Carolina, while operating as Piedmont Flight 22 from Asheville, North Carolina, to Roanoke, Virginia. According to the NTSB report (AAR68AJ, dated September 5, 1968), a twin-engine Cessna 310 (N3121S, c/n 35069) arriving at Asheville from Charlotte, North Carolina, reportedly moved into the flight path of the climbing airliner, for reasons that were never determined. Sadly, both aircraft were destroyed, with an unfortunate total loss of eighty-two lives. This accident held the dubious distinction of being the first major accident to be investigated by the then newly formed National Transportation Safety Board (NTSB).

Certification

The Boeing 727-100 series was certified by the Federal Aviation Agency on December 24, 1963, after the most rigorous testing program ever undertaken in the airline industry. During the course of the program, a total of 103,650,000 data points were prepared and distributed to the engineering staff for analysis. To process these data, 2,100 hours of time using Boeing's then-state-of-the-art IBM 7094 computer was required, as well as 80,000 man-hours to thoroughly interpret and document the results. Among the four test ships, 1,143 hours of flight tests were conducted both for Boeing and FAA purposes. Amazingly, all of this transpired between the first flight, which

occurred on February 9, 1963, and the certification date: a time span of just ten and a half months.

On February 1, 1964, Eastern Airlines inaugurated revenue passenger operations with the 727. After the 727 entered service, the airlines began to take notice of an interesting phenomenon: the airplane wasn't just efficient—it was more efficient than the performance charts indicated. Joe Sutter, chief of engineering on the 727, was initially cautious about making this public. Peter Morton, who was Boeing's liaison to British West Indies Airways (BWIA), explained:

> The drag polar that we got from aero staff was really interesting. Sutter gave orders not to use anything but the predicted drag polar. So, the airplane actually went into service using predicted drag in the Operations Manual. I had two customers, BWIA and American. BWIA wanted to fly the airplane at long-range cruise speed, and the airplane had much-better performance in long-range cruise than predicted, by a margin of 5 or 6 percent. American didn't care about long-range cruise. They were up against Braniff, who was flying the 707-227 between Dallas and New York, and they wanted to go fast because the 227 was fast. The predicted max cruise thrust would give you 0.83–0.84 Mach. But when they set that max cruise thrust, it would go 0.87 Mach, and American was happier than a clam with that! I was out in the field with these guys, and I kept sending messages back, saying, "The customers are asking what is wrong with the Ops Manual? It doesn't work for long-range cruise, and it doesn't work for high-speed cruise. What is going on here." Finally, it came out that Sutter did not want to reveal the fact that the airplane was 7 percent better than book on drag.

America's newest jet–coming your way soon!

It's the new 727, by Boeing. Swift, quiet, the 727 is the nation's first short-range jetliner. It goes into service within weeks.

The 727 is a sleek three-engine jet that can operate with ease from short runways. It will be able to serve cities now bypassed by the big jetliners, adding hundreds of cities to the jet networks of the world. In addition, the 727 will bring an unprecedented level of speed, comfort and convenience to short-range air travel.

When you go by Boeing 727, "getting there" will be an exhilarating part of your trip.

As the newest member of the Boeing family of jetliners, the 727 is backed by the experience gained in more than one billion miles of 707 and 720 jet experience. Here are the airlines that have already ordered 140 Boeing 727s: American, Ansett-ANA, BWIA, Eastern, Lufthansa, TAA (Australia), TWA and United. **BOEING 727**

Courtesy of the Boeing Company

The truth was that the airlines were already very happy with the "book" performance of the 727, and it was off to a great start saleswise. The fact that the 727, in the wild, outperformed the book no doubt added to the popularity of this amazing aircraft.

This was just the beginning of the long and successful career of the 727, which was destined to become one of the most loved jetliners of all time. As we will explore in the following chapters, the Boeing 727 airliner went on to set the standards for future airliners and was instrumental in pioneering many of the technologies that have made today's outstanding air carrier safety record possible.

The 727QC

Boeing had noticed the great success of the 727-100 airplane in passenger operations and also saw the need for a cargo-capable airplane, smaller in size than the 707, which could dependably operate in and out of smaller municipal airports year-round. Many customers wanted an airplane that could fly passengers by day and cargo at night, while others wanted to be able to use the airplane as a "combi" configuration of half passenger and half freight on the cabin deck.

Studies showed that typical aircraft utilization of a "convertible" 727 could be increased to eleven and a half block hours per day, compared to the eight hours that was typical for the standard 727-100 aircraft. This higher utilization could still allow an estimated four and a half hours per day for cabin conversion and routine maintenance. A full-scale cabin mockup was specially constructed to test the viability of the new convertible 727 and to establish operational times for conversion, loading, and unloading of passengers and cargo.

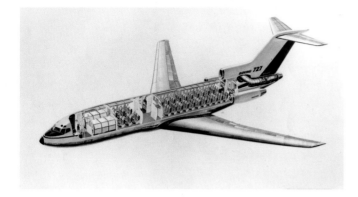

The 727QC could also be configured in a part cargo, part passenger "combi" configuration. *Courtesy of the Boeing Company*

The answer to this need was the 727QC (Quick Change), which was introduced in 1965. The aircraft could be readily converted back and forth between passenger and freight, utilizing a crew of eight technicians. Like the 707 freighters, the 727QC was equipped with a large 91-by-134-inch main deck cargo door, forward of the left wing. This large, top-hinged door was hydraulically operated through the electrically powered "B" hydraulic system. Naturally, this door was installed primarily to allow the expeditious loading of containerized cargo, but it also allowed the quick-change capability. The passenger seats, flooring, and galley equipment were modified to be easily removable by using the standard cargo-loading ground equipment. The 727QC was equipped with a roller flooring system that allowed palletized seats or cargo to be moved in any direction once onboard the aircraft. Reinstalling the passenger accommodations was just as quick, with seats and galleys clicking into place by using specially designed pallet locks that transferred any acceleration loads directly to the aircraft's floor structure. Total conversion time, given appropriate manpower, could occur in just thirty minutes.

United Airlines was an early 727QC customer. This special truck allowed for an expeditious conversion to and from passenger configuration, using palletized seats and galleys. *Courtesy of the Boeing Company*

The floors of the cargo-carrying 727 feature roller assemblies for easy loading and unloading. *Author's collection*

Maintaining the standard appearance of the cabin when the aircraft was being used for all-passenger operations was important both to Boeing and the airline customers, so the presence of the cargo door was visually minimized as much as possible. Sharp-eyed observers could, however, detect the nonstandard spacing of the windows required for structural purposes near the edges of the large cargo door. To enhance passenger comfort, electrically heated blankets were even built into the sidewalls near the door for additional insulation during high-altitude flight.

When the cabin, or a portion of it, was being used for cargo operations, the overhead passenger service units (PSUs) did not need to be removed or disconnected but simply folded up toward the ceiling. A customer-specified option to fold the hat racks and PSUs down along the sidewalls was also available for operators who required the vertical cabin height. A 9G barrier net, with proper attach points, was provided to protect the cockpit and forward cabin from cargo shift during abnormal situations. The attach points were recessed and utilized fittings built into the barrier net. These were simply inserted and then locked into place with manual rotation of the attachment fitting.

A total of five different configurations were possible, including an all-cargo format, three different "combi" possibilities, and an all-passenger format. In the cargo role, up to eight 88-by-125-inch cargo containers could be accommodated, with a total upper-deck volume of 4,560 cubic feet available and an allowable payload weight of 44,400 pounds. In this configuration, all seats and galleys were completely removed to provide the required space. In the "combi" roles, the carriage of slightly smaller 88-by-108-inch cargo containers was required to allow access between the passenger cabin in the aft portion of the aircraft and the cockpit, along the

This 727-51C (N491US, c/n 18899, l/n 256) demonstrates the ease of loading large pallets through the aircraft's main deck cargo door. *Courtesy of the Boeing Company*

The flight line at Boeing's Renton facility in March 1964, with several early 727 examples being readied for flight and delivery. *Courtesy of the Boeing Company*

Trans World Airlines was a strong customer for the 727. This aircraft, N850TW (c/n 18569, l/n 36), was delivered to TWA on April 29, 1964. *Courtesy of the Boeing Company*

Lufthansa's D-ABIR (727-30, c/n 18933, l/n 185) is seen with an Iraqi Airways Trident 1E (YI-AEC, c/n 2129) in Prague, Czechoslovakia, during the mid-1960s. *Courtesy of Petr Popelar*

port side of the cabin. A two-container configuration allowed the retention of the midship galley and use of the R1 (galley) door, accommodating seventy passengers aft of the cargo/passenger cabin partition. If three containers were required, the partition was moved aft of the midship galley and the R1 door, causing the removal of an additional fourteen passenger seats and galley relocation to the aft cabin. The maximum number of cargo containers allowed in the "combi" configuration was four. This loading still provided accommodations for fifty-two passengers and placed the cargo/passenger compartment partition just forward of the four required overwing exits. Since the passengers were seated in the aft portion of the aircraft, the ventral airstairs were available for emplaning and deplaning. The aircraft could also be operated normally in a typical all-passenger configuration of ninety passengers (optionally 131 with high-density seating).

On the standard 727-100 configuration, the number of passengers was typically limited by seats rather than by weight, even with full fuel tanks. The use of large cargo containers on the 727QC meant that the cabin could potentially cause the aircraft to reach weight limits prior to becoming volume limited. Because of this, the 727QC was offered with an option to increase maximum takeoff weight to 169,000 pounds through structural improvements to the airframe, though this did come with a small operational price. The use of this higher weight limited the maximum indicated airspeed to 350 knots (vs. 390 knots), restricted the permissible forward end of the center-of-gravity range to 11 percent MAC (vs. the standard 10 percent MAC), and required a maximum of flaps position 30 for landing. Even with these more-restrictive limits, the 727QC proved to be a popular option among airlines. The structural enhancements brought forth by this airplane provided the basis for the later advent of the stretched 727-200.

600 miles takes one hour up here,

or all day down here.

An hour's rest in a Boeing jet can take you as far as a long day's drive in your car.

Compared to driving, you gain a *day* for every hour you fly aboard a Boeing jet. Boeing jets give you extra time to spend *there*. They bring every part of America, and all the world, within easy reach.

And if you've never flown before, you'll enjoy an exhilarating new experience.

You'll discover why even veteran air travelers find Boeing jet flight the most enjoyable part of their trips.

Boeing jets have carried more than 120 million passengers. They serve 301 cities in 121 countries, and average a takeoff or landing every 13 seconds, around the clock. Boeing jets have set more speed and distance records than all other jetliners combined.

Next trip, fly Boeing.

Now flying Boeing jets: *Air Congo, Air France, Air-India, Air Madagascar, All Nippon, American, Ansett-ANA, Avianca, BOAC, BWIA, Braniff, Continental, Eastern, El Al, Ethiopian, Flying Tiger, Indian, Iran Air, Irish, JAL, Japan Domestic, Lufthansa, MEA, National, Northeast, Northwest, Olympic, PIA, PSA, Pacific Northern, Pan American, Qantas, Sabena, Saudi Arabian, South African, TAA, TAP, TWA, United, Varig, Wardair Canada, Western, World.* In service later: *Aerolineas Argentinas, Air Asia, Alaska, American Flyers, Braathens, Caledonian, Frontier, Mexicana, Northern Consolidated, Pacific, Piedmont, Southern Air Transport, Wien Air Alaska.*

BOEING JETS
World's first family of jets: 707 · 720 · 727 · 737

Courtesy of the Boeing Company

Japan Air Lines took delivery of JA8307 (727-51, c/n 18874, l/n 166) on July 15, 1965, with a lavish ceremony. The same aircraft is seen in flight prior to delivery. *Courtesy of the Boeing Company*

This is a beautiful study of Lufthansa's D-ABIN (727-30, c/n 18369, l/n 125) on a predelivery flight. This airplane served with the German airline until January 1981. Subsequently, it served with the Oman police before being operated by Hewa Bora Airways. *Courtesy of the Boeing Company*

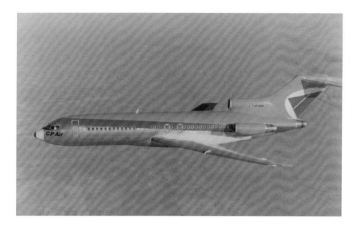

Canadian Pacific Airlines was rebranded as CP Air, and an attractive new livery was introduced. This airplane, CF-CPN (c/n 20327, l/n 798), was delivered to the carrier in March 1970. *Courtesy of the Boeing Company*

OK-TGX was a 727-51 (c/n 18798, l/n 93) that began life with Northwest Orient Airlines as N462US before sale to Air Terrex. The aircraft is seen here in the Czech Republic during 1992. *Courtesy of Petr Popelar*

This photo shows a typical delivery interior for the 727-100 series. Later interior modifications included flush passenger service units (PSUs) and larger overhead bins with doors to prevent luggage from falling. *Courtesy of the Boeing Company*

The rear cabin of an early 727-100-series aircraft. The flight attendants' jump seat is attached to the aft entry door for the ventral airstair. *Courtesy of the Boeing Company*

The Boeing 727-100 in Service

The British West Indies Airways Adventure with Peter Morton

It was 1963; Peter Morton, a young Boeing engineer, had recently transferred from his first job as a flight crew ground instructor to Flight Operations Engineering. This was the Boeing department that published performance and operations manuals for customers and assisted airlines in the introduction of jetliners to commercial service. Here are Peter's recollections between July 1964 and mid-1965, of an adventure culminating in the delivery of British West Indies Airways' third 727-100 airplane (9Y-TCQ, c/n 18796, l/n 108), nonstop from Seattle to Kingston, Jamaica:

As a newly minted flight operations engineer, I had waited impatiently to be assigned the responsibility to support

airline 727 introductions. I had taught systems and performance of the 727 in the ground school and knew the airplane intimately. My boss, Peter Gallimore, assigned me two airlines; American Airlines and British West Indies Airways (BWIA). The former had me acting as a "consultant" to a sophisticated and competent engineering staff at AAL; they knew all about putting new transport aircraft into service and had done it many times before: the Electra, the 707-100, and the 720B. All they wanted from me was explanation about kinks in the 727 fuel mileage charts, why the airplane drag was lower than predictions, and to help them strategize what to do with the unexpected ability of the airplane to cruise much faster than anticipated from Dallas to New York, where they were competing against Braniff's "hot rod" 707-220 airplanes.

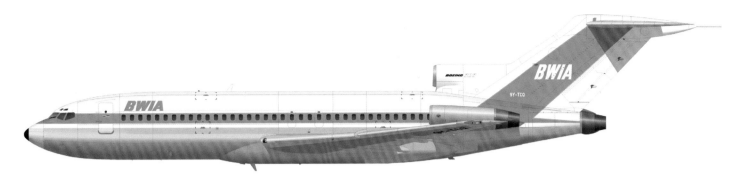

Courtesy of Jennings Heilig

BWIA was a different matter entirely; their turbine experience consisted of operating a small fleet of British Viscount turboprops, and that of a few senior pilots who flew a leased BOAC 707 three times weekly from New York to the airline headquarters in Port of Spain, Trinidad. As the Boeing flight operations engineer, I worked with BWIA's limited staff and the pilot group to set airline flight operations policy. I flew with every crew member on every route to be served with their three-airplane fleet to make sure the operation was safe and efficient. I also had to deal with implementation of their minimum-equipment list; given their British heritage, they called it the "allowable-deficiencies list." Trinidad was a member of the Commonwealth, so it was a hybrid regulatory situation: a US-certified airplane would fly in an operation regulated by a somewhat cranky British CAA officer. It was a challenging assignment; one I will never forget.

Unlike American Airlines, BWIA did not want to fly the 727 fast. They wanted to fly it far. There was a daily "milk run" through the West Indies Trinidad–Barbados–Antigua–Puerto Rico–Kingston–Montego Bay–Miami, and back. No airplane problem, except it strained the airline's ground crews to maintain schedule performance.

It was the New York service replacing the leased BOAC 707 that would challenge the airplane and flight crews. The airplane was sold based on a preliminary drag level at a maximum gross weight of 153,000 pounds. What Boeing delivered was a jetliner with 7 percent better performance and a maximum gross weight of 161,000 pounds. On my first planning visit to Port of Spain, Trinidad,

Braniff International Airways operated the Boeing 707-227 on routes competing with American Airlines. Although the -227 was a fast jet, the 727 was able to compete favorably with the older airplane. *Courtesy of the Boeing Company*

A BWIA 727-78 is readied for departure from the Boeing flight line. Note the full nose-up position of the horizontal stabilizers and the open inboard main landing gear doors, which are normally closed except during maintenance. *Courtesy of the Boeing Company*

Author's collection

months before 727 deliveries, I flew from New York on the BOAC 707, and no sooner had we reached cruise altitude when the crew "invited" me to the cockpit for an inquisition about 727 performance. They had looked at the performance planning numbers and were [unconvinced as to the ability] of the airplane to fly from Antigua to Idlewild (now JFK) airport with sufficient reserve fuel to cope with traffic arrival delays. Once in Trinidad, I was asked to meet with the pilot union leaders to help the airline deal with a mild revolt against management for having purchased an airplane that seemed inadequate to the job.

Introduction of the first delivered airplanes between Trinidad and Miami went relatively well, but it was becoming clear that something dramatic had to be done to gain flight crew confidence in the long-range operation of the 727. The same lower-than-predicted drag that allowed AAL's 727 to cruise at Mach 0.87 manifested as a significantly lower fuel burn at long-range cruise. Coupled with the increased gross weight, it amounted to better than an hour of holding capability at Idlewild. Pilots don't do as well with abstractions as they do with demonstrations, so BWIA management asked me to help with something that might overcome pilot skepticism: create marketing buzz and bring media attention to their new fleet of 727s.

BWIA branded itself as THE West Indian Airline. Though headquartered in Trinidad, a lot of traffic was generated in Kingston, Jamaica. So, we decided to deliver

the third airplane nonstop from Seattle to Kingston (about 2,900 nautical miles) and set about planning public relations, logistics, and technical details. A much-longer flight than Antigua to Idlewild (about 1,600 nautical miles), it really was a stretch for the 727, and the longest 727-100 flight then on record.

Peter Morton and Boeing's marketing staff set out to sell the 727 to the BWIA pilots and quell any doubts about the capabilities of the 727, and they were able to gain good public relations in the balance.

The flight from Seattle to Kingston required a fair amount of preparation to ensure that the flight would be a success. A few days prior to the flight, members of the media who were to be onboard were invited to Seattle for plant tours, briefings, and the delivery ceremony for BWIA's newest jet. It was simply a great opportunity for Boeing to extend goodwill and then to let the 727 prove itself to the world.

First and foremost, safety could not be compromised in any way. The aircraft was serviced with cold, high-density jet fuel, which allowed another 1,000 pounds to be squeezed into the fuel tank volume. Prior to departure, the crew coordinated with Air Traffic Control to obtain direct routing for the flight. Initially, the flight was filed from Seattle to Miami with the intention of refiling their flight plan and continuing to Kingston, provided that there was a safe amount of fuel remaining (with adequate reserves) as they crossed into Florida.

The flight departed Seattle early in the morning under the command of Capt. Keith Maingott. Peter Morton (a fully rated flight engineer and ground school instructor on the 727) monitored from the observer's seat, making certain that optimum power settings were constantly being used.

In the cabin, a total of twenty-eight passengers were aboard, including six people from the media, along with Boeing and BWIA VIPs. The cabin crew consisted of two former Trinidad beauty queens, and BWIA executive Bill Sapey ensured that there was enough martini mix onboard to keep everyone happy, and he was reported to enjoy quite a few himself. A good time was being had by all.

The entire cockpit crew were Jamaican natives, including Morton, who just happened to be born in Kingston and still had family there. As the aircraft passed over Tallahassee, Florida, a fuel audit was conducted and calculations were rechecked. It was determined that the fuel load was good, and the aircraft contacted ATC and changed their destination to Kingston. The flight landed safely in Jamaica and was treated to a great reception, for which Morton's mother was present. Capt. Maingott was interviewed after the flight and was asked if he thought they might not make it. He replied, "I never doubted it. I do observe that it is a good thing Bill Sapey was drinking martinis and not kerosene!" Peter Morton continued:

The PR and technical data from the delivery flight did its job; confidence in the 727's ability to fly Antigua to Idlewild was now OK among the flight crews. I flew with every crew on their first Antigua–Idlewild operation; I remember that month as an exhausting experience.

Operationally, there was one significant challenge regarding the airport facilities in Antigua that brought about an interesting work-around when service commenced with the 727. Peter Morton recounts:

INTRODUCING THE UNHEARD-OF AIRLINE.

British West Indian Airways.

Recently, we kicked off a big advertising and marketing program. Business has been unheard-of ever since.

We're promoting not only ourselves, but our home as well. A whole vacation area. Not just one or two islands that a lot of people are already tired of. Not a few hotels that are almost always overbooked.

We're selling the "unheard-of" Eastern Caribbean. Offbeat islands that are easy to reach, and within most travelers' budgets.

For 29 years now, BWIA has been flying to the Caribbean. Today, we've more jets and more seats than ever before.

Every morning our new 707 Sunjets leave New York for Antigua, Barbados, Trinidad. And arrive in time for same-day connections to the smaller island sun spots. Our 727 Sunjets fly nonstop daily to Barbados, and through to Trinidad.
Plus new through service to Tobago three days a week.

On June 6th we start new Miami Sunjet express service nonstop to Antigua, and direct to Barbados and Trinidad. We also have Sunjets direct to Jamaica, Grand Cayman and St. Lucia.

The in-flight service is unheard-of, too. Inside and out, our planes reflect the cheerful, warm attitude of the islands. As do our girls' new uniforms. The food and drink is somewhere between the Caribbean and heaven.

Be prepared. We won't be unheard-of for long.

BWIA

Author's collection

But there was one more wrinkle . . . the airport apron at Antigua was not level, and no matter how we parked the 727, we could not fill the tanks. We were 500 pounds short, equal to several minutes of holding at Idlewild during a period when ATC arrival delays were common. What to do? By scribing a line on the apron that would level the wings, we had only to raise the nose and the airplane would be level. My good friends in maintenance at Antigua built themselves a wooden ramp. When the 727 would arrive to load fuel for Idlewild, the pilots kept the engines running. A baggage truck would come out on the ramp, dragging a strange wooden contraption; the mechanics would nudge it up to the nose gear and then motion the pilot to spool up thrust until the nose gear was on the ramp. Great ingenuity, if primitively expressed.

I'll close with a true story that probably no one will believe. It was a time long before locked cockpit doors, and informal access was common. We were loaded up and taxiing to the runway for departure at Antigua, and a passenger burst into the cockpit. "Is this airplane going to Montreal?" he said. The captain replied, "No, we are going to New York." We taxied back to the terminal, unloaded the passenger, put the nose gear on the wooden ramp, topped off the fuel, and departed. Arriving in the New York area, the traffic was formidable, and we held for over an hour and—you guessed it—diverted to Montreal. This is what I love about aviation; impossible stories abound. Even though I was there, I have to pinch myself to remember it as reality!

Cruzeiro Do Sul operated eight 727s, including this late model 727-100-series airplane. PP-CJF (c/n 20419, l/n 815) was equipped with upgraded JT8D-9A engines that developed more thrust at high-density altitudes. *Courtesy of the Boeing Company*

Seen with United's updated paint scheme at Los Angeles International Airport, N7025U (727-31, c/n 18317, l/n 88) poses in front of the iconic "Spider" in the early 1970s. This aircraft ended its career flying for Federal Express. *Courtesy of the Boeing Company*

Avianca operated many secondhand 727-100-series aircraft, sourced from different carriers. This unidentified ship carries the temporary, or possibly fictitious, registration of HK-727X. *Courtesy of the Boeing Company*

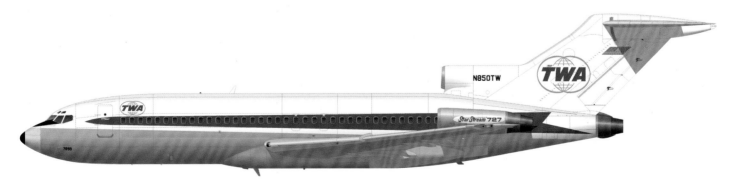

Courtesy of Jennings Heilig

N727AL (727-172C, c/n 19807, l/n 575) was delivered to the carrier on May 31, 1968. This aircraft subsequently saw service with Southeast Airlines, Fleming International, Flying Tigers, and Purolator Courier before being stored in Pontiac, Michigan, in 2002. *Courtesy of the Boeing Company*

N8102N (727-25, c/n 18253, l/n 11) was a very early example, having first flown on September 10, 1963, prior to FAA type certification. *Courtesy of the Boeing Company*

Eastern was an important early 727 operator. This aircraft, (N8102N, c/n 18253, l/n 11) was an early example that first took flight on September 10, 1963. After operating for Eastern, this aircraft was leased to the Nicaraguan carrier Aeronica, before being operated by the government of Liberia. *Courtesy of the Boeing Company*

China Airlines operated this 727-109 (B-1818, c/n 19399, l/n 380) until August 1982, when it fell to the scrapper's torch in Hengshan, Taiwan. This angle shows the slight upward deflection of the wing, even during unaccelerated flight. *Courtesy of the Boeing Company*

This 727-171C (c/n 19860, l/n 599) was delivered to Trans International Airlines on July 5, 1968, registered as N1728T. This aircraft later saw service with Braniff International and Lloyd Aéreo Boliviano. *Courtesy of the Boeing Company*

Alaska Airlines was another long-standing operator of the 727. This 727-081 (N124, c/n 18821, l/n 124) was originally delivered to All Nippon Airways as JA-8301 and was subsequently purchased by Pacific Southwest Airlines (PSA) and leased to Alaska Airlines in June 1972. *Courtesy of the Boeing Company*

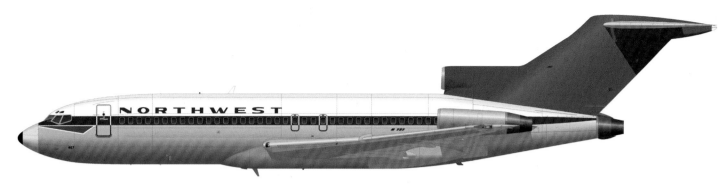

An artist's impression of N467US as it appeared on the day of the D. B. Cooper hijacking. *Courtesy of Jennings Heilig*

Courtesy of the Boeing Company

Skyjacked: The Mystery of Northwest Orient Flight 305 and D. B. Cooper

On the afternoon of November 24, 1971, Northwest Orient flight 305 began boarding at the Portland (Oregon) International Airport. Nothing seemed out of the ordinary as the aircraft, N467US (Boeing 727-51, msn 18803, l/n 137), was boarded by thirty-six passengers and serviced for a scheduled flight to Seattle, Washington. On this evening, however, this jetliner would become the proverbial Pegasus for one of the most storied and baffling mysteries in the history of aviation.

Presenting a twenty-dollar bill at the Northwest Airlines ticket counter, a dark-complexioned, tall man who identified himself as Dan Cooper purchased an open-seating ticket on the short flight to Seattle. Dressed in a dark suit and tie, Cooper stood alone in the boarding area with an attaché case, waiting to board the delayed flight. He settled in row 18 in the aft cabin, just prior to the aircraft's departure at approximately 15:00 local time.

Shortly after flight 305 became airborne, Cooper summoned the attention of one of the flight's stewardesses, Florence Schaffner, and quietly slipped her a note that read, "I have a bomb here, and I would like you to sit next to me." Once she sat down next to him, the man, polite and respectful in demeanor, indicated that he would detonate his explosive device unless he received a $200,000 ransom package. Additional to this requirement, he also made the very interesting request for four parachutes. While this request was being coordinated, Capt. Bill "Scotty" Scott kept the airplane in the air. Once assurance was received that Cooper's demands had been met, the aircraft landed at the Seattle Sea-Tac Airport. The flight's crew kept the situation quiet and did not alert the other passengers.

Funds were procured from the SeaFirst Bank, along with the parachutes. Different types of parachutes were provided, including both sport and military C9-type devices. Once these demands were met, Cooper allowed the other passengers and all but one stewardess to leave the aircraft. The remaining stewardess, Tina Mucklow, spent

An aircraft, identical to the D. B. Cooper airplane is seen in flight over the Pacific Northwest. This 727-51 (N461US, c/n 18797, l/n 90) primarily served with Northwest Airlines throughout its twenty-eight-year service life, but was leased for short periods to both PSA and Mexicana. Today, the aircraft resides at East Coast Aero Tech in Bedford, Massachusetts. *Courtesy of The Boeing Company*

most of the time sitting next to Cooper and was very observant, noting small details such as what type of cigarettes he smoked, where he obtained his matchbooks, and his physical features. During a press conference seventy-two hours after the event, she stated, "He was not nervous. He seemed rather nice other than he wanted certain things to be done. He never tried to harm myself. . . . Although he was impatient a few times, he was never cruel, or nasty, or impolite to me in any way." Complications occurred during the fueling of the aircraft, which required three trucks to be dispatched to the aircraft. This precipitated a delay, which caused Cooper considerable annoyance.

Cooper appeared to have knowledge of the Boeing 727 that was not normally available to the general public. He requested that the pilots fly at a reduced airspeed after departure, and specifically asked for the wing flaps to be set to position 15. He also understood how the ventral airstairs operated, knowing that they could be lowered in flight at reduced airspeed, which was not common knowledge at the time. He was offered instructions as to the use of the parachutes, but he indicated that he did not need to read them. Whoever Cooper really was, he had certainly done his homework and was extremely thorough. Requesting a southbound flight path, and due to the 727's limited range with the flaps set to 15, Reno, Nevada, was decided on as the next destination.

The flight departed Sea-Tac at 19:33 local time with Cooper, Stewardess Tina Mucklow, Capt. Scotty Scott, First Officer Rayaczak, and Flight Engineer Harold Anderson onboard. The flight waged southbound, following the Victor 23 airway toward Portland. Very soon after takeoff, Cooper requested that Mucklow return to the cockpit and remain there, as he attempted to deploy the ventral airstairs. It is surmised that air loads were somewhat hampering his efforts. He soon discovered that aided by his body weight on the

stairs, the assembly would deploy far enough for him to egress, along with the bulky equipment and possibly one or two bags of money, depending on the popular theories. The time of Cooper's departure from the aircraft is not positively known but was most likely between 20:10 and 20:15. This was based on the nose-down pitching motion the aircraft made during this period. It is thought that the partially deployed airstair on the lower portion of the aft fuselage was deflecting the passing slipstream, causing the pitching felt by Rayaczak, who was flying the aircraft by hand.

Due to the D. B. Cooper hijacking, as well as several follow-on copycat incidents, all passenger 727s were modified by adding the "Cooper switch," indicated by the red arrow. Simple in operation, the vane rotated as airflow increased during takeoff and mechanically locked the airstair closed. *Author's collection*

No further word was heard from the cabin, and the aircraft landed uneventfully in Reno, Nevada. After parking the aircraft, the crew examined the cabin and found no sign of Cooper, but his clip-on tie and cigarette butts remained, along with the unused parachutes. It appeared that Cooper had selected the military-issue C9 chute for use, which may have been a significant clue as to his background. The following day found thirty agents scouring the suspected drop zone near Woodland, Washington. No traces of Cooper or his belongings were found.

Soon after the Cooper hijacking, a series of similar acts were committed, with the 727 being the natural choice for such operations due to the ventral airstair. Boeing quickly designed a lock, known as the "Cooper switch," which was an aerodynamic vane attached to a mechanical lock. When the aircraft moved through the air at above 80 knots, air loads rotated the vane to activate the lock, which blocked the deployment of the airstairs in flight.

For over eight years, the trail was cold. Then in February 1980, a recreating family found some rolls of bills shallowly buried in the sand on the banks of the Columbia River at Tena Bar. This was only a small amount of the money taken by Cooper's heist that night in 1971, but the serial numbers on the decomposed bills matched those given to the hijacker. Tena Bar was a significant distance from the flight path of the aircraft, which stirred multiple theories. As of 2018, the Federal Bureau of Investigation had cleared over six hundred suspects but thus far has not been able determine the real identity of the man known as Dan Cooper.

The World Airways Da Nang Evacuation

As the Vietnam War was coming to a close in March 1975, Edward Daly, the hands-on leader of World Airways, based in Oakland, California, engaged in a humanitarian mission to evacuate refugees from Da Nang, Vietnam. Da Nang is located just south of the 17th parallel, and close to the Demilitarized Zone that divided North and South Vietnam. The city was under siege from the North, with many women and children in harm's way. With cooperation from the US Embassy, Daly employed three of World's Boeing 727s and began operations between Saigon and Da Nang on March 26 and 27 to evacuate nearly 2,000 people. A true leader in every sense, Daly was personally onboard as many of the fights as possible. The boarding process was chaotic, as panicked people swarmed the airplane.

On the morning of March 28, due to safety concerns, the US government withdrew support for the operation. Ed Daly, who was in outward disagreement with the decision, joined Capt. Healy and

his flight crew and boarded one of World's 727-173Cs, N693WA (c/n 19507, l/n 449). Along with four members of the news media to bring the situation to light globally, the aircraft departed Saigon for Da Nang. Reportedly, the control tower in Saigon refused to allow the aircraft to depart, but Healy had a radio failure and departed anyway. This flight, as were the earlier operations, was intended to evacuate women and children from the war-torn city. After a flight of less than an hour, '693 descended into Da Nang. Aircraft from Air America attempted unsuccessfully to warn the crew, via radio communication, of the chaos and degrading situation that was in progress at the airfield.

As the airplane landed and slowed to a stop on the ramp, the ventral airstair was deployed and the harrowing situation began. Instead of onboarding the women and children as intended, the aircraft was mobbed by soldiers, pushing the women and children aside to save their own lives. Daly fought them off, but there was no stopping the onslaught of men pushing their way onto the airplane. Two of the media members, who had exited the aircraft to get footage and coordinate with local officials, were unable to reboard in the ensuing riot. Hundreds pushed their way onto the airplane as the aircraft began to taxi. Those who could not board began firing on the airplane while it was moving down the taxiway with the still-extended airstair dragging on the concrete. Grenades were thrown at the aircraft, badly damaging the trailing edge flaps and wings of the airplane.

Knowing that the airplane was severely overloaded, but not certain by how much, Healy reached the end of the taxiway and pushed the thrust levers all the way up. Dozens of warning lights were illuminated in the cockpit, and with no time to get onto the runway, Healy elected instead to use the taxiway for departure. The badly damaged 727 roared down the taxiway, striking three small radio sheds in the process and running over anything remaining in its path. The 727 struggled to become airborne just as the last of the paved surface passed beneath the main landing gear tires. The jet remained mere feet above the surface, clawing to gain airspeed in the cushion of air provided by ground effect. Healy noted that there was a strange resistance on the flight controls, which he could not explain, but the aircraft remained controllable. The main landing gears refused to retract, while the nose gear followed commands from the cockpit. With the lower-deck cargo doors indicating open, the crew was unable to pressurize the cabin and was limited to a flight altitude to 10,000 feet. Given that jet engines are much less fuel efficient at low altitudes, combined with fuel leaking out of the aircraft's wing tanks, the aircraft was critically low on fuel. Another World Airways 727 came up alongside '693, assessed the damage, and gave Healy a report as to the condition of his aircraft. Dozens

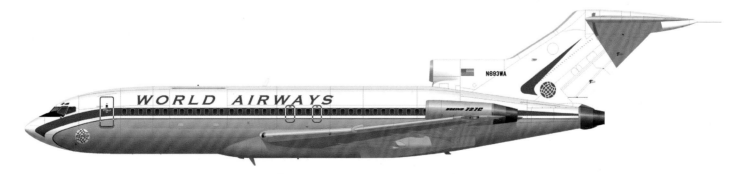

An artist's impression of N693WA, the aircraft involved in the Da Nang evacuation. *Courtesy of Jennings Heilig*

of people could be seen in the open baggage compartments, clutching aircraft components and control cables in the main landing gear wells, explaining the unusual feedback in the flight control system. The ventral airstair was still partially extended, and the portside inboard trailing edge flaps were badly damaged.

Healy was able to land the crippled jet on the long 14,000-foot runway in Saigon, with many of the aircraft's systems impaired. Once the aircraft came to a stop, the passenger count in the aircraft's cabin tallied at 268 people, of which, sadly, only eight were the intended women and children. Many escaped from the baggage compartments and wheel wells before a conclusive tally was made, but it was estimated that there were likely 360 people onboard and that the aircraft was at least 20,000 pounds overweight. This particular aircraft normally had accommodations for 105 passengers. Given this, it was a miracle that the aircraft, in its badly damaged state, was capable of becoming airborne, much less completing the flight to Saigon. Despite the sadness of events, this was perhaps the most extreme test of capability and durability for Boeing's 727.

Ed Daly, the leader of World Airways, was personally onboard the day of the flight and was wounded in the ensuing riot. *Author's collection*

Ed Daly, still undaunted by the experience, ordered supervised evacuations of orphans later that month and paid for the operation. The cost was estimated at over $2 million, and immigration fines levied against him exceeded $200,000, but because of the brave efforts of Daly and his crews and the unique capabilities of the Boeing 727, thousands were given a chance for survival and a new life.

The 727 High Dive

On April 4, 1979, Trans World Airlines Flight 841, operated by N840TW (c/n 18905, l/n 160), departed John F. Kennedy International Airport at 20:25 local time for Minneapolis–St. Paul. While en route at 39,000 feet over Saginaw, Michigan, Flight 841 suddenly departed controlled flight into a spiraling dive, losing 34,000 feet in sixty-three seconds. The aircraft recovered less than 5,000 feet above the surface due to the recovery efforts of the flight crew. The investigation began probing into what would become one of the most interesting and highly debated airline events of all time.

This postcard shows N840TW resting at the Indianapolis International Airport, years before the incident over Saginaw, Michigan. *Author's collection*

Due to aircraft damage incurred during the upset, Trans World Flight 841 made a no-flaps emergency landing at the Detroit Metro Airport at 22:31 local time. The aircraft was missing the #7 leading edge slat panel, the #10 spoiler panel, and the right inboard flap track fairing. The fuselage showed signs of tension field wrinkles due to high g-loads both forward and aft of the wing attach points. This extensive damage to the airframe categorized the event as an "accident," although everyone onboard survived the ordeal. The assessment of the cockpit voice recorder (CVR) was impossible because it had been erased by the flight crew during their postflight activities and checklist. This may seem suspect, but at the time it was fairly commonplace for flight crews to habitually erase the CVR after the completion of a "successful" flight. Culturally, pilots were uncomfortable with the somewhat recent installation of the CVR systems, even if they could not legally be used for non-accident-related, punitive purposes. Many pilots included pressing the ERASE button as part of their postflight cockpit switchology flow. It is therefore plausible that a pilot could do this flow without being specifically mindful of preserving the recorder data after being distracted by a stressful event.

While the Lockheed Aircraft Services A-109D flight data recorder (FDR) gave some useful data, early units such as this recorded only a few parameters, inherently limiting the information it could yield. What information the FDR did provide was both amazing and a testament to the design and incredible strength of the Boeing 727 airframe.

According to the FDR data, at 21:47 hours, TWA Flight 841, with a total of eighty-nine souls onboard, departed controlled flight when the #7 leading edge slat extended while the airplane was cruising at Mach 0.80 at 39,000 feet. The slat remained extended, significantly increasing the camber of the right wing. This caused the air above the airfoil to accelerate, and likely created a shockwave on the wing that interrupted the production of lift. Despite full-left-roll control inputs applied by the pilot, the aircraft rolled to the right, with the nose dropping well below the horizon toward a vertical, nose-down

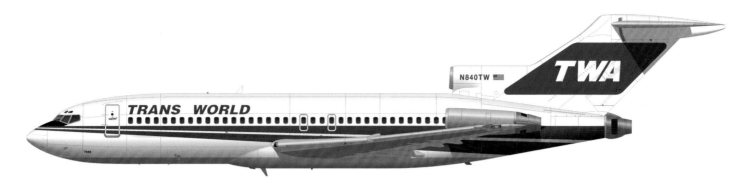

N840TW was the aircraft involved in the "High Dive" incident. The flight data recorder indicated that the aircraft had experienced six times the force of gravity during the dive recovery—nearly twice the design load limit for the 727. *Courtesy of Jennings Heilig*

attitude. Airspeed and Mach number increased along with g-forces as the aircraft dove toward the terrain below. Realizing that the situation was desperate, the captain chose to extend the landing gear, regardless of the airspeed being well in excess of the maximum landing gear extension speed. Immediately after the landing gear deployed, it is believed that the extended #7 slat departed the aircraft. The flight crew's action of extending the landing gear, along with the departure of the #7 slat from the airframe, allowed the recovery of the aircraft to controlled flight. A successful emergency landing ensued with no fatalities. The maximum Mach number recorded during the recovery was 0.96, and the loads waged on the airframe were as high as 6 g. Given that airliners are certified to a maximum of 2.5 g, with an ultimate design load of 3.5 g, this was an amazing airframe capability.

The big question was this: How did only one slat extend, and why? As far as the NTSB was concerned, taking into account the workings of the 727 high-lift systems, this type of failure was virtually impossible. In theory, any remote possibility of the slats being engaged in an uncommanded extension would have also brought out slats #2, #3, and #6 as well.

It was known to veteran 727 pilots that the wing of the 727 could gain a significant aerodynamic improvement at high altitudes by slightly extending the trailing edge flaps to position 2. Opening the leading edge slat circuit breaker was imperative, in order to prevent the unwanted extension of the slats while conducting this nonstandard and illegal "technique." The NTSB believed that the crew had possibly intended to accomplish this procedure to gain additional fuel economy improvements due to their long forty-five-minute taxi, and the attendant 1,500-pound fuel burn prior to departure. The safety board's theory was that the crew had inadvertently allowed the slats to deploy and, realizing the error, had retracted the flaps in an attempt to remedy the debacle. The #7 slat was found to be rigged incorrectly and skewed slightly, which, along with the high aerodynamic loading, caused it to jam in the extended position, even though slats #2, #3, and #6 retracted properly. This was believed by the safety board to have caused the asymmetric lift situation that forced Flight 841 to depart controlled flight.

The flight crew, to this day, fervently denies that they had deliberately, or unintentionally, caused the extension of the #7 slat, and that it was a mechanical malfunction of the aircraft's systems. The absolute, unrefuted truth will probably never be known for sure due to the limited information resources available, but the NTSB concluded the following:

The Safety Board determines that the probable cause of this accident was the isolation of the No. 7 slat in the fully or partially extended position after an extension of the Nos. 2, 3, and 6 slats, and the captain's untimely flight control inputs to counter the roll resulting from the slat asymmetry. Contributing to the cause was a preexisting misalignment of the No. 7 slat, which, combined with the cruise condition air loads, precluded the retraction of that slat. After eliminating all possible individual or combined mechanical failures or malfunctions which could lead to slat extension, the Safety Board determined that the extension of the slats was the result of the flight crew's manipulation of the flap/slat controls. Contributing to the captain's untimely use of the flight controls was distraction due probably to his efforts to rectify the source of the control problem.

It is interesting and noteworthy that not all members of the board agreed completely as to the path taken to determine the probable cause. Board member Francis H. McAdams added to the NTSB report:

Although I voted to approve the Board's report, which concluded that the extension of the leading edge slat was due to flight crew action, I do so reluctantly.

The report as written, based on the available evidence, i.e., the analysis of the flight data recorder, the simulator tests, the flight tests, and the tilt table tests, appears to support the Board's conclusion. However, I am troubled by the fact that the Board has categorically rejected the crew's sworn testimony without the crew having had the opportunity to be confronted with all of the evidence upon which the Board was basing its findings. At the time of the first deposition, the following evidence was not available to the crew or the Board: the flight data recorder analysis, the results of the simulator and flight tests, and the tilt table tests. Although the crew was deposed a second time, their testimony was limited to one issue, i.e., the physical location of the flight engineer at the time of the incident. I had recommended that since the Board was ordering a second deposition, it could be conducted "de novo" so that the crew would have been aware of all of the evidence. The Board did not agree.

Furthermore, I do not agree that a probable cause of this accident, as stated by the Board, was "the captain's untimely flight control inputs to counter the roll resulting from the slat asymmetry." In my opinion, the captain acted expeditiously and reasonably in attempting to correct for the severe right roll condition induced by the extended slat.

Regardless of the cause of this event, the 727 structural design that Jack Steiner and his team had created was proven to be more than robust. Even more impressive was that N840TW was repaired and continued to fly with the airline until October 1988, when it went on to fly for Express One, Emery Worldwide, and Charter America before being stored in 2005.

An Alaska Airlines 727-90C (N797AS, c/n 19169, l/n 320) demonstrates the aircraft's ability to land on slippery and frozen runways during poor weather conditions. The absence of standard Alaska Airlines titles indicates that this photo was taken during the aircraft's lease to BP Alaska in the late 1970s and early 1980s. *Courtesy of the Boeing Company*

N798AS (727-90C, c/n 19170, l/n 332) wears Alaska Airlines' Golden Nugget livery while being loaded at Nome, Alaska. Much later, on June 8, 2001, this aircraft was hit by a missile while landing at Luena, Angola. The 727 landed safely, was repaired, and reentered service with Transafrik International as S9-BOG. *Courtesy of the Boeing Company*

Alaska with Reeve Aleutian Airways

When bush pilot and entrepreneur Robert "Bob" Reeve arrived on the Alaskan aviation scene in 1932, he was already an accomplished pilot, albeit in a very different environment. Reeve had been a pilot with Panagra Airways, operating in the challenging South American environment. At one point, he was assigned Air-Mail Route 9, which stretched more than 1,900 miles from Lima, Peru, to Santiago, Chile, making the run famous for being, at the time, the longest scheduled route in the world. If this was not enough, Reeve used a 1928 Fairchild to complete the route in twenty hours, largely under the cover of darkness, using a whiskey compass for navigation. Reeve continued to fly this route after transitioning to the speedy Lockheed Vega until January 1932, when he wrecked the aircraft on the airstrip in Santiago, Chile.

Fearing termination by Panagra for the accident, he left South America as a stowaway on a steamship and headed for Alaska. Undaunted by his setback with the Vega, Reeve set out to make his way in Alaska, a land known for dangerous flying, where only the most skilled and fortunate survived for the duration. This was a land where whiteout conditions occurred on a moment's notice, obscuring rugged terrain and often forcing unscheduled landings on sandbars, beaches, and small clearings. It was in this environment that Reeve Aleutian Airways got its humble beginnings with its first company-owned airplane, a Fairchild Model 51, based in Valdez. Profitability eventually came for Bob Reeve and his company, with an ever-expanding fleet of capable aircraft.

The company grew with the use of several aircraft types and by 1946 was providing service with surplus Douglas C-47 (DC-3) airplanes, which were being offloaded by the military following the end of World War II. By the early 1950s, Reeve expanded his company's capabilities by adding Curtiss C-46s, as well as the larger, four-engined Douglas DC-4s and DC-6s. The operation continued to grow and even extended the route structure well out into the Aleutian Island chain.

The Curtiss C-46 was the mainstay of Reeve's fleet for many years before being replaced by more-modern equipment. *Courtesy of Piergiuliano Chesi via Wikimedia Commons*

In 1968, Reeve began to operate turbine equipment when the company acquired its first Lockheed L-188 Electra (N1968R, c/n 2007). This aircraft was followed by more Electras as the company moved into the 1970s.

N1968R became somewhat famous while being operated as Reeve Flight 8 on June 8, 1983. The aircraft had departed Cold Bay, Alaska, bound for Seattle, Washington. While climbing to altitude,

An artist's impression of N832RV (727-22C, c/n 19098, l/n 318), which was christened "Tilly." This aircraft, along with sister ship N831RV (c/n, 19093, l/n 293), was originally delivered to United Airlines. The two aircraft share the same operator history, being subsequently utilized by Wien Air Alaska and Flying Tigers before being operated by Reeve Aleutian Airways in 1984. *Courtesy of Jennings Heilig*

Reeve Aleutian Airways, Inc.

ANCHORAGE CITY TIMETABLE

Schedule Effective May 18, 1998

TO/FROM	LEAVE	ARRIVE	FLIGHT	STOPS	FREQ.	SERVICE
TO: ADAK	8:25 a	11:25 a	721	1	TU/TH	S
FROM: ADAK	12:05 p	4:25 p	722	1	TU/TH	S
TO: BETHEL	7:30 a	9:00 a	181	0	MO/FR	
	10:30 a	12:05 p	181	0	SA ONLY	
	5:15 p	6:25 p	723	0	EXCEPT SA	
FROM: BETHEL	9:45 a	11:15 a	182	0	MO/FR	
	12:40 p	2:10 p	182	0	SA	
	7:05 p	8:10 p	724	0	EXCEPT SA	
TO: COLD BAY	10:10 a		721	0	TU/TH	S
	?:35 p		725	0	MO/WE/FR	S
	?00 p		725	1	SU	S
			726	1	MO/WE/FR	
			722	0	TU/TH	
			726	1	SU	
			187	1	MO/WE/FR	S
			185	0	TU/TH/SA	S
			?8	0	MO/WE/FR	S
				0	TU/TH/SA	S
				0	MO thru FR	S
FROM: D.				0	MO thru FR	

RESE_____S:

1-9_____

1-8_____Toll Free

Courtesy of Rob Sherry

an unusual vibration was noted by the cockpit and cabin crew. Vibration rapidly increased as the #4 (right outboard) propeller parted company with the aircraft and, while still spinning, passed underneath the forward fuselage, slicing its way through the lower structures. The blades severed the engine controls, depressurized the cabin, and severely limited the pilots' controllability of the aircraft. The pilots shut down the #2 engine to allow the airplane to descend for landing due to the unusability of the throttle controls, which were jammed. Altitude was controlled by retracting the landing gear to allow a shallow climb and extending it to initiate a descent. Miraculously, Captain James Gibson, First Officer Gary Lintner, and Flight Engineer Gerald "Moose" Laurin brought the stricken aircraft in for a successful emergency landing at the Anchorage International Airport. Remarkably, not a single person was injured onboard the aircraft, and the aircraft was repaired to fly another day.

While the dependable C-46s soldiered on, they were starting to show their age, making it apparent that a replacement needed to be considered. The Japanese company NAMC offered a twin-engine turboprop airliner called the YS-11, which Reeve deemed perfect for the role. Beginning in late 1972, the YS-11 deliveries signaled not only the slow retirement of the company's C-46s, but also their DC-4s and DC-6s. The YS-11s served well for over a decade, but the need for pure jet equipment became a priority for Reeve in 1984.

After considering the Boeing 737, among others, the company settled on the procurement of two Boeing 727-22QCs, purchased from Wien Air Alaska. These airplanes were capable of being operated in cabin configurations with various volumes of cargo and passenger seats, using palletized passenger cabin components that could be locked directly to the cargo floor (see "The 727QC" in chapter 3, page 87, for further details on this capability). The 727 was the first American jetliner to be specifically approved for operations into unimproved gravel airstrips, allowing Reeve Aleutian to operate the type up to 1,500 miles out into the island chain. Given the low purchase price of these aircraft, profits were good, even when considering the additional fuel burn of the big jet over turboprop equipment or newer 737s.

Flying the 727

Reeve's captain John Fredenhagen began with the company by flying the Curtiss C-46. He shared some of the more interesting insights about flying the 727 for Reeve Aleutian Airways in the 1990s:

Courtesy of Rob Sherry

Courtesy of Rob Sherry

We flew to Adak Naval Air Station out in the Aleutian Islands, a thousand miles from Anchorage, with some fairly precipitous terrain. Circling approaches there were always entertaining. Along with that were very strong winds from all points of the compass on any given day. You had to prepare for the potential for strong winds and the need to circle around the hills close to the airport. Another airport that was entertaining was Red Dog Mine up by Kotzebue. We did a charter flight there once a week, and it was a gravel strip a little over 5,000 feet. It had a nonprecision approach . . . landing into a canyon, and the missed-approach point was 6 miles away. At the missed-approach point, we had to make a decision to fly visually into the canyon and land on the short gravel runway. It was very sporting. We had another gravel airport in the Aleutians at Saint Paul Island. The runway was made up of volcanic cinder material. We had to be very judicious about using the 727 there, but Red Dog Mine was just a straight gravel environment. We used the same gravel technique at both places.

On final approach the engineer was pretty busy. We used flaps 30 for landing even though we could have used flaps 40, but we just experienced too much gravel damage to the flaps at that setting. We just used flaps 30 and took the airspeed penalty, so to speak, and the landing-distance penalty. It wasn't very much, and it outweighed the damage to the flaps. We landed flaps 30 with the packs off and the doors shut, bleeds off. Then we only reversed the center engine, and that was quite a coordinated effort with a fairly short runway to boot! It was totally instinctual for the captain to reach for all of the reverser levers as soon as you touched down. The engineer actually had to hold the outboard reversers down to prevent the captain from [putting them] into reverse. One of the other companies, Northern Air Cargo, was operating 727s in and out of Red Dog as well, and they [destroyed] both pod engines reversing there because of foreign-object damage. We practiced that procedure in the simulator every time we went, because it was something that we didn't do all of the time, but when you did it, you had to be proficient. I developed a crew coordination item with my engineers, because I noticed that it was so instinctual to grab all of the reversers. When I would pull the power to idle and touch down, I would tell the engineer to select the center reverser. I guarded the outboard reversers and let him reverse the center engine because he could do a much-better job with his eyes on the engine instruments. He could bring the reverse lever right up and set max reverse, and I could continue to keep the airplane straight with braking and so forth.

Takeoffs on gravel were just a "packs off" procedure. We had another procedure for departing in heavy crosswinds to keep the center engine from compressor stalling. As we turned around into the wind at the end of the runway, we'd stand the throttles up to 70 percent, and when they were all stable, we advanced the power to max on the outboards. At the call "airspeed alive," the engineer would set the center engine to max. It was a bit unorthodox, but it seemed to work well. It certainly made the engineer work a lot.

Capt. Fredenhagen flew both the Lockheed L-188 Electra and the Boeing 727 for Reeve Aleutian Airways in this demanding environment. He shared his insights into the strengths and weaknesses of both airplanes:

The fact was that the cargo-carrying ability was almost the same. With the 727, you could get up and above all of the turbulence and fly faster, but for the Electra, it didn't matter. It was such a smooth airplane because the wing was about 80 percent washed by the prop wash, so it wasn't terribly affected by turbulence. Of course, it had 4,000 horsepower per engine, so it could get up and above anything handily. It could go around from balked landings . . . just push the throttles up and point it at the moon. The fuel consumption wasn't much different down low or up high.

On the 727, like all jets, the fuel consumption is such an issue. You are always fighting for a higher altitude, and that level of planning always had to exist. "Well, do we go down or stay up here?" We never had that conversation about the Electra. We could go down and take a look at it . . . it's not going to cost us any more fuel. We would never do that with a jet.

Russian Operations

In 1995, Reeve saw an opportunity with the warming relations between Russia and the United States and the furtherance of the oil industry. The 727 was put to use on routes into the former Soviet Union, which supplied the crews with ample adventures. Captain Fredenhagen recalled:

We started flying a once-a-week trip to Russia for Marathon Oil on a charter basis. That ranks with probably the most adventure I ever had flying an airplane. The Russians had enticed Marathon Oil to look at the oil prospects over in Sakhalin Island, just off the north coast of Japan. We could do it with our -100s with a tech stop a Petropavlovsk. So, we did a couple of proving flights there and decided that . . . the quality of the fuel and airport services was such that we could do it. It was going to take having a Russian-speaking coordinator with us. So, we did that and got to be great friends—definitely a necessity. I got to fly quite a few of those trips, and among other unexpected things, the runways in Russia are made out of concrete blocks set end to end and side to side. There were these seams . . . it's universal with all of those runways over there. If you ever look at a Russian airplane, the tires and shock absorbers are huge. Those cracks are a real jolting experience. One time we were departing from Petropavlovsk, and thankfully it was the last leg going home. . . . After bouncing down the runway and barely able to read the instruments, I rotated and the copilot's airspeed indicator fell out, not just the instrument, but the insides of the instrument! The glass had broken and all of the insides fell out! That was different! Thankfully, it didn't take out the rest of the pitot static system. We had to put up with things like that every time we went over there. We would bring back a whole log sheet of write-ups because the runways had brutalized the airplane so badly.

While the 727 brought modern, high-speed jet transportation to the table, it clearly operated with some liabilities. For example, the YS-11 could land reliably on a 3,500-foot runway that a jet captain wouldn't dare consider for normal operations. One of the handicaps that the Electra possessed was the lack of an antiskid braking system. Tires could easily be blown because of braking that was too aggressive for the conditions. Conversely, the 727's antiskid systems automatically prevented blown tires in the field, even under the most-demanding conditions, but required somewhat longer runways than the turboprops.

While the 727 was approved to land on unimproved runways, the use of special pilot techniques was required. This capability brought jet service into communities that had never experienced such luxuries. Until the advent of the Boeing 737 with the Unimproved Runway Kit, the 727 was the jet-powered Monarch of the Arctic. The 727 was able to carry higher loads without modifications and without the need for additional ground support equipment from these primitive, ice-covered fields.

Reeve Aleutian Airways had a long and storied history, but in the late 1990s, the financial health of the company began to wane. The closure of the Adak military base was a major blow to profitability, since much of the government charter business vaporized. During the same time period, increased competition from Alaska Airlines and Markair (both 737-200 operators) cost Reeve business opportunities. Finally, Reeve's elderly fleet of aircraft began to require mandatory aging-aircraft inspections and maintenance, which was quite costly. While purchasing and operating older aircraft may have been a good short-term decision, it was proving to cause Reeve serious problems in the long run. After attempts to recapitalize and restructure the company, Reeve ceased operations on December 5, 2000, signaling the end of the legendary Alaskan carrier.

Courtesy of the Boeing Company

The Unducted-Fan (UDF) Studies

In the late 1970s and early 1980s, fuel prices were increasing by large factors and were a major reason why high-bypass turbofan engines were being installed on traditional airframes such as the 737 and DC-9. The airlines felt the squeeze, especially with the deregulation of the US airline industry looming on the horizon. General Electric teamed up with SAFRAN to create an engine called the GE36 Unducted Fan, which was a hybrid of sorts, drawing on turbofan and turboprop technology. This power plant, which used the General Electric F-404 core as a basis, added additional turbine stages to directly drive two sets of contrarotating, scimitar-shaped blades. Likely for marketing reasons, the engines were not labeled "Turboprops" and instead acquired the moniker "Unducted Fan" or "UDF."

Boeing explored the next-generation airplane designs in the 150-passenger size class and formed a major project called the 7J7. This concept was intended to be a new-technology, highly efficient jetliner using the 25,000-pound-thrust-class GE36-B22A "Unducted Fan" power plant. Failure analysis, consequential to possibly losing a blade, suggested a tail-mounted configuration to protect the fuselage, wing fuel tanks, and systems. This made the 727 a logical test bed for the UDF, resulting in perhaps the most unusual application ever involving a 727. Boeing purchased a 727-063 (c/n 19846, l/n 555) from the Peruvian carrier Faucett to conduct UDF engine testing. On the 727 test bed, a GE36 replaced the number 3 engine, and flight testing was conducted as a joint Boeing-GE program. Fuel efficiency showed a nearly 60 percent reduction over conventional power plants, but the noise from the contrarotating unducted fan created a loud and uncomfortable passenger cabin. While great in concept, the 7J7, combined with the GE36 power plant, simply had too many

Another view of the Boeing/GE UDF test bed. After testing was finished for the UDF project, this aircraft was painted in a fictitious Midwestern Airlines paint scheme and used to create the plane crash scene in the 1992 movie *Hero*. *Courtesy of the Boeing Company*

A model of the 7J7 concept, which was being marketed to several airlines, including SAS. *Courtesy of the Boeing Company*

The Boeing 7J7 high-efficiency concept. *Courtesy of the Boeing Company*

disadvantages to outweigh the fuel savings during the mid-1990s, when fuel prices began to fall. Additionally, the time required to develop the aircraft was thought to be too lengthy for market demands. Concurrently, Boeing was working on the stretched 737-400, which would arrive on the market scene much sooner and was projected to be quite fuel efficient in its own right. The combination of these factors led to the cancellation of the 7J7 program, but research and development conducted with fly-by-wire technologies were incorporated into the later Boeing 777 program. Additionally, it is interesting that the UDF story is not necessarily over. The UDF is still being explored by engine manufacturers, using novel blade shapes and unequal blade spacing to address noise issues while retaining fuel efficiencies.

The Restoration and Last Flight of Ship One with Bob Bogash

My involvement with E1 (Ship One) began actually with E3—the third airplane—in September 1963. E1 and E2, of course, were around at the Flight Center at Boeing Field, being tested. E1 went on to complete 727 flight testing and was delivered to United in 1964—unique until the 777—since Boeing usually retained the first airplanes for follow-on testing-and-development activities. One reason was that the first airplane had a lot of "stuff" inside that made it hard (read "expensive") to convert into a deliverable configuration. Another was that the first airplane usually also had a lot of engineering/manufacturing "issues" associated with actually converting the early engineering drawings into a physical product. Often, things didn't exactly fit together as intended. Nevertheless, E1 was refurbished into a certified configuration and went into service with UAL. As became apparent during our preparations for her last flight, everyone at United knew she was the first airplane and left their "marks of Zorro" graffiti in every nook and cranny.

During her career, she accumulated 64,495 hours, made 48,060 landings, and flew an estimated three million passengers. While United paid $4.4 million for the airplane, she in turn generated revenues of more than $300 million during her service life.

In 1984, I was the chairman of the Aircraft Acquisition Committee at the Museum of Flight in Seattle—I have been an active volunteer there for more than fifty years. One day, on a business trip to Chicago, while taxiing in after landing, we passed N7001U–E1. I excitedly pointed her out to my seatmate, who failed to see the excitement. Later that year, Boeing rolled out the last 727, #1832, in a ceremony

in Renton. We tried to get E1 for the occasion, but United couldn't spring her off the line. With the last 727 having been built, and E1, a 727-100, being over twenty years old, I could see the handwriting on the wall. Her days were numbered and her future likely lay either with some small operator in a Third World location, or in the desert, to be followed by beer can heaven. I decided that this could not be allowed to happen, and I needed to do something preemptively.

I approached the two top guys at UAL, Ed Carlson and Dick Ferris, and asked for the airplane—upon retirement, of course (I did the same with Lord King—chairman of British Airways—asking for a Concorde). Both United and British Airways agreed! Fast-forward six years to January 1991. United retired E1, painted her in her as-delivered livery, and flew her on a last revenue flight to Seattle. After a ceremony at Boeing Field, she was ferried to Paine Field in Everett (site of her first landing), for interim storage. The museum had no room at Boeing Field for her (and other large aircraft).

Interim turned out to be a lot longer than I anticipated. In 1995, I retired from Boeing and began working on E1 in earnest, with the goal of flying her down to the museum at Boeing Field—which now had a place for her. The only thing that lay in my way were parts—you see, UAL had removed essentially all the serviceable parts, including the engines, to support their in-service fleet. She was airworthy when she flew in, so—it seemed—all that was needed was to reinstall the missing hardware. Long story short, that task consumed the next twenty-five years.

UAL provided some of the missing hardware, but most came from six donor airplanes—primarily two, one from FedEx and one from Clay Lacy. And in the end, FedEx provided three airworthy engines (and a huge amount of support). Dozens of people supported the effort, but two individuals in particular, Steve Huemoeller, a retired UAL mechanic, and T. C. Howard, retired Boeing engineer, were my main workhorses.

As the years rolled by, many with little activity on the airplane, two other issues arose. One was deterioration of the airplane from just being out in the elements. This continually increased our Statement of Work. The other impediment came from the museum management, who, looking at the airplane and its deteriorating condition, questioned the feasibility of actually flying her again. Discussions were held about disassembling her and moving her by surface, or even scrapping her in place and using a substitute airplane, a 727-200 already at the museum's main campus. My little band and I—we kept a stiff upper lip and worked on diligently, with the intention of making a last flight a reality, while the museum management ebbed and flowed in their support of such an activity. Quietly, sometimes, we wondered ourselves.

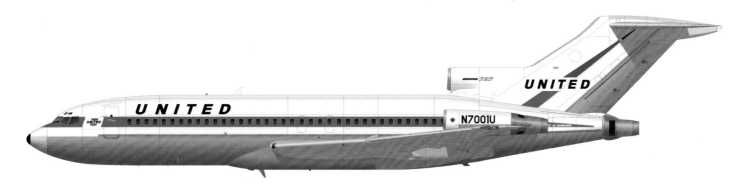

Ship One is seen in its current configuration as displayed at the Museum of Flight's Pavilion. The addition of FedEx hush kits, as evidenced by the extended tailpipes, was a legal requirement for the 26-mile ferry flight from Paine Field to Boeing Field in 2016. *Courtesy of Jennings Heilig*

Eventually, after a lot of behind-the-scenes lobbying, the museum agreed—in January 2015—to support restoration for a ferry flight. My argument was that I could fly it cheaper than they could move it by road—and we did! I am proud they had the confidence in my management and aviation skills to bring home the bacon one more time—I had done this also in 2003 with the 737 Prototype. In the end, we came in under budget, and at about half the cost of road transport.

The summer of 2015 was a busy one. We cleaned and repainted the airplane and received and built up three engines received from FedEx for the flight. Then, in January 2016, our real work began as we started the process of "waking up the airplane." We were waking up an airplane that first flew fifty-three years earlier, and that had been "sleeping" for the past twenty-five years. For me personally—I began my affair with her thirty-two years earlier—in 1984, if not way back in 1963. I knew—just knew—that she was still an airplane that had the Magic of Flight embedded in her genes, and we intended to let her experience that magic one more time. And we would savor the experience along with her. It is, in a nutshell, why I do what I do.

People who know me or hear my many talks know that I continually talk about airplanes as "Living Things," not just a collection of glass, rubber, steel, and aluminum. A measly "machine." Airplanes have Souls. This airplane certainly has one. People who design, build, fly, or work on airplanes don't have to be told that. And, after sleeping for a quarter of a century, much of it lonely, unnoticed, and unloved, in the dark winter rains and the warm summer nights, she was, once again, as in the days of her youth (and our youth), the center of attention—prodded and probed, coddled and pampered, as a beehive of activity surrounded her still-beautiful body. She knew all this, of course, and responded by coming alive and proving to all who were watching that her heart beat still.

During January and February 2016, we overcame many challenges as we brought her electric, fuel, hydraulic, flight control, and engine systems back to life. She experienced many firsts during that time— first time in twenty-five years inside a hangar, first time her engines ran, first time she moved under her own power. Finally, on March 2, 2016, she rolled down runway 16R at Paine Field, gathered speed, and lifted off, returning—if only for one last brief moment in time— to her home in the sky.

Thousands of people watched her departure and arrival, and millions followed our progress on the internet. Those people, and those who worked on her during her fifty-plus years, are the Ghosts I speak of so often—the Ghosts who have surrounded her from conception. If you close your eyes, you can see all of them from here. Like the ballplayers coming out of the cornfield.

And the one continuum, the one constant in this fable, is the airplane. Our airplane. The living, breathing thoroughbred that she is, working hard alongside her human partners. As those people came and went, she continued and endured. It was she that was the one common thread in this half-century tale of activity. Even in her quarter century of retirement, her spirit lived on as her admirers worked hard to let her taste the freedom of the skies yet one more time. And, in the end, they succeeded. From my seat in her cockpit, I felt her shake her mane and swish her tail, and I knew that she was smiling.

If you should come and visit our airplane and go aboard, pause and look around, close your eyes for a moment, and see them, all of them—her ghosts—including, yes, all of us who will soon enough also fade back into the cornfield. Her ghosts of past and present. Like those who came before, we will be her ghosts someday, while she endures. Our legacy will have been to be part of her life. Thanks to lots of hard work, and belief by the management and trustees and volunteers of this great museum, we will have made this possible. We have created and preserved something of beauty that will survive us. Not many things in life can we say that about. But we can fade

Ship One was restored at Paine Field prior to her last flight home. *Courtesy of Bob Bogash*

ROBERT BOGASH | PHOTO

ROBERT BOGASH | PHOTO

Ship One on final approach to Boeing Field on March 2, 2016. The aircraft was flown in a landing gear-down, flaps 5 configuration for the entire 26-mile flight. *Courtesy of Bob Bogash*

into our cornfield content in the knowledge that we have played a part in her life and allowed her to slumber contentedly. For—as we who awakened her over the twenty-five-year journey know so well— she will only be sleeping. You who visit her in the Aviation Pavilion will know assuredly, as we have proven unequivocally, that the miracle of flight still resides in her graceful wings, and in her lovely body, an airplane's heart beats—still.

For more info, a very detailed history of this airplane with hundreds of photographs can be found on my website here: www. rbogash.com/ual727tx.htm

Further study of the restoration and historic last flight of Ship One can be found in *United 727 N7001U: The Restoration and Last Flight* by crew chief Terry "TC" Howard.

The 727-100 series had proven to be an incredibly capable airplane, from busy metropolitan airports to gravel runways in the Arctic, surrounded by inhospitable terrain. This airplane set new standards for aircraft flexibility, efficient development, and manufacturing. With the ever-increasing passenger numbers, the jet age was in full swing. Advances made for the later JT8D engines produced by Pratt & Whitney promised higher thrust levels that could be maintained to higher altitudes. With these factors in mind, Boeing began to explore ways to make the 727 more efficient and desirable to the airlines of the world.

Ship One lifts off for the first time in twenty-six years, for the short flight from Paine Field to Boeing Field. *Courtesy of Jim Larsen / Museum of Flight via Bob Bogash*

Ship One receives the traditional water cannon salute at Boeing Field as she is taxied into the Museum of Flight parking lot. *Courtesy of Ted Heutter / Museum of Flight via Bob Bogash*

Ship One was the airplane that started the Boeing 727 story. It is fitting that she has been lovingly restored and preserved by the Museum of Flight at Boeing Field in Seattle, Washington. *Courtesy of the Boeing Company*

4

The Boeing 727-200 Series

A Need for More Capacity

In late 1965, after just two years in service, the Boeing 727 had proven itself to be both reliable and efficient. Even so, engineers desired to build on its success by increasing capacity to reach a wider customer base. More available seats would permit better seat-mile costs, an idea that was gaining momentum. In fact, even during the initial design of the 727-100, the possibility of developing a version with a maximum capacity of more than 131 passengers was envisioned. Working under Don Finlay in the preliminary design group, engineer Peyton Autry had quietly conducted much of the initial research on a "stretched" 727 concept.

During the production of the short-body 727s, fatigue test data were used to integrate structural enhancements into the construction of newer 727s on the production line. These additions, along with strengthened landing gears, allowed for a gross weight increase for the 727C without sacrificing the original structural margins built into the aircraft. The 727C required this additional weight capability because the original 160,000-pound maximum takeoff weight left the airplane weight restricted when operating in high-density cargo configurations. Boeing used these enhancements to increase the

These are early artist's conceptions of the 727-200. Note the midship galley door and oval center-engine inlet, similar to the 727-100 configuration. *Courtesy of the Boeing Company*

maximum takeoff weight to 169,000 pounds, thereby expanding its utility in the cargo role.

Although this weight increase was made available for the 727C, there was not enough cabin space to take advantage of the extra lifting ability on a passenger-only configuration, making an extended fuselage the next logical step. The idea was quickly gathering inertia because, unlike the time frame of Autry's initial studies in 1965, the economics of a stretched fuselage were becoming more favorable. Dick Ault of Western Airlines was a vocal critic of many of the older-technology features of the Boeing 720. He noted that the 727, along with the 737, featured many advancements airplane wide. He had noticed improvements in fuel gauging, cockpit lighting and instrumentation, electrical-wiring design, flight control systems, structures, and corrosion proofing available with the 727. Modular component installation facilitating ease of maintenance and the addition of an auxiliary power unit (APU) were also major attractors for the 727 over the older 720. Ault specifically favored the design advancements of the 727 in these areas and expressed this on numerous occasions to Boeing personnel.

Even with the overwhelming evidence that the days of the four-engine 720B and its higher operating costs were numbered, many at Boeing still resisted building the 727, and later the 727-200, because it effectively meant early obsolescence for the 720B. Time would show these fears to be well founded, as airlines looking to add a new airplane in this class rapidly began placing orders for the 727-200 instead of the 720B. Boeing, however, wanted to create an airplane that used current state-of-the-art technology to compete favorably for the foreseeable future, and the 727-200 was the answer.

While the operating costs of the 727-100 compared favorably to the first-generation jetliners, competitive forces emerged when Douglas began selling two airplanes with better seat-mile costs than the 727-100; namely, the "stretched body" DC-8-60 series and the new DC-9 twin jet. Both the DC-9 and the long-bodied DC-8-60 series were selling fairly well during this time frame, constituting a serious marketing threat for Boeing. There was also an air of internal competition between the 727 and the new Boeing 737, because although the 737 was smaller, it could carry 80 percent of the passengers allowed by the 727-100 series at lower seat-mile operating costs. Initially, the 737 was slow to sell in the market, mainly due to its late start as compared with the DC-9, further complicating Boeing's predicament. Boeing did not wish to allow their successful 727 to lose market share to these new competitors, but simultaneously desired to move it out of the way of the emerging 737. If these were not enough to cause concern, there were rumblings of a new European organization, called Studiengruppe Airbus, which was determined to combine the strengths of multiple aircraft manufacturers from the European continent in building a new, superior jetliner.

Even though the 727 design capitalized on its many strong attributes, such as an exceptionally high-lift wing and relatively long-range capability, this question remained: Could Boeing tap into enough of these strengths to create an excellent seat-mile-cost jet that increased revenue capacity without sacrificing too much performance?

In 1965, Jack Steiner issued a memo that effectively kicked off the new 727-200 with a fuselage lengthened by 160 inches. If need be, this length increase could be reduced as necessary to meet the La Guardia takeoff performance requirements. Soon, however, the drive for even more capacity eclipsed the full-up La Guardia capability, which in the big picture would have been akin to "the tail wagging the dog." By September 1965, the specification for the 727-200 had been amended to include a 240-inch "stretch" of the fuselage structure, with a 10-foot extension just forward and another aft of the wing carry-through structure. To expedite emergency passenger egress via inflatable slides and the servicing of the aft-cabin galleys, two service doors, one on each side, were added to the design just forward of the pod-mounted engines. The 727-200 retained the ventral airstair from the -100 and also continued to offer the forward (L1) door airstair as an option. While the 727-100 had exceptional range capabilities within its class, the 727-200 design goal was to transform a small portion of that range into additional revenue capacity.

Boeing 727-200 Fuselage and Cabin Configuration

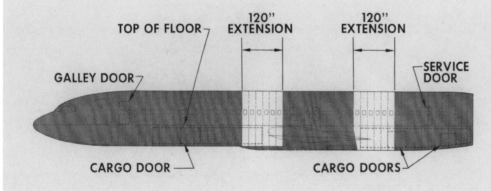

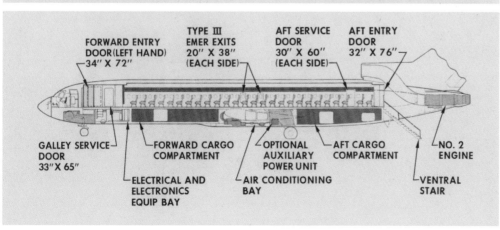

Courtesy of the Boeing Company

Lew Wallick (*right*) during a 727 demonstration flight with United Airlines' Weldon E. "Dusty" Rhoades. Rhoades was Gen. Douglas MacArthur's personal pilot during World War II. *Courtesy of the Boeing Company*

Steiner encouraged input from many airlines on the specifications for the new 727-200, with United Airlines being a prime contender. Initially, United's Weldon "Dusty" Rhoades indicated that they were interested in preserving the range capability for flying their 727-200s from Chicago to the West Coast of the United States. At this point, Boeing was planning a 240-inch fuselage expansion and indicated to Rhoades that their range requirement would be difficult with anything more than a 120-inch total stretch. Initially, Rhoades was fairly adamant that this range potential was a first priority. The tide began to change, however, after Rhodes met with his senior airline management. He later returned to meet with Steiner on July 9, 1965, and acquiesced on the range issue, apparently seeing greater value in the larger cabin.

Subsequent to United's agreement on the 240-inch increase, Boeing continued to work with interested carriers in firming up the specification. American was initially favorable to the 240-inch increase, but Eastern was still sitting on the fence with the 727-200.

An artist's rendition of the 727-200 in Northeast's new paint scheme. *Courtesy of the Boeing Company*

With United and American showing enough interest to proceed, though, Steiner reached a firm configuration for the new jet on July 19, 1965. He presented the details to Bill Allen with a projected launch date of September 1, 1965, and a projected certification goal of September 1967.

Events occurred rapidly as the new design developed. American Airlines, Northeast, and United were involved in the process as Boeing listened and designed the airplane. This is when an interesting turn of events transpired. On August 10, 1965, Northeast Airlines submitted an order for six 727-200s and an additional six short-body 727s. This sent shockwaves throughout the industry, since Northeast was a relatively small airline compared to the "normal" launch customers. American Airlines kept in good humor about it but gave Boeing a bit of a ribbing. Pan American, on the other hand, was upset not to be in the 727-200 loop. In a late 1965 letter to Harold Mansfield, author of *Billion Dollar Battle*, Steiner recalled:

> Pan American was incensed by it, claiming that there was an unwritten law that Boeing always shows its new models to Pan American first. In this case we hadn't even kept Pan American up to date. American made a big joke of it and the caustic comments are just now abating. However, I don't believe it has any bearing or effect on the program.

Ruffled feathers aside, the Boeing 727-200 program was now rolling forward with Bill Clay as the chief project engineer. This being said, because of the unusual circumstances of the Northeast deal, Boeing's 727-200 team needed to carefully navigate through a potential minefield. For the 727-200 to be a success, at a minimum, the airplane had to have the blessing of both American and United, without alienating Northeast. The key was clear communication with all involved parties during the intricate task of building a new version of the 727.

On September 27, 1965, American Airlines issued an order for twenty-two 727-223 jetliners, with the agreed-on 240-inch fuselage stretch configuration. Soon thereafter, American came back to Boeing, strongly urging that Boeing reduce the fuselage stretch from 240 inches to 200 inches, likely because of performance constraints. Naturally, this caused a major debacle since Boeing had already committed to build the 240-inch airframe for Northeast. The tightrope was getting higher as the issue went all the way up to Boeing's director, John Yeasting, who had an emergency meeting with American's representative, Mr. Hogan, to work out the issue. During the same time period, Pratt & Whitney's R. L. Rouzie worked with Boeing to create the JT8D-9 model, a new version of the JT8D. Since the -9 could produce up to 14,500 pounds of thrust, it was the needed compromise that allowed the 240-inch stretch to meet American's performance requirements. Because of effective project management and administration, three companies came together in a very confined time period to meet a challenge that would have otherwise created serious problems for all involved. Another victory had been won for the 727, and its 240-inch improvement abided.

The Pratt & Whitney JT8D-9

Still, some customers were concerned that the new 240-inch stretched aircraft would be a "runway lover." Instead of reducing the length of the 727-200, Boeing went to Pratt & Whitney, builder of the JT8D engine, in search of the answer. The Connecticut-based engine builder doubled efforts to produce a version of the engine that increased engine thrust from 14,000 to 14,500 pounds. As mentioned above, this power plant was the JT8D-9 and, with the possibility of even higher-thrust versions becoming available, eased Boeing's concerns that the 727-200 would be, as Jack Steiner termed it, a "lead sled." The JT8D-9 differed from the -1 and -7 in having improved blade shapes in the first, second, and seventh compressor stages. To accommodate the extra thrust, the diffuser case and the low-pressure turbine (N1 spool) shaft were reinforced. Advanced alloys were employed in the production of the first-stage turbine disk and the second-stage turbine vane supports.

Not only was the extra 500 pounds of thrust significant, equally so were the newly improved thermal limits of the JT8D-9. The maximum thrust available on many jet engines, especially during the early parts of the jet age, was limited below the maximum rated thrust when either altitude or ambient temperatures were increased. In practice, this meant that the JT8D-1, even at sea level, could make rated thrust only below 59 degrees F. At temperatures higher than this, the engine would reach its thermal limits before reaching its rated thrust limit. This reduced performance, particularly in places such as Denver, Colorado, where both altitude and temperatures often worked against airplane performance, especially in the ever-important engine-out scenario. The JT8D-9 engine, though, could deliver its full-rated 14,500 pounds of thrust up to 84 degrees F at sea level, providing an enormous performance advantage.

Not only was additional cabin space provided by the 727-200's fuselage "stretch," but valuable underfloor cargo compartment volume was also gained, with an increase from 900 to 1,450 cubic feet. To allow quick loading and unloading, the design of the two cargo doors (both fore and aft) was altered from inward opening to doors actuating outward and up. An optional third, 32-by-48-inch inward-opening door was made available to allow bulk loading after the container cargo in the aft compartment had already been loaded. Last-minute hand loading of late-arriving bags was also still possible due to the lower part of all three openings being within 5½ feet from ramp level.

From the outset, the 727 was designed to require a minimum amount of service equipment for normal operations. The early addition of an auxiliary power unit (APU) and the aircraft's approval for "powerback" procedures (using reverse thrust to back away from the gate, versus requiring an aircraft tug) were evidence of this design philosophy. Due largely to an engineering request made by American Airlines, Boeing designed a system for the 727-200 that used a structure that articulated out of the baggage door openings. This device provided a cable hoist to load containerized cargo, without any ground-based equipment. Each container could hold 78 cubic feet and 1,750 pounds of cargo for expeditious loading. This was offered as an option, but the hoist proved to be somewhat troublesome in service and was short lived in operation. Although this one feature was less than successful, it did show that Boeing was constantly attempting to improve their product.

The La Guardia compromise was not the only concession accepted to create the 727-200. The 727-100 was typically range limited by fuel tank capacity due to the lower weights involved. The 727-200, due to higher aircraft weights, along with increased passenger and baggage payloads, became more of a classic range versus payload aircraft. The original 1967 version of the 727-200 still performed

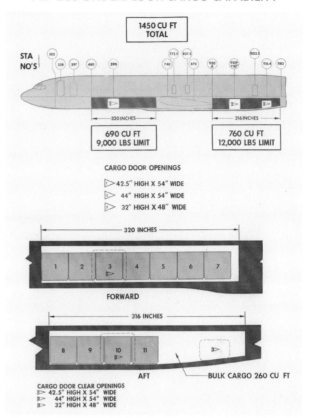

727-200 UNDERFLOOR CARGO CAPABILITY

The fuselage extensions, both fore and aft, significantly increased the baggage capacity of the 727-200. Note the second door added to the aft compartment. *Courtesy of the Boeing Company*

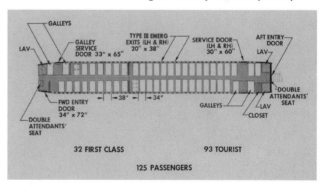

727-200 Low and High Density Cabins (1968)

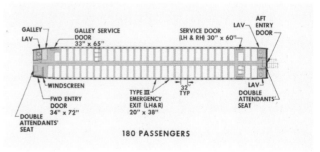

Courtesy of the Boeing Company

The optional cargo loader is shown here, demonstrating its ease of use. Although a great feature in concept, the system proved troublesome in service. *Courtesy of the Boeing Company*

factor. This was a gamble that the engineers had to accept, provided that the aircraft's performance numbers and operational usefulness were not hampered too severely. In hindsight, this additional capacity turned out to be a very good decision.

An Airplane for All Seasons

The 727-200 was, like the 727-100, designed to be operational in challenging weather conditions, day or night. While possessing all the same ice and rain protection features of the 727-100, the -200 featured a more capable autopilot system: the Sperry SP-50 Mod Block IV. The 727-200 was certified straight "out of the box" with Category II (1200 RVR and 100-foot decision altitude) automatic-landing capability. This autopilot was a dual-channel system with redundant pitch channels, flare couplers, and roll monitors, which provided more precise instrument landing system (ILS) approach tracking than the earlier generation Mod Block III units delivered on the 727-100. Additionally, pilots were provided early warning of any critical flight instrumentation malfunction via the standard equipment Collins FD-108 flight director and 54W-1D instrument comparator systems. At the end of a low-visibility approach, sighting the runway in poor conditions prior to touchdown was required. To aid in this, the rain repellent system was retained from the 727-100, but the use of a new type III repellent fluid allowed for better rain mitigation, which lasted up to five times longer in harsh weather conditions.

very well and did not sacrifice much range in providing accommodations for forty-four additional passengers. When compared to the standard 727-100, using a 0.84 Mach cruise speed, the 727-200 sacrificed 650 nautical miles of range, while reducing the cost per seat-mile by 21 percent on a typical 500-nautical-mile flight. The 727-200 economics were even more dramatic when the carrier was willing to outfit the aircraft with a high-density layout, typically allowing a flight to pay for itself with an unheard-of 29 percent load

Lew Wallick has a 727 lined up on the runway, awaiting a departure clearance. Wallick was well respected and known to be an outstanding pilot. The test instrumentation on the glare shield is noteworthy. *Courtesy of the Boeing Company*

Building the 727-200

Three 727-200 fuselage sections share the floor with several 727-100 sections, making the longer fuselage of the -200 series quite apparent. *Courtesy of the Boeing Company*

Air Canada's first 727 (C-GAAA, c/n 20932, l/n 1069) is prepared for final assembly inside Boeing's Renton assembly hall. This aircraft was later operated by Federal Express as N221FE. *Courtesy of the Boeing Company*

Three 727-200 series aircraft in final assembly. Special devices are seen installed on the aircraft's tail in the foreground to aid with control rigging. *Courtesy of the Boeing Company*

727-200 models are receiving their final touches prior to having engines mounted; 737-200 airplanes are sharing the line. Today, the same factory is being used for 737 MAX production, but the airplanes move nose to tail down the line, on three lines. With Boeing's adoption of Lean Manufacturing, inspired by Toyota, this factory is capable of producing fifty-two 737s a month. *Courtesy of the Boeing Company*

This view of a nearly completed 727-200 shows the additional aft baggage door and the effective Fowler trailing edge flaps. *Courtesy of the Boeing Company*

A completed 727-200 rolls toward the paint shop. Producing three different types on the same floor meant tight quarters with equipment parked nearby. *Courtesy of the Boeing Company*

Occasionally, the 707 airframe would make an appearance or two on the Renton assembly hall floor during the late 1970s through 1994, often in the form of the AWACS platform ordered by the USAF and NATO. *Courtesy of the Boeing Company*

A 727-200 aircraft is seen being painted in the Renton paint shop. This example is a much-later aircraft (727-2L5 5A-DIA, c/n 21050, l/n 1108), which served with Libyan Arab Airways for seventeen years before colliding with a MiG-23UB on December 22, 1992, while on approach to Tripoli, Libya. *Courtesy of the Boeing Company*

727-200 Flight Test

The first Boeing 727-200-series aircraft was originally intended to be a production aircraft and was built as such. Adorned in Boeing's then-typical yellow-and-brown demonstrator colors, N7270L (c/n 19536, l/n 433, Effectivity QA001) was also the first to fly in the flight test program. On July 16, 1967, ground testing began with the required taxi, air-conditioning, and engine evaluations. It was noteworthy that even with the revised center-engine inlet and S-duct, engine surges, often called compressor stalls, were still experienced while accelerating the engine during crosswind conditions. As mentioned in chapter 3, the JT8D is an engine that can be prone to compressor stalls, especially when mounted in the 727's number 2 position. Compressor stalls are caused when there is an uneven buildup of pressure within the engine's compressor. To eliminate this, a surge bleed valve (SBV) is used to eliminate this uneven buildup of pressure by slightly "unloading" the compressor until the engine is accelerating normally. It was found that the SBVs were mistakenly disabled, though, which was quickly corrected as the aircraft moved through the task list toward first flight.

On July 27, 1967, N7270L became airborne for the first time, under the command of Capt. Lew Wallick, Copilot D. C. Knutson, and Flight Engineer C. R. Cummings. The airplane was loaded to the middle of the center-of-gravity range at 31 percent MAC, with a gross weight of 133,137 pounds for the initial tests. The crew flew the airplane as slow as 103 knots, and as fast as Mach 0.45 at 10,000 feet. Stability tests were also conducted with the yaw damper off to evaluate the airframe's unaugmented yaw stability. A safe landing followed at Paine Field, and the airplane was expeditiously prepped and flown again the same day. The second flight was generally successful but was plagued with cabin pressurization system problems and test instrumentation issues both with the trailing cone and the trailing "bomb" used for instrument calibration.

Four days later, further exploration of the aircraft's yaw stability and propensity for Dutch roll continued to be evaluated at the higher altitudes and speeds with the yaw damper systems off. Like the -100 series, the Dutch roll tendency was more pronounced at high altitudes and high speeds, but due to the vertical stabilizer having an extra 10 feet of leverage on the -200, the onset of instability generally occurred at higher altitudes for a given airspeed / Mach number. At 35,000 feet, Dutch roll was deemed "slightly damped" at Mach 0.65, but when accelerated to Mach 0.78, it became "slightly divergent," indicating some measure of instability without yaw damper augmentation.

The entire speed range of the airplane was explored, with the aircraft eventually reaching indicated airspeeds of 520 knots, which was well in excess of normal operating limits. Aerodynamic stalls were also evaluated, with special attention given to the loads imposed on the tail of the airplane, particularly at the forward, nose-heavy end of the CG spectrum. Slam engine accelerations at high altitudes were still found to cause compressor stalls on the center engine. This was likely due in part to the aircraft systems that usually do not require bleed air extraction from the center engine, making the condition more probable. Like the -100 series, the -200 had vortex generators in the S-duct to help mitigate this unwanted characteristic.

The crew that flew the 727-200 on its first flight, led by Capt. Lew Wallick. *Courtesy of the Boeing Company*

The first takeoff of the 727-200 series, with a date well planned on 7-27-1967 (American convention for July 27, 1967). *Courtesy of the Boeing Company*

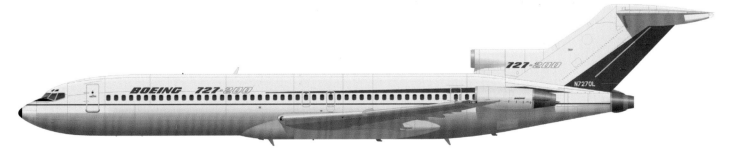

Courtesy of Jennings Heilig

These were reconfigured, and twenty-two sensors were installed in the throat of the S-duct. Engineers monitored the sensors and noted significant improvement during subsequent flights. With repeated testing, airflow stability of the center engine was achieved to a reasonable standard. That being said, airlines were known to install the newest engine on a particular aircraft in the number 2 position, since engines exhibiting wear from use tended to be much more susceptible to compressor stalls.

Boeing test pilot Tom Twiggs at the controls of a 727. *Courtesy of the Boeing Company*

While the program was not without some minor issues, the aircraft itself was more or less a known quantity, which was basically a simple fuselage "stretch" from the 727-100 with little in the way of system changes. Boeing gained Type Certificate approval for the 727-200 series on November 29, 1967, after an intensive and thorough flight test program that lasted just over four months.

Meeting the Design Goals

One of the major design goals for the 727-200 was to achieve maximum parts commonality, with as few design changes as possible when compared with the 727-100-series airplanes. This criterion saved substantial capital in research and development, production, and line operations because of parts commonality. By the time the 727-200 design was locked in, the two versions shared 79 percent component commonality. This also extended into the cockpit, with the aircraft's operation and systems being nearly identical, having only some minor systems and ergonomic differences. An unrestricted and clear view of the instrument panel was improved by revisions to the pilots' seats and a slight resizing of the control yokes.

Until the end of 727-100-series production, the two versions shared the floor at Boeing's Renton assembly hall. The last -100 series aircraft produced (c/n 20533, l/n 869) was delivered to a nonairline customer on November 3, 1971. *Courtesy of the Boeing Company*

727-100 and 727-200 Comparison (1968)

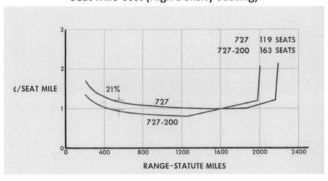

	727-100	727-200
Overall Length	133 feet 2 in.	153 feet 2 in.
Wingspan	108 feet 0 in	108 feet 0 in
Maximum Taxi Weight (pounds)	161,000	170,000
Maximum Takeoff Weight (pounds)	160,000	169,000
Maximum Landing Weight (pounds)	137,500	150,000
Maximum Zero Fuel Weight (pounds)	118,000	136,000
Typical Empty Weight (pounds)	86,300	94,607
Maximum Indicated Airspeed (knots)	390	390
Maximum Mach Number	M .90	M .90
Typical Passenger Capacity	119	163
Total Cargo Volume (cubic feet)	900	1,450
Standard Fuel Capacity (U.S. Gallons)	7,174	7,174

Seat-Mile Cost (High Density Seating)

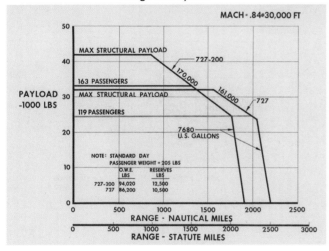

Range vs. Payload

These charts offer a comparison of the 727-100- and early 727-200-series aircraft. *Courtesy of the Boeing Company*

As of 1978, the operational center-of-gravity (CG) range for the 727-200 was the largest of any of the existing jetliners of the period. This wide range of loaded-aircraft balance points meant that there was additional flexibility with regard to where cargo was loaded and where people sat in the cabin. This desirable characteristic meant better on-time numbers and reduced instances where a departure was delayed while relocating either people or cargo.

Even given the large range available, the 727-200 was fairly tail heavy when sitting empty, or nearly so. This was because two-thirds of the passenger seats and all of the center tank (#2) fuel was forward of the typical aircraft balance point. In the absence of these items being onboard, there was always concern that the 727 might decide to become a tail-sitter, which risked damaging the aircraft. In fact, there was a close call around 1968 when a brand-new 727-200 was being delivered to National Airlines. The 727 had very effective brakes, and the pilot brought the airplane to a stop, perhaps a bit more abruptly than intended. As the airplane rocked after the expeditious halt, the nosewheels bounced completely off the ground before returning to their intended place on the ramp. This incident was an attention-getter and pushed forth the procedure that the ventral airstairs be deployed when the aircraft was parked. Although not widely publicized, there were even certain 727 configurations where a few hundred pounds of lead ballast were affixed to the forward pressure bulkhead to help null this potential issue.

The 727-200 Begins Revenue Flight Operations

Northeast Airlines was the surprise launch customer for the 727-200 series and took delivery of their first "stretched" machine on December 11, 1967. This aircraft (727-295, N1641, c/n 19446, l/n 471) was finished in the beautiful "Yellowbird" paint scheme, introduced by the company just a short time before. The very next day, National Airlines took delivery of their first 727-235 (N4730, c/n 19450, l/n 464), and the race to be the first to operate the aircraft in service was on! On December 14, 1967, Northeast Airlines provided the world's first 727-200 service with N1641, under the command of Captain Clark Willard, on routing from Miami, Florida, to New York's Kennedy Airport. Flight attendant Barbara McCormick was part of the crew that day and shared the experience:

> I don't remember a thing taking place in the gate area. It was a scheduled flight of the 727-100, and that morning we had a change of aircraft. We knew it was coming, but we didn't know when. We had all been checked out on it inside, but we didn't know when we would get the go-ahead,

Northeast Airlines operated the first-ever 727-200 service, with the aircraft sporting the carrier's attractive new paint scheme. *Courtesy of Jennings Heilig*

and I know that it was a race, so to speak, between National and Northeast of who was going to take off first. That was it! The chief pilot in Miami took the left seat. I think the normal captain for the flight moved over to the right seat. It wasn't until we were taxiing that the captain actually came out and said that it was the inaugural flight of the 727-200. Everybody cheered and everybody paid attention.

Barbara McCormick was a member of the crew that operated the first revenue service of the 727-200. *Courtesy of Barbara McCormick*

Little did anyone involved know that this event, devoid of media coverage, would be of paramount significance. The 727-200 program went on to be extremely successful for Boeing. In fact, the 727-200 series continued to sell well when other aircraft in the Boeing stable, notably the 737 and 747, were stagnating due to the economic climate during the late 1960s and early 1970s. According to Jack Steiner, the 727-200 program was completed exactly on budget, while meeting or exceeding every performance promise made to the customers.

N751VJ (727-2B7, c/n 20303, l/n 793) was delivered to Allegheny Airlines in March 1970 but served with the carrier for only seventeen months before being transferred to Braniff International as N405BN. *Courtesy of the Boeing Company*

Northeast Yellowbirds

You'll wish we flew everywhere.

Author's collection

American Airlines was a significant operator of the 727-200-series aircraft and operated N843AA (c/n 20984, l/n 1121) starting in May 1975, until being withdrawn from use by the carrier on April 10, 2001. At the time, this aircraft had operated 42,930 flights, totaling 69,317 hours. *Courtesy of the Boeing Company*

Pacific Southwest Airlines took delivery of N550PS on March 30, 1973, shortly after this photo was shot. Note that the airplane is missing the trademark smile that was normally painted on the nose of PSA's aircraft. It was the airline's tradition not to paint the smile on the aircraft until the carrier had officially taken possession of the airplane. *Courtesy of the Boeing Company*

N556PS (727-214, c/n 21513, l/n 1365) seen in flight, sans smile, prior to PSA taking delivery of the aircraft on July 18, 1978. This aircraft went on to serve with Piedmont Airlines and USAir before being converted into a freighter for Kitty Hawk AirCargo. *Courtesy of the Boeing Company*

This Pacific Southwest Airlines 727-214 looks more the part, properly equipped with a big grin. *Courtesy of the Boeing Company*

Competing with the Wide-Bodies: The "Wide-Body Look" Interior Program of 1969

The 1969 "Wide-Body Look" interior increased the volume of the overhead storage space and created a more modern, spacious feel in the passenger cabin. *Courtesy of the Boeing Company via Chuck Ballard*

Scarcely more than three years after the 727-200 debuted, wide-body aircraft designs such as the 747, DC-10, and L-1011 were coming to fruition. In Europe, the Airbus A300 was in the preliminary design phase. These airplanes would soon be in the world market and could have cost the 727 a substantial portion of its market share. Wide-body jetliners offered more-spacious cabins, putting narrow-body airplanes such as the 727 in a vulnerable position.

In an effort to hold on to the upper end of the 727's market, Boeing set about to make the narrow-body cabin as spacious and modern as possible. In 1969, Boeing began to market their Wide-Body Look interior program, which was intended to be offered straight from the factory on new-production 727-200s, and also as a cost-effective retrofit for existing 727-200, 707-320B, and 707-320C models. The kit replaced the sidewall panels, ceiling, overhead bins, and passenger service units with modernized, modular parts. This resulted in an increase of passenger headroom, creating the impression of a larger cabin.

The cabin lighting was also redesigned with overhead and sidewall florescent bulbs to establish a roomier look, while making use of modern materials that would meet the future FAA safety requirements pending at the time. In addition to this, great effort was put forth to lower sound levels through the use of sound suppression and revisions to the airplane's air-conditioning distribution systems, producing ambient noise reduction of 1–2 dB for aisle seat passengers. The new enclosed, latching overhead-bin configuration also supplied some measure of sound dampening just by the nature of their new design.

Brackets and attachments that transmitted the overhead-bin loads to the fuselage structure were also redesigned, allowing higher weight capacities than the previously existing "hat racks." The new passenger service units (PSUs) were flush with the ceiling over the passenger seats, equipped with three reading lights, gasper air outlets, and attendant call systems. Each seat row was equipped with four automatically deployed passenger oxygen masks, one for each seat and an extra for lap-held children. Each was specifically designed to make use of preexisting electrical connections and plumbing to the bottle-pressurized oxygen system. The spacing of the PSUs was

adjustable, with the addition or subtraction of blank panels to allow for variable seat pitch configurations.

The simplified sidewall panels, which replaced the early multipiece units, extended from floor to ceiling and incorporated sliding window shades, similar to the original equipment. The panels were recessed around the windows to contribute to the "big airplane" look of the cabin.

Extensive use of florescent lighting provided effective cabin illumination. *Courtesy of the Boeing Company via Chuck Ballard*

The increased headroom is evident in this photo. *Courtesy of the Boeing Company via Chuck Ballard*

The covered overhead bins were added for safety, as well as to enhance the clean look of the cabin. The Wide-Body Look interior was also available for retrofit on existing 727-200 and 707-300B/C aircraft. *Courtesy of the Boeing Company via Chuck Ballard*

To allow a relatively easy conversion, the existing four-, five-, or six-abreast seating could be retained, along with the galley installation. Conversions typically took place during the course of heavy maintenance checks, where the aircraft was already largely disassembled. Because of this, aircraft downtime was minimized and the passenger experience aboard the 727 was considerably enhanced. The first airlines to operate 727s with the new interior installed were Lufthansa and Air Algerie, both of which introduced the "Wide-Body Look" in 1971.

The 727-200 Advanced

In January 1971, Boeing issued a document titled "727 Product Development Program," which outlined the objectives for a new version of the 727-200, the 727-200 Advanced. During the late 1960s and early 1970s, the first generation of wide-body jetliners had made their debut and were popular with the traveling public. On the other hand, the world economy had entered a downturn, and orders for these airplanes stagnated to some extent. Boeing had spent millions of dollars researching how to improve the 727 to keep the aircraft's sales steady and strong. Much effort was spent on larger and higher-weight 727 concepts, known as the 727-300 and the 727-XX (see chapter 6 on page 168). During these unusually hard times, Boeing, instead of spending enormous sums of money on these possibilities, took the conservative approach, with the feeling that it would be more profitable to work with the existing 727-200 airframe to improve it to the maximum extent possible.

As discussed earlier in this chapter, while the standard 727-100 was typically range limited by available fuel volume, the basic 727-200 was normally load limited, which generally required a less-than-full cabin to allow completely full fuel tanks. Naturally, the addition of long-range fuel tanks, offered as a factory option, significantly highlighted this characteristic. In response to the situation, a factory retrofit was offered to increase the maximum takeoff weight from 170,000 pounds (or optionally 173,000 pounds) to 183,000 pounds, resulting in the 727-200 Advanced. In order to facilitate this, the standard airframe was modified as follows:

- additional reinforcement to strengthen the station 950 bulkhead
- replaced main-gear torsion link assembly with upgraded units
- replaced main landing gear wheels and tires with heavy-duty 50 × 50 units

- replaced four #2 fuel tank pumps with higher-capacity pumps with revised tubing
- replaced standard airspeed indicators with dual Vmo indicators

While these modifications required an average of 1,900 man-hours to accomplish, they greatly increased the maximum payload range of the aircraft, opening up the possibility of new routes for the 727-200. Increasing the number of passengers onboard, along with the attendant heavier baggage weights, required much-higher zero fuel weights (ZFWs). As its name implies, the ZFW is the actual weight of the loaded aircraft without fuel. Increasing this weight or the maximum takeoff weight (MTOW) requires further structural modifications, and in the case of the 727-200 Advanced, more-conservative speed limitations to be observed. As mentioned, a dual Vmo airspeed indicator was part of the modification. This instrument had a moving redline indicator that reflected limit speeds listed below, dependent on the actual weight of the aircraft. At light weights (typically below 172,000 MTOW or 136,000 ZFW), the 727-200 could be operated in "Mode A," which required only the use of standard speed limitations (notwithstanding ICAO airspace speed limits). The more conservative "Mode B" speed limits were in effect when operating above these weights.

MODE "A" LIMITATIONS		
Vmo (Maximum Indicated Airspeed):	Sea Level	380 knots
	5,000 feet	389 knots
	10,000 feet	398 knots
	15,000 feet	404 knots
	20,000 feet	409 knots
	21,500 feet	411 knots
Mmo (Maximum Indicated Mach Number):	Above 21,500 feet	.90 Mach
MODE "B" LIMITATIONS		
Vmo (Maximum Indicated Airspeed)	Sea Level	350 knots
	5,000 feet	352 knots
	10,000 feet	355 knots
	15,000 feet	359 knots
	20,000 feet	363 knots
	25,000 feet	369 knots
	26,500 feet	372 knots
Mmo (Maximum Indicated Mach Number)	Above 26,500 feet	.90 Mach
		.88 Mach*
*Some model versions vary		

Author's collection

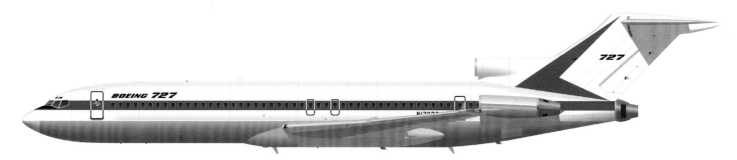

For marketing purposes, N1787B (727-276, c/n 20553, l/n 991) was painted in the standard Boeing test livery for only a few days before being repainted in Trans Australia Airlines colors and reregistered as VH-TBH.
Courtesy of Jennings Heilig

The 727-200 in the Wild

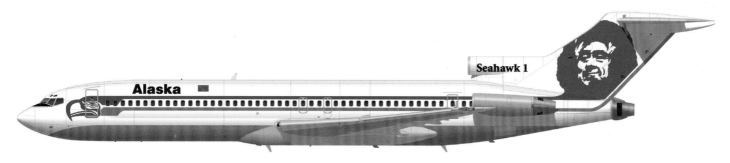

Alaska Airlines modified their standard paint scheme to show support for the Seattle Seahawks football team. *Courtesy of Jennings Heilig*

Air Canada operated C-GAAQ (c/n 21626, l/n 1472) until 1979, when it was converted for use as a freighter for Federal Express. *Courtesy of the Boeing Company*

An Air Florida 727-200 departs. Air Florida began service in 1971 and continued to operate until 1984. *Courtesy of the Boeing Company*

An American Airlines 727-223 is seen receiving finishing touches prior to its first flight. *Courtesy of the Boeing Company*

N261US (727-251, c/n 19980, l/n 706) first took flight on March 20, 1969, and spent its entire career with Northwest Airlines. *Courtesy of the Boeing Company*

An interesting shot of the number 1 engine as seen from below the inboard aileron. *Courtesy of the Boeing Company*

N7251U (727-222, c/n 21398, l/n 1296) served its whole operational career with United Airlines before being stored in October 2001. *Courtesy of the Boeing Company*

Delivered to National Airlines in 1968, N4744 (727-235, c/n 19464, l/n 553) was named "Donna" per the carrier's long-standing tradition of naming each aircraft after a company flight attendant. This aircraft ditched short of the runway at Pensacola, Florida, on May 8, 1978, while operating as National 193, killing three of the fifty-eight people onboard. *Courtesy of the Boeing Company*

Libyan Arab Airlines operated 5A-DAH (727-224, c/n 20244, l/n 650) for under two years before it was intercepted by a pair of Israeli F-4 Phantom II fighter jets after straying from its approved flight plan while operating as Libyan Arab Airlines Flight 114. After multiple attempts demanding that the aircraft land, the fighters fired on the airliner, and it crashed shortly thereafter with only five survivors. *Courtesy of the Boeing Company*

Hughes Airwest changed to this bright-yellow livery after one of the carrier's DC-9s experienced a midair collision with a McDonnell F-4 Phantom II in 1971. Because of this distinctive paint scheme, the airline adopted the slogan "Top Banana in the West." *Courtesy of the Boeing Company*

The Greek national carrier Olympic Airways took delivery of SX-CBB (727-284, c/n 20004, l/n 678) on January 16, 1969. The aircraft was originally named "Queen Anna Marie" but was later renamed "Mt. Pindos." *Courtesy of the Boeing Company*

USAir used variations of the Allegheny Airlines paint scheme for several years after the branding change. The aircraft seen here, N760AL (c/n 21953, l/n 1516), first flew on July 13, 1973. *Courtesy of the Boeing Company*

D-AHLT (c/n 21851, l/n 1551) flew for Hapag-Lloyd for less than four years before being handed over to Tunisair in 1983. *Courtesy of the Boeing Company*

Alitalia was an early-marketing-target carrier for Boeing. The Italian airline, after several years, did eventually become a loyal 727 customer. I-DIRI (c/n 21265, l/n 1226) left the fleet in 1984 and subsequently served with PEOPLExpress, Continental, and Kelowna Flightcraft Air Charter before finally being scrapped in 2015. *Courtesy of the Boeing Company*

All Nippon Airways was an early 727 customer, having operated several examples both of the 727-100 and -200 series. JA8355 (c/n 21474, l/n 1378) served with the carrier until August 18, 1978, when it flew the last revenue 727 flight for ANA. *Courtesy of the Boeing Company*

Singapore airlines operated ten 727s in fleet with the Boeing 737 and the larger Airbus A300. *Courtesy of the Boeing Company*

Air France operated F-BOJA (727-228, c/n 19543, l/n 541) from 1968 until 1991, accruing a total flight time of 42,626 hours. *Courtesy of the Boeing Company*

HC-BHM (c/n, 22078, l/n 1644) was delivered from Boeing to Transportes Aéreos Militares Ecuatorianos (TAME) on September 30, 1980, via the Fuerza Aerea Ecuatoriana (Ecuadorian air force) and served its entire operational life with the state carrier. *Courtesy of the Boeing Company*

Iraqi Airways was initially a Hawker Siddeley Trident 1E operator but much later operated a total of fifteen 727-200s from various sources. YI-AGM (c/n 21119, l/n 1203) was purchased directly from Boeing on May 7, 1976, and served with the carrier before being stored in 1991. *Courtesy of the Boeing Company*

An unidentified Syrianair 727-294 is seen departing Renton. Syrianair purchased a total of seven 727s from Boeing between 1976 and 1981. *Courtesy of the Boeing Company*

7T-VEW (727-2D6, c/n 22375, l/n 1723) was delivered to Air Algerie on March 11, 1981, and served its entire operational career with the airline before being withdrawn from service in 2005. *Courtesy of the Boeing Company*

Weight and balance calculations done mathematically are somewhat time consuming and can create a time crunch for the person responsible just prior to pushback from the gate. Some carriers, such as Eastern Airlines, were allowed to streamline the calculations a bit by using a nomograph and an appropriately scaled center-of-gravity chart. Starting at the point where "operating empty weight" and "empty center of gravity" cross in the lower left-hand corner of the chart, the nomograph was used to draw in the lines for total fuel, followed by total cargo bin weight, sliding down the scale for rear cargo bin weight, then forward passengers, aft passengers, and finally back to the fuel trace to depict burn-off. If the aircraft was within the allowable envelope for takeoff and zero fuel, then it was within structural weight and balance limits.

On the basis of the indicated takeoff weight, the performance charts were then consulted and the Takeoff Data Card was populated by the flight engineer. At a glance, this showed the pilots all the applicable data parameters for the takeoff. The EPR (a measurement of engine thrust) numbers were calculated on the basis of atmospheric conditions and annotated for the different phases of departure. Notice that two were listed (e.g., EPR 1.92/1.94); the first was for the pod engines (#1 and #3) and the second for the center engine (#2). The reason for this was that the bleed air demands for the pod engines were higher than those of the center engine, so therefore it was typical to have slightly different settings. The applicable flap and elevator trim settings were recorded, along with V1 (takeoff decision speed), Vr (rotate speed), and V2 (takeoff safety speed). The speeds for flap retraction would vary with weight and thus were also listed for each takeoff. In case of an emergency return, the fuel dump time required to bring the weight down to maximum landing weight (in this case, five

minutes) was computed and indicated on the lower right corner of the card.

Similar calculations were conducted by the flight engineer in preparation for landing. The landing weight was calculated by simply subtracting total fuel used from the takeoff weight. This number was then compared to the structural maximum landing weight for the aircraft, and the landing-performance charts were consulted to determine stopping distances. The 727 was designed to operate at high weights into smaller runways and had strong capabilities in this regard. However, on shorter runways, allowable landing weights were reduced significantly if antiskid braking or automatic spoilers were inoperative. For example, a 727-225 landing on Runway 4 at New York's La Guardia would typically have a 28,300-pound landing-weight penalty if the antiskid braking system was inoperative with wet-runway conditions. In many cases, this situation might require landing at a different airport with a longer runway.

After the determination was made that the landing was within performance limits, flap extension and approach speeds were derived from charts and listed on the Landing Data Card. In the event of a go-around, the EPR settings were also notated for quick reference in case a missed approach became necessary.

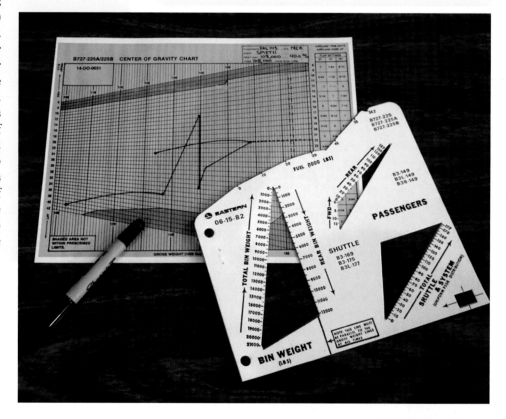

With the passenger counts, cargo bin weights, and total fuel aboard determined, this system was used to quickly confirm that the aircraft was within weight and balance limits both for takeoff and landing. *Author's collection*

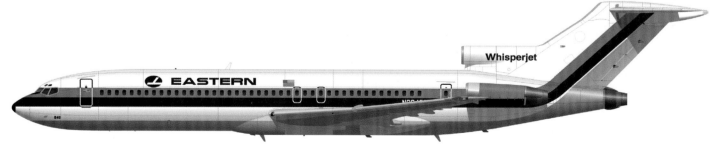

Courtesy of Jennings Heilig

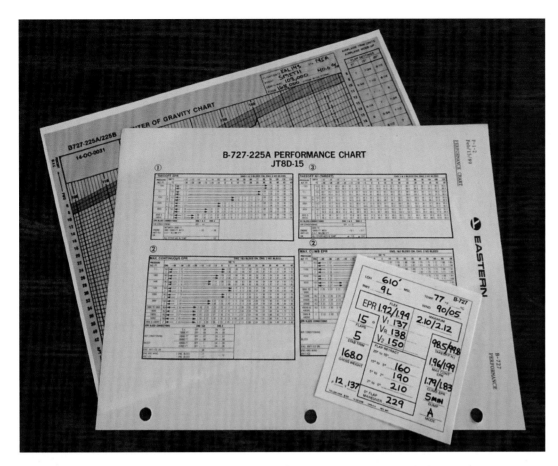

Once the takeoff weight was calculated, the flight engineer would consult the performance charts to determine the engine thrust EPR settings, flap setting, and appropriate V speeds. V1 is takeoff decision speed, Vr is the speed at which the nosewheels are raised from the runway, and V2 is the optimum initial climb speed with an engine failure. The EPRs are mismatched because of the differing bleed extraction requirements of the pod engines versus the center engine. *Author's collection*

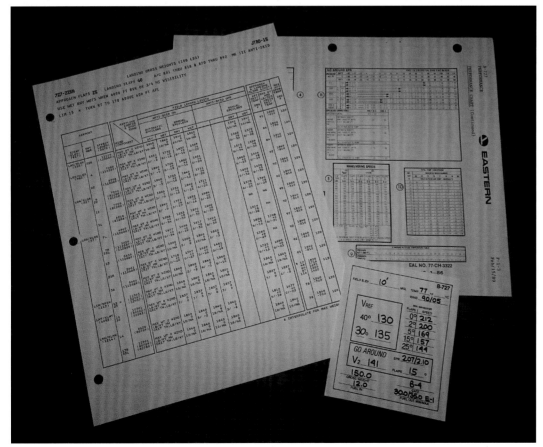

Landing-performance numbers were calculated by the flight engineer by using runway-specific performance data along with the aircraft charts. Changes in aircraft weights require different minimum (maneuvering) speeds for each flap setting to ensure that safe airspeeds are maintained. Vref is the minimum approach speed for the associated flap setting. Additives of 5–20 knots are applied to this number to account for wind and gusty conditions. Go-around thrust (EPR) and flap settings are calculated in advance in case of a last-minute missed approach. *Author's collection*

The rollout ceremony for the 1,000th 727 occurred with N474DA (c/n 20751, l/n 1000). This aircraft spent its entire operational life with Delta Air Lines after being delivered from Boeing on January 4, 1974. *Courtesy of the Boeing Company*

The 1,000th 727 is seen taxiing at Renton with the standard Delta paint scheme applied. Note the "1,000th 727" logo on the forward fuselage. *Courtesy of the Boeing Company*

The Turkish carrier Turk Hava Yollari operated several 727-200s alongside their fleet of Boeing 707s, DC-9s, DC-10s, and Fokker F27 turboprops. TC-JBG (727-2F2, c/n 20981, l/n 1086) is seen on the flight line at Renton being prepared for delivery alongside two other ships for the airline. *Courtesy of the Boeing Company*

YU-AKA (727-2H9, c/n 20930, l/n 1044) served with JAT before being reregistered as TC-AKD with Talia Airways. This aircraft crashed into high terrain during a ferry flight in Cyprus on May 31, 1974. *Courtesy of the Boeing Company*

The Sterling Airways Sale

The highest weight variant of the 727-200 Advanced came into existence because of the needs of Sterling Airways. Sterling was a Danish charter operator started by Eilif Krogager in 1962 with two ex-Swissair Douglas DC-6Bs to service the needs of his Denmark-based travel agency. Over time, the company grew and eventually began providing jet service with the use of Sud Caravelles, the first of which, a Caravelle 10B3, was delivered in 1965. By 1971, jet operations had expanded with Caravelle VIRs and "stretched" Caravelle 12s, but soon even more capacity was required. Sterling operated the Caravelle on the Stockholm–New York route in an exceptionally uncomfortable high-density seating layout of 28-inch pitch. Because of the range limitations of the Caravelle, which was designed as a short-to-medium-range jetliner, a planned fuel stop was always required. During a publicity event, the company's leader, Anders Helgstrand, was met by a reporter with microphone in hand. When asked if his customers minded the fuel stop, he responded, "To the contrary, they are grateful!"

Levity aside, Sterling began searching for just the right airplane in the early 1970s. Representatives from Airbus, Boeing, and McDonnell Douglas were called on to present their offerings for an aircraft with high-density seating to fill the carrier's needs. Boeing representative Fred Mitchell remembered pitching the 727-200 Advanced to Sterling:

> I had a lot of interesting assignments . . . and one of the assignments was when I was doing interiors for companies if they were interested in airplanes. We would send a specialist team out with a sales guy, and there were areas where we would allow them to customize the interior and the avionics a bit. We would try to get them to pick from a catalog. I made a lot of those trips, and there was one in particular on the 727, where we called out a few guys: Ves Zommers and the marketing guy, Don Hufford. So, they called me over and said, "We are thinking about a high-gross-weight version of the 727." It was 208,000 pounds, and they said that a potential customer, Sterling, was looking for new airplanes. McDonnell Douglas was in there with the DC-8, Airbus was there with the A310, and we wanted to go in with a 727 that would have to go down to the Canary Islands, from Copenhagen on charter operations.

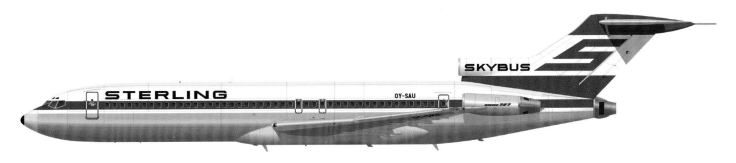

Courtesy of Jennings Heilig

Sterling operated a fleet of Sud Caravelles prior to the introduction of the high-gross-weight 727-200 Advanced aircraft to their fleet. *Author's collection*

Sterling was a one-man airline. One guy, Anders Helgstrand, ran everything. He was chief pilot, president of the airline, everything. So, they said, "You need to come over and do an interior." I was somewhere else at the time, and I got this wire: "You have to come out to this airline because we think he is really serious, and it has to be the highest density we can put in the airplane"—189 passengers in this case. So, we got up there and they said, "We are glad you are here. We are going to go out to dinner at his place, and he really wants to talk airplanes. Take notes because we don't have an interior. He has just decided that he is going to buy an airplane." What was happening, really, was that the competition was coming in to his office the next morning at 7:30. We had to give him a pitch and get him to sign. This was our time to lay something on the table.

We had some fantastic people whose job was to build

a rapport with the customer, and I think we are very straight forward and the customers trusted us. So we got out there, and the first thing he said was "Take all of your clothes off! I have got the sauna going." His house was right there on the Bering Sea, with a sauna and a big pool. He brought out a case of cold beer and threw it into the sauna. So, we all got in there and he started. "OK, how many passengers?," and we said, "175." Helgstrand demanded, "189, Fred; that's what I want!" I said, "Oh jeez; I will work on it." "No," he said, "I need a commitment tonight!" Then he started in: "Will it do the mission?" My teammates were telling me, "Yeah, sure; it will do the mission." He said, "OK, what is the price?"

After an hour, I was on the floor with a rag over my head! I said, "Jeez, give him what he wants!!" So, we had finished a whole case of beer, and holy cow, we were sweating away. So, he opened the door and said, "OK!," and we all jumped into the pool. We were all splashing around, and there was his wife making dinner for us. "Oh, thank God, we're done and we can have dinner and go back and try to draw up an airplane interior." He said, "I don't like the price. Back to the sauna!" So, we were there for another half hour. Finally, he decided, "OK, that is pretty good." We went up and had dinner and we had drunk a lot by now. He said, "I need you guys in my office at seven o'clock tomorrow morning, and you need to have the arrangement, the LOPA [author's note: LOPA stands for layout passenger accommodations], and Ves; we are going to need to sign something, and you guys, here is the range for the mission and that is it! Have a good night!" So, we got a cab and we went back to the hotel room with a blank piece of paper, and Ves said, "Jeez, maybe we ought to call Jack, Jack Steiner, who runs the place. . . . He doesn't know about this." Then he said, "Should we call Gray first?" I said, "Gray, that's Pratt & Whitney." He said, "Well he doesn't know that we have committed him to a new engine!"

Sterling's OY-SAU (727-2J4, c/n 20764, l/n 960) wearing a temporary Boeing test registration, N1779B, during flight test. Note the instrument calibration "bomb" attached to the lower fuselage, just aft of the wing trailing edge. This could be lowered on a cable into clean airflow to get accurate air data values. The small cone trailing from the vertical stabilizer's bullet fairing serves the same purpose and eventually replaced the "bomb." *Courtesy of the Boeing Company*

We were concerned about the aircraft weight. I happened to have a slide rule with me, and I did a few numbers on my old slide rule, and we said we could make it all right with lots of gas. We hadn't called anybody! It was just us!

When we arrived the next morning, Helgstrand greeted us: "You have to get in here early, because I am going to commit to Airbus, because of politics, for the A310." Then he said, "After a while (I am going to put enough in there so that I can get out of it) and I will just let it quietly go away. I will buy your airplane. Douglas, I will tell, 'Thanks, but no thanks.' Now, get out of here and leave that LOPA and whatever we signed." We went back home and called Gray and he had a fit! I don't know what Jack ever said; I wasn't in that meeting, but we sold the airplane!

Sterling took delivery of their first 727-2J4 Advanced (OY-SAU, c/n 20764, l/n 960) on November 15, 1973, after over three months of testing while registered as N1779B. Sterling took delivery of two more aircraft in the following weeks and ultimately purchased a total of eight 727s directly from Boeing.

This situation shows the strength of the corporate culture at Boeing during this time period, which encouraged and empowered representatives in the field to use their best judgment in making the difficult choices needed to clench the deal. This was especially important in those days where immediate communication with headquarters was often difficult, if not impossible. Jack Steiner is said to have not been upset by such decisions and was always looking to improve the capabilities of the Boeing products. Fred Mitchell continued:

We have had some very strong guys that were absolutely committed to Boeing. It is their life, and they take it as theirs. Each one takes it as theirs. I am talking about our bosses and people down through the ranks. They are willing to take risks.

This culture was not just tribal within the 727 program, since similar field decisions were also made in other Boeing programs, with similar successes. Bill Allen, Boeing's president during these years, led by example in being willing to take carefully calculated risks to ensure the advancement of the company.

By 1981, versions of the 727-200 Advanced had been certified with no fewer than three structural versions of the wing and four different engine options, yielding the following capabilities:

In addition to the structural modifications to allow these higher operating weights, airplane climb performance had to be considered as well. On each and every takeoff, calculations are made that assume that an engine failure will occur at the most inopportune time imaginable: after takeoff decision speed (V1) and before raising the nose up to continue the takeoff at rotation speed (Vr). Under this condition, the 727 will be required to continue the takeoff on two of its three engines, while clearing all obstacles in the departure path by specified margins. On many takeoffs, this is the parameter that limits maximum takeoff weights, particularly at high field elevations and ambient temperatures when terrain is a factor.

The Pratt & Whitney JT8D engine continually evolved since its service debut on the very first Boeing 727s. In fact, this engine became one of the most loved and successful aero engines in history, building a reputation for rugged dependability and bulletproof operation. One mechanic expressed his fondness of the engine and its brute robustness

The 727 on the Presidential Campaign Trail

Jimmy Carter disembarks from "Peanut One" during his successful campaign on September 8, 1976, at Pittsburgh, Pennsylvania. *Library of Congress*

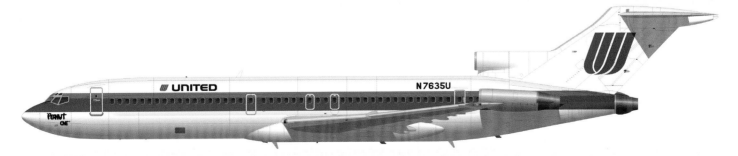

American president Jimmy Carter (1977–1981) leased United Airlines' N7635U (727-222, c/n 19908, l/n 653) during his presidential campaign. The name "Peanut One" was chosen because of Carter's involvement in the peanut-farming business. *Courtesy of Jennings Heilig*

by saying, "You can throw a bunch of rocks into a running JT8D and it will blow sand out the back!" While this was likely a bit of an exaggeration, it shows the respect that airline mechanics had for these engines. On the basis of this reliability, the JT8D was modified throughout the years to allow higher internal temperatures and pressures, thereby providing increases in thrust accordingly.

	Standard wing		Intermediate wing		High GW wing
	Basic	Option	Options		Option
Maximum taxi weight, lb	185 800	191 000	195 500	197 700	210 000*
Maximum takeoff weight, lb	184 800	190 500	194 800	197 000	209 500
Maximum landing weight, lb	154 500	154 500	154 500	154 500	161 000
Maximum zero fuel weight, lb	138 000	140 000	140 000	140 000	144 000
Engine/thrust, lb					
JT8D-9A/14,500	−9A**				
JT8D-15/15,500		−15	−15		
JT8D-17/16,000		−17	−17	−17	−17
JT8D-17R/17,400	−17R	−17R	−17R	−17R	−17R
Passenger capacity					
10%/90% at 38/32-33 in. pitch, 4/6 abreast			145		
All tourist, 32-33 in. pitch, 6 abreast			161		
All tourist, 32 in. pitch, 6 abreast			178		
All tourist 29/30 in. pitch, 6 abreast (exit limit)			189		
Fuel capacity, U.S. gallons					
Basic fuel		8090	8060		8105
Auxiliary fuel – one tank			860		
– two tanks			1670		
– three tanks			2480		
Cargo capacity – cu ft					
No auxiliary tanks			1525		
One auxiliary tank			1320		
Two auxiliary tanks			1130		
Three auxiliary tanks			810		

* Subject to noise limits
** JT8D-9A basic

This chart shows the different gross-weight and engine options available for the late-model 727-200 Advanced aircraft. *Courtesy of the Boeing Company*

The Pratt & Whitney JT8D-17R

The most powerful of the small-fan JT8D series was the -17R. This engine increased allowable thrust from 14,500 pounds (for the -9) to 17,400 pounds, although to save wear on the engines, the alternate takeoff thrust value (16,400 pounds) was normally used for takeoff. Because of the typical use of alternate takeoff thrust settings, the -17R employed another feature devised especially for the high-gross-weight 727s, which provided an automatic performance reserve (APR) system. The APR was designed to automatically increase engine thrust to 17,400 pounds on the remaining two engines in the case of an engine failure during takeoff and initial climb. When the aircraft was so equipped, the APR system was armed for every takeoff, provided both of the following criteria were met:

- Wing flaps set to a takeoff position (flaps 5–25)
- All engines operating above 70 percent N1 fan speed (>6,000 rpm)

Once these conditions existed on takeoff, a green APR ARMED light would illuminate on the flight engineer's panel to indicate that the system was active.

The performance increase provided by the JT8D-17R's APR system allowed for higher payloads or more fuel to be carried (or both), particularly out of climb-restricted fields. In order to create the JT8D-17R, starting with the base -17 engine, the following modifications were made:

Enhanced materials:
- Second-stage fan blades
- Third-, fifth-, and sixth-stage compressor blades
- Second-stage turbine stator vanes
- Diffuser fan duct fairings

Reinforced components:
- Tenth-stage compressor disk
- Third-stage turbine disk
- First- and second-stage fan case and rear turbine fairing containment

Modified components:
- Second-stage fan blade tip relief cut
- Seventh and eighth stator vanes recambered
- Spacers shortened between ninth- and tenth-stage and tenth- and eleventh-stage compressors
- Lengthened bolt holes on inlet case
- Takeoff thrust reset mechanism added to fuel control unit

N363PA (727-221, c/n 22535, l/n 1764) is seen during a predelivery flight. This aircraft, christened "Clipper Racer," was a late example of the Advanced model, equipped with the highest-thrust JT8D-17R engines. *Courtesy of the Boeing Company*

Republic Airlines absorbed Hughes Airwest during the merger mania after deregulation in the late 1980s. The modernized Republic paint scheme was based loosely on the North Central Airlines livery and still featured "Herman the Duck" on the vertical stabilizer. This aircraft, N715RC (c/n 22019, l/n 1584), is seen just prior to the official merger. *Courtesy of the Boeing Company*

Air Jamaica took delivery of 6Y-JMA (c/n 21105, l/n 1158) on August 22, 1975. This aircraft remained in service until December 20, 2016, when it crashed shortly after takeoff from Puerto Carreno, Colombia, for Bogotá, Colombia, operating as a cargo flight for Aero Sucre. *Courtesy of the Boeing Company*

Eastern Airlines branded their 727s and DC-9s as "Whisperjets." When the 727 entered service, it was much quieter than the pure turbojet aircraft that were prevalent at the time. Like many 727s, this airplane (727-225, c/n 21288, l/n 1234) went on to serve with Federal Express before being donated to the Spartan School of Aeronautics in Tulsa, Oklahoma. *Courtesy of the Boeing Company*

Another late-model 727-200 (N79746, c/n 22449, l/n 1756) is seen in the attractive livery of Continental Airlines. *Courtesy of the Boeing Company*

Landing the 727

The 727 was a unique airplane by design, with several characteristics that were a departure from its predecessors. In cruise flight the 727 was fast and exhibited low drag numbers, but on approach it was able to rapidly descend with the high-lift systems and landing gear extended. This, combined with the somewhat slow spool-up time for the JT8D from idle thrust, meant that the pilot needed to time the addition of approach power correctly. One other important observation about the 727 is that the pilot could not hear the engine noise in the cockpit. This is a cue to which many pilots had become accustomed, but the cockpit of the 727 did not offer this nuance to an unfamiliar pilot. A high sink rate, along with a late decision to increase thrust from idle, could have catastrophic consequences. The first 727 accident along these lines occurred on November 11, 1965, with United Airlines Flight 227, while attempting an approach in to Salt Lake City, Utah. The aircraft (N7030U, c/n 18322, l/n 130) made ground contact over 300 feet prior to the runway threshold, costing the lives of forty-three of the ninety-one people onboard. Shortly thereafter, on February 4, 1966, an All Nippon Airways 727-81 (JA8302, c/n 18822, l/n 126) crashed short of the airport during approach to Tokyo's Haneda Airport. While it cannot be verified, due to a lack of flight-recording hardware, it was certainly suspected that a similar cause was likely. It was found that crews operating the 727 were much more apt to have high sink rates on approaches due to the aircraft's capabilities. Retraining airline crews to specifically avoid this situation remedied the issue, leading to a much-improved safety record for the 727. Boeing test pilot Brien Wygle remembered landing the 727:

> When I was flying the 727 . . . I thought it was perfectly normal, but maybe it was experience on the B-47, B-52, and the Dash 80 that prepared us for that. Certainly, if you close the throttles at full flap, it is going to come down sharply.

Flaps 40 was the most extended flap setting, which offered slightly lower approach speeds than flaps 30. However, because of the higher induced drag, this configuration yielded aggressive descents if the thrust was left at idle. In response to this, some carriers, such as Trans World Airlines, took further precautions by locking out the flaps 40 selection entirely and instead exclusively used flaps 30 for normal landings.

Due to the highly swept wing, the 727 has a main landing gear that places the wheels a fair distance aft of the airplane's center of pitch rotation, causing the airplane to be a bit different during the last few feet of the approach. A sharp pitch up, right at the last second, causes a downforce on the tail prior to the wing's angle of attack, increasing its lift to check the aircraft's descent. The downforce, combined with the main landing gear's aft position, causes the main landing gear wheels to be smashed onto the runway with a hard, less-than-satisfying "thump." Many of the more experienced 727 pilots used a procedure commonly referred to as the "roll on" technique. The pilot arrests most of the descent rate passing through about 10 feet. Then, just prior to touchdown, the pilot eases the yoke forward. This has the opposite effect of allowing the wheels to gently slide onto the runway—that is, if the pilot's depth perception and timing are just right. More times than not, as the following piece by 727 pilot Len Morgan points out, the 727 does not give away smooth landings.

GREASERS WHEN LANDING A 727? NOT LIKELY.

The Three-Holer rewards a firm touchdown.

BY LEN MORGAN

Landing is the most interesting phase of flight in any airplane. In some ways it is the most challenging, particularly for a pilot unhappy with anything less than the delicious slide of rubber on concrete so aptly described as "painting it on."

The smoothness with which an airplane can be transformed from sleek flying machine to ungainly ground vehicle depends on several factors, most of them beyond a pilot's control. Take its landing gear: The DC-4 had large tires and long struts; hold it a foot off the runway with the nose up a few degrees and it would settle ever so softly onto the ground, making you look better than you were.

But "soft" landing gears are heavy, require large storage wells and therefore annoy designers whose last concern is flattering pilots. So they made the DC-6 noticeably stiff-legged. You could pull off a good landing in a -6 but a "greaser" was rare. The same was true of the Connie. The Electra was downright humbling; for gear it seemed to have cast-iron wheels and I-beam struts. A remarkable plane in many respects, it could loosen your fillings on arrival no matter how hard you tried. The 707, on the other hand, would often reward an attentive driver with a gentle touchdown. (And the 747 was an absolute delight, I would learn quite a few years later.)

I'd wondered how Boeing's novel trijet would compare. What an absolutely marvelous airplane! The 727 was more pilot-friendly from the first day than any other transport in my logs. It was easy to learn. The ground school was a snap and my flight training was completed days ahead of schedule without the customary simulator warm-up. Not everyone, however, found transition to the "Three-Holer" to go as smoothly. This is not to say I was sharper than average. Far from it; I am a slow learner. I breezed through 727 training simply because I had already flown the 707.

Qualifying on *that* brute was something else. It was almost three times the weight of the Electra I had been flying. It was ponderous, accelerated slowly even at maximum power and hurtled along at the bottom of descent with power at idle. Unless you stayed miles ahead of it on letdown, there was no option but to request a 360 while speed dwindled, a common embarrassment among newcomers to jet flying.

Something we piston drivers never appreciated until we lost it was the braking provided by idling props. The turbojet developed considerable shove even with thrust levers back against the stops. Precise speed control on final was extremely important. The 707 floated 1,000 feet for every 10 knots of excess speed over the fence. This could get you into trouble at a marginal field like Kansas City Municipal when braking action was reported as fair to poor.

The 707 was heavy on the controls until you learned to trim it. And, of course, we had to cope with its (then) astounding weight and blazing speed using the same instruments and navigation gear installed in piston equipment. The only computers in early jet cockpits were between the pilots' ears. Yet after 200 hours I felt completely at home in the new marvel and wouldn't have swapped it for a seat on the Stock Exchange.

This background provided a tremendous edge during transition to the 727, which is not to say it was a scaled-down version of its big sister. Boeing's new baby had rear-mounted engines, two rudders, four ailerons, 14 spoiler sections, 26 flap panels, nosewheel brakes and a tail skid. But the hydraulic, electrical and fuel systems were nearly identical to the 707's, as was the cockpit layout.

In everything I had previously flown, powerplant performance was monitored as much by listening as by what the gauges reported. The 727 cockpit was eerily quiet; in contrast, you were scarcely aware of engine thunder even at takeoff thrust. This took some getting used to.

In flight the 727 was a dream, light on the controls and delightfully responsive. Descent, approach and landing techniques came easily to anyone with 707 experience. When a radar controller requested an expedited descent, you eased back on the "speed brake" lever that deployed the flight spoilers and down you came like a load of sand. You could lose altitude at 4,000 fpm and faster if you dropped the gear. The

JAY VERGENZ

same trick in a 707, while safe and legal, caused an uncomfortable shuddering that made nervous passengers look out the windows.

Descent and approach posed no problems once you got the feel of the 727. Our descent drill was: idle thrust and Mach .80 from cruising level to 320 knots, then 320 to 10,000 feet, below which the speed limit was 250. The flight engineer noted weight and computed a reference speed (VREF), which was 1.3 times stalling speed with landing flaps. Depending on weight, VREF was 115 to 125 knots.

At five to 10 miles from the outer marker flaps were extended "on schedule." At 200 knots, the "Flaps 2" handle position extended a pair of leading-edge slats on each wing and dropped trailing-edge flaps two degrees. At 190 knots, "Flaps 5" dropped all remaining leading-edge slats and flaps and extended trailing-edge flaps to five degrees. At 160 knots "Flaps 15" was selected and at 140 you moved the flap control to "Flaps 25." The idea was to cross the outer marker with flaps extended 25 degrees and speed nailed on 140 knots. There was nothing to it after a bit of practice.

When the glideslope came alive you dropped the gear and landing flaps, reduced speed to VREF plus 10 and tidied up the cockpit for arrival. Small power adjustments thereafter kept speed and sink rate where they belonged from outer marker to airport— and it was important that they were closely monitored.

Decaying airspeed or increasing sink rate had to be immediately set right, particularly below 500 feet. Any combination of low speed, excessive rate of descent or spooled-down engines was potentially lethal. There was more than one disastrous 727 undershoot before this deadly combination was fully appreciated. You had to stay well ahead of the 727 at all times which, of course, means it's no different from any other airplane, large or small.

One thing we old piston drivers had to learn was that jets don't touch down on the numbers. Instead, you aimed them at a point 1,000 feet down the runway. That seemed like a waste of perfectly good concrete but it made sense in that it prevented a pilot a trifle low from dragging his wheels through the approach lights. The natural urge to "duck under" when breaking out of a 100-foot overcast had to be suppressed.

"Hold what you got" was the ironclad rule regarding descent rate once the runway came into view. (I must digress at this point. I can already hear the hoots of men and women pilots in Africa, South America and polar regions who routinely shoehorn 727s and other jets into short gravel strips where planting the mains on the numbers is imperative. My admiration for those gutsy troops is unbounded.)

It's said that a good approach offers the best shot at a good landing and I believe that's true. So you had best fly the Three-Holer precisely "on profile," properly trimmed, with speed and descent rate right on the money down to the runway threshold and ease off the power. What then? If you were landing on one of Portland, Oregon's incredibly smooth runways and it was wet from recent rain and it was one of your best days, you just might slick it on. But it was foolish to bet on it.

At most airports our passengers knew when flight ended. The touchdown was firm, though not uncomfortably so, and often produced a short skip. A sudden sink during flare in the stretched 727-200 could sometimes be offset by releasing back pressure on the wheel. This lowered the nose and slowed the descent rate of the rear-mounted main gear, avoiding a jarring arrival. Sounds crazy but it worked. The Three-Holer rarely embarrassed its pilots on landing; neither did it often reward them with a greaser—and that's a comment, not a complaint. You'll never hear anything but praise from me about Boeing's magnificent Model 727. □

Courtesy of Flying Magazine

Emergency Egress

N7625U (727-222, c/n 19542, l/n 586) is seen in flight during a predelivery shakedown flight. United Airlines ordered their early 727-223s with additional emergency exits installed just forward of the wing, one on either side, to aid in emergency egress of the high-capacity aircraft. Later, United decommissioned the additional exits as seating density was reduced. Although the painted door outline was removed, these early airplanes are discernible by noticing the nonstandard window spacing in this area. *Courtesy of the Boeing Company*

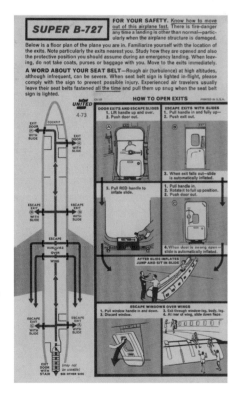

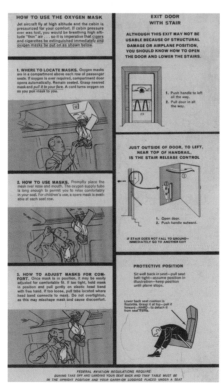

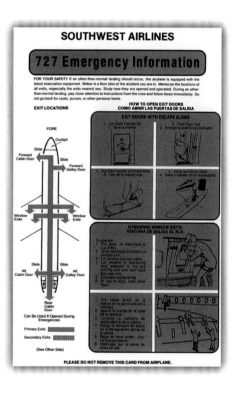

This 1973 United Airlines safety card details the additional midship escape hatches and their operation. The Southwest Airlines safety card shows the more common standard 727-200 exit configuration. *Courtesy of Southwest Airlines and author's collection*

The forward galley (R1) door is detailed in its normal at-the-gate, disarmed configuration, with the slide girt bar detached from the fittings on the floor. *Courtesy of the Boeing Company*

The standard passenger configuration for the 727 has two overwing exits on each side of the aircraft. They are plug-type exits that must first be pulled inside the aircraft, then either left in the cabin or rotated sideways and discarded onto the wing. *Courtesy of the Boeing Company*

The starboard aft galley (R2) door. This mockup does not appear to have a slide installed as it would in operation. *Courtesy of the Boeing Company*

The aft cabin exit door to the ventral airstairs doubled as seating for two flight attendants during flight. This exit opens inward and is a plug-type door. *Courtesy of the Boeing Company*

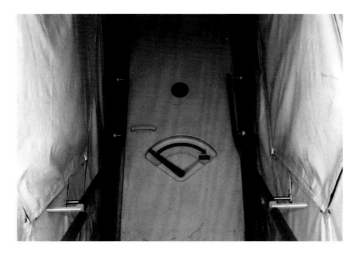

The aft cabin exit door as seen from the ventral airstair. This door was not equipped with a slide, but emergency egress was possible by using the ventral airstair, provided that the aircraft rested on its main landing gears. *Courtesy of Southwest Airlines*

The Flying Kings

JY-ADR (727-2D3, c/n 20885, l/n 1055) was an earlier aircraft with JT8D-9 engines and was known to be somewhat more performance limited than ALIA's newer 727-200s. *Courtesy of the Boeing Company*

King Hussein occupies the captain's seat and is seen preparing for departure aboard JY-ADU (727-2D3, c/n 20886, l/n 1061), christened "City of Amman." He is accompanied by Boeing's Sandy McMurray (*right seat*), and Les Bish in the flight engineer's seat. ALIA's chief pilot, Amin Husseini, is in the fourth observer seat. *Courtesy of the Boeing Company*

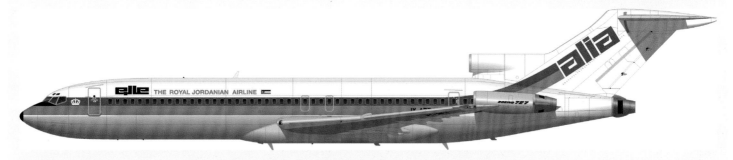

King Hussein of Jordan used ALIA's 727-200s as personal transports and often flew the aircraft himself, since he was an experienced pilot. JY-AFT (727-2D3, c/n 22268, l/n 1641) is shown as it appeared upon delivery to the airline on July 22, 1980. *Courtesy of Jennings Heilig*

King Hassan II wrote of the incident his memoir, *The Challenge*:

Royal Air Moroc purchased the Boeing 727-200 to further the operation of the state's airline and also for use as a personal transport for King Hassan II. Unrest was prevalent on August 16, 1972, when his 727-2B6 (CN-CCG, c/n 20471, l/n 848) was intercepted by four Northrop F-5 military fighter jets that demanded the aircraft land at the air base in Kenitra. King Hassan II, an experienced pilot, took control of the 727 and refused to divert, continuing to Rabat as planned. The rebel pilots attacked the king's aircraft with cannons blazing, injuring passengers in the cabin.

CN-RMP (727-2B6, c/n 21298, l/n 1246) was similar to the aircraft that was attacked. This ship flew with Royal Air Moroc from 1977 until 1998, when it was purchased by Kalitta Leasing and subsequently operated by Custom Air Cargo and Kalitta Charters. *Courtesy of the Boeing Company*

Author's collection

Because we refused to obey them, the fighters opened fire on us. Although we veered about, we could not avoid a direct hit. Some passengers were wounded, and I gave the orders for them to be tended as well as possible. We were extremely lucky that our petrol tanks were not hit, although a rocket narrowly missed them; we were lucky not to be in flames. Although hit several times and losing altitude at an alarming rate, we continued our course towards Rabat. The attacking pilots circling around us seemed to have lost their sang-froid. Major Kouera, who had run short of ammunition in his fighter, tried to ram us. He later came down by parachute in the sea near Rabat; when he was rescued, he told everything. Our Boeing was riddled with bullets, its landing gear demolished and its tyres punctured, but it managed to land at the end of the Rabat runway. (pp. 152–153)

Author's collection

Some accounts indicate that King Hassan himself, in a moment of quick thinking, transmitted on the radio, "Stop firing! The tyrant is dead!" The fighters, believing that they had succeeded in their mission, broke off and returned to base. In reality, both King Hassan II and his trusty 727 survived the incident, although the aircraft suffered a depressurized cabin and multiple areas of battle damage during the attack. Cannon fire from the fighters had struck the empennage, with one directly penetrating the spar structure of the vertical stabilizer. Subsequent to the ambush, King Hassan II was so grateful for the 727's rugged durability that he bestowed upon the aircraft an award called Wissam al-Arch (Order of the Throne) for its distinguished service, above and beyond what could be expected.

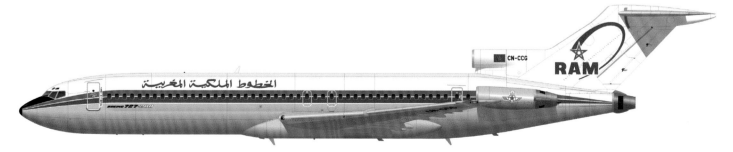

Courtesy of Jennings Heilig

Author's collection

Trijets from behind the Iron Curtain

During the 1960s and 1970s, the Soviet Union's airline services were blossoming, and new, modern aircraft designs were sought by Aeroflot and the Soviet government to expand service. Although most Soviet designs were unique, some of the aircraft configurations from the West were employed because the aircraft were designed to similar specifications. One such configuration was the rear-mounted, three-engine option, first developed by Sir Geoffrey de Havilland and made successful by the Boeing 727. In this section, we will explore three such aircraft that proved to be of significant service within the Soviet Union.

The Yakovlev Yak-40

The Yak-40 was much smaller than the Boeing 727 but used a similar tail design. This particular aircraft (c/n 9620247) was a later model that featured a thrust reverser for the center engine and higher-thrust power plants. In 1988, this aircraft was lost in a takeoff accident at the Sofia-Vrazhdebna Airport, Bulgaria, while operating for Hemus Air. *Courtesy of Petr Popelar*

The Yakovlev Design Bureau traces its roots back to 1927, when it designed and built the first AIR-2, a two-seat biplane featuring a single ADC-Cirrus power plant of a modest 60 horsepower. The bureau, headed by Aleksandr Sergeyevich Yakovlev, went on to produce many significant military aircraft during the Second World War, as well as during the Cold War and post–Cold War periods.

On April 30, 1965, the Yakovlev Design Bureau, which previously specialized mainly in military aircraft, was chosen to engage in the design and production of a three-engine jetliner. This airplane, which became the Yak-40, was designed to replace antiquated, propeller-driven airliners such as the Ilyushin IL-14P and the Antonov An-2. In order to fulfill this role, the Yak-40 needed to possess special short- and unpaved-field capability. Although the Yak-40 was much smaller than either the Trident or the 727, a similar trijet configuration was chosen with two aft-mounted, podded turbofan engines. A third engine was buried in the aft fuselage, complete with an S-duct installation and ventral airstair provisions. The Ivchenko AI-25 turbofan engine, rated to 3,310 pounds of thrust each, was chosen to power the new jetliner, which had a seating capacity of thirty-two passengers and a maximum takeoff gross weight of 35,000 pounds. Later versions of the aircraft came standard with the AI-25T engine, uprated to 3,860 pounds of thrust and with a thrust reverser added to the center engine. Because of the need for extreme short-field takeoff and landing capabilities, the Yak-40 featured a high-aspect-ratio wing with very little sweep. This not only sacrificed cruise speed but also forced the designers to place most of the passenger cabin forward of the wings.

In many ways, the Yak-40 was ahead of its time and was essentially one of the first designs similar to today's successful Regional Jet aircraft. It also possessed incredible short-field performance, with a published takeoff distance of 2,346 feet (715 meters). The later models, featuring the thrust reverser, produced an even more impressive landing distance of just 1,805 feet (550 meters)!

The Yak-40 proved to be successful, and production continued from 1966 through 1981, with a total of 1,011 aircraft produced. Aeroflot, the Russian national airline, operated Yak-40 service extensively to 276 destinations within the Soviet Union. Many different versions were built, including an adapted long-range export variant (the Yak-40D), cargo-passenger "combi" (the Yak-40K), and VIP specialized airplanes. Even bold concepts were explored, such as a vertical takeoff and landing (VTOL) version. This concept incorporated eight vertically mounted Kolesov RD36-35 turbojet engines, four in the forward fuselage and four in the tail, with the removal of the center engine and ventral airstair. The two podded engines were to be retained for forward thrust. This airplane, clearly borrowing some technology from Yakovlev's Yak-38 VTOL jet, was never produced, but it showed how the bureau left no stones unturned during research and development.

The Yakovlev Yak-42

In 1972, Aeroflot, impressed with their in-service experience operating the Yak-40, issued a specification to the Yakovlev Design Bureau for a short-to-medium-range jetliner with a capacity for 100 to 120 passengers. Some requirements for the new aircraft were similar to those issued for the Yak-40, including good short- and unimproved-runway capabilities. The first Yak-42 (CCCP-1974, c/n 01001) emerged in 1975 as an aircraft similar in configuration to the earlier Yak-40, but flying on a slightly swept wing of 11 degrees measured at one-quarter chord. Once again, the majority of the passenger cabin existed forward of the wing, but another airfoil, swept to 23 degrees, was installed on the second prototype (CCCP-1975, c/n 1002) and all subsequent production aircraft. The Lotarev (Ivchenko Progress) D-36 high-bypass-ratio turbofan engine was selected, with a maximum thrust of 14,330 pounds, quite similar to the early JT8D engines. While the Yak-42 was dimensionally similar to the 727-100, it lacked

The Yak-42 definitely bears some configuration similarity to the Boeing 727. The aircraft seen here (c/n 11840202) was built in 1978 and displayed at the Paris Airshow in 1981. *Courtesy of Petr Popelar*

the lifting capacity, full cabin range, and speed of its American counterpart.

Author's collection

After a lengthy gestation period, the Yak-42 entered service on May 15, 1979. Before long, however, difficulties with the aircraft type were on the horizon. The Yak-42 featured a variable-angle-of-incidence horizontal stabilizer to allow a wide range of speeds with adequate pitch control. In order to set the angle, a jackscrew assembly was provided, giving the pilot (or autopilot) precise speed control. On June 28, 1982, an Aeroflot Yak-42 (CCCP-42529, c/n 110400104) suffered a failure of the jackscrew assembly, causing the horizontal stabilizer to become completely uncontrollable. The aircraft crashed near Mozyr', Belarus, with the loss of all 132 people aboard. The entire Yak-42 fleet was grounded while the cause could be determined and a solution found. The jackscrew was discovered to have failed due to metal fatigue, and the mechanism was redesigned. The modified Yak-42 fleet reentered service in 1984, but significant damage was done to the airplane's reputation, and the expected production run of 2,000 aircraft was never realized. Although the exact number is unknown, it is estimated that roughly 200 Yak-42 airplanes were completed in a production

Author's collection

run that continued until 2003. Even though the Yak-42 was never seen as a commercial success, it did demonstrate the viability of the three-engine, T-tail design shared in common with the Boeing 727.

This Yak-42 (4L-TGG, c/n 4520423116579) was operated in the attractive livery of Airzena Georgian Airways. *Courtesy of Petr Popelar*

The Tupolev Tu-154 used pods to house its rearward-retracting main landing gear. Note the limited space between the landing gear pods and the side-mounted engines, which created challenges in loading and servicing the aircraft. With the 727-100 series being much shorter than the Tu-154, this was a major concern and caused a redesign of the main landing gear while the 727 was in early development. *Courtesy of Petr Popelar*

ЯК-42	YAK-42
Скорость – 750 км/час	Speed – 750 km per hour
Дальность – 3000 км	Range – 3,000 km
Высота – 9000 м	Altitude – 9,000 m
Количество пассажирских мест – 100–120	Seating capacity – 100/120

НАШ ДЕВИЗ – СКОРОСТЬ, КОМФОРТ, ГОСТЕПРИ-ИМСТВО!

AEROFLOT STANDS FOR SPEED, COMFORT, HOSPITALITY!

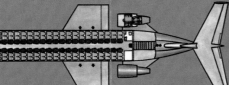

During the first half of the 1960s, the Soviet Union's Ministry of Civil Aviation sought to replace the aging IL-18 four-engine turboprop and the country's first jetliner, the Tupolev Tu-104. These aircraft were becoming overshadowed by advances in aircraft design from the West. The new airplane needed the ability to operate from an 8,202-foot-long runway with a passenger capacity of 150 to 160, and to travel at least 1,729 nautical miles.

Following the design and limited production of the Tupolev Tu-144 supersonic jetliner, the new design became known as the Tu-154, with Aleksander Shengardt as the project chief designer. In addition to the requirements already specified by the Ministry of Civil Aviation, he set additional requirements for the use of advanced high-lift devices and fully powered flight controls, while reducing pounds-per-square-foot loading on taxiways and runways, thereby making more airports accessible to the new machine.

In 1968, less than one year after the 727-200 entered service with Northeast Airlines, the Tu-154 first took to the air from the airfield at Zhukovski on October 3. The airplane was nominally larger than even the highly stretched 727-200, with a length and wingspan of 157 feet and 123 feet, respectively. The resemblance to the Boeing jet was striking, and unlike the Yak-40 and later Yak-42, the "Tupe" was as fast

This Soviet brochure shows details of the Yak-42. *Author's collection*

This Cold War–era brochure from Aeroflot highlights the modern cockpit and hospitality aboard the Tu-154. *Author's collection*

as the 727 at high altitudes, with a maximum Mach limit (Mmo) of M.90, and under some rare circumstances, such as with certain 727-200 airframes, operating under high-gross-weight "B Mode" limits, the Soviet machine was marginally faster. At low altitudes, however, where maximum indicated airspeed (Vmo) reigns versus Mach number, the Tu-154 airframe was limited to a much-slower speed of 310 knots. The first Tu-154 models featured three Kuznetsov NK-8-2 engines producing 20,943 pounds of thrust, while the later Tu-154M made use of the higher-thrust Soloviev D-30KU turbofan engines of 23,148 pounds of thrust, allowing higher takeoff weights up to 229,281 pounds, well in excess of even the later high-gross-weight 727 models.

The wing had a large surface area with an anhedral (downward inclination toward the wingtip) of 1.17 degrees but, like the 727, made use of high-lift devices and triple-redundant fully powered flight controls. As was considered during very early research and development for the 727, the main landing gears retracted rearward into pods mounted on the trailing edge of each wing. To provide for lower pavement loads, a six-wheel "bogie" configuration was used for the main landing gear, along with a dual wheel nose gear.

The Tu-154 was designed with a service life goal of 30,000 flying hours or 20,000 flight cycles, with a longevity of twenty-three years. Passenger service began on February 9, 1972, but it soon became apparent that the alloy (V95) used for the lower wing structure, while showing good strength statically, began showing signs of fatigue early in the aircraft's service life. This material was not robust enough to successfully tolerate fatigue due to repetitive flight cycles. The decision was made to redesign the lower wing box structure, using more-appropriate alloys for newly built aircraft. To reduce twisting forces to the wing, the ailerons were reduced to nearly half their original size. Roll control was more heavily augmented by flight spoilers, which exert their control forces farther inboard, further reducing fatigue. A retrofit program was concurrently initiated to replace the wings of aircraft already in service, at great expense.

Once the wing fatigue issues were solved, the Tu-154 went on to enjoy a successful service career, not only within the Soviet Union but also in many countries both inside and outside the Soviet Bloc. Some examples of the Tu-154 were modified from standard configuration for use during cosmonaut training, as VIP transports, and for cargo operations. One aircraft, CCCP-85035 (c/n 73A035), was converted from Tu-154B standard to test the use of alternative fuels and was redesignated as a Tu-155. This aircraft was equipped with one Kuznetsov NK-88 engine (starboard pod position), which was designed to operate either on liquid hydrogen, liquid natural gas, or traditional fossil fuels. Operations with this test-bed aircraft began in 1989, but by the early 1990s, the decline of the Soviet Union brought the program to a premature end.

The Tupolev Tu-155 was a modification of the Tu-154 jetliner, designed to test alternative fuels. *Courtesy of Artem Katranzhi via Wikimedia Commons*

The Tu-154, like its twin-jet predecessor, the Tu-134, enjoyed a lengthy service life within Russia that spanned over forty-four years. The type brought modern, high-speed jet transportation to many cities and towns around the world. However, all good things do come to an end. On December 25, 2016, a Tu-154B-2 (RA-85572, c/n 83A-572) crashed into the sea shortly after departure from the Adler/Sochi Airport, with a loss of all ninety-three people onboard. The flight, operated by the Russian Ministry of Defense, was carrying the world-famous Alexandrov Ensemble Russian Armed Forces Choir to the Latkia-Khmeimim Air Base in Syria. Theories of terrorist involvement and mechanical malfunctions of the aircraft's flap system were circulated haphazardly before a thorough investigation could be completed. Once due diligence had been conducted, it was found that the most plausible cause was spatial disorientation of the captain, who was the flying pilot at the time, which likely was exacerbated by fatigue issues. Although the accident was eventually determined to be due to human factors, the Russian government called for the permanent removal of all remaining Tu-154 aircraft from passenger

service, largely spelling the end of the contribution of this significant aircraft in Russian aviation history. Sources do indicate, however, that as of 2018, the Tu-154 continues to be operated in limited quantities by Air Koryo in the Democratic People's Republic of Korea.

Continued Marketing Efforts

While Boeing created the 727-200 for a specialized niche, it was also flexible enough to be truly successful. Even though the 727 stood on a foundation of strength, continued marketing efforts were constantly pursued. Boeing personnel sometimes even took predelivery aircraft to visit key customers. Such was one endeavor in February 1976, when Boeing leased a Trans Australia Airlines 727-276 (VH-TBL, c/n 20951, l/n 1101) to visit key customers in the Far East, using the airplane's cabin as a venue for presentations that put forth all the strong attributes of the aircraft. These types of marketing efforts were accomplished several times during the production life of the 727.

VH-TBL rests in Kuala Lumpur (ICAO: WMKK) during the 727-200 marketing tour. *Courtesy of the Boeing Company*

Singapore was also visited during the tour; Singapore Airlines was an important customer for Boeing. Through the decades, the carrier has operated many Boeing jets, including the 707, 727, 737, 747, 757, 777, and 787. *Courtesy of the Boeing Company*

Enthusiasts and airline employees admire the convenience offered by the 727's ventral airstair. *Courtesy of the Boeing Company*

The cabin of VH-TBL was temporarily set up to provide presentations to invited guests during the tour. *Courtesy of the Boeing Company*

This photo shows part of the standard 727-200 Advanced wing paint scheme. The leading edges and ailerons (both inboard and outboard) were bare aluminum, and the trailing edge, except for the ailerons, was painted Boeing Grey. The center section of the wing was coated with Coroguard, an epoxy-based paint that was impregnated with metallic particles and inhibited corrosion. *Courtesy of the Boeing Company*

The DC-9 Super 80

The Boeing 727, with its high cruise speed and short-field capabilities, remained largely unchallenged for nearly two decades. McDonnell Douglas was utilizing the "pincher effect" against the 727 by marketing the larger, longer-range DC-8-60 series and the smaller DC-9 twin jet to put the "squeeze" on Boeing. In Europe, the de Havilland (later Hawker Siddeley) Trident was too small to truly compete, although often being mistaken for a 727 because of the similar three-engine configuration. The closest aircraft that became available in the early 1970s was the Dassault Mercure, which was similar in seating capacity to the 727. This aircraft, however, employed only two JT8D-15 engines (instead of the 727's three) and was thus underpowered. Because of this, the otherwise advanced Mercure design lacked the lifting capability to match the long range of the 727, especially with a full cabin.

By the late 1970s, two important metrics began to catch up with the 727 design. The first was the public outcry about airport noise. The small-fan JT8D engines (particularly the uprated JT8D-17 and -17R models) created enormous amounts of noise, both at takeoff thrust and while on approach. The second issue was fuel consumption. Unrest in the Middle East had driven increases in jet fuel prices, leading the airlines to require more-fuel-efficient aircraft for their fleets in order to keep costs down. Airline deregulation, which was also occurring during the late 1970s in the United States, was another contributing factor in forcing airlines to tighten their belts. Prior to this, the long-standing government control over fare prices virtually ensured airline profitability, regardless of running costs. With deregulation this was no longer the case, and airlines were forced to compete in an open market. Profitability was ensured only for airlines that had the most cost-effective operations, with much of this efficiency being found in the ever-important selection of new aircraft.

The McDonnell Douglas DC-9 was a fine aircraft but offered more competition to Boeing's 737 than to the significantly larger 727-200. Seeing the need for a quieter and more efficient replacement for the 727, McDonnell Douglas made its move and launched the stretched DC-9 Super 80 (later rebranded as the MD-80). As we will see in chapter 6, simply changing engines on the 727 to create a more modern derivative was not easily achievable because of the S-duct design of the center engine inlet. Even a modest change in engine

Swissair was the launch customer for the DC-9 Super 80 (later known as the MD-80) series. HB-INU (c/n 49358, l/n 1294) was delivered to the carrier in 1986. The MD-80 series effectively replaced the 727 on many routes due to its quieter operation and improved specific fuel consumption. *Courtesy of Petr Popelar*

The Dassault Mercure was a great aircraft by many measures but had the wrong blend of lifting ability versus range; thus only twelve examples were constructed. *Author's collection*

fan diameter would drive a complete redesign of the entire tail section of the 727. The DC-9 design, with no center engine and podded, side-mounted engines, made for relatively simple adoption of larger engines when compared with the legacy 727.

During the early 1970s, Pratt & Whitney began to see further potential for their successful and "tough as nails" JT8D engine and endeavored to develop a higher-bypass derivative. This engine, based on the core of the standard JT8D, added a new enlarged, two-stage fan section. The new engine, marketed as the JT8D-200 series, was markedly quieter due to the additional air volume, which completely bypassed the engine's core. This larger amount of air, mixed with the jet exhaust from the core prior to being expelled out of the jet pipe, created a significant reduction in ambient noise levels. Additional benefits of the compressor redesign also created more fuel-efficient power and additional maximum takeoff thrust. This engine was a home run for McDonnell Douglas, because not only was this engine superior to the older JT8D variants, it possessed a fan diameter increase from 40 to 49 inches. The Long Beach manufacturer knew that this would be a challenging adaptation with the Boeing 727.

Stretching the fuselage of the DC-9 still presented many challenges for McDonnell Douglas, because an airplane is more than just engines; the body and wings have to be adapted to suit the new configuration. Boeing's Joe Sutter, who was deeply involved in the development of the 727 and spearheaded the 737 and 747 programs, commented on the difficulties faced with the DC-9 Super 80 development:

> You have your cockpit and your load-carrying passenger seats up front. If you wanted to stretch the airplane, you couldn't do it effectively. The MD-80 was a typical example of this. Even with a modest increase in engine weight, the fuselage was all in front of the wing. It becomes unbalanced very quickly . . . and you can't grow the airplane very easily. The future is limited.

Each one of the JT8D-200 series engines weighed nearly 1,000 pounds more than the traditional small-fan version. This additional weight caused most of the fuselage stretch to occur ahead of the wing, as Sutter indicated. Every airplane design employs a set of compromises, and the Super 80 was no different. Despite the challenges,

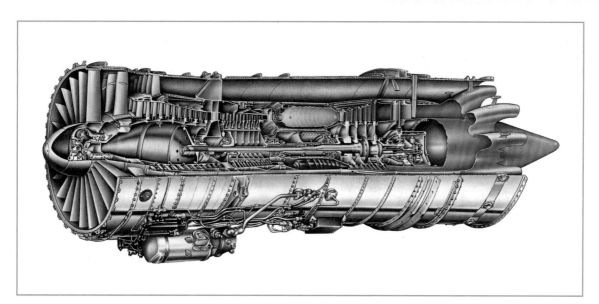

A cutaway drawing of the refanned JT8D-200-series engine. *Courtesy of Pratt & Whitney*

the reductions in fuel consumption and noise made the airplane very popular. The Super 80 entered service with Swissair on October 5, 1980. Many airlines followed suit, buying the aircraft to supplement and eventually replace many of the 727-200 aircraft in service. Airlines such as Pacific Southwest Airlines (PSA) and American Airlines were key examples of the 727 replacement effect caused by the introduction of the DC-9 Super 80. Because the stretched airplane's passenger capacity sat in between the 727-200 and the 737-200, airlines such as AirCal also used the Super 80 to replace their fleet of original-series 737 aircraft. Until Boeing introduced the ultra-fuel-efficient and quiet 737-300 in the mid-1980s, the Super 80 enjoyed a serious market advantage in its size class for nearly half a decade. Although there were challenges with weight and balance for the new DC-9 Super 80, the aircraft was a fierce competitor for Boeing and especially the 727. As years passed, aircraft retirements accelerated, with many 727s being relegated to cargo and foreign-airline operations.

Soon to be delivered to Air France, F-GCDC (727-228, c/n 22083, l/n 1605) is seen on a test flight over a smoking Mt. St. Helens on April 16, 1980. The volcano erupted less that forty-eight hours later, shedding a vast amount of the mountaintop in the process. *Courtesy of the Boeing Company*

N362PA (727-2D4, c/n 21856, l/n 1536) was painted in Ozark Airlines colors but was never taken up by the airline. This aircraft was subsequently repainted and served with Pan Am as "Clipper Frankfurt," later being renamed "Clipper Wide Awake." After the demise of Pan Am, this aircraft was modified as a freighter and flew for Federal Express as N288FE.

Western Airlines was a significant operator of the 727. N2807W (727-247, c/n 20579, l/n 886) was delivered to Western on May 12, 1972, and transferred to Delta Airlines during the merger of the two carriers on April 1, 1987. *Courtesy of the Boeing Company*

Kuwait Airways acquired 9K-AFA (727-269, c/n 22359, l/n 1652) from Boeing on September 25, 1980. In 1990, this aircraft was seized by the Iraqi government and operated for Iraqi Airways before being returned to the government of Kuwait in 1991. *Courtesy of the Boeing Company*

This retouched photograph depicts a 727 in British Caledonian colors, created for marketing purposes, although the British carrier never ordered the 727. *Courtesy of the Boeing Company*

It is a little-known fact that Southwest Airlines flew 727-200-series aircraft, leased from its rival, Braniff International. N406BN (727-291, c/n 19991, l/n 521) was leased from March 1, 1979, until January 1980, to provide temporary seat volume. *Courtesy of Southwest Airlines*

N406BN shown at the gate in 1979 with an experimental logo, which was not adopted fleetwide. *Courtesy of Southwest Airlines*

The Saga of TWA Flight 847

June 14, 1985, began as a normal day for the crew of Trans World Airlines Flight 847, with passenger service from Athens, Greece, to Rome, Italy. The weather was crystal clear, with a storm system having

Volume IX, No. 6   August 1983

Let's Go For It—Together!

Dear Fellow Employee:

Because I have been asked so many questions by so many of you concerning two recently instituted programs at Southwest Airlines, I thought it might be appropriate to address these two subjects in the form of an open letter to all employees.

Fleet Expansion

It is true that we have leased two 727-200's from People Express. We were given our "pick of the lot" from the Braniff airplanes not yet refurbished in People's livery, and we selected the two aircraft recommended by our Maintenance Department. Both these airplanes will be introduced in connection with our September 22nd schedule change and they will basically be used over longer-haul routes. We were able to secure very favorable lease arrangements with People in return for our arrangement to provide certain facilities and services for them. Each 727 lease is for one year, with an option to renew for an additional year. We are not currently negotiating for any other 727's. The reasons for our election to utilize the 727-200 are quite simple:

1. *The rental cost per seat per year is $4,429.00, as compared to a money cost of approximately $13,770.00 per seat per year for a new 737-200.*
2. *The price of jet fuel is down and appears stable.*
3. *Our 737-300's do not begin arriving until the end of 1984, and the 727 is a much more marketable long haul aircraft than the 737-200.*
4. *With the cessation of the FAA's slot control program, if we do not serve some of the more attractive, longer routes within our present system, our competitors will do it for us.*

In our continuing efforts to be a "good neighbor" to the homeowner groups concerned with noise at Love Field, the 727's will not be scheduled into or out of Love Field. They will remain overnight at Houston and will be maintained by Southwest at Houston.

Competition is the name of the game and, as you all know, Southwest has always prided itself on being a frontrunner in that game. Today is no exception — our aggressive September 22nd schedule will serve to reinforce that reputation!

In addition to the two leased 727-200's, we have also signed leases for three 737-200's. These leases will be for shorter periods of time and will more than likely terminate when our first quarter 1984 new 737-200's are delivered. In the interim, however, these leased planes will allow us to "beef up" our present schedules in many of our city-pair markets where we have had gaps attributable to slot constraints (such as San Antonio-Houston, San Antonio-Dallas, Austin-Houston, Austin-Dallas, and Lubbock-Dallas), as well as allow us to institute San Francisco-San Diego service which many of you have been wanting to do for a long time.

We will be offering extremely competitive fares over our new routings . . . very attractive frequencies . . . an aggressive advertising, marketing, and public relations campaign . . . dependable "on-time" performance . . . and the best employees in the industry — employees who are renowned for being warm, courteous, and cooperative, who continually accommodate our passengers in an efficient, quick, and friendly manner, and who constantly spread their own brand of SOUTHWEST SPIRIT (unmatched by any competitor, regardless of what may appear in other carriers' advertising) to our valued customers.

The Southwest Airlines company paper *Luv Lines* detailed the reintroduction of the 727-200 to augment the existing fleet of 737-200 equipment prior to the arrival of the new 737-300. Ultimately, Southwest leased six ex-Braniff 727-200s from PEOPLExpress between 1983 and 1986. Those aircraft were N551PE (727-227, c/n 20072, l/n 982), N561PE (727-227, c/n 21043, l/n 1113), N563PE (727-227, c/n 21045, l/n 1133), N564PE (727-227, c/n 21118, l/n 1167), N566PE (727-227, c/n 21242, l/n 1196), and N569PE (727-227, c/n 21245, l/n 1202). *Courtesy of Southwest Airlines*

moved through just two days prior. Capt. John Testrake, First Officer Phil Maresca, and Flight Engineer Christian Zimmermann were operating N64339 (c/n 20844, l/n 1065), a 727-231 Advanced model, for the short journey. After a normal departure and climb from Athens, loud banging was heard from the cabin. Pounding began on the cockpit door with increasing intensity until the door's lower blowout panel (provided in case of a cabin depressurization event) gave way, allowing hijackers to gain access to the cockpit.

Courtesy of Jennings Heilig

The cockpit crew of TWA 847 consisted of (*from left to right*) First Officer Phil Maresca, Capt. John Testrake, and Flight Engineer Christian Zimmermann. *Author's collection*

The two hijackers were Shiite Muslim extremists, coordinated by Hezbollah. Their goal was to gain an alliance with Amal, a larger and slightly less radical Shiite Muslim group, while attempting to gain release of other Shiites being held in Israel. It was later discovered that a third hijacker did not make it onto the airplane and was detained by Greek officials. The hijackers, described by Testrake as young men in their late teens or early twenties, spoke no English. However, it was soon discovered that one of them did know German, as did the flight's purser, Uli Derickson. The men, armed with a large-caliber handgun and grenades, demanded that the aircraft be diverted to Algiers, Algeria. The aircraft had only 17,000 pounds of fuel aboard and thus did not have enough fuel for the journey, so a landing in Beirut was negotiated instead. Upon arrival, the control tower at Beirut refused landing clearance to TWA 847 but relented when the crew insisted, being low on fuel by this point.

This 727-231 (N54341, c/n 21628, l/n 1454) is similar to the aircraft involved in the hijacking but displays the early outlined Trans World titles. *Courtesy of the Boeing Company*

While on the ground in Beirut, the aircraft was refueled and the release of seventeen women and two children was negotiated. Unfortunately, the treatment of the remaining passengers and crew became more extreme and abusive. Under these conditions, the aircraft departed for Algeria. The routing between Beirut and Algiers tested the range capability of the 727-200, with the added difficulty of there being no navigation airways in the region. This caused the

pilots to rely largely on dead-reckoning techniques, navigation using heading and time, corrected for forecasted wind, to complete the flight. The routing took TWA 847 over Cyprus, Crete, and Malta; north and just offshore of Tunisia; and farther west into Algiers, a total of 1,624 nautical miles. Arrival in Algeria did not provide the hijackers with the support that they demanded, as negotiations in Arabic over the aircraft's VHF radios became more and more heated. The captors became more violent with the passengers and also with Zimmermann, the flight engineer. The hijackers were able to negotiate refueling with the release of twenty-one more passengers, who were freed for "humanitarian reasons." When the fuel truck arrived at the aircraft, the fuel attendant refused to provide fuel without payment. They finally accepted Uli Derickson's Shell credit card to load 6,000 gallons of jet fuel into the tanks. The abuse of those left onboard continued to increase as the aircraft departed once again for Beirut.

When they arrived back over Beirut, their landing clearance was again refused, and this time the runways were blockaded. When the crew of TWA 847 indicated that they were going to land regardless because of fuel constraints, permission was finally granted, and one runway was opened while the flight circled on the little fuel reserve that remained. The aircraft landed and remained on the runway, where negotiations to gain support from Amal continued to fizzle. Sadly, in the early morning before dawn, one of the passengers who had been singled out by the terrorists for especially harsh treatment, US serviceman Robert Stetham, was executed and left on the runway. While demands for Amal support continued, the aircraft was taxied to the fueling ramp, where it was provided with fuel and meals by Middle East Airlines. Soon thereafter, several additional hijackers were brought onboard.

The terrorists learned that a possible Israeli raid was imminent, and became very motivated to leave Beirut. The destination was once again Algeria, and following their second arrival in Algiers, fuel was demanded and obtained by using Derickson's Shell credit card. The third hijacker, who had been detained in Athens, was permitted to join the hijacking as negotiated by the hijackers via radio communications. As provided by these negotiations, fifty passengers and the five flight attendants were released, leaving American men as all of the remaining hostages.

Along with the third original hijacker, a new terrorist leader, known as "Jihad," assumed control of the hijacking and, fortunately, was more moderate regarding the treatment of the hostages still onboard. On one occasion, he had passengers and the flight engineer role-play and scream into the microphone to have his demands met. Jihad indicated to Capt. Testrake that he wished to fly the aircraft to Aden, Yemen, but it was soon calculated that it was well outside the range of the aircraft and that a fuel stop would be required. There was discussion of going to Tehran, Iran, a course of action about which Testrake was deeply concerned. A compromise was made in returning to Beirut for a third time to refuel and then continue on to Aden via another, yet-to-be-determined fuel stop. At this point, Testrake, Maresca, and Zimmermann began to talk when they were left alone in the cockpit about somehow disabling the aircraft to end the incessant flight demands.

Again, the 727 departed for Beirut, and while en route, Testrake covertly attempted to contact other TWA aircraft that possessed long-range high-frequency (HF) radios to obtain information on the political implications of landing in Tehran. His thinking was that if the hijackers could obtain safe haven there, that course of action might bring the ordeal to a close. Unfortunately, he was unable to get useful information before the flight was back over Beirut. TWA 847, for the third time, was on approach after further negotiation with the control tower and landed safely.

Knowing that the hijackers understood little about the workings of the 727, Zimmermann began to "create" aircraft malfunctions to prohibit further flights. Beginning this deception early, the crew expressed to the hijackers that the engines were in bad shape because they were not receiving regular maintenance and needed to be overhauled. Upon touching down in Beirut, Zimmermann secretly cut fuel to engine 2, followed by engine 3 as they taxied in, drawing significant attention to the fact that the engines were "failing" and the aircraft could no longer fly. Jihad suggested that they receive replacement engines from Middle East Airlines, but Testrake pointed out that MEA's Boeing 707s used a different engine and that it would be of no use.

The hijackers, believing that they were truly stuck on the ground, took the remaining passengers from the aircraft to locations unknown to the crew. Only the pilots and the hijackers remained on the aircraft, using the auxiliary power unit for electricity and air-conditioning. When fuel became low from the nonstop APU use, the #1 engine was started and the aircraft was taxied to the fueling stand for replenishment.

American president Ronald Reagan holds a high-level meeting to help find a solution to the hijacking, which lasted more than two weeks. *Courtesy of the United States government*

The crew hostage situation had gone on for fourteen days when first officer Maresca was bitten, presumably by a spider, which resulted in a serious infection. A doctor from Middle East Airlines came to examine him and immediately ordered that he be taken to the American hospital in Beirut for treatment. Within minutes, he was off the aircraft and on his way to safer surroundings. After a total of seventeen days, Testrake and Zimmermann were taken from the aircraft to an apartment in downtown Beirut, where they were interviewed by reporters who appeared to be friendly with the Amal. After being allowed to sleep, the two were moved to a schoolyard, where they were eventually joined by the rest of the hostages, who were being held in remote locations in Beirut, most by the Amal and four by Hezbollah. Together, they were taken to Damascus, Syria, where they were released and flown to West Germany, finally leaving after seventeen days of captivity. The aircraft, N64339, went on to fly

for the airline for several more years and was even the test airplane for TWA's experimental "Project Skinny" bare-metal livery. Further, this aircraft operated TWA's last revenue flight from New Orleans, Louisiana, to St. Louis, Missouri, on September 3, 2000, bringing a thirty-six-year relationship between Trans World Airlines and the Boeing 727 to a close.

On July 2, 1979, Boeing rolled out the 1,500th 727 and celebrated the achievement with much fanfare and speeches made by prominent Boeing officials. N7297U was owned by United Airlines throughout its entire operational career but was leased to Northeastern International Airways in 1985. *Courtesy of the Boeing Company*

Author's collection

The End of the Line: The Last 727s

Courtesy of Jennings Heilig

Boeing delivered the last passenger 727 to USAir on April 6, 1983. Registered as N779AL, this aircraft (727-270, c/n 23052, l/n 1817) served with the carrier until March 1987, when it changed hands and continued to be operated by Sterling Airways (as OY-SBI) until 1994. After being stored for over two years, the aircraft was operated by Champion Air as N697CA, beginning in late 1997. Subsequently, this aircraft was placed in storage in Opa Locka, Florida.

Federal Express was the recipient of the last fifteen 727 airframes produced, which were delivered as pure freighters straight from the factory. All these airplanes were equipped with the upgraded Pratt &

Whitney JT8D-17A engines and integral tail stands (in addition to the airstair) to prevent tipping during cargo loading. The last of the breed N217FE (a 727-2S2F, c/n 22938, l/n 1832) was christened "Sonja" by the carrier and first flew on August 28, 1984. This historic aircraft was upgraded with the Valsan engine and winglet conversions and is still operating in dependable service with Oil Spill Response, registered as G-OSRA. Along with sister ship G-OSRB (c/n 22929, l/n 1823), Oil Spill Response uses 727s to aid in mitigating the environmental effects of maritime oil spills with the use of onboard chemical sprayers.

Last Passenger 727
Produced by Boeing
Delivered to USAir
April 6, 1983

Boeing Advanced 727-200
Line Number 1817
Delivery Number 1816
Serial Number 23052
Registry N779AL
Pratt & Whitney JT8D-17AR

Courtesy of Jennings Heilig

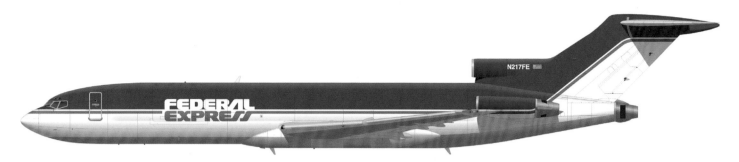

Courtesy of Jennings Heilig

N217FE was the last 727 produced and is seen here leaving the paint shop. *Courtesy of the Boeing Company*

This landmark aircraft marked the end of 727 production, with 1,832 aircraft completed. *Courtesy of the Boeing Company*

Courtesy of the Boeing Company

Last Scheduled Boeing 727 Passenger Service

Courtesy of Jennings Heilig

On January 13, 2019, the last scheduled passenger flight of the Boeing 727 was completed, marking the end of an era. The aircraft, EP-ASB (727-228 Advanced, c/n 22082, l/n 1603), operated this historic flight as Iran Aseman Airlines Flight EP851 from Zahedon, Iran, to Tehran, Iran. The aircraft, nearing its thirty-ninth birthday at the time of the flight, began life with Air France in 1980 and served with the French national carrier until 1991.

the first jet airliner fully approved for commercial operations from unimproved (gravel) runways. In all, a total of 1,832 Boeing 727s of all types were built.

In the next chapters, we will explore the efforts put forth by Boeing and others to modernize the 727 and continue production of this beautiful airplane. This interesting journey ultimately led to the creation of the new-technology Boeing 757.

Conclusion

The Boeing 727 was a magnificent achievement for Boeing and the thousands of people involved in the success of this tremendous aircraft. The 727 was the first civilian jet airliner to exceed the 1,000-sales threshold and remained the bestselling jetliner in history until later eclipsed by the Boeing 737 series. Additionally, it was the first airplane to have an auxiliary power unit together with self-contained airstairs and single-point refueling capability, giving the 727 less dependence on ground equipment. Pioneering features such as perforated intake shrouds and the use of the jet-mixing principle made the airplane significantly quieter than all others in operation at the time. This paved the way for the 727 becoming the first jet approved for routine operations from the noise-sensitive La Guardia Airport. The 727 was equally at home in more-rural locales, being

Lufthansa applied this attractive experimental finish to D-ABCI (727-230, c/n 20430, l/n 830) prior to the aircraft's removal from their fleet in 1986. *Courtesy of Petr Popelar*

Aftermarket 727 Modifications

Boeing continually improved the 727 design throughout its production run, successfully extracting every ounce of performance possible with the existing airframe and engine combination. As the airplane grew, environmental noise footprints became more of a public issue. This, along with a desire for increased fuel efficiency, caused aftermarket modifiers to enter the picture to extend the service life of the 727 airframe.

By modern standards, the first-generation, stock Pratt & Whitney JT8D engines were loud—very loud. This noise crisis was becoming quite apparent as time passed. In fact, the Federal Aviation Administration in Oklahoma City had a large picture of a JT8D hanging on the wall, with the very visible title underneath: "Public Enemy Number One." Quick to notice this, modifiers deployed several different methods to create stopgap solutions.

Raisbeck Quiet

Raisbeck Engineering, famous for the high-lift wing flap designs of its founder James Raisbeck, recognized that other modification companies were offering expensive fixes for the noise issue and sought a more affordable solution to enable the 727 to comply with the increasingly stringent noise rules. The noise issues were not just a factor on takeoff because of the higher power settings, though; they were also an issue on landing approaches. While other companies were focused solely on upgrading and retrofitting newer engines along with hush-kitting their tailpipes, Raisbeck saw another way to achieve similar results.

The modification was offered in three different versions, dependent on the needs of the airline customer and the weights at which the aircraft was being operated. TWA, an early customer, was utilizing a relatively low-maximum-weight version of the 727-200. Under normal circumstances, the 727 was approved for landing with flaps at position 30 (or 40, depending on the version of the aircraft), with position 25 as an "emergency only" landing selection. Raisbeck found that by limiting the landing flaps to position 25, the 727's approach noise footprint was markedly less and did not significantly increase landing distance. The only modifications needed for the airplane itself were to block off the position 30 and 40 detents on the flap lever and to modify the aural warning computer. James Raisbeck explained the situation:

> We modified and installed an available Boeing computer box, which compared the EPRs [engine thrust] of the three engines. Thus, the airplane became smart enough to know when it was taking off and when it was landing, even though the flaps were set at 25 degrees, and the otherwise noncancelable gear-warning horn was silenced after takeoff when the gear was raised. That constituted our Lightweight Noise Abatement System, met Stage 3 noise requirements, and was a cost-effective solution for many airlines using that model 727. That system sold for $695,000 and made it possible to keep those airplanes in service.

Other customers, such as American Airlines, were operating midweight versions of the aircraft. These required more-substantial modifications to obtain the same results due to the higher thrust-setting requirements for heavier aircraft, particularly on takeoff. Raisbeck discovered that by modifying the maximum travel of the extended leading edge slats, both takeoff and approach noise levels could be effectively mitigated. By reoptimizing the slat extension to

"KEEP'EM FLYING"
727 STAGE 3 By RAISBECK
THE SIMPLE SOLUTION!

- 103 Raisbeck Stage 3 727s in operation worldwide as of February 2000

- Customers include American Airlines, TWA, Pan Am, AllCanada Express and Avensa, among others

- Kits priced from $695,000 to $1,295,000

- Installation time from 30 to 215 man-hours

- Continued full support from Boeing and Pratt & Whitney

Contact: Susan Stahl
Vice-President, Marketing
Raisbeck Commercial
Air Group

Tel: 206-722-2020
Fax: 206-722-1892
Email: sstahl@raisbeck.com
www.raisbeck.com

RAISBECK
COMMERCIAL AIR
GROUP INC

Author's collection

a "less extended position," drag was considerably reduced while still providing good lift characteristics. This configuration, since it included eight new leading edge slat actuators and associated hardware, cost the airline $1.295 million per aircraft and one week of downtime. Even so, it was still much cheaper than the options from other modifiers, which could run more than $5 million each and required up to six weeks of downtime.

For the reconstituted Pan Am, which was operating the 727 at very high gross weights, Raisbeck offered the above modifications along with the inclusion of noise suppressors inside the jet pipes. This addition reduced engine noise at the increased thrust levels required for the operation of these aircraft at higher weights, and cost $1.695 million per ship set.

Raisbeck was able to abate many of the noise issues that the 727 was experiencing for much-lower cost, without adding substantial weight to the aft-mounted power plants on the 727-200, which was already prone to being tail heavy. Raisbeck's aerodynamic solution was a win-win for the airlines and environmentalists and allowed the 727 to have a longer service life than may have been otherwise possible. Overall, several hundred were sold both in the US and internationally.

The Dee Howard 727-100QF Quiet Freighter

The Dee Howard Company was started by Durrell U. "Dee" Howard as an aircraft modification firm, which found its beginnings modifying the venerable Lockheed Ventura and Lodestar twins into modernized executive transports. After years of success with corporate and private transports, Howard turned his sights on the jet noise problem and began looking for solutions to keep these otherwise good airplanes in the air while abiding by ever-tightening noise restrictions. Although Dee Howard wished to move exclusively into engine nacelle and thrust reverser design, other firms, such as Rohr, were already well established in the field. To allow the development of his nacelle systems without head-on competition with the larger companies, Dee Howard focused on retrofitting modern power plants to existing airframes.

During this period, Rolls-Royce was intent on providing a new-technology replacement for the aging Pratt & Whitney JT8D and introduced the Tay Mk. 620-15 high-bypass turbofan engine, rated to 13,320 pounds of thrust. Although based on the proven Rolls-Royce Spey Mk. 555 core, the Tay was highly modified. A larger twenty-two-blade fan section provided a much-higher bypass ratio than the Spey, increasing fuel efficiency while sharply reducing noise

Durrell U. "Dee" Howard, founder of the Dee Howard Company in San Antonio, Texas. *Courtesy of the Dee Howard Foundation*

levels. Similar to the Spey, the new engine retained a twelve-stage high-pressure compressor driven by a two-stage turbine section.

Dee Howard wished to interface the Tay engine with the 727-100 airframe but needed more thrust for ideal performance capability. Howard traveled to Great Britain, and Rolls-Royce agreed to create an uprated version capable of 15,400 pounds of takeoff thrust. The new engine, the Tay Mk. 651-54, featured a 2.92-to-1 bypass ratio and yielded a specific fuel consumption (lb./hr./lb. of thrust) of 0.69, which was roughly a 12.6 percent improvement in fuel efficiency over the legacy JT8D-7. However, there was a compromise, since the Tay was notably more thrust limited at higher altitudes. This could potentially demand lower cruising altitudes under certain high-weight conditions when the temperatures aloft were relatively warm.

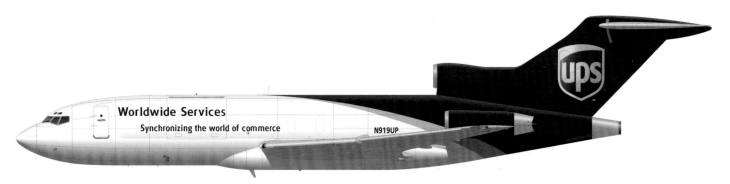

Courtesy of Jennings Heilig

One of United Parcel Service's 727-100-series freighters undergoes the Dee Howard QF conversion, which required extensive modification to the aircraft's vertical stabilizer and aft fuselage. *Courtesy of the Dee Howard Foundation*

All things considered, Dee Howard saw great potential with this engine for increasing longevity of the Boeing 727-100-series airframe. The noise contour for the reengined 727 was greatly reduced, being nearly 79 percent smaller. Additionally, fuel efficiency improvements extended the aircraft's range by nearly 300 nautical miles. The new power plant was approximately 310 pounds heavier than the JT8D, which, along with other required modifications, added 1,208 pounds to the aircraft's operating empty weight (OEW). The main challenge, however, was the change in fan diameter from 40.4 to 44.7 inches. While the pod-mounted #1 and #3 engines required a new cowl and thrust reverser system, these could be added with relative ease when compared to the center #2 engine. Dee Howard engaged in a complete redesign of the S-duct to accommodate the increase in airflow volume required by the new turbofan engine.

The provision for reverse thrust on the 727-100QF was provided on the pod-mounted engines only. The standard 727's pneumatically actuated thrust reverser system was replaced with a TR6510 target-type, hydraulically activated system, drawing power from the aircraft's 3,000 psi hydraulic system A. An additional accumulator was added to provide redundant emergency pressure in case of a system A failure. The center engine was equipped with an acoustically treated, non-thrust-reversing exhaust nozzle.

The modifications were not just limited to the power plant installation and related systems. The 727-100QF was also outfitted with the Collins electronic flight instrument system (EFIS), which replaced the original analog attitude and horizontal-situation indicators in front of both pilots. The flight engineer panel changed little in function with the exception of instrumentation and switch changes related to the Rolls-Royce power plants.

The primary customer for the Dee Howard 727-100 Quiet Freighter was United Parcel Service, which ultimately went on to operate fifty-one modified aircraft. Since some of these aircraft began life as passenger or "combi" airplanes, they still had provisions for cabin windows. UPS began to look for new ways to generate more revenue with the 727 fleet during off-peak times. UPS contracted PEMCO World Air Services to convert five of their 727-100QF aircraft interiors to the 727-100QC standard with palletized interiors. In this way, the aircraft would be used to conduct cargo transport during the week and fly passenger service on the weekends. Only four and a half hours would be required for the complete conversion (see "The 727QC" in chapter 3, page XXX, for more details) from freight to passenger modes, or vice versa. With this capability, UPS operated passenger operations with five aircraft: N946UP (c/n 19721, l/n 490), N947UP (c/n 19722, l/n 493), N949UP (c/n 19417, l/n 468), N950UP (c/n 19718, l/n 474), and N951UP (c/n 19850, l/n 497), all of which had once flown with Eastern Airlines as standard 727-25C aircraft delivered by Boeing. Flights began in 1997 and continued until late 2001, with service to such exotic destinations as Aruba and

This photo shows a comparison of the standard 727-100 (*foreground*) and the modified 727-100QF. Note the larger-diameter intakes of the QF model. *Courtesy of the Dee Howard Foundation*

Cancún on behalf of cruise ship companies. The experiment came to an end on September 3, 2001, just eight days prior to the 9/11 attacks. It was a great experiment in aircraft utilization, but UPS ultimately decided to return to flying freight exclusively. UPS's fleet of fifty-one 727-100QF airplanes soldiered on for several more years, with the last one finally being retired in August 2007.

It is noteworthy that UPS was not the only customer for the Dee Howard 727 treatment. A corporate operator, Westfield Aviation, converted an ex–American Airlines 727-23 (N727WF, c/n 20045, l/n 596) to the 727-100QF standard, while retaining a corporate interior and sporting the Valsan / Quiet Wing winglet retrofit package.

XA-FIE (727-264, c/n 21072, l/n 1145) was delivered new to Mexicana on June 23, 1975, and was given the name "Cancun." The fairing on the upper surface of the aft fuselage that houses the repositioned automatic direction finder (ADF) is discernible in this view. *Courtesy of the Boeing Company*

This corporate 727 (727-23, c/n 20045, l/n 596) was modified with QF modification, and Valsan / Quiet Wing winglets. This aircraft was originally delivered new to American Airlines in 1968. *Courtesy of the Dee Howard Foundation*

The Dee Howard 727-100QF program is one of the more complex 727 supplemental type certificate (STC) modification options for the 727, largely due to the extensive modifications involved. These were primarily the adaptation of the center-engine S-duct and major revisions to the engine-mounting hardware required for the Rolls-Royce engines, which shared no commonality with the JT8D equipment that they replaced. The modification was expensive to accomplish but very successfully brought the aircraft into compliance with the strict requirements of Stage 3 noise certification standards.

The Mexico City Factor

One of the more exciting 727 modifications involved operations out of Mexico City International Airport, which is nestled in a high-altitude mountain valley and routinely tests the performance capabilities of many airplanes. Under most circumstances the 727-200 was able to climb acceptably from the Mexican capital without issues. However, this changed when the national carrier, Mexicana, wished to fill their 727s with a full complement of passengers and capitalize on the fairly long range of the aircraft for flights deep into the United States. High-altitude airports cause performance issues for airplanes because the air is naturally thinner, requiring the aircraft to travel faster over the ground to gain the same lift as at sea level in zero-wind conditions. The engines also commonly produce less thrust at high-density

A total of six rocket engines were installed in the aft wing root fairings. This caused the repositioning of some hydraulic system B components and the ADF antenna to make space. *Courtesy of the Boeing Company*

altitudes, which is made worse by high ambient temperatures. The hot and high scenario requires the aircraft to accelerate to a higher speed and climb away with less available power to safely complete the maneuver.

All air carrier aircraft must be able to lose an engine at takeoff decision speed (V1) while still on the runway and continue their takeoff while clearing obstacles and terrain, with established buffers on every departure. Mexicana desired to take advantage of the high-gross-weight capabilities of their 727-200 series aircraft, but under high-weight conditions with the JT8D available at the time, an acceptable climb gradient was not possible for the first portion of the climb-out. The operation sought help and obtained the assistance of a company called De Vore, which specialized in providing military-style standby rocket engine systems to civilian users.

Author's collection

While never having been fired with an engine failure in service, the rocket assist system was thoroughly tested to verify operation and performance. Boeing had extensive experience using similar systems on the B-47 strategic bomber. *Courtesy of the Boeing Company*

This rare photo shows the repositioned ADF antenna (*green arrow*) and the special aft wing-to-body fairing designed to cover the unique rocket motors (*red arrow*). *Author's collection*

De Vore, in concert with Boeing, modified several of Mexicana's 727-200 aircraft with this rocket-powered system. Six Aerojet 15KS-1000-A1 thrust augmentation units, literally rocket engines, were mounted in the aft wing-to-body fairing areas, three on each side of the aircraft. The aft wing-to-body fairings are normally home to the B-system hydraulic pumps and reservoir on the left side, and the automatic direction finder (ADF) navigation hardware on the right side. To accommodate the installation, the B-system hydraulic components were moved forward into the air-conditioning pack bay, while the ADF antenna was moved to the top of the rear fuselage, under a long fairing. Naturally, a fire control system was required and added for the area around the rocket engine mountings. The entire conversion took approximately 1,800 man-hours to complete and added 1,250 pounds to the empty weight of the airplane.

Under normal three-engine conditions, the 727 climbed well, but if an engine failure occurred during takeoff and initial climb, these rockets would come in to play. If activated, the rocket engines would fire in an automatic sequence, activating two at a time. Approved only for flaps 15 takeoffs, although other settings were proposed and tested, the rockets would provide enough thrust to help the aircraft through the initial climb segments to meet the performance requirements. Other than during certification, this system was never used "for real" with an actual engine failure (although industry lore does tell the story of the system accidentally activating on the ground once, which likely got some unwanted attention!).

Valsan

The 727RE (Reengine)

During the late 1980s, a large portion of the 727 fleet was still operational and flying for airlines and operators around the world. Boeing delivered the last 727, destined for Federal Express, on September 18, 1984. The Boeing 757, an airplane featuring high-bypass turbofan engines and an advanced wing design, had much-improved specific fuel consumption characteristics over the 727 and other jetliners from earlier generations. Fuel prices were ever increasing, and, with airline deregulation looming on the horizon in the United States, airlines would soon be competing in a free market without

government price control. This brought fuel economy into a highly valued state, causing a bit of a conflict of priorities for the airlines, since the latest model 727-200s produced were less than a decade old and still years away from being sent out to pasture. This led aftermarket companies such as Valsan to explore the possibilities of using new technology to update the 727 design.

In the late 1980s, Valsan began looking at ways to use existing engine technology to improve the 727 and give it a new lease on life. The McDonnell Douglas MD-80-series airplanes had been in service for nearly a decade utilizing the refanned Pratt & Whitney JT8D-217 and -219 engines. Using the same basic engine core as the earlier JT8D-17 engines, with minor modifications, an entirely new, larger fan section was added. Since the refanned engines provided more thrust from the fan, the thrust level increased from 17,000 pounds each to 20,000 pounds for the -217 and 21,000 pounds for the -219 versions. The specific fuel consumption was substantially lower than the earlier JT8D engines, while the additional bypassed fan air considerably reduced engine noise.

The new engine's fan and inlet diameter was 8 inches larger than the standard engine on the 727. This meant that unless a modifier wished to rebuild and enlarge the center engine duct, the center engine needed to remain unchanged. The new engines could be installed in the pod positions with relative ease, however. Valsan elected to provide an acoustically treated exhaust for the original center engine, while installing engines and pods that were virtually identical to those on the MD-80. The new engines each weighed roughly 1,000 pounds more than those being replaced, which, combined with the additional thrust available, required Valsan to modify the aft fuselage to provide additional structural strength. Since the JT8D-217 and -219 engines required accessory lines and ducts that were somewhat larger than the earlier engines, all new pylons were also engineered and installed.

The difference in performance between a modified and unmodified 727 was astounding. The 727-200 was often performance limited under "hot and high" conditions, which commonly occurred at airports such as Denver's Stapleton Airport, which sits more than 5,000 feet above sea level. With an outside air temperature of 100 degrees F, a standard 727-200 was limited to a takeoff weight of roughly 146,000 pounds due to runway and climb constraints. A Valsan-modified airplane, though, could provide an additional 29,000 pounds of lifting capability under the same conditions. Equally important, the Valsan airplane was up to 8 dB quieter when compared to a standard 727 during takeoff and climb-out. This brought the airplane into compliance with the new Stage 3 noise limits, which were soon to be put into effect at many airports around the world. Overall fuel burn reductions of 10–15 percent were realized through the more efficient generation of power. Additionally, because the airplane could climb 23 percent faster, there was an increase in the percentage of the flight spent at optimum cruise altitudes. This naturally expanded its range by roughly 400 nautical miles over a standard 727-200 aircraft.

Although the engine modifications added roughly 3,300 pounds to the operating empty weight (OEW), the performance benefits, along with an extremely fast modification time of less than thirty days, the 727RE program provided the answer that many operators, such as Federal Express, were seeking. The 727RE program was subsequently purchased and marketed by Rohr (a subsidiary of BF Goodrich), which is well known for making engine cowlings and thrust reverser systems.

The Valsan / Quiet Wing Winglet Modification

Not content to stand on the laurels of the advances made possible with the 727RE program, Valsan looked for additional ways to harvest efficiencies from the 727 airframe. All conventional-winged aircraft use the Bernoulli effect to create low pressure above the wing, thereby causing the relatively high-pressure air beneath to seek equilibrium and move toward the lower-pressure air on top. Since the wing is in a position to block this migration of air from high to low pressure, the wing is lifted as it flies through the air. Some of this air inevitably spills around the wingtip, which creates a tornado-like vortex. Since this unwanted effect causes a significant amount of drag, engineers used winglets on the aircraft's wingtips as a counter. Winglets move the wake vortice outward and upward somewhat while harnessing some of the energy to create a small measure of forward thrust, reducing induced drag. Valsan designed a winglet modification for the 727 that replaced the OEM wingtip while providing the structural modifications required for safe, dependable operation. The first aircraft was modified with the newly designed composite winglets and flown in 1992.

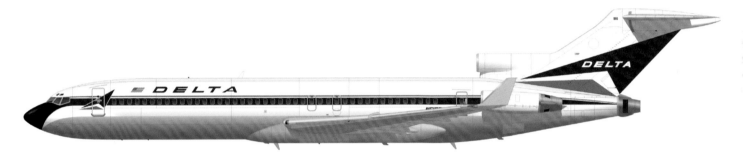

Delta Air Lines operated N510DA (727-232, c/n 21312, l/n 1330) along with N511DA (727-232, c/n 21313, l/n 1347) with winglets in the late 1990s. Note the serial numbers versus line numbers in this situation, which is interesting. The construction numbers are issued in order batches, while the line numbers are in order of production. *Courtesy of Jennings Heilig*

BF Goodrich and Rohr later held the rights to the Valsan JT8D-200-series engine retrofit, dubbed the "Super 27." Note the lack of a thrust reverser on the center engine, which was a standard small-fan JT8D, equipped with a special noise-attenuating tailpipe. *Author's collection*

There goes another

SUPER 27

BFGoodrich

This former United Airlines 727-22 (N7024U, c/n 18316, l/n 80) was used as the test bed for the Valsan / Quiet Wing winglets. The system generated efficiency gains of 6 percent with improved lifting performance.

The winglet was tufted with yarn to observe the local airflows around the surface.

The idea of using "winglets" to reduce drag was known, but to what extent was widely questioned. Wind tunnel data generally did not show a large improvement in drag with winglets because of Reynolds-number scaling effects, which involve using a scale model in the wind tunnel, which in turn presents differences in airflow and boundary layer thickness when compared to a full-scale aircraft. Computational Fluid Dynamics, a discipline using high-powered computers to model aerodynamic data, took into account the correct scaling of the airfoil/winglet combination and predicted substantial improvements in drag with the use of winglets.

The winglets are of composite construction, using graphite and epoxy layups. The outer skin of the surface is formed with a Nomex honeycomb layer bonded to the assembly. The winglet is then attached to the existing wing structure, with minimal structural changes.

As part of the winglet modification program, Valsan also took advantage of another known idiosyncrasy of the 727, which was a bit unusual. At high altitudes, it was known that if the trailing edge flaps were slightly extended, without the extension of the slats, the 727 could attain a higher cruising altitude and thus gain a measure of fuel efficiency not otherwise possible. As part of the winglet modification, the trailing edge flaps were modified to take advantage of this effect, and the ailerons were drooped slightly. This allowed slightly higher lift coefficients, which reduced drag and sometimes allowed higher cruising altitudes. Efficiency was not the only benefit gained with the trailing edge droop system though. The drooped trailing edges redistributed some of the structural loads imposed on the wing, offsetting much of the additional aerodynamic load created by the winglet itself.

The 727 winglet program, marketed today by Quiet Wing, provides up to a 6 percent improvement in fuel consumption, naturally translating into a similar increase of the maximum range. Additionally, takeoff performance is significantly enhanced, with up to an 18,000-pound increase in allowable payloads, and reduced CO_2 emissions are said to be positive byproducts of the winglet modification program.

Two-Pilot 727 Programs

In the early 1980s, Ronald Reagan formed the Presidential Task Force on Crew Complement. This group of industry experts was assembled to look at the possible safety ramifications of eliminating the flight engineer position on new airliner designs, effectively reducing the cockpit crew to just two pilots. While advances in technology and changes in traditional aircraft systems design could certainly automate many of the functions typically left to the flight engineer, the pilot and flight engineer unions had a different opinion, arguing that the third person's assistance was critical to safety. The argument that three minds were better than two certainly appeared from the outside to make logical sense, but airlines and aircraft manufacturers begged to differ and felt that the two-person cockpit was easily as safe as one with three. After weighing all the data and studying historical accident statistics, the Task Force concluded that two-pilot operations were as safe and, under non-normal circumstances, slightly safer than the traditional three-person-crew airplane. This was the case largely because of easier communication when only two people are involved, and there is less of a tendency to "troubleshoot" the system, increasing the risk of degrading the aircraft state further. In the midst of these studies, it was also proven that the ability of the flight engineer to spot traffic from their typical position in the cockpit was more or less nonexistent because of view angles through the windows versus the flight path of the airplane through the air.

Airplanes such as the Boeing 737 were designed to be operated by a flight crew of two, with a "set it and forget it" type of system that substantially reduced pilot workload while the plane was in flight. Other systems, such as the electrical system, provided automatic bus switching in the event of power source failures, leaving the pilots free to fly the aircraft and to run non-normal checklists on a time-permitting basis. Prior to the definitive findings of the task force, many airlines operated aircraft designed for two pilots with a flight engineer in the observer's seat, due to union pressure. The findings of the task force concluded that this was no longer necessary, and three-crew practices in two-pilot airplanes soon went to the wayside. A two-crew configuration offered airlines a substantial operating-cost advantage over three-crew airplanes such as the Boeing 727.

Shortly after the Presidential Task Force on Crew Complement concluded, a company called Page Avjet worked in conjunction with the famed flight instrument manufacturer Kollsman to explore the possibility of converting the three-person 727 cockpit to a two-person operation. The planned conversion, dubbed the "Boeing 727 Series Two-Pilot Flight Deck Conversion," was not intended to be a simple "Let's move everything from the flight engineer's panel to the pilot's overhead panel" conversion. When Boeing designed the 737 in the mid-1960s, its systems were made similar to the 727's where possible, but several changes were implemented to the electrical, fuel, and pneumatic systems to reduce pilot workload. Page Avjet clearly saw value in designing the two-person 727 cockpit as similar to the 737 as possible, so the proposed placement of the overhead systems was nearly identical to that of the 737, which would aid pilots in transitioning between the two airplane types.

One example of a high-workload item on the 727 was the fuel system. Managing this system kept the flight engineer quite busy, particularly during takeoff and climb, in keeping fuel tank quantities within prescribed limits while still ensuring positive fuel feed. The fuel system was to be automated with a triple-redundant computerized system, which would autonomously maintain the quantity limits but would provide a warning if the automatic system malfunctioned, so that the pilot could take manual control. While the 727 was designed with the ability to dump fuel in the event of an emergency, the progress of the fuel jettison needed to be carefully monitored by the flight engineer to avoid dumping too much. On the Page Avjet design, the dump limit could be set digitally, and the system controlled the process without the need for pilot intervention.

The electrical system was another that featured proposed changes to provide automatic bus transfer, eliminating the need for manually paralleled AC generator frequencies to make the system much more self-sufficient. This was allowed by modifying the electrical bus into a split system, similar to that of the 737, so that only one generator could supply AC power to a bus at a time.

Labor-intensive non-normal procedures, such as manual landing gear extension and alternate flap operation, were designed with electrically operated and controlled backups to reduce workloads. The original flight engineer panel on the 727 was much larger than the overhead panel, necessitating that Page Avjet redesign several panels. Likewise, reducing the number of required switches by combining multiple functions to a single switch could reduce the size requirement for the panel while simplifying operation. Where possible, push-button switches were to replace the traditional "throw" switch hardware, to create similarity with other newly designed airplanes.

To truly bring the 727 cockpit up to the state of the art, an electronic flight instrument system was included in the design, replacing the mechanical artificial horizon and horizontal situation indicators. With all these changes, it was hoped that new life could be breathed into the 727 airframe and reduce operating expenses, while significantly modernizing the airplane. The Page Avjet modification was marketed to carriers such as Delta Air Lines while it was presented to the Federal Aviation Administration for supplemental type certificate approval. Although much research and development time was spent on the Boeing 727-Series Two-Pilot Flight Deck Conversion project, it is not believed that any modified aircraft were ever flown.

After Page Avjet's failure to launch in 1987, five years later the World Auxiliary Power Company (WAPCO) came to the table with a similar plan to extend the life of the 727 and bring better economics to operators. The modifications proposed by WAPCO focused on removing the need for the flight engineer while maintaining minimal changes to the aircraft's basic systems. The goal of the two-crew 727 pilot workload being in parity with that of the 737-200 was the foundation for the design.

The proposed overhead panel bore some similarity in format to the 737-200, but most flight engineer's systems panels were left unchanged and simply moved to positions on the overhead panel. These systems included air-conditioning, anti-icing, hydraulics, fuel dump control, and pressurization. This was a slightly more minimalistic approach than was seen from the failed Page Avjet design, but, similarly,

high-workload systems were automated with modified cockpit panels. The electrical system was modified to allow automatic switching of essential power and bus tie contactors, mitigating much of the workload normally required of the flight engineer. The completely redesigned fuel control panel was to incorporate configuration warnings for the pilot to expedite corrections before errors would become critical. Several auxiliary system controls were placed in other locations, such as the cockpit sidewalls, outboard of the pilots, to allow easy reach while not expanding the already crowded overhead panel.

WAPCO also offered this modification to 727 operators, while pursuing FAA supplemental type certificate approval. Unfortunately, like the Page Avjet modification, it is not believed that any 727s ever entered service with the WAPCO modification. One can speculate as to why neither of these seemingly valuable modifications ever saw the light of day. These concepts came along late in the life cycle of the 727, the youngest of which was already eight years old at the time of WAPCO's application to the FAA. Another primary factor was that neither of these companies were directly supported by Boeing, causing additional engineering and research that required high levels of reverse engineering to make the ventures successful. Meanwhile, Boeing was building both the 757 and 737 "Classic" series, which were far quieter and fuel efficient, making carriers lean more toward replacing their 727 equipment than modifying an aging airframe.

The 727's lifespan was truncated to a large extent due to high specific fuel burn and oil prices during the period. Additionally, compared to the modern engines that were becoming commonplace in the late 1980s and early 1990s, the JT8D engine was loud and Stage 3 noise regulations were threatening the viability of the 727 for the foreseeable future. The limited perceived lifespan of the 727, due largely to these two factors, likely made both the Page Avjet and WAPCO solutions too expensive to be offset by the revenue savings garnered by eliminating the flight engineer. In the end, the two-pilot 727 was not meant to be. However, it is noteworthy that such feats have since been successfully completed on other aircraft types. FedEx operated the three-pilot McDonnell Douglas DC-10, alongside a sizable fleet of more-modern two-pilot McDonnell Douglas MD-11 freighters. Seeing many years of potential service for their DC-10 fleet, FedEx elected to have these airplanes modified to MD-10 standard, which eliminated the flight engineer position and made the pilot-aircraft interface similar to that of the MD-11.

Conclusion

We have studied examples of several aftermarket vendors who worked to extend the useful life of the robust and venerable Boeing 727 airframe. Attempts to increase performance while reducing operating costs and noise footprints were made in earnest, with some measure of success. At the same time, while not interested necessarily in modifying existing airframes, Boeing also spent many years attempting to modify the standard 727 design into a new and more efficient derivative for production. This interesting story, and how the follow-on Boeing 757 came to be, will be looked at in detail in the following chapter.

6

The Proposed
Boeing 727 Derivatives

The 1969 727-300 and 1971 727-XX Concepts

As early as November 1965, while the 727-200 was still in early development, Jack Steiner considered a larger 727, perhaps even with twin high-bypass turbofan engines envisioned for future development. Following the debut of the 727-200 in 1967, it became clear to the powers at Boeing that more capacity was needed and that continued growth of the successful 727 airframe was desirable. By this time, the newly formed Airbus Industrie consortium was developing the A300 wide-body twin jet. Many at Boeing felt that a higher-capacity 727 version would allow good competition in the market with the upcoming A300. Furthermore, an airplane of this size would fill the market gap between the wide-bodied McDonnell Douglas DC-10 and Lockheed L-1011 trijets, and the more compact 727-200-series airplanes.

By May 1969, Boeing had developed a concept known as the 727-300, designed to carry up to 189 passengers with a maximum takeoff weight of 208,000 pounds. This concept was a major redesign of the 727 airframe, versus a simple fuselage "stretch."

A standard 727-200 model (*top*) is compared with a scale model of the proposed 1969 727-300, a high-bypass turbofan twin using the General Electric CF6-50 power plant. *Courtesy of the Boeing Company*

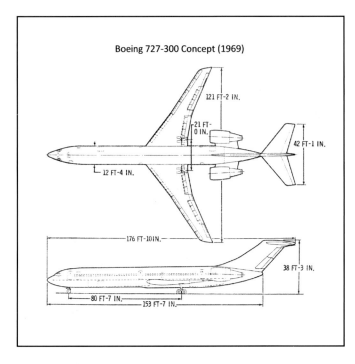

Boeing 727-300 Concept (1969)

121 FT-2 IN.

21 FT-0 IN.

42 FT-1 IN.

12 FT-4 IN.

176 FT-10 IN.

38 FT-3 IN.

80 FT-7 IN.

153 FT-7 IN.

Courtesy of the Boeing Company

The 1969 727-300 concept was intended to take advantage of the emerging high-bypass engine technology under development by General Electric for the DC-10. This engine, the CF6, would become available in July 1970 and was much quieter and featured specific fuel consumption projections that were superior to the low-bypass JT8D engines in use on the 727 fleet. As an option, the Rolls-Royce RB211-22 was also offered, with projected engine availability being slightly later in October 1970. During this time,

engine noise impact on the neighborhoods surrounding major airports around the world was becoming a very hot topic, so this configuration was seen as providing a large advantage for selling the new design in the worldwide market.

Using the 727 airframe as a twin jet dictated a substantial redesign of the aft fuselage and empennage of the aircraft in order to eliminate the center-engine S-duct, and to provide stronger mountings for the larger podded turbofan engines, one mounted on either side of the rear fuselage. Although it appears that the idea was to retain as much of the vertical-stabilizer structure from the legacy airplane as possible, modified horizontal stabilizers were planned to compensate for the required airframe changes.

The heavier aircraft weights involved pushed forth the need for additional wing area. A new wing center section was proposed that would add a total of 13 feet to the wingspan by utilizing two 6.5-foot inboard wing root extensions. Outboard of the new wing root section, the existing 727 wing design remained largely unchanged except for the required movement of the main landing gear bay into the new inboard wing root structure. This new design, with the additional wing area, was estimated to yield approach speeds up to 10 knots less for a given landing weight than the standard 727-200 wing. Due to the increased aircraft weight and concerns about wheel loading, a new four-wheel "bogie" main landing gear based on the Boeing 720 design was integrated into the concept. Wheel and brake assemblies were to have commonality with the Boeing 737 to reduce production expense and allow parts interchangeability while also supporting lower maintenance costs.

The 727-300 was scheduled to achieve FAA certification in late 1972, but, alas, the aircraft was never built. Boeing attempted to get the pulse of the industry and even offered to develop a wider version of the 727, known internally as the 727-XX, with seven-abreast seating. While an interior mockup for the 727-XX was constructed in 1971, high costs and lack of substantial interest played key roles in the decision not to proceed with the program. Additionally, during this time frame Boeing had costly development programs that had not yet reached financial equilibrium because of stagnating sales with the 737 and 747 programs. Boeing's Bruce Florsheim explained:

> During the period of 1969–1971, US airline orders tanked. The airlines just could not afford new jets. To get 727 sales going again, Jack Steiner worked with the airlines and created the 727-200 Advanced. The features on the Advanced came at low cost compared with a 727-300, and so efforts on the 727-300 were put aside.

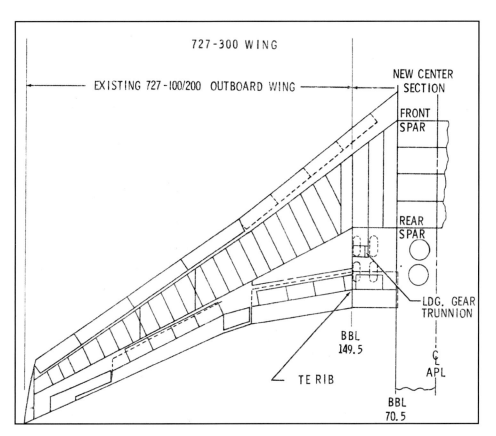

727-300 WING

EXISTING 727-100/200 OUTBOARD WING

NEW CENTER SECTION

FRONT SPAR

REAR SPAR

LDG. GEAR TRUNNION

BBL 149.5

TE RIB

APL

BBL 70.5

This diagram details the root extension of the wing to acquire the requisite wing area for the proposed gross-weight increase. *Courtesy of the Boeing Company*

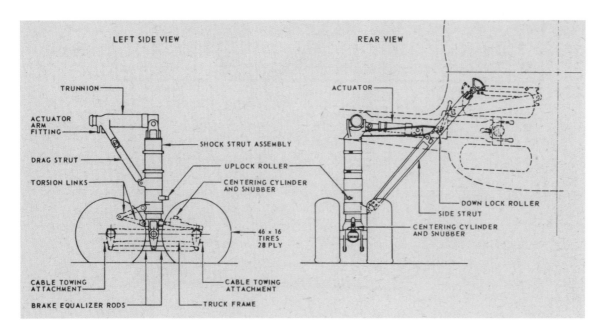

LEFT SIDE VIEW

TRUNNION

ACTUATOR
ARM
FITTING

DRAG STRUT

TORSION LINKS

SHOCK STRUT ASSEMBLY

UPLOCK ROLLER

CENTERING CYLINDER
AND SNUBBER

46 x 16
TIRES
28 PLY

CABLE TOWING
ATTACHMENT

CABLE TOWING
ATTACHMENT

BRAKE EQUALIZER RODS

TRUCK FRAME

REAR VIEW

ACTUATOR

DOWN LOCK ROLLER

SIDE STRUT

CENTERING CYLINDER
AND SNUBBER

The main landing gear design for the 1969 727-300 concept was based on those used on the Boeing 720. *Courtesy of the Boeing Company*

Launching a major redesign during this period was deemed prohibitively expensive for the company. As a stopgap measure, Boeing instead launched the Advanced 727-200, essentially a modernization of the extant 727-200 airframe, which required minimal expenditures during this difficult time of financial recession (see "The 727-200 Advanced" on page 125).

The 1973 727-300B Concept

After Boeing decided that it was not financially viable to produce the 1969 and 1971 Boeing 727 derivative concepts, engineers explored options with marketing to increase the capacity and lift of the 727 airframe with minimal modifications. In the first quarter of 1973, new "stretched" 727-300 concepts were being studied to make a larger capacity 727 model marketable. Several iterations were explored, mostly focused on an approximate 180-inch stretch to the fuselage.

One of the main concepts that showed promise was known internally as the 727-300-S15H and marketed as the 727-300. While the 1969 727 concept featured major changes to the wing and the empennage, the new directive was to minimize these expenses while attaining a majority of the original goals. Boeing studied the possibilities and surveyed airline interest.

The most important attribute of the 727-300 was the lengthening of the fuselage to accommodate more seats and cargo. This stretch was designed to be executed entirely within Section 44: the portion of the fuselage that mates with the wing structure. Within this section, one 120-inch extension was designed forward of the wing box, while another 60-inch plug provided balance behind the wing structure. This left the forward fuselage, Section 43, and the aft fuselage sections, Sections 46 and 48, largely unmodified except for some additional structural enhancements. As with so many of Boeing's cost saving decisions, the stretch would retain much of the component and manufacturing commonality.

A model of the proposed 727-300B. *Courtesy of the Boeing Company*

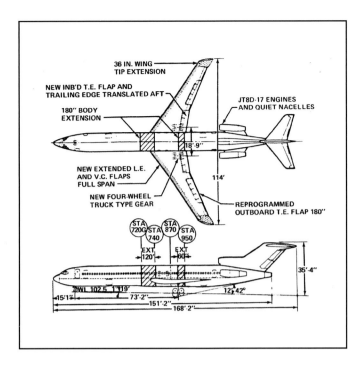

The 1973 Boeing 727-300B (727-300-S15) concept was intended to incorporate a substantial fuselage stretch beyond the dimensions of the 727-200. *Courtesy of the Boeing Company*

A full-scale mockup of the 1973 Boeing 727-300B concept was constructed to confirm the fitment of parts in a 3-D environment. Today, the use of advanced computer programs such as CATIA largely eliminates the need for full-scale mockups. *Courtesy of the Boeing Company*

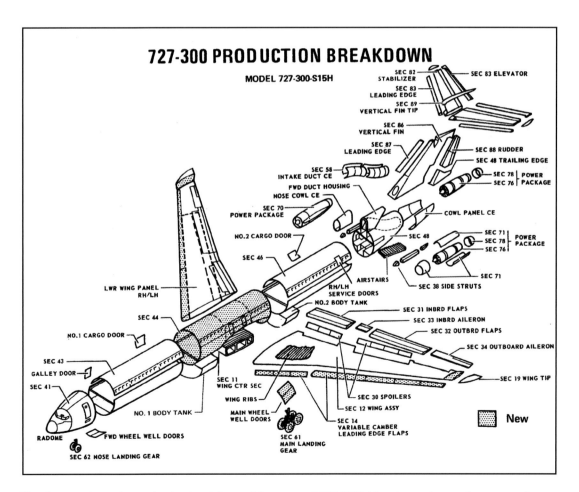

This diagram shows the production breakdown of the proposed 727-300B. Note the section numbers, most of which are common to other Boeing aircraft types as well. *Courtesy of the Boeing Company*

This is a mockup of the right main landing gear for the 727-300B. *Courtesy of the Boeing Company*

Due to the higher gross weight and concern about tire loads and braking effectiveness, a four-wheel bogie main landing gear was devised that featured wheels and brakes from the Boeing 737, similar to the 1969 concept. This assembly, when retracted, would require more center-section wheel well space. The 60-inch length increase of the aft portion of section 44 served a dual purpose, since it was also designed to accommodate this additional required wheel well volume.

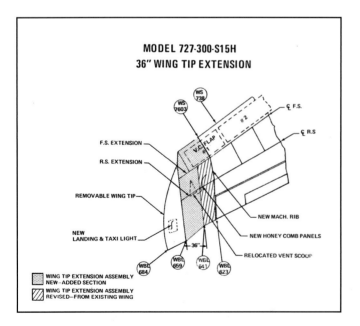

The expansion of the wing area required for the proposed 727-300B was gained by adding a 3-foot extension to each wingtip and additional area to the trailing edge between the inboard aileron and the fuselage. *Courtesy of the Boeing Company*

Wing area on the 727-300 required expansion so that takeoff and landing performance would not be substantially hampered by increased speeds. In order to accomplish this, the standard high gross weight 727-200 Advanced wing design was modified with 36-inch, bolt-on wingtip extensions. The inboard trailing edge flap assembly was also amended and translated aft with a revised 90-degree trailing edge. This type of wing modification allowed for an increase in wing area as well as providing additional space for the new, larger main landing gear. Due to this change, the inboard spoilers and associated hardware installations were moved aft, which in turn caused design changes to the inboard wing structure. Some technology was drawn from the Boeing 747 leading edge device configuration. Variable-camber leading edge Krueger flaps were used to replace the existing rigid Krueger flaps and outboard-mounted slats. Like the 747, these devices were stowed in the lower leading edge area during high speed flight. While stowed, these panels contoured to the bottom of the wing, which was fairly flat. During takeoff, approach, and landing, they were extended in concert with the trailing edge flaps. During the deployment process, these flexible panels would extend and become more curved, re-cambered by the extension hardware into a more rounded shape for maximum lift.

The 727-300B wind tunnel model exhibited a strong propensity for the deep stall characteristic. *Courtesy of the Boeing Company*

Ship Two (c/n 18464, l/n 2) was retained by Boeing for use as a test bed for its entire operational life and was reregistered as N1784B in 1971, prior to conducting the 727-300B wing trials. Vmu tests were carried out with full-span, variable-camber Krueger flaps installed. Note the additional tail skid attached aft of the pod-mounted engines to protect the center engine tailpipe. *Courtesy of the Boeing Company*

There were also additional revisions incorporated into the new design. The proposed wing modifications propagated minor changes to the wing-to-body fairings, and the main landing gear doors needed to be lengthened to accommodate the larger main landing gears. In order to maximize range, an additional center tank cell was planned for installation forward of the wing box structure. Due to the extended length and added fuselage height above ramp level provided by the new landing gear units, the ventral airstair, which was initially retained in the design, was reconfigured to be slightly longer. In the interest of minimal design changes, particularly to the complex Section 48 and the incorporated Number 2 engine S-duct, the 727-300 was to retain the standard JT8D powerplants, with the highest thrust ratings

available. A change to a higher bypass engine would alter the diameter requirement of the S-duct and potentially create an avalanche of expensive design modifications.

During the same time period, Boeing engineers considered adding some of these developments to the existing 727-200 airframe, as it was still selling quite well. Known as the 727-200B, this concept was intended to incorporate the leading edge devices and 36-inch wingtip extensions of the 727-300, optimizing lift over the stock 727-200 wing. This high lift configuration, combined with the three-foot wingtip extensions and the revised inboard trailing edge was tested extensively on Ship Two, which had previously been re-registered as N1784B and repainted in the attractive white and red Boeing demonstrator paint scheme. Soon thereafter, flight testing began for the new 727-200B and -300 wing configuration.

Alan Mulally, an aerodynamics engineer with Boeing at the time, shared his experience with flight testing the new 727-300 wing on N1784B. The deep stall phenomenon experienced first-hand by Lew Wallick on the 727-100 program was still fresh in the minds of the flight test pilots as Mulally explained:

We had the 727-100 and then we stretched it to the 727-200. Then we had this idea, because it works really well in airplane design, to stretch the vehicles and get all of the performance out of them. We decided that we were going to stretch it again, but we needed some powerful leading edge devices to be able to fly the extra weight at the lower speeds. So, we came up with the idea of putting [on] these leading edges, these powerful Krueger flaps that are on the 747 . . . variable-camber Krueger flaps. So, we were going to put them on the wing of the 727.

Now, one design challenge for a T-tail airplane is what we call "deep stall." At high angles of attack, you can get a lot of turbulence off the wing when it starts to stall, and it can blanket the tail, which makes it very hard to control the airplane. And Lew was this fantastic pilot . . . just fantastic . . . he kind of adopted me and told me what I needed to know. And, so I ended up being assigned to be the stability control engineer for this flight test. I was part of the team that was doing all of the wind tunnel testing . . . figuring out how to scale it up to the Reynolds number of flight. He took me aside a couple of times and explained to me this characteristic of this deep stall. He also shared with me that he had actually been in a deep stall, lost a lot of altitude, and didn't know if he was going to get out of it during the original design [727-100]. So, I knew he was serious about this, and my seriousness was ever increasing. Then, we were getting ready to lay out the flight test, and

he said, "You know, I think it would be really good if you go with me on this flight to check out the stall speeds." I'm going, "You've got to be kidding me!" He said, "I want you to sit right behind me in the jump seat, and we are going to put the instrumentation on angle of attack across the whole front end. And I want you, as we get closer and closer to the stall speed at every flap, read out the angle of attack, right in my ear, so that I know exactly when to push over because the airplane wasn't going to stall. I said, "OK, got to go now, got to check my numbers."

For a week, I don't think I went to bed! I checked every calculation. It was the best experience I could have ever had. So, we get ready to go fly and he gets me one of those cool jackets and I am sitting on the jump seat. We started

Ship Two is shown in layup with inboard slats and outboard variable-camber Krueger flaps installed on the leading edge. *Courtesy of the Boeing Company*

The main landing gear was extended on this aircraft to replicate the taller units of the proposed 727-300B, as evidenced by the airstair extension being used. Note the extended partial-span, variable-camber Krueger flaps and redesigned inboard trailing edge flaps. *Courtesy of the Boeing Company*

to do the first stall, and we slow down and slow down and I am reading the numbers of the angle of attack. I am saying, "Ten, twelve, FOURTEEN, NOW!" And he pushes the airplane over and he said, "Alan, you are scaring the [heck] out of me!" I will never forget it! I said, "I am really sorry, Lew." He said, "I want you to talk slowly, and quietly. You say the numbers and I will do the flying. Ready?" Just like so many neat leaders at Boeing . . . it was a great experience. He was a fabulous, fabulous pilot!

By May 1974, additional modifications to the 727-300 had been instated, the most significant of which was the shift from full-span variable-camber leading edge flaps to a hybrid configuration. This setup retained the variable-camber leading edge flaps on the outboard portions of the wing, but added larger slat assemblies to the inboard sections. It was also in this timeframe that the ventral airstair was deleted from the design, never to re-emerge throughout the rest of the program. A planned maximum takeoff weight of 210,500 pounds was envisioned with the use of the JT8D-17R engine in conjunction with the Automatic Performance Reserve (APR) system.

Ship Two is seen conducting Vmu tests with inboard slats and outboard variable-camber Krueger flaps installed. This particular set of tests created a stir when sparks caught the dry grass next to the runway on fire! *Courtesy of the Boeing Company*

More Power and the 1974 Boeing 727-300B

Boeing and United considered using the new "re-fanned" JT8D-217 series engines to meet the objectives of higher fuel efficiency while mitigating some of the noise problems generated by the JT8D-17R engines. At the higher thrust settings, the -17R engine produced some supersonic flow in the exhaust which created additional "shock cell" noise. Even so, the 727-300 with -17R engines was estimated to provide a seat-mile fuel reduction of 6–8 percent over the 727-200. With the addition of the re-fanned JT8D-200 series, an improved 12–16 percent fuel savings per seat mile was anticipated along with a modest noise reduction. Engineers also began using the availability of these higher-bypass engines to explore the possibility of adding

additional length to the fuselage, above and beyond the 180-inch stretch already on the drawing board, with an increase to 220 inches (160 inches forward of the wing and 60 inches aft). A takeoff weight bump to 223,000 pounds and capacity for a maximum of 215 passengers could theoretically be achievable.

Several different airlines showed keen interest in the stretched 727-300B concept including Braniff, Swissair, Trans Australia Airlines, and Western Airlines. Each was monitoring Boeing's progress while considering larger aircraft such as the A300, DC-10, and L-1011. Conversely, it was believed that some operators in the more remote locations might still favor the 727-200 because of its comparatively long range. United Airlines was viewed as a key customer for the program because of the large number of airplanes that would likely be ordered, lowering project risk for Boeing. In late October 1974, United's Board of Directors authorized a cooperative study with Boeing to develop specifications for the new aircraft and was seemingly resistant to the procurement of additional wide body aircraft. This concept was marketed as the 727-300B, primarily to United Airlines.

United used an interesting performance metric for determining if the new design would be a complimentary fit with their fleet. The study condition was to operate the 727-300B from Allentown, Pennsylvania's Lehigh Airport to O'Hare International Airport in Chicago, Illinois. It is believed that this route was chosen because Allentown had a short runway, and thus constituted a worst-case scenario for a heavy airplane. Boeing analyst George Kanellis was responsible for estimating and compiling the data to present to United Airlines management. The data delivered on May 6, 1975, was based on the 727-300B version which was 220 inches longer than the 727-200, with the high lift wing, and Pratt & Whitney JT8D-217 engines. The operating empty weight (OEW) was estimated at 129,400 pounds with a takeoff conducted from the short 6,185-foot runway at Allentown. The flight performance was calculated with enough fuel for the route to Chicago, plus forty-five minutes legal reserve, United Airlines' standard additional contingency fuel of thirty minutes holding fuel, and ample alternate airport fuel to Detroit. Five years of statistical data was used for departure airport meteorological conditions and winds aloft for takeoff and cruise performance estimates. The charts shown overleaf use the historic July–September conditions for 8:30 am (top) and 4:00 pm (bottom) departure times.

The analysis showed that the aircraft would be takeoff weight limited much of the time, only being able to carry the full 157 passengers 78 percent of the time during the early departure, and only 45 percent of the time during the typically warmer afternoon departures. It was found that more load reliability could be gained if United restricted passenger boarding to a total of 141 passengers. Under these stipulations, the likelihood of meeting the performance requirements for the morning and afternoon departures were an improved 93 percent and 85 percent respectively. Still, there would be times when customers might be left behind in this worst-case scenario. Kanellis indicated that the estimated performance of the 727-300B on this test-case route, along with the proposed aircraft's economics, were likely the decisive factors leading to the demise of the program. Takeoff and approach noise was also a contributing factor. Soon after this timeframe, in the late 1970s, noise was becoming an increasingly important consideration which would undoubtedly have affected the potential sales of the 727-300B. This would have been true even with the new JT8D-217 engines as quieter, higher-bypass engines were already under development and more restrictive noise regulations were on the horizon.

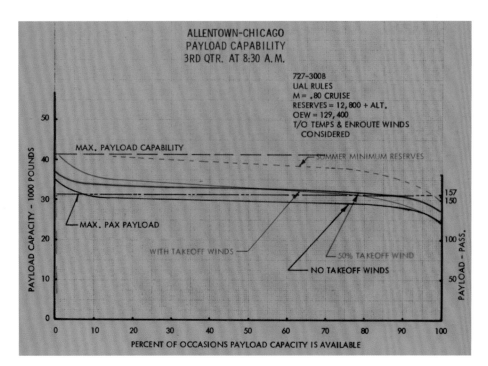

ALLENTOWN-CHICAGO
PAYLOAD CAPABILITY
3RD QTR. AT 8:30 A.M.

727-300B
UAL RULES
M = .80 CRUISE
RESERVES = 12,800 + ALT.
OEW = 129,400
T/O TEMPS & ENROUTE WINDS
CONSIDERED

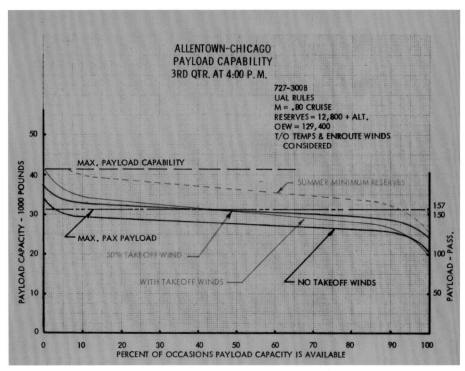

ALLENTOWN-CHICAGO
PAYLOAD CAPABILITY
3RD QTR. AT 4:00 P.M.

727-300B
UAL RULES
M = .80 CRUISE
RESERVES = 12,800 + ALT.
OEW = 129,400
T/O TEMPS & ENROUTE WINDS
CONSIDERED

Courtesy of the Boeing Company via George Kanellis

The End of the 727-300

Notwithstanding the proposed addition of re-fanned JT8D-217 engines, there were other inherent issues with the 727-300B design. The variable-camber Krueger flaps were very effective at producing high lift at relatively low airspeeds. While this was the desired effect of the wing design, it caused stability problems if one of the Krueger flap panels either failed to deploy or was damaged by a bird strike. Boeing engineer Larry Timmons explained:

Jim Kraft was the guy bearing the bad news about one Krueger flap missing: a bird could take out a Krueger flap.

With one Krueger flap missing, the airplane rolled very smartly. So, then the Krueger flaps were cut in half. All of a sudden, you have all of these mechanisms, and it got really ugly in a hurry. That was another contributor.

In the interim, United was likewise showing some interest in the blooming 7X7 program, which would later become the Boeing 767. United intended to make a go/no-go decision by February 1975, but due to instability in the economy during the period, it was delayed until August 28, when United's chairman, Edward E. Carlson, made the decision not to purchase the 727-300B. He indicated the reasons for this were the uncertain economy, the meteoric rise in fuel costs, and the possible looming effects of airline deregulation. Statements made by Edward Beamish, United's senior vice president for corporate planning, mirrored these sentiments, indicating that the 727-300B did not embody enough additional fuel efficiency to make it a sound investment for the carrier. With this decision made, the direct follow-on 727 derivative studies came to a close later that year.

Boeing engineer Larry Timmons shared some additional reasons for the demise of the 727-300 program, placing more weight on the airport noise constraints being imposed:

The 727-300 was going to be all things to all people. It was going to have tremendous short-field characteristics, be as fast as lightning, and be kind of quiet. The JT8D-200s were not particularly quiet and mostly on the sideline . . . it was noisy. At any rate, I believe that program was killed by, number 1, the noise rule. Number 2, the airplane became everybody's pet project. . . . Some said, "We don't need the D. B. Cooper door anymore, so let's take that out. Well, now we have space in the back end, so let's do some things about the S-duct," and it rolled on from there. Finally, it became a new airplane. It lost sight of the original objective, which was a quick entry into an improved airplane. Obviously, the fuselage couldn't get any longer without putting a root insert in so the gear could be bigger and longer. The whole thing was pretty much up against its design limits, so it was canceled.

Soon after this timeframe, the airlines and airport authorities came under greater pressure from the public and the FAA to mitigate aircraft noise as much as possible. The JT8D-17R engine, being the version with the highest exhaust velocity, produced additional noise due to the shock-cell phenomenon. To many of the people involved, it was becoming apparent that a highly-modified derivative, if not a whole new airframe, was going to be required to gain market share. The engineering staff was challenged with selling an expensive and involved airplane development program to Boeing's upper management. The Pratt & Whitney JT8D low-bypass turbofan was an amazing engine at the time of its arrival into the marketplace and, when

compared to existing pure turbojet engines of the period, was considered to be "quiet." Eastern Airlines even branded their airplanes "Whisperjets" to showcase this as a boon for public relations. Nonetheless, by the mid-1970s, the newer high-bypass engines from General Electric, Pratt & Whitney, and Rolls-Royce were substantially raising the bar on noise pollution and fuel economy.

Bruce Florsheim provided additional information explaining why the 727-300 was not ultimately pressed into production:

After the 1973 oil crisis, the airlines were starting to recover, and United, which was considered as the prime launch customer for any 727-300, wanted a simple stretch of the 727-200 Advanced with uprated engines and one stop transcontinental range. . . . There was little interest from the other US carriers, and Boeing was unwilling to produce what would have become a custom airplane for United.

In Jack Steiner's 1978 *Case Study in Aircraft Design: The Boeing 727*, he stated:

In the first quarter of 1973, we initiated a less ambitious improvement derivative program called the 727-300, which raised the gross weight, installed a more powerful engine, and lengthened the body still further. This version lasted until about September 1974, when major airline customers decided that the advanced version of the present JT8D engine, then being considered, constituted a significant noise risk.

Given the situation with noise, fuel burn, and runway performance, engineers began the research and development for what would essentially become an entirely new airframe: the 7N7. Concurrently, as late as November 1975, there was a team working on a 727 derivative concept which was still on table. Dubbed the 727-300-S68F, this design was to be further stretched and incorporate the new CFM56 turbofan engine under development by General Electric and SNECMA, in a joint American and French partnership. The concept looked

The 727-300 S68F concept was based on the use of three CFM56 high-bypass turbofan engines, which would force a significant redesign to the vertical stabilizer and aft fuselage due to the requirement for a wider center-engine S-duct. *Courtesy of the Boeing Company*

muscular, with intakes expanded from 40 inches for the JT8D to roughly 60 inches for the wider girth of the CFM engine's high-bypass fan. These super quiet and efficient engines would solve some problems, while creating other potential issues when married to the 727 airframe. The combination of a longer body and bulkier engine pods would likely lead to further handling issues during low speed flight and stalls. Furthermore, the entire Section 48 (aft fuselage) would need a significant redesign to accommodate the expanded S-duct, mitigating much of the cost savings enjoyed by building a "simple derivative" airframe. The 727-300-S68F was also destined to fall by the wayside, signaling the end of the line for the legacy 727 airframe.

According to the InterAvia Airletter (No. 8620) dated October 29, 1976, Boeing's Bob Norton indicated that research and development for the 727-300 program cost Boeing $48 million. While this was a substantial expenditure, it was far more cost effective than launching a program that could potentially fall short of success. Additionally, these studies produced valuable information which could be applied to the development of future airplanes.

The 1975 Boeing 7N7 Concept

Following the discontinuation of the 727-300 concepts, emphasis was redirected to an aircraft that needed to feature a new wing design and wing-mounted high-bypass turbofan engines. The airlines made

it clear that a high-technology wing design was required to launch a program that would have considerable sales success in the evolving world airline market. The challenge was twofold, since not only did this new aircraft need to be sold to the customer, but first and foremost, engineering needed to sell the idea of building an entirely new airplane to Boeing management.

During the 1975 Farnborough Airshow, Boeing issued press release S-1775, which detailed a new 727/737 derivative concept known as the 7N7. Riding on the shoulders of this release was the public announcement of an entirely new twin-aisle design called the 7X7, which ultimately became the Boeing 767. The 7N7 was intended to accommodate passenger capacities ranging from 120 to 180 passengers, with a nonstop range of 1,500 to 2,000 miles. The engines being considered for the low-weight version of the new airplane were the new CFM56 and Pratt & Whitney JT10D high-bypass turbofan engines. To accommodate a heavier version, the General Electric CF6-32, a refanned version of the McDonnell Douglas DC-10 power plant or the Rolls-Royce RB211-22 (a modification of the Lockheed L-1011 power plant) were once again being considered.

Throughout the course of the 7N7 studies, different versions of the concept were scrutinized by separate groups, but they all had one thing in common: they were considered "derivatives." This was tactical, because airplane manufacturers equate "derivatives" with "less expensive to develop," versus an all-new airplane, which would require significant research-and-development expenses long before reaching the market.

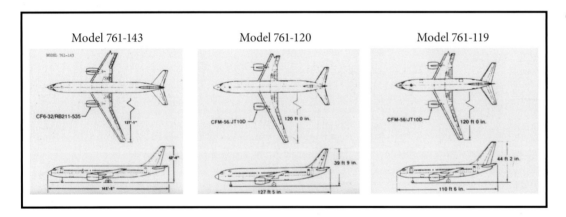

Courtesy of the Boeing Company

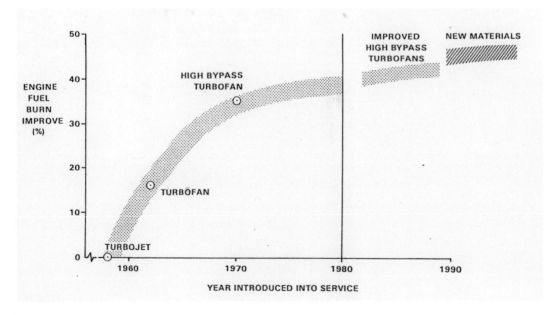

This chart shows the significant reduction of specific fuel consumption brought by the use of high-bypass turbofan engines. *Courtesy of the Boeing Company*

By late 1976, the 7N7 concept had three different flavors, each offering varying range and passenger capacities. Each of these designs featured a fuselage-mounted conventional tail design that appeared to be based on that of the 737-200 Advanced, and the typical 727/737 nose and forward body sections.

The largest of these was Concept 761-143, which was envisioned as having an overall length of 145 feet, 6 inches; a high-aspect-ratio wing spanning 127 feet, 1 inch; and the ability to carry 180 passengers over 1,800 nautical miles. A four-wheel bogie main landing gear setup was planned for this version, with both the CF6-32 and RB211-22 turbofan engines seen to be ideal matches to this heavier, long-range airframe.

Another option in the 7N7 procession was Concept 761-120. This design was slightly smaller, accommodating 160 passengers over a nonstop distance of 1,600 nautical miles. The fuselage layout was a shorter 127 feet, 5 inches, with a slightly smaller wing than Concept 761-143, which spanned 120 feet and required only twin-wheel main landing gears because of the lower planned maximum gross weight.

The smallest variant was the Concept 761-119 design, which used the same wing planform and twin-wheel setup as the 761-120, but with a fuselage length of 110 feet, 6 inches and an operational range of 1,300 nautical miles. The Pratt & Whitney JT10D and the CFM56 high-bypass turbofans were considered the best options for these two lighter designs. Interestingly, with the exception of the shorter projected range, both designs bore a strong resemblance to the much-later 737 Next Generation series of jetliners, which became wildly popular with airlines worldwide following their service debut in the mid-1990s.

These concepts persevered through the 1977 time frame, being developed concurrently with the new twin-aisled 7X7, which later became the Boeing 767 aircraft design. The 7X7 was poised to tackle the market between the larger DC-10 and L-1011 trijets, and the smaller 727 and future 7N7. All the while, the 7X7 would compete directly with the Airbus A300, already in service, and the A310, which was still under development at the time. During this period, the intercontinental 7X7 was envisioned as a trijet, smaller but similar in configuration to the L-1011.

This photo shows the early three-engine Boeing 7X7 concept model. *Courtesy of the Boeing Company*

Because there were multiple teams working on the 7N7 and 7X7, the progression of the 7N7 design was not completely linear. While some engineers were designing an airplane with a conventional, low-set horizontal-stabilizer design, there were still some who felt it would be beneficial to have the airplane remain a derivative of the successful 727. By this point in time, tail configuration aside, most had acquiesced, realizing that the design required twin, wing-mounted, high-bypass turbofans that dictated the need for a new, high-technology wing design. A new wing had also become common to most if not all post-1975 7N7 permutations, with the 727-300 moniker having forever vanished into the ether. Even with this, there were still efforts in the engineering department that focused on retaining a 727 empennage, complete with the high-mounted horizontal stabilizer sans the center engine duct. Murray Booth explained the situation:

The 727 team wanted to build a low-cost derivative. The internal selling-point program costs and scheduled resources told the proponents of the T-tail that the smartest way to get to the 7N7 was to build a low-cost derivative of the

This 7N7 configuration still possessed the traditional Boeing narrow-body cockpit and a modified 727 tail structure. *Author's collection*

727. That's how the T-tail got started. They hung on to that belief, and once you decide that that is what you are going to do, you can come up with reasons why that is a good idea for marketing. It looks more like a derivative.

By this time, the 7N7 design had evolved from a 737 lower fuselage section both forward and aft of the wing, back to the 727 configuration with a deeper baggage compartment depth behind the wing, while retaining the 727/737 forward fuselage cross section, as evidenced from Boeing drawings. Boeing designer Jack Wimpress had a late-night meeting with T. Wilson, then the CEO of Boeing in late 1978. This signaled the change from the 727-derivative T-tail to a conventional tail design, thereby terminating nearly all commonality between the 7N7 and the 727, with the exception of the fuselage cross sections. Wimpress recounted the event:

So, I was set to write the requirements for pitch stability. I was under a lot of economic pressure to keep the T-tail, so I kept trying to think of a reasonable requirement for a T-tail pitch stability requirement, trying to work through the dynamics to have a reasonable airplane. I remember being in the middle of this and looking at the drafting table with a T-tailed airplane when T. Wilson came by, the CEO of the company. And he sat down and I explained what we were worried about trying to save the 727 tail. His comment was "I wouldn't bust my ass to save the 727 tail!"

When T. Wilson came by and made that comment to me, I thought, "What other major company is there, as big as Boeing, where the chief executive officer would sit down with an engineer and talk. I thought, boy, that is one of the reasons it is great to work at Boeing!

Kenneth Holtby, vice president and general manager of the 7N7/7X7 programs, was described by Joe Sutter as "quiet, but firm" and a "very, very good designer." Holtby was never known to raise his voice, because it was unnecessary. People listened because of his knowledge, judgment, and expertise. No table pounding was required. Jack Wimpress continued:

This image is from a McDonnell Douglas brochure given to PSA during the late 1970s showing their ATMR concept designed to replace the 727 and compete with the future 757. This aircraft, slated to become the DC-11, never left the drawing board. *Courtesy of the Boeing Company*

So, finally Holtby said to me, "Jack, you are writing your requirements around your configuration!" That was very, very good insight. So, I went back and said, "Well, what you really want, if you are in trim, anything you can pull into, you can push out of." Now, that is a good requirement! Simple, but absolutely definitive. The airplane is absolutely safe unless you mistrim it or something. He said, "There is only one way that will work . . . the tail has to go on the bottom. Otherwise, you can't meet that requirement." That is a good requirement on any airplane.

Murray Booth, a strong proponent of the conventional tail on the 7N7, commented during a 2018 interview: "Don't put a T-tail on it unless you have to!" Although the 727 was engineered in such a way to mitigate the deep stall and locked-in-stall characteristics experienced by the BAC One-Eleven and the Hawker-Siddeley Trident jetliners, it did create a possible pitch stability problem when operating at the edge of the flight envelope. The new thought process at Boeing took this into account and did not want to risk any adverse flight characteristics. Any aerodynamic drag benefits or commonality reaped from the use of the 727's T-tail were not found to be worth the trade-off.

In the end, the 727 had very little commonality with the 757. With the 7N7 and 7X7 teams working on their designs in parallel, an ingenious idea was proposed. Would it be possible to have systems and cockpit commonality between the 7N7 and the larger 7X7?

757/767 Cockpit Development

The original 767 cockpit featured a flight engineer panel. A handful of very early 767s were delivered in this configuration at the airline's request, but these aircraft were later converted to the more familiar two-crew configuration. *Courtesy of the Boeing Company*

757 project engineer Peter Morton shares his experience with the 7N7/757 transition:

As I reminisce about the 757 flight deck evolution and its relationship to the 767, a few powerful memories emerge.

It starts when Phil Condit, the 757 chief project engineer, invited me to join him for lunch to see if I was interested in an assignment as senior project engineer on his airplane, which was on the verge of being launched. Its name was just evolving from "7N7" to 757. I asked Phil two questions:

"What's the crew complement?" This query has to do with what kind of challenge is involved in the assignment...a three-person crew with a flight engineer like the 707, 727, 747, and the then configuration of the 767 is an interesting, but not compelling challenge. Phil replied, "It is a two-person crew flight deck."

Next question was "To whom do I report?" A two-person flight deck involves direct negotiation with every engineering group in order to manage systems workload and meet FAR Part 25 certification criteria. If the 25-person flight deck group is buried administratively as part of, say, the 200-person electrical organization, that sort of negotiation becomes difficult, if not impossible. Phil replied, "You report to me."

I said, "I'll take the job!"

There were problems. The 767 had a completely new cockpit structure; basically a "wide body" at the pilots' station. It had plenty of room to install the new cathode-ray-tube flight instruments. The 757 flight deck was the same as the 727, with interference between the structure and the new cathode ray tubes. There was aerodynamic noise inherent in the 727 that had not been fixed since the days of the 707. Naturally, the flight crew accommodations were inherited from the 727.

Then magic happened in an incredibly short period of time. Some of these highlights were the following:

- Doug Miller and Avtar Mahal from Product Development and Aerodynamics put their heads together and thought we could splice the 767 cockpit structure to the 757.
- The pilot's union objected to the 767 two-person crew on the basis of flight safety and demanded that the 757 change to a three-person crew.
- The Department of Transportation formed a task force to investigate the relative flight safety of two- and three-person-crewed aircraft and found the former just as safe, possibly safer.
- The 767 launch customers asked to switch to a two-person crew.
- My boss and I sold the company on the possibility of refining the 767 and 757 designs to accommodate a common pilot type rating.
- On the shop floor, Clifford Coomes said he could create a conversion shop to change the first thirty 767s to two-person crew configurations and preserve the contract delivery schedule.

I've never seen anything like it. The company, its customers, and the FAA all pivoted with agility and speed to produce the first common type-rated airplane pair, Boeing gained a significant market advantage, and we never looked back. This was the most satisfying technical assignment I ever had."

"Two airplanes, one learning curve. It's a way to cut training costs, boost productivity."

"Each step up the flight crew training ladder represents a major investment in training, in training equipment, and in time away from the job.

"One way to lower those costs, and still grow, is to make it easier to move from one airplane to the next. That's exactly what commonality does in the Boeing 757/767 family. The flight decks of both airplanes are virtually identical; so are the flying characteristics. Pilots trained in one can fly the other and, with about four hours of classroom training, be certified to fly both.

"Commonality also reduces maintenance training and the maintenance burden, reduces spares, makes double use of ground support equipment—and can save millions in simulators.

"The 757/767 family. It's another way Boeing puts advanced technology to work for its customers."

—Peter M. Morton
*Director, Customer Training
Boeing Commercial Airplanes*

BOEING

Peter Morton and his team were instrumental in achieving the common pilot type rating for the 757 and 767. This was a first in the airline industry and saved airlines untold millions of dollars in training expenses and crew utilization. *Courtesy of the Boeing Company*

Allowing the common type rating for pilots saved research-and-development expense while creating seamless pilot transition training between the two aircraft types. Ultimately, as Morton pointed out, this became the path of least resistance with the 7N7. The cockpit of the larger 7X7 was grafted onto the existing 727/737 forward section of the 7N7 by changing the nose profile and canting the control cabin floor down 2 degrees. Doing so allowed a common cockpit with good aerodynamic qualities. Because of this decision, when the 7N7 and the 7X7 were certified as the 757 and 767, respectively, crew qualification training was greatly simplified and the two aircraft were granted a common type rating approval for pilots. This merely required "Differences" training, which was allowed only for aircraft derivatives within a common aircraft type (e.g., 727-100 and 727-200) prior to this certification. Today, many airlines have pilots who are dual qualified concurrently on the 757 and 767. This is significant because these are two completely different aircraft designs, but they feature systems and cockpit commonality that make the aircraft nearly equivalent from the pilot's perspective.

Thus, the final versions of the 7N7 that led to the Boeing 757 no longer bore any resemblance to the legacy 727. While the 727 continued to serve passenger and cargo roles for years and are still in service with very limited numbers as of 2020, the 7N7 transformation into the 757 marked the end of the long and successful lineage of the Boeing 727. With that being said, the contribution of the 727 lives on through the technological advancements centered on this magnificent airplane. Today, many of those advancements and the exemplary safety record enjoyed today are, in part, owed to the contributions of the Boeing 727.

The final 757-200 configuration bore no resemblance to the 727 airframe. *Courtesy of the Boeing Company*

Technology and Safety

Windshear

Many airliners have been lost to a phenomenon known as windshear, which was identified as the primary factor in over 600 deaths and nearly 250 injuries between 1964 and 1986. In Advisory Circular AC-00-54, the Federal Aviation Administration defined severe windshear as "A rapid change in wind direction or velocity causing airspeed changes greater than 15 knots and/or vertical speed changes of greater than 500 feet per minute."

Microbursts are believed to occur in roughly 5 percent of all thunderstorms and generate extreme windshear, thereby making them a leading cause of low-level windshear accidents. A microburst is a narrow, rapidly descending column of air that exits the storm's cloud base and is generally less than 3,000 feet across. As the microburst nears the ground, its progress is impeded by the terrain, causing it to fan out in all directions. Typically, the thunderstorm itself is all too obvious to the pilot, but until the advent of modern detection systems (reviewed later in this chapter), the pilot was likely unaware of the existing microburst or how severe the conditions might be in reality.

Courtesy of the Boeing Company

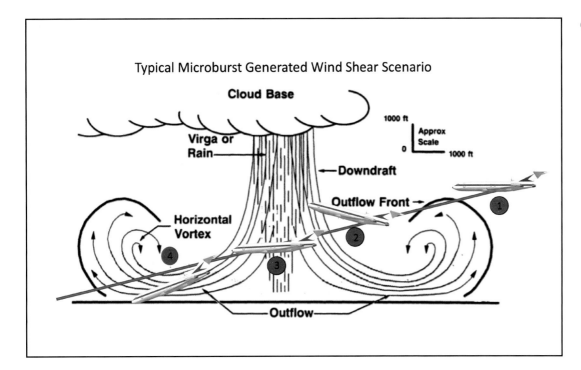

Typical Microburst Generated Wind Shear Scenario

As seen in the microburst diagram above, the aircraft is entering the situation at position (1). All parameters seem normal and the aircraft is on a stable glide slope to the landing runway. Proceeding to position (2), the aircraft experiences a strong headwind gust. Since the aircraft has a significant amount of inertia, this is experienced as a sharp increase in indicated airspeed. Due to this, lift is increased, and the aircraft naturally begins to seek a nose-high attitude. This occurs because of the aircraft's static stability and inherent tendency to return to the trimmed airspeed. To correct airspeed and return to the glide path, the pilot will tend to reduce thrust and force the nose down, thereby increasing descent rates. This becomes the first nail in the proverbial coffin, since the pilot might be tempted during extreme encounters to reduce thrust to idle, unspooling the engines. Keep in mind that jet engines require from three to eight seconds to spool back up sufficiently to produce meaningful thrust. The aircraft continues to position (3), where it is likely unspooled and suddenly encounters a strong downdraft along with sharply decreasing airspeed. The pilot advances the thrust levers, but in this situation, it is too late and the engine spool-up takes far too long. The nose of the aircraft generally wants to drop, further increasing descent rates. At position (4), the engines are starting to spool, but airspeed is decreasing too rapidly for the aircraft to recover during a severe encounter. The consequences of this situation are all too often catastrophic. Please note that an aircraft lifting off from a runway at position (3) would be representative of the worst-possible aerodynamic situation: low altitude and rapidly decreasing airspeed.

Windshear characteristically exists whenever wind speed or direction changes over a short distance, and can also be manifested occasionally by mountain rotors. Although the microburst is often identified as the most severe form of windshear, mountain rotors can generate severe windshears that are insidious and often completely invisible to the unwary pilot. Mountain rotors are formed on the lee side of mountain ranges and create horizontally rotating eddies of air, which are invisible even to modern radar systems because they are commonly devoid of condensed moisture content.

In desert areas during the late afternoon, dust devils are abundant and appear to be a very low-altitude phenomenon. The only part of the funnel visible to the naked eye is the portion that has picked up dust and debris. The truth is that they can extend a thousand or more feet into the atmosphere while generating intense localized areas of windshear, the effects of which are explored in the following sidebar.

Engineer and later Boeing CEO Alan Mulally was the manager of the Windshear Task Force at Boeing. The task force was set up to devise innovative pilot techniques and, later, advanced instrumentation to help make windshear survivable. On May 31, 1984, United Airlines Flight 663, a Boeing 727-222 (N7640U, c/n 19913, l/n 672), commenced departure from Denver Stapleton (DEN). Denver is famous for severe weather created by the confluence of warm, moist air from the southwest and cold air from the north. This, combined with the Rocky Mountains' topography, often leads to extreme weather and unpredictable wind currents. As the 727 departed Stapleton Field, an extreme windshear was encountered, causing a significant loss of airspeed and lift immediately after leaving the runway. Nine years previously, a Continental Airlines 727 crashed after being pushed back onto the ground under similar circumstances while departing Stapleton. The following is a transcript of an interview that occurred during the 2015 Pathfinders Awards Banquet held at the Museum of Flight in Seattle, Washington:

Peter Morton: Now I want to go to another topic . . . another special assignment for you, and it was called "Windshear." You were instrumental in the Boeing initiative to address this issue because it was a really serious safety issue, not just for Boeing. There was a flight of a United Airlines 727 that took off from Denver, and [United Airlines president] Dick Ferris called [Boeing president] Frank Schrontz (who is here in the audience), and he said, "Thank you. You just saved 172 lives!" So, tell us that story.

BOEING COMMERCIAL AIRPLANE COMPANY

SEATTLE, WASHINGTON 98124

F. A. SHRONTZ
PRESIDENT

June 4, 1984

Mr. Alan Mulally

Dear Alan,

It came to my attention that you had personally participated in the briefing received by the first officer of the UAL 727 which experienced a severe wind shear incident on May 31. I also heard that the survival of the airplane was attributed to the heightened awareness of altitude indications that is, among other parameters, an objective of your briefing.

It is not often in this business that one is able to make such a direct and positive contribution to the safety of our products, and I know you must be feeling a keen awareness and pride in that contribution. In this case, I am aware that the effectiveness and quality of the communication that took place was the product of many months of diligent hard work in your role as Wind Shear Task Force Manager. You have handled this assignment with drive and imagination, as you did your previous effort on the effects of airplane wing contamination. It is not easy to distill the widely varying opinions and facts that bear on these kinds of issues into a succinct and effective message for the user of our products. The May 31 wind shear incident proves that it can be done, and you did it. I am pleased to congratulate you on your success.

Keep up the good work. At the heart of our long term business success is our reputation for technical concern and diligence. Contributions such as yours show that we can continue to excel in this vital area.

Sincerely yours,

Frank Shrontz

peh

A DIVISION OF THE BOEING COMPANY

Courtesy of the Boeing Company via Alan Mulally and Peter Morton

Alan Mulally: We had had over twenty serious accidents associated with windshear. Airplanes fly with respect to the air. . . . A neat thing about airplanes that are statically stable, like all of our airplanes, is that if you get away from the trimmed speed (especially like on a takeoff), the airplane, by itself, will try to return to the trimmed speed. Airplanes are magic! But when you are trying to take off and climb, you have to really watch the rate of climb indicator and speed so that you can keep the airplane climbing, because it is called a TAKEOFF! We studied it and studied it, and what we figured out was that when the air moved away from the airplane, with this characteristic of the airplane to return to its trim speed, actually was lowering the nose. Because the nose was up, the pilots couldn't see that unless they really saw the rate of climb indicator, they could actually end up descending into the ground. At the time, [there was] another neat thing about Dick Taylor, who was the general manager of the division. When we figured this out on the simulator . . . I called Dick because he was a pilot and he stood for technical excellence. I said, "Dick, you have to come over here and fly this on the simulator." He did, and the same thing happened to him that happens to a lot of people, and he got it just like that. He said, "What do you think we should do?" I said, "We just need to teach the pilots to use the maximum capability and give them some instrumentation so that they have some confidence that they are not going to stall the airplane, because the airplane has a lot of capability." So, that is what we did. We went down to a number of the big airlines to teach them how to do this. The pilot on the 727 that you mentioned was actually in the training . . . he really got it. We gave him some windshear models, and he flew through it and kept pulling the nose back and made a successful takeoff. So, a couple of weeks later, he was in Denver and ran into windshear. He knew exactly what to do and used all of the capability of the airplane. The pictures that we have of it . . . he just burned the grass all the way down past the runway. He kept it going and going and up. He got up a little bit in altitude and was going to pressurize the airplane, and he couldn't pressurize it. So, the procedure was that he needed to take the airplane back. When they got on the ground, they saw that he had [approach] light structures stuck in the bottom of the 727 because he went all the way along, past the runway, but he saved the airplane, because he used the capability . . . saved the airplane and the lives. It was just fantastic! A really neat thing about this is that Boeing went to work on the instrumentation to give them these visual aids, and we haven't had a major windshear accident since.

Peter Morton: But wait, there's more. This is a Paul Harvey moment.

Alan Mulally: We didn't practice this, Peter!

Peter Morton: No, we didn't. I think you will enjoy it. This connects Dick, his son Steve, and you. Let's hear the story from the start from Steve.

Steve Taylor [comes to the stage]: So about twenty years after that, Alan, windshear training and guidance systems were traditional among all airplanes. I was a pilot in Boeing executive flight operations, and you were my passenger.

Peter Morton: The passenger was the CEO!

Steve Taylor: Alan happened to be the CEO of Boeing Commercial Airplanes at the time, and we were landing in Palm Springs. Palm Springs is known for some amazing gusty winds. As we were coming in on final, I looked out and saw a dust devil coming across the airport, and I thought back to my training . . . this is a bad idea! So, I made the decision to go around. I thought, "This is easy." We were at about 1,000 feet, and I thought, "No problem." At about the time that we had brought up the gear and brought up the flaps, we ran into a 45-knot windshear. The bottom fell out, and the airplane just basically felt like it had dropped from the sky. In my thirty-five years of flying, that was the one occasion where I really was not sure what the outcome was going to be. So, Alan, while you also saved 172 lives on United, you saved a few that are a little closer to home!

Alan Mulally: Now that you said that, I remember I yelled up at you and said, "Great job, Steve! How many knots did you lose?"

Steve Taylor: He was more excited about whether I had matched his record in the simulator!

Peter Morton: So, twenty years . . . you invent something and twenty years later it saves your life. That's pretty cool!

The knowledge gained from the efforts of industry leaders such as Alan Mulally and Dick Taylor ultimately led to the inclusion of integrated systems to avoid not only windshear but aircraft collisions with terrain, caused by a variety of situations. A system known as the Ground Proximity Warning System (GPWS—sometimes pronounced "jip wiz") was introduced to mitigate the hazards of terrain contact, regardless of the possible causes.

Ground Proximity Warning System (GPWS)

The first versions of GPWS (sometimes also referred to as Terrain Avoidance Warning System or TAWS by ICAO) used inputs from the aircraft's avionics system to determine if there was a terrain contact hazard. These inputs were radio altitude, barometric altitude, Mach number, indicated airspeed, glide slope (Instrument Landing System descent path), and the position of the flaps and landing gear.

The Mk. II GPWS system had several modes that sensed hazardous conditions on the basis of inputs from the aircraft's avionics. The activation of the following modes, except for mode 6, was accompanied by a red GPWS light:

MODE 1: The aircraft has excessive closure rate with the ground, resulting in "SINK RATE" and possibly "PULL UP, PULL UP" aural warnings.

MODE 2: The aircraft has excessive closure rate with terrain, resulting in "TERRAIN, TERRAIN" and possibly "PULL UP, PULL UP" aural warnings.

MODE 3: Loss of altitude immediately after takeoff, resulting in a "DON'T SINK" aural warning

MODE 4: The aircraft is too low either for the landing gear or flap configuration, resulting in a "TOO-LOW GEAR" or "TOO-LOW FLAP" aural warning. Rapidly rising terrain underneath the aircraft (sensed by radio altimeter), resulting in a "TOO-LOW TERRAIN" aural warning.

MODE 5: The aircraft sinks below the glide slope path on an Instrument Landing System (ILS) approach, resulting in a "GLIDE SLOPE" aural warning with an associated amber BELOW G/S light.

MODE 6: Descent below the decision altitude as set by the pilot on an instrument approach, resulting in a "MINIMUMS, MINIMUMS" aural alert. This mode is advisory in nature and would normally be heard if the runway environment is sighted and the pilot elected to continue with a landing. Therefore, this alert did not illuminate the red GPWS light.

With the exception of mode 6, these warnings could be caused either by windshear, an improper flight path, or improper configuration. If windshear was involved, the first-generation GPWS systems did not specifically call out the windshear condition itself, but typically called out one or more of the above to alert the pilot that terrain contact was likely without corrective action. With the activation of a "PULL UP, PULL UP" warning, the pilot was trained to immediately apply emergency thrust, to pitch up to a target pitch (usually 15 to 20 degrees, depending on aircraft model), and to tolerate momentary activation of the stall-warning stick shaker. Without further guidance, this was the best means of maneuvering the aircraft as close to the optimum lift to drag speed (L/D max) as possible, providing the highest chance of escaping the windshear.

The first-generation GPWS/TAWS systems were a strong step forward in the advancement of aviation safety, but there were still some weaknesses inherent in the system. First was the lack of positive windshear identification, since the system warned the crew only once the flight path had degraded significantly. Second was the fact that the system used radio altitude (height above terrain directly beneath the aircraft) and was not forward looking. There were several instances on specific airways when aircraft would clear terrain ahead at a legal altitude, but a steep rise in terrain directly beneath the airplane would give false "PULL UP, PULL UP" warnings. The answer to these two primary issues was the new-technology EGPWS.

Enhanced Ground Proximity Warning System (EGPWS)

In 1997, Honeywell installed the first certified Enhanced Ground Proximity Warning System. One key difference between the GPWS and EGPWS systems was made possible through the use of the global positioning system (GPS) and a detailed onboard terrain database. This addition to the system greatly reduced the possibility of false warnings because the system became "smart" enough not only to know where it was, but also where it was going above the terrain.

The second major improvement was a seventh mode that looked at the air data and other aircraft parameters to identify times when the aircraft was actually encountering severe windshear. This system gave the pilot a positive identification of the threat, in most instances before the flight path was severely degraded. When windshear was detected, a "WINDSHEAR, WINDSHEAR" aural warning sounded and a red WINDSHEAR indication would appear in front of the pilot. The pilot, in turn, would immediately set emergency thrust

and begin the escape maneuver perhaps seconds earlier than with the older GPWS installations.

Today, modern jetliners also incorporate windshear escape guidance into the aircraft's flight director systems. When the EGPWS system provides a windshear warning that the aircraft is actually in windshear, the flight director pitch bar guides the pilot to the exact pitch attitude needed to utilize every bit of the airplane's performance capability. This is important because during windshear encounters, the conditions and the aircraft's kinetic energy are in a dynamic state of change.

Predictive Windshear (PWS)

The aircraft radars used on today's jetliners are extremely good and can see weather nearly twice as far ahead of the aircraft as older units of just a few years ago. These radar systems have an additional capability that uses the radar's imaging to detect disturbed air ahead of the aircraft, such as microbursts, and then alerts the crew of the danger in one of two ways. If the threat is directly in the flight path of the aircraft during departure, it will issue a "WINDSHEAR AHEAD" aural warning, or a "GO AROUND, WINDSHEAR AHEAD" voice warning if the aircraft is on approach. The pilot will be better prepared and will have increased the distance of the aircraft from the ground prior to encountering the microburst, which is an enormous additive to safety.

If the PWS senses weather ahead, but not directly in the flight path of the aircraft, the PWS system will advise the pilots with a "MONITOR RADAR DISPLAY" caution. The radar display will automatically display the area that is generating the caution, to enhance situational awareness.

The PWS system is an effective warning system for microburst and thunderstorm windshear threats, which are often not completely visible to the pilot in advance. However, there is one caveat for PWS to be effective—there must be precipitation or particulate matter in the air. Other phenomena such as dry mountain rotors will likely not be sensed by the system.

The GPWS, EGPWS, and PWS systems were developed in response to numerous accidents and incidents that cost countless lives prior to these innovations. While windshear is still a viable threat, pilots today are equipped with modern tools and training to effectively deal with this hazard, making commercial aviation far safer than in years past.

Traffic Alert and Collision Avoidance Systems (TCAS)

The hazards of midair collisions have been known and identified since the early years of aviation. As air carrier aircraft became more numerous and airspace traffic saturation increased, it was logical that collisions became more numerous. Several landmark accidents occurred, the first of which was the 1956 midair collision of United Air Lines Flight 718 (a Douglas DC-7, N6324C, c/n 44288, l/n 540) and Trans World Airlines Flight 2 (a Lockheed L-1049 Super-G Constellation, N6902C, c/n 4016) over the Grand Canyon. This was a high-profile accident that spawned vast research efforts. All told, 128 people perished in the accident, making it by far the worst aviation disaster up to that time. This accident brought to light the need for advances in technology to mitigate the collision hazard as much as possible.

Prior to testing and rule-making changes regarding wet-runway stopping performance pioneered by N127 (Boeing 727-61, c/n 19176, l/n 290), the performance data used by airlines led to many runway excursions. The work done by this crew of FAA, US Air Force, and industry engineers and pilots in October 1971 led to the greatly improved runway safety statistics that we currently enjoy. Less than two years after this photograph was taken, N127 was involved in a midair collision with a Cessna 172K (N78297, c/n 17257557) over Yukon, Oklahoma, on July 27, 1973. The Cessna contacted the horizontal stabilizer of the 727, removing most of the surface on one side of the jet's vertical stabilizer. Unfortunately, three people perished aboard the Cessna, which was rendered uncontrollable by the collision, but amazingly the crippled 727 made an emergency landing in Oklahoma City (ICAO: KOKC) despite seriously compromised pitch control. *Courtesy of the Federal Aviation Administration via Capt. Tom Imrich*

PSA Flight 182

Although there had been technological advances in Air Traffic Services' (ATS) radar systems, accidents still occurred with full radar information available to the controller. In the terminal area, many times aircraft are cleared for a "visual approach," which requires adequate in-flight visibility and for the pilot to visually acquire nearby airborne traffic. In this situation, when traffic is called "in sight," to the air traffic controller, the responsibility of traffic avoidance is transferred to the pilot. Such was the situation on the morning of September 25, 1978, when Pacific Southwest Airlines Flight 182, operated by a Boeing 727-214 (N533PS, c/n 19688, l/n 589), was approaching San Diego's Lindbergh Airport from the east. A Cessna 172M (N7711G, c/n 17265788) was on an instrument-training flight with a flight instructor in the right seat and the student pilot in the left seat. As is normal during instrument flight training, the left-seat student was wearing a hood, essentially an oversized sun visor used to block all view outside the aircraft. This is done to simulate flight in clouds, leaving the right-seat instructor pilot to assume responsibility for traffic avoidance.

ATS called out the Cessna traffic to PSA 182 and was acknowledged to be in visual contact by the crew. As the approach continued, the PSA crew lost visual contact with the Cessna. According to the NTSB investigation findings, it is believed that the yellow-painted Cessna was below the PSA jet and was likely blending in with the houses on the final approach course to Runway 27. The cockpit voice recorder revealed that the crew was discussing among themselves that they had lost visual contact with the Cessna and believed that they had already passed the light airplane. During this time, however, the Cessna was directly in the path of the Boeing 727 and seemingly invisible to the jetliner's crew. PSA 182 would have been visible for a short period through the left-side window of the Cessna, but with the left-seat pilot wearing the training hood and himself likely blocking the view out the left window for the instructor, the accident unfolded.

After being transferred to the Lindbergh tower frequency, the crew of PSA 182 became more concerned about the Cessna and transmitted to the controller, "Okay, we had it [the Cessna] a minute ago . . . I think he's passed off to our right." The tower controller believed that he had said, "I think he is passing off to our right." This naturally led the controller to assume that there was still visual contact, even though neither of the aircraft's pilots were capable of seeing the other. At 2,600 feet, the Cessna contacted the right wing of the PSA 727, causing the aircraft to be lost 3 miles northeast of Lindbergh Field. One hundred forty-four people perished, including seven on the ground. Solutions needed to be found.

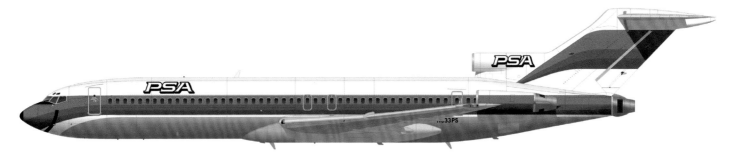

Courtesy of Jennings Heilig

Development of TCAS

The Federal Aviation Administration used two 727-100-series aircraft for safety research. This airplane (N40, 727-61, c/n 19854, l/n 628) was used to conduct testing for the development of TCAS. In late August 1980, FAA test pilot Capt. Tom Imrich and his crew flew multiple operations in busy airspace surrounding New York's La Guardia and Kennedy airports to validate the system. *Courtesy of the Boeing Company*

Although ATS controllers perform extremely well in a remarkably difficult job, this accident proved the need for real-time collision avoidance technology completely independent of ATS. The new system needed to provide one final safety net to preclude a midair collision. As early as 1971, proposals were made to develop collision avoidance systems (CAS).

The use of altitude-encoding transponders became more commonplace and were installed to allow ATS to positively identify an aircraft, reliably track it, and also to monitor the aircraft's altitude. Normally an aircraft's transponder is interrogated by ATS radar systems, which display the relevant information on the controller's screen. One of first systems developed utilizing this capability was the Beacon-Based Collision Avoidance System (BCAS). These early systems were highly affected by other radio frequency transmissions, which seriously reduced reliability. As air traffic volume continued to rise, the BCAS systems became increasingly problematic due to this phenomenon.

TCAS Implementation and Operation

In the wake of the PSA 182 accident, the US Congress enacted a law in 1981 setting the Federal Aviation Administration on a mission to encourage the development of an improved BCAS system. Later on, this effort evolved further, eventually being renamed by J. Lynn Helms, the FAA administrator at the time, and became known as the Traffic Alert and Collision Avoidance System or "TCAS," as it is known today.

Even the first versions of this BCAS and TCAS equipment interrogated other nearby aircraft transponders and were completely independent from ATS radar. This important element allowed TCAS to successfully operate even if outside any ATS radar contact, or if ATS radar contact was lost or unavailable, such as at lower altitudes. With this feature, TCAS would operate normally on oceanic tracks, at low altitudes, and over remote land areas or Arctic regions that did not have any radar surveillance services. Based on these aircraft-to-aircraft interrogations, the system provided the pilot with a depiction of azimuth, distance, and altitude differential data, along with an aural warning that traffic was near and a possible threat. The concept behind the alerting system is called tau, which allowed the calculation of slant range between the subject aircraft, divided by the closure rate, to give an equivalent of a nearest possible collision time. Due to the widely varying speeds of different aircraft, and differences in possible collision trajectory geometry, a more relevant method was used to ensure separation, to be calculated within the TCAS system as a projected collision-warning time, related to an estimated closest approach.

Initially, TCAS was planned to provide only a traffic advisory (TA), which merely alerted the crew of the presence of a potential traffic conflict. This was often shortly followed by a resolution advisory (RA), which suggested appropriate pilot action to avoid a collision. Sometimes the system went directly to an RA. In this case, the pilot could easily be confused by being suddenly confronted by an RA with no precursor warning, possibly generating concern about whether the advisory was real and necessary or a false warning. In other instances, the pilot could be confused as to which nearby aircraft actually was the one posing the collision threat. To solve this, it was believed important for TCAS to also provide the pilot with a "full-time" display of nearby traffic if the pilot desired to have that information displayed on the cockpit instruments. That way, the pilot was given sufficient information ahead of time, useful for visually acquiring the intruding aircraft or seeing the situation develop if in IMC, to make it possible to conduct an avoidance maneuver with confidence on the basis of the cockpit traffic display information. With the display of nearby traffic, even without a visual sighting of the conflicting aircraft, or if in IMC, the pilot could then instantly follow the RA, knowing it was the safest course of action. This type of alerting before any TA or RA was posted is now known in TCAS as display of "proximate" traffic. It is either displayed continuously at the pilot's option or at least pops up on a cockpit display well before a TA or RA is posted.

On a typical TCAS system today, when an intruding aircraft is calculated by the system to pose a threat, twenty to forty-eight seconds from the estimated closest point of approach, the system issues an aural and visual advisory. Eventually, if the conflict persists, an aural and visual warning will be observed. The display assists the pilot in maneuvering to miss the intruder and to underscore the need to look outside to visually acquire the intruder.

This capability was a major improvement in technology and safety but, in the early days, still had significant limitations of a pilot not knowing where to look, not being able to spot a conflicting aircraft, or not knowing where the conflict aircraft was in instrument meteorological conditions (IMC). Yet more troubling, the pilot had little to no precursor threat development information to assess the conflict situation before an avoidance RA instruction was issued. Visual conditions needed to exist in order to allow the threat aircraft to be sighted. Maneuvering instantly based solely on a surprising

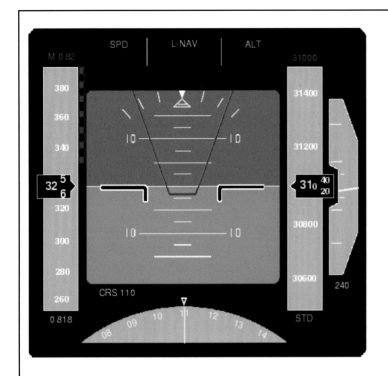

Pitch Cue Implementation

Vertical Speed Tape Implementation

This diagram shows a typical TCAS II Resolution Advisory guidance with modern displays. The pitch cue implementation (*left*) shows a calculated pitch attitude required to avoid the intruder aircraft. This indicates that the aircraft must pitch down to be below the red V-shaped box. On the right, another method of giving the pilot RA pitch guidance involves the use of the vertical-speed indicator. The aircraft must be pitched down until the vertical-speed indicator on the right side of the screen shows a descent rate in the green band. Today, many aircraft incorporate both of these methods. *Courtesy of the Federal Aviation Administration via Tom Imrich*

RA, without visual acquisition, was not an ideal situation in a real-time environment. Before the final mandatory TCAS equipage rule for air carriers was issued, this limitation and concern about the original TCAS concept of not having traffic information were widely recognized. Therefore, requirements for the addition of "proximate traffic" depiction, along with TAs and RAs, became an integral part of TCAS.

Noting the limitations of the TCAS systems, by December 31, 1993, an evolution of the proposed TCAS II was mandated and required to be installed on all commercial aircraft with more than thirty-one passenger seats. Later, it was recognized that smaller air transport aircraft with fewer than thirty-one seats would benefit from and in fact needed this type of collision protection too, so a simplified and less expensive version of TCAS was developed that provided only TA information. When that system was introduced for regulatory compliance for smaller transports, it was identified as TCAS I, with the original TCAS, which was anticipated being required for the larger air carrier passenger transports, renamed TCAS II. Both TCAS I and TCAS II were initially encouraged for voluntary adoption by general aviation (GA) and by turbine-powered air cargo operators. However, later large turbine-powered air transport cargo operators also fell under the TCAS equipage mandate per Federal Aviation Regulation (FAR) 121.356, issued on April 1, 2003. TCAS I shares many of the features of TCAS II, but TCAS I does not provide RAs. Development was not entirely concurrent, with what is now called

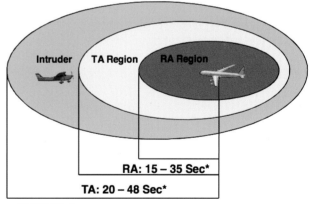

Courtesy of the Federal Aviation Administration

TCAS II long predating TCAS I. That being said, the symbology and many of the concepts, including the use of tau, remain.

With TCAS II, in a typical traffic encounter the crew receives a TA with an aural "TRAFFIC, TRAFFIC" warning and a display of traffic azimuth, range, and altitude differential to assist in visual acquisition. If the situation deteriorates further and the point of closest approach falls within an approximate fifteen to thirty-five seconds, the TCAS II system issues an RA. The purpose of the RA

Typical TCAS II Retrofit Display

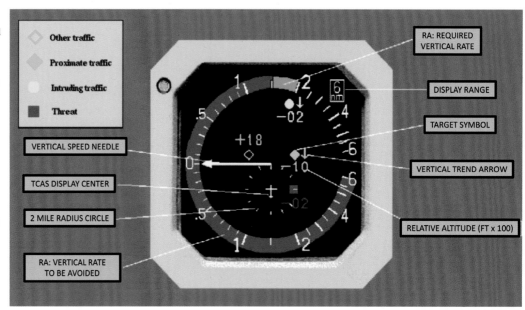

Other Traffic, altitude unknown. Unfilled diamond in white or cyan

Proximate Traffic, 1100 feet above and descending. Filled diamond in white or cyan

Traffic Advisory (TA), 900 feet below and level. Filled yellow/amber circle.

Resolution Advisory (RA), 500 feet below and climbing. Filled red square.

RA: REQUIRED VERTICAL RATE

DISPLAY RANGE

TARGET SYMBOL

VERTICAL TREND ARROW

RELATIVE ALTITUDE (FT x 100)

VERTICAL SPEED NEEDLE

TCAS DISPLAY CENTER

2 MILE RADIUS CIRCLE

RA: VERTICAL RATE TO BE AVOIDED

Other traffic
Proximate traffic
Intruding traffic
Threat

Courtesy of the Federal Aviation Administration

function is to separate the aircraft by using differential altitude. This is accomplished by issuing the pilot a clear pitch-maneuvering command, such as "CLIMB, CLIMB," "DESCEND, DESCEND," "ADJUST, ADJUST," or "MAINTAIN, MAINTAIN." Regulatory provisions set forth in FARs 91.123a and 91.221 allow pilots to respond as required to TCAS II commands, irrespective of an ATS clearance, because it is intended to be that last line of defense against midair collisions when the human element has otherwise failed. Once the aircraft is on the required trajectory, and when able to do so, the crew reports compliance with the RA to the ATS controller. Once the traffic is no longer a factor, the system issues the advisory "CLEAR OF CONFLICT." This indicates to the pilot that the aircraft can return to the originally cleared altitude. These early TCAS II systems, retrofitted into legacy aircraft such as the Boeing 727, provided an instrument display that included traffic and TCAS commands, as well as vertical speed (IVSI). The TCAS-capable display replaced the original inertial vertical-speed indicator (VSI or IVSI). This electronic screen added to the VSI shows a traffic display overlay on a digital representation of an otherwise analog VSI display. Red and green arcs on the outer VSI scale assist the pilot in attaining the ideal vertical speed and thus pitch settings to resolve the conflict. Other installations additionally added a display of traffic information on cockpit weather radar CRTs, some even with the capability to depict the barometric "absolute" altitude of nearby traffic instead of "relative altitude," as selected by the pilot.

The TCAS II system gives optimum performance when both of the conflict aircraft are equipped with the system. This allows both TCAS II systems to communicate electronically with each other in providing a mutual solution. For example, two coaltitude TCAS II aircraft moving toward each other in opposite directions would generate coordinated but opposite-direction RA commands. One would receive a "CLIMB, CLIMB" command, while the other would receive a "DESCEND, DESCEND" resolution. When only one aircraft possesses TCAS II capability, the system calculates closure information and issues the optimum command to the pilot only on the basis of the known self-aircraft's trajectory. For non-altitude-reporting transponder-equipped aircraft, TCAS can issue only a nearby traffic advisory.

The Boeing 727 was a popular jetliner from the 1960s through the 1990s, serving with numerous airlines. Consequently, they were involved in some of the landmark accidents that led to the development of the TCAS technology. The 727 test aircraft owned and operated by the FAA also was key both in TCAS development and in recognition of the importance of including nearby proximate-traffic information in the eventual TCAS regulatory requirement.

The 727 design also endured long enough to reap the benefits of this important technology with GPWS, windshear protection, and TCAS. Hundreds of lives and many aircraft have undoubtedly been saved by the efforts of those within the airline and aviation manufacturing industry, working with regulatory authorities and ICAO, hand in hand with avionics vendors, to provide the GPWS, windshear, and TCAS solutions. The attendant safety record that we enjoy aboard airline aircraft today is due to the collaborated efforts and teamwork between organizations and dedicated individuals to develop these systems.

Expected Pilot Response

"Traffic, traffic"

Example: "Climb, Climb"

Example: "Adjust Vertical Speed, Adjust"

Upon TA

- Utilize traffic display to help visually acquire threat
- Do NOT deviate from ATC clearance based solely on TA or traffic display

Upon RA

- Respond to initial RA <u>within 5 sec</u>
- Respond to increase rate and reversal RAs within 2.5 sec
- Pitch change ~2° enroute, ~5 - 7° on approach for Climb/Descend RAs
- Required response is moderate (1/4 g or less for an initial RA)
- Most autopilots do not meet TCAS design criteria - the autopilot should be disengaged prior to RA response

Upon Weakening

- Prompt response to "Weakening RAs" which command a reduction in vertical rate once sufficient vertical miss distance is attained

If RA contradicts ATC clearance, comply with TCAS RA

- **FAA guidance (AC 120-55C) allows non-response to TCAS RAs under certain conditions:**
  - Responding would compromise safety (some air carriers require response except in this case)
  - Pilots have visually acquired the correct threat aircraft and can maintain safe separation
  - Misidentifying the wrong threat aircraft or misjudging separation can occur and increase collision risk

Courtesy of the Federal Aviation Administration

Because of the dedication and teamwork of aviation industry professionals, many of the hazards of the past are largely mitigated today. Improved pilot training along with systems like TCAS, EGPWS, and PWS have been major contributors to the safety record that the industry currently enjoys. *Courtesy of the Boeing Company*

Boeing 727 Systems and Technical Data

Knowledge of systems information on the Boeing 727 will increase understanding of how the aircraft was designed and is operated in the real world. The basis of this analysis is the 727-100 series, with significant differences for the 727-200 presented at the end of each section. A pictorial walk-around inspection is also provided at the end of this chapter for further exploration.

Electrical

The 727 features a robust, redundant, and failure-tolerant electrical system that supplies power to all the aircraft utilities. The system, as a whole, supplies both 115-volt alternating current (AC) power and 28-volt direct current (DC) to the aircraft systems. Both the AC and DC supply systems are separated into multiple buses so that a single failure does not affect the entire system. Likewise, redundant items onboard the airplane are typically powered from different buses, so that at least one, or more, depending on which aircraft system is involved, remains operational at all times. The electrical control panel is located on the upper portion of the flight engineer's panel. The condition indicators and control switches are logically arranged to represent the item's location on the electrical schematic whenever possible, to make them operationally intuitive. Each portion of the electrical system will be looked at to obtain an understanding of its operation and function.

AC Power Sources

Engine Generators
Each engine turns an AC generator, driven by the high-pressure (N2) spool accessory drive. The generators are designed to provide 115-volt, 400-cycle AC power to the aircraft, with a maximum output of 34 kilowatts (kW) each. These generators are essentially electromagnets that produce the required voltage by passing within proximity to one another. This requires some electrical-field "excitation" to be provided in order for the generator to provide useful power to the system. This excitation is allowed only when the respective generator FIELD switch is in the CLOSED (connected) position, as indicated by the respective amber FIELD light being extinguished. Moving the FIELD switch to TRIP will effectively disable the associated generator.

Constant-Speed Drives
In order to produce power at the proper 400-cycle frequency, the generator units must turn at exactly 6,000 rpm. Since the engines produce variable thrust, they must naturally be operated over a wide range of rotational speeds, making a direct gear drive to the generators impossible. To solve this problem, the 727 uses constant-speed drives (CSDs) that are driven by each engine's N2 spool to turn a generator at a constant speed, using a liquid drive. This drive speed, and thus the output frequency of the associated generator, can be manually adjusted within a small range. The flight engineer uses this function during procedures where multiple generators are powering the bus tie. The flight engineer accomplishes this by using the frequency control knobs located under each generator's kW output gauge on the lower portion of the panel, while monitoring the synchronizing lights located on the lower right corner of the electrical panel. Once syncing is complete, the system functions without further intervention, provided that everything is operating normally.

Each CSD has an amber LOW OIL PRESSURE light and a DISCONNECT switch. A low oil pressure indication is normal when the respective engine shuts down, but with the engine running, this would constitute a non-normal condition. To avoid damage to the

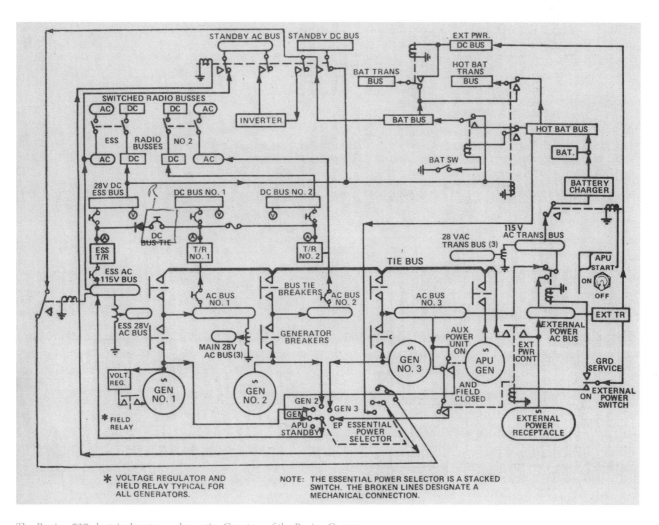

The Boeing 727 electrical system schematic. *Courtesy of the Boeing Company*

The electrical control panel at the flight engineer's station. *Author's collection*

CSD and engine accessory drive, the checklist will lead the flight engineer to activate the DISCONNECT switch. This action mechanically disconnects the CSD from the engine accessory drive, resulting in the affected generator becoming inoperative, an action that is not reversible while in the aircraft is in flight.

External Power and APU Power

With the engines shut down on the ground, AC power can be supplied to the aircraft buses either from airport-supplied external power or by using the onboard APU. Most operations start with the use of external power, which is plugged into the aircraft via a receptacle on the right side of the nose, located below the first officer's side window on the lower fuselage. With this plugged in and operational, the external power switch can be selected to the "ON" position to supply AC power to the aircraft's electrical system.

The APU employs a generator identical to the engine generators, but since the APU operates at a constant speed, the APU's generator is geared directly to the APU accessory drive system and a CSD is not required. Once the APU is started and up to speed, it becomes selectable in powering the electrical system until the engines are started prior to the commencement of taxi operations.

Main AC Power System

Typically, with the engines running, each engine generator drives its respective AC bus after it has been connected by moving that generator's GEN switch to the CLOSE position. Once this has occurred for all three generators, each one independently powers its own AC bus, provided that the sync bus tiebreakers are open (i.e., not connected). For example, engine 1 drives generator 1, which is normally connected to AC bus 1.

During normal operations, however, the sync bus is connected to all three AC buses through three BUS TIE switches. These are generally left in the CLOSED position, with the respective amber BUS TIE light extinguished. This connection to the sync bus allows all three engine generators to "parallel power" the aircraft, evenly sharing the electrical loads. This way, if there is a failure of one or more generators, the sync bus allows the remaining generator(s) to continue powering the other AC buses. In these situations, high-draw nonessential loads, such as galley power, are turned off per the non-normal checklist by the flight engineer to reduce the workload on the remaining generator(s). The sync bus also provides the necessary means to connect APU and external power to the electrical system during times when the aircraft requires normal system power on the ground with the engines shut down.

DC Power System

The 727 has many systems that are not compatible with AC electrical power, so an equally capable and redundant DC power system is provided. Since all the generating power that the aircraft produces is 115-volt AC, the addition of transformer rectifiers (TRs) to the system to convert this AC power into 28-volt DC power is required. The 727 has three TRs for this purpose: TR1, TR2, and TR3. Under normal circumstances, AC bus 1 feeds TR1, which directly feeds DC bus 1, while AC bus 2 feeds TR2, which directly feeds DC bus 2. This system shoulders the nonessential DC electrical loads for the aircraft. TR3 receives AC power through the rotary ESSENTIAL POWER SOURCE switch located in the middle of the flight engineer's electrical panel, and routes current to the essential DC bus, covered in depth later in this chapter. If TR3 were to fail, the high-priority loads from the essential DC bus can be provided by TR1 and TR2 through a diode that allows current flow only to the essential DC bus, preventing any reverse feeding of TR3 power to nonessential systems. The essential DC bus also provides DC power to the aircraft's battery bus, battery transfer bus, and hot battery transfer bus. The aircraft's battery, which is normally kept charged by AC bus 3 through a battery charger, can supply power to these buses in the absence of normal ship power.

The Essential Power System

The 727 was designed to allow safe operation of the aircraft, even after multiple electrical malfunctions. High-priority items that are deemed "essential" for safe flight are powered by the essential power system, giving it its functional name. The source for electrical power is selected by the flight engineer via the rotary ESSENTIAL POWER SOURCE switch. In flight, this can be set to draw from any operating engine generator, although it is normally selected to GEN 3. This is because, unlike generators 1 and 2, generator 3 is not the wired power source of a TR and therefore has more load capacity for operating the essential buses. It is important to note that essential power can be supplied by any engine generator, the APU, or external power. The procedure of "protecting essential power" is well known to 727 flight engineers and constantly emphasized. Before changing or disconnecting a power source, the flight engineer must select another source of essential power to avoid depowering important items.

The flow of essential power is provided by the selected generator or external power source and proceeds to the essential AC bus for supplying the high-priority AC power items. The essential AC bus provides AC power to the emergency AC bus and to TR3, which in turn provides 28-volt DC current to the essential DC bus. The essential DC bus provides power to the emergency DC bus, as well as the battery transfer bus, and the hot battery transfer bus through the battery bus.

The Emergency Power System

The emergency power system, referred to as the "standby system" by some airlines, is designed to provide power to items that will allow a crew to make a successful emergency landing if a complete failure of the AC generating systems on the aircraft were to occur. Under this condition, all the AC, DC, essential AC, and essential DC buses would be left completely unpowered, with the aircraft battery as the sole source of power. Since the battery is rated for a minimum of only thirty minutes, power is supplied only to the emergency DC bus, the battery buses, and the static inverter. The static inverter effectively does the opposite of a TR operation in providing 115-volt AC power from a 28-volt DC source; in this case, the battery bus. In this way, the static inverter converts battery power for use by the emergency AC bus. The items on these buses, powered by the battery, consist of the captain's basic instrumentation, navigation, and the #1 VHF communications radio. Power is preserved to these items so that an emergency approach and landing can be attempted. Because of this fail-safe electrical design, along with the "manual reversion" capability of the flight control system (see "Flight Controls" on page 200), and the ability for the engines to suction-feed fuel without boost pumps, the 727 was designed to remain safely flyable, even after extreme systems failures.

727-200 Difference

The 727-200 series uses Sundstrand 40 axial-gear-differential drives for constant-speed generator rotation, but operation from the cockpit is otherwise similar.

Hydraulics

As part of the 727's requirement for high lift and low approach speeds, the aircraft employs a fully powered flight control system. The 727's hydraulic system provides the power source and redundancy for these controls as well as other systems, such as landing gear extension and retraction, wheel brakes, and even ventral airstair operation.

The 727 hydraulic system typically utilizes the standard Skydrol 500 (BMS 3-11) hydraulic fluid, contained in three reservoirs. These reservoirs supply ample fluid to hydraulic system A, hydraulic system B, and the standby system. Each reservoir is named according to the system it supplies, with a balance line connecting the system A, system B, and standby reservoirs. The balance line is coupled near the top of the system A reservoir to prevent a leak in system B or the standby system from depleting the entire system A reservoir. The standby system reservoir is located near that of system A in the ventral airstair area, while the system B reservoir and pumps are located in the servicing compartment, inside the aft, left-side wing-to-body fairing. A filling port, a hand pump, and quantity gauges in this compartment allow for fast and easy hydraulic fluid servicing at ramp level by using the aircraft's balance line system.

The flight engineer's hydraulic system panel. *Author's collection*

Hydraulic System A

The hydraulic system that shoulders the highest working loads is system A. This system is powered by variable-displacement pumps that are mechanically driven by the #1 and #2 engine accessory drives. These pumps supply 3,000 psi of hydraulic pressure to the system and can be electrically deactivated and isolated from the system through shutoff and isolation valves in the event of a pump leak or engine fire. If an engine-driven pump fails to produce at least 1,200 psi, the amber LOW PRESSURE light will illuminate.

The system A hydraulic reservoir has a capacity of 4.4 gallons and is slightly pressurized through the use of bleed air from engines

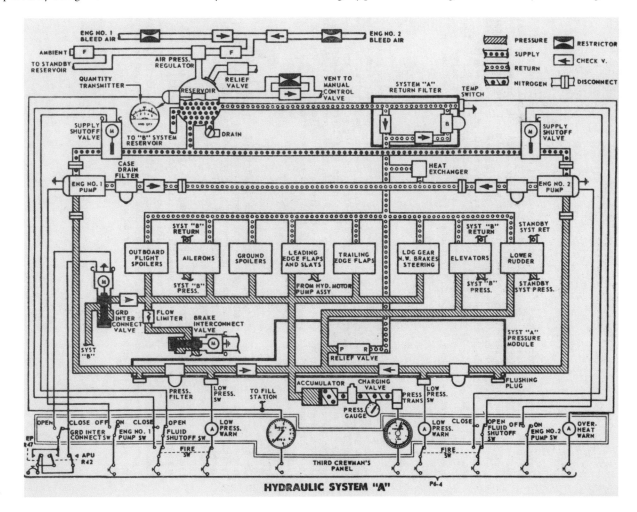

Courtesy of the Boeing Company

#1 and #2 to prevent fluid from foaming at high altitudes. From the reservoir, the engine-driven hydraulic pumps work in unison to pressurize the system. Any excess fluid volume produced by the pumps is returned to the reservoir via a heat exchanger in the #3 fuel tank. Pressurizing fluid creates heat, and this action cools the system fluid while warming the fuel in the right wing. Despite this cooling system, an amber OVERHEAT light is provided with a sensor at the reservoir return line as a precaution.

The following systems are powered by system A:

- ailerons
- elevators
- lower rudder
- ground spoilers
- outboard flight spoilers
- trailing edge flaps (primary)
- leading edge flaps and slats (primary)
- landing gear retraction
- landing gear extension (primary)
- nosewheel steering
- nosewheel brakes (optional)
- main wheel brakes (alternate)

Hydraulic System B

Basic flight control redundancy and systems requiring lower fluid volumes to operate are managed by hydraulic system B. The reservoir for this system has a capacity of 2.9 gallons and is partitioned in such a way as to allow for a small quantity of fluid to be left in the event of a system leak. This fluid is reserved for alternate extension of the leading edge

devices in conjunction with the standby system, which will be discussed under "Flight Controls." Two electrically driven hydraulic pumps provide system pressure similar to system A at 3,000 psi, but at a significantly decreased fluid volume. Each pump can be deactivated by shutting off electrical power via the associated ELEC PUMP switch and is equipped with a respective amber LOW PRESSURE light that alerts the flight engineer of a pump failure. Each pump is also equipped with a high temperature switch that is wired to a common amber OVERHEAT light, informing the flight engineer that troubleshooting must occur to determine which pump is generating the OVERHEAT indication. Like system A, system B also employs a pressure accumulator, which is located in the right-side main landing gear well.

Since system B can be easily powered on the ground through the use of the APU generator or external electrical power, a ground interconnect valve is conveniently provided. This valve allows system B pressure to pressurize system A for maintenance purposes without the need to run an engine. It is controlled by the GRD INTERCON-NECT switch located on the flight engineer's panel and can be opened only if there is either APU or external electrical power supplied to the aircraft. Since neither the APU nor external power is available in flight, these safeties prevent inadvertent selection during flight operations.

The following equipment is powered by system B:

- ailerons
- elevators
- upper rudder
- inboard flight spoilers
- main landing gear brakes (primary)
- ventral airstair

Courtesy of the Boeing Company

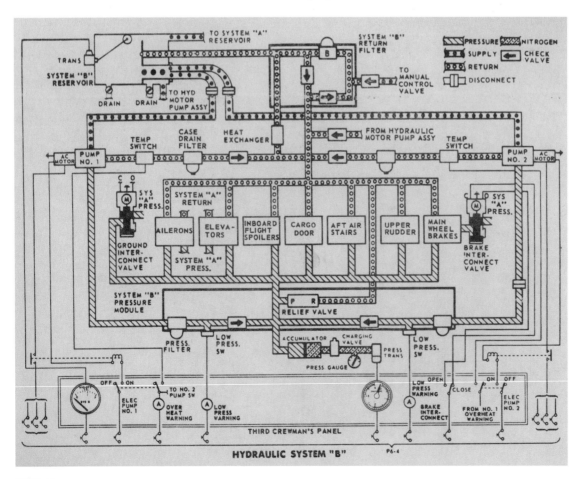

HYDRAULIC SYSTEM "B"

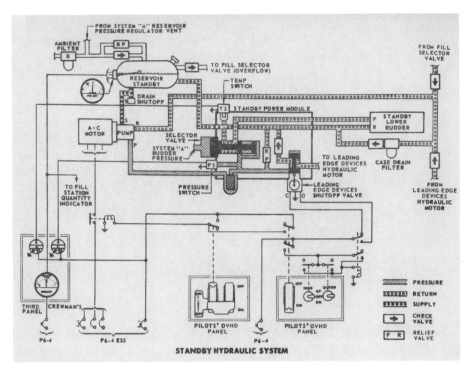

STANDBY HYDRAULIC SYSTEM

The Standby System

Due to the aerodynamic design of the 727, loads are too high on the rudder surfaces to allow for manual reversion, as discussed in chapter 3. Since the primary flight controls (ailerons, elevators, and rudders) must be triple redundant for safety reasons, the aerodynamics engineers looking at the 727 wind tunnel data realized early on that a third "standby" hydraulic system was required to provide adequate failure tolerance for yaw control. A smaller 1.35-gallon reservoir is provided for the system, which is compatible either with Skydrol 500 or MIL-H-5606 fluid types.

The standby system employs a single, electrically driven hydraulic pump to drive the standby rudder power control unit if system A pressure is lost to the lower rudder panel. On the pilot's overhead panel, if the RUDDER SYS A switch is set to OFF, the standby system is automatically selected because the switches are mechanically tied together. This causes the standby-system electric pump to become activated, supplying hydraulic control pressure to the standby rudder actuator.

The standby system is also used to provide backup actuation of the leading edge slats and Krueger flaps in the event of a system A failure. The standby system is automatically activated when the ALTERNATE FLAPS switch is selected to ON. This allows alternate extension of the leading edge devices by using system B reservoir reserve fluid pressurized by a hydraulic-motor pump assembly driven by standby system pressure. Once this system is used to extend the leading edge devices, though, they cannot be retracted until maintenance action is performed on the ground.

727-200 Advanced Difference
An additional ambient air vent line is installed between the system A and standby system reservoirs.

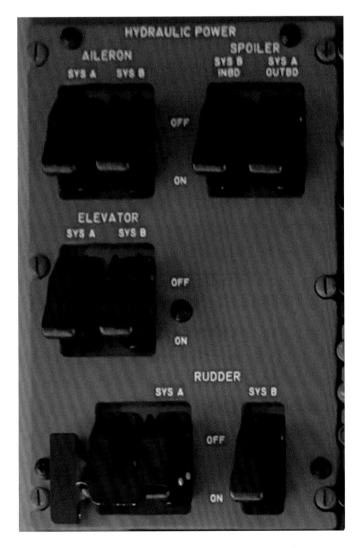

The panel that controls hydraulic power to the flight control systems is located on the pilot's overhead panel. *Author's collection*

The alternate flaps control panel is located on the pilot's overhead panel. *Author's collection*

Flight Controls

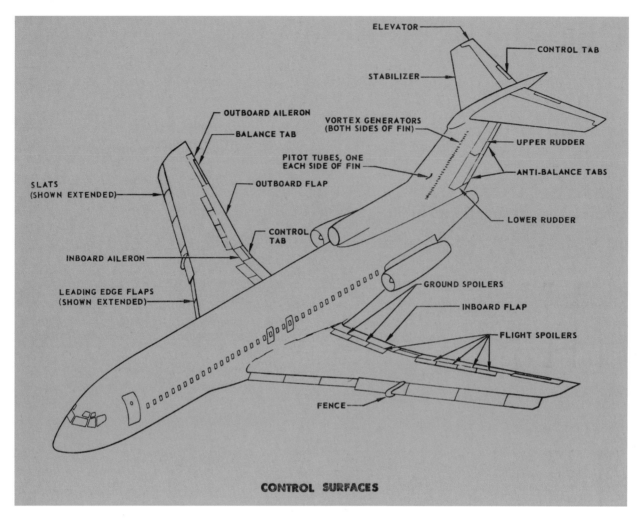

Courtesy of the Boeing Company

Courtesy of the Boeing Company

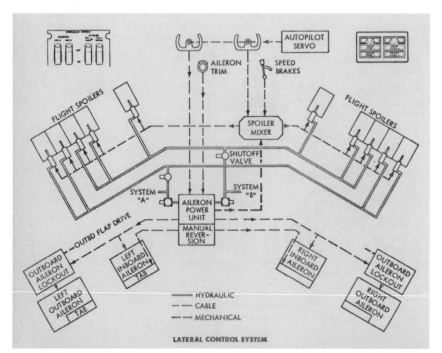

Lateral Control

The lateral-control system bears some similarities to the 707, the most obvious being the use of four ailerons. Each wing employs an outboard aileron located near the wingtip along with an inboard aileron located closer to the fuselage, situated between the inboard and outboard trailing edge flap assemblies. At low speeds (i.e., with flaps extended), both the inboard and outboard ailerons work in unison to provide the desired aircraft handling. During high-speed flight with the flaps retracted, the outboard ailerons are no longer required and are locked in a neutral position. This arrangement helps the aircraft structurally because during flight at high Mach numbers, it prevents twisting forces from being leveraged on the outboard portions of the wings. Five flight spoilers on each wing are used to slow the aircraft in flight and to dump lift after landing. Additionally, the flight spoilers work in unison with the ailerons to enhance roll control. Let's imagine that a pilot is on approach with the flaps extended and wants to bank the aircraft to the left. He turns the yoke to the left, causing the inboard and outboard ailerons on the right wing to deflect downward, thereby increasing lift on that wing. Conversely, both ailerons on the left wing deflect upward along with the flight spoilers, thus decreasing lift. This inequity of lift between the left and right wings causes the aircraft to bank; in this case, to the left. The spoilers help reduce lift and add some element of drag to the downward-moving wing, helping to nudge the nose in the intended direction of the turn and null out any natural adverse yaw tendency.

In contrast to the 707, though, the 727 flight control system is normally operated hydraulically with the use of dual power from the two primary hydraulic systems—system A and system B. In the very unlikely event of a total loss of both systems, a cable-driven backup is provided for the ailerons. This system uses balance panels and control tabs attached to the inboard ailerons, which are manually displaced by the pilot through the control yoke. The control tabs are on the trailing edge of the respective aileron and use aerodynamic forces to displace them. With the flaps extended, the outboard ailerons are slaved to the inboard ailerons via aileron bus cables. This mode, called "manual reversion," occurs automatically if hydraulic pressure is lost, and results in a slightly heavier control feel for the pilots.

Yaw Control

Yaw control, or control about the vertical axis, is primarily controlled by the 727's large and effective dual-rudder installation. The rudder system employs independently actuated upper and lower panels, each with an antibalance tab to increase control effectiveness. Most swept-wing jets exhibit some measure of a tendency called "Dutch roll." If not properly damped out, this tendency can cause alternate rolling and yawing, which amplifies and can lead to a loss of aircraft control and possible structural failure. While the 727 airframe was designed to naturally dampen out much of this tendency, it was also equipped with dual yaw damper systems to ease aircraft control and to optimize passenger comfort. The 727's yaw dampers use a gyro system that senses even the slightest nudge of Dutch roll and

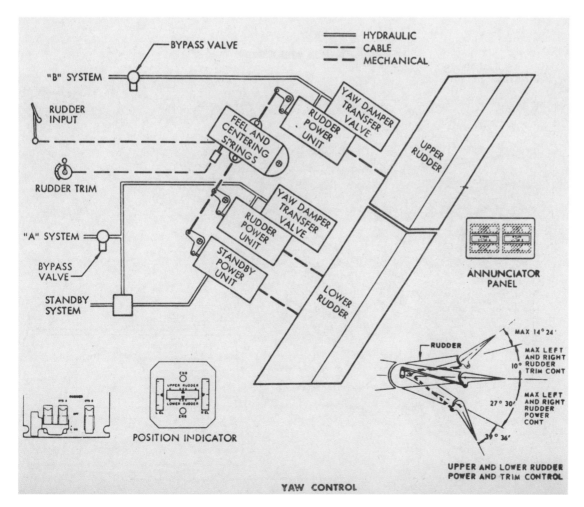

Courtesy of the Boeing Company

automatically provides a small rudder movement to null out the motion. This is done without any feedback to the pilot and is working in the background at all times.

The upper and lower rudder panels are powered independently by system B and system A, respectively. In the event of a loss of both systems, a third electrically driven standby hydraulic system is employed to restore rudder control, but only to the lower rudder. If the standby hydraulic system is the only power source for the rudder, both yaw damper systems are also lost. Since there are three hydraulic power sources, manual reversion is not required on the 727 rudder system.

Pitch Control

The 727 uses two elevator surfaces to effect pitch control for all flight operations. Each elevator, left and right, employs separate hydraulic actuators and, like the ailerons, is powered both by the A and B hydraulic systems. The loss of either system A or B does not change the functionality of the elevator system. A cable-driven manual reversion mode becomes automatic only if both hydraulic pressure sources fail. Both elevators are also equipped with balance panels to reduce manual-control forces for the pilot in the absence of hydraulic boost.

The horizontal stabilizers themselves feature a variable-incidence angle that is manipulated via a jackscrew and dual electric motors. One of these motors is operated by an electric trim switch located on the outboard horn of each pilot's yoke. The other operates at a slower speed and allows the autopilot to automatically trim the stabilizers to maintain an in-trim condition at all times. If both of the electric motors become inoperative, the pilots can use the manual trim wheels located on each side of the cockpit center pedestal. Connected to the stabilizer jackscrew via a cable-and-drum system, these manual trim wheels mechanically reposition the stabilizer during an emergency.

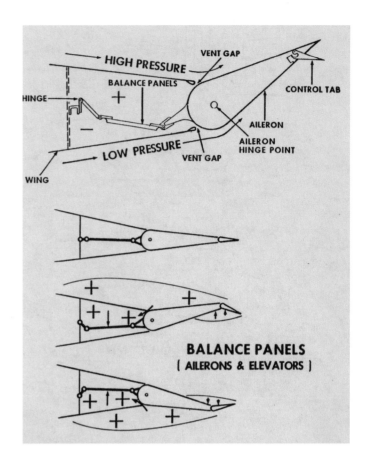

The balance panels located forward of the control surfaces use the differential air pressure above and below the surface to provide lighter control forces for the pilot during manual-reversion flight. *Courtesy of the Boeing Company*

Courtesy of the Boeing Company

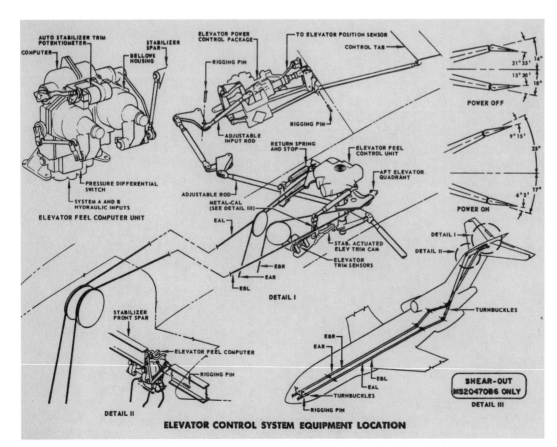

ELEVATOR CONTROL SYSTEM EQUIPMENT LOCATION

Flaps and Slats

The 727 incorporates a very effective and redundant high-lift flap and slat system. Each wing is provided with an inboard and outboard triple-slotted trailing edge flap system. These flaps are a Fowler-type design that increases lift and effective wing area as they translate aft and down. The inboard and outboard flap pairs are operated by independent jackscrew-type deployment systems, which are normally powered by system A hydraulics. Separate gauges are located on the pilot's center panel and labeled OUTBOARD and INBOARD. Each gauge has two needles for the left and right positions, which normally move together, with one on top of the other as the flaps extend and retract. If an asymmetry is detected between either pair of flap panels, the system will automatically discontinue additional movement.

The flap position gauges and leading edge position indication lights are located near the center of the pilots' instrument panel. *Author's collection*

The leading edge Krueger flap panels (three per wing) and slats (four per wing) are automatically actuated in response to the position of the trailing edge flaps. When the trailing edge flaps are in the up position, all slats and Krueger flaps are retracted. When the trailing edge flaps are selected to position 2, slat panels 2, 3, 6, and 7 sequence to the extended position. As the trailing edge flaps are extended farther, the remainder of the slats and all of the Krueger flaps extend. When the leading edge devices are either in motion or not in a commanded position, an amber LE FLAPS light illuminates below and slightly to the right of the INBOARD FLAPS position gauge. Once in the extended position as commanded, the green LE FLAPS light will illuminate to indicate proper operation. When all flaps are selected to UP and all leading edge devices are retracted, both the amber and green LE FLAPS lights are extinguished.

Alternate extension of the trailing edge flaps can be conducted in the absence of normal system A pressure. The trailing edge flaps are operated by an electric-motor-driven backup, while the standby hydraulic system provides power to extend the leading edge devices. By moving the guarded ALTERNATE FLAPS switch to ON, the standby system electric pump is activated, the INBD and OUTBD flap switches are armed, and normal hydraulic pressure is isolated from the system.

Momentary actuation of either the INBD or OUTBD switches will open the leading edge standby shutoff valve. Standby system pressure operates a hydraulic motor that uses a small amount of reserve system B fluid to extend the devices. Once the leading edge devices are extended, they cannot be retracted. When holding the INBD and OUTBD flaps switches to DOWN, the trailing edge flaps are slowly extended by electrically driven motors. Releasing the switches to the spring-loaded OFF position allows the trailing edge flaps to be stopped at any intermediate position desired. Alternate flap operation does not provide for any automatic asymmetry protection that differs significantly from the normal system.

Speed Brakes

As previously mentioned, the flight spoilers are used to augment roll control automatically in conjunction with the ailerons via a spoiler mixer. The flight spoilers can also be used symmetrically as speed brakes through the use of the SPEED BRAKE handle, which is located between the two pilots, to the left of the thrust levers. Pulling this handle aft provides variable speed brake deployment to assist in descending or slowing the aircraft. While in flight, speed brake use on the 727 is strictly allowed only with the wing flaps retracted. An aural horn will sound if the flaps and speed brakes are deployed simultaneously while airborne. When the SPEED BRAKE lever is pulled aft (past 10 degrees) after the aircraft touches down or during a rejected takeoff, the ground spoilers fully extend to place as much weight on the main landing gears as possible to enhance braking action.

The speed brake handle is located between the pilots, just to the left of the thrust levers. *Author's collection*

Landing Gear and Brakes

The 727 features a fully retractable, tricycle-type landing gear system with an incorporated tail skid. Using hydraulic system A pressure, the nose landing gear is steerable up to 78 degrees to either side to provide directional control via the captain's tiller. Steering up to 6 degrees is allowed through the use of the rudder pedals.

Landing gear extension and retraction are normally powered by hydraulic system A. The system also includes fairing doors, which completely enclose all three landing gear wells while the aircraft is in flight.

Retraction

Landing gear retraction is controlled by the LANDING GEAR lever on the pilot's center panel. Once weight is off the wheels, a solenoid lock in the handle disengages, allowing the handle to be moved into the UP position, beginning the retraction sequence. When the nose landing gear is retracted, the forward nose gear doors, which are normally closed with the gear extended, open mechanically via a cable drive. Once fully open, the landing gear is hydraulically retracted. When the nose gear is fully retracted, the forward nose gear doors will sequence closed. If the aircraft is equipped with optional nosewheel brakes, pressure is automatically applied to stop the rotation of the wheels.

Each main landing gear is equipped with an outboard landing gear door that is mechanically articulated by the landing gear's motion. The inboard landing gear doors are normally closed when the gear is extended, but during retraction, these doors are hydraulically opened prior to movement of the landing gear legs, and the mechanical down lock is disengaged. The gear is then retracted hydraulically and braking is automatically applied to the wheel brakes to stop wheel rotation. Once the gear is safely locked in the up **position, the inboard doors are commanded to close.** The tail skid is electrically retracted with the landing gear. While the landing gear is in transit, the red NOSE GEAR, LEFT GEAR, RIGHT GEAR, and DOORS lights illuminate until the landing gears are up and fully locked, and the doors are secured closed. The pilot can then move the LANDING GEAR handle to the OFF position, which removes hydraulic power from the system.

The landing gear control and indication panel is located between the pilots on the instrument panel. *Author's collection*

Extension

Positioning the LANDING GEAR lever to the down (DN) position begins the extension sequence. The red NOSE GEAR, LEFT GEAR, RIGHT GEAR, and DOORS lights illuminate while the landing gear is in transit. Landing gear extension occurs in the reverse order compared to the retraction. The forward nose gear doors and inboard main gear doors are first sequenced open, followed by the extension of the landing gear legs. The landing gears employ an over-center locking system, which mechanically holds the landing gear legs in the down position. The forward nose gear doors and inboard main landing gear doors sequence closed, and the red DOORS light extinguishes. Once all the landing gears are properly extended and locked, the green NOSE GEAR, LEFT GEAR, and RIGHT GEAR lights remain illuminated.

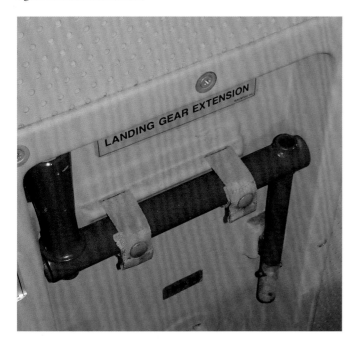

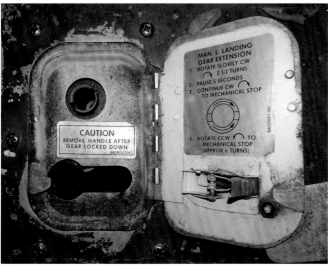

The manual-gear-extension handle is stored on the aft bulkhead in the cockpit. Three manual-gear-extension sockets are located on the floor of the cockpit, just forward of the entry door. *Author's collection*

The landing gears can be manually extended by the flight engineer via a cable-driven system if system A pressure or normal landing gear operation (or both) is lost. A crank tool is secured to the aft cockpit wall, which is dismounted and used for this purpose. Located in the floor of the cockpit, just forward of the cockpit door, there are three small doors that cover the manual-extension sockets for each gear leg. By carefully following the direction placard and the non-normal checklist, the manual extension is accomplished. In this situation, the tail skid will not extend and the inboard main landing gear doors will remain open.

The main landing gear viewer can be used to visually confirm that the gear legs are down and locked if the indication light system for landing gear position were to fail. When the two red lines seen in the inset are aligned, the gear is confirmed down and locked. *Author's collection*

In the event of a loss of power to, or a malfunction of, the landing gear position indicator lights in the cockpit, a landing gear viewer system is provided as a backup. A viewer for the nose gear is located in a compartment on the floor of the forward galley area, approximately 4 feet aft of the cockpit door. The main landing gear viewers are located on either side of the aisle, roughly 5 feet behind the rearmost overwing exits. When looking through the viewer (each of which has a sight glass focused on the respective landing gear), the flight engineer can see the aligned white and red stripes, indicating that the down lock for that particular landing gear leg is properly engaged. The inset on the photo above depicts a proper down-and-locked indication, as seen through the viewer.

Brakes

Brakes are actuated by the pilot exerting pressure on the tops of the rudder pedals. The left pedal controls the brakes on the left landing gear, with the right pedal doing the same for the right landing gear. Each wheel assembly incorporates a multiple-disc-brake provision to allow powerful braking action for the 727. The main landing gear wheel brakes are normally powered by hydraulic system B, with backup power supplied by system A through the brake interconnect valve, and, failing that, a 1,000 psi brake pressure accumulator. An antiskid system is employed to prevent wheel lockup during times of heavy braking. The system senses an impending wheel lockup and momentarily reduces pressure to that wheel until traction is restored.

Some 727 aircraft are equipped with nosewheel brakes for additional short-field performance. Hydraulic system A pressure is metered to the nosewheel brakes when the antiskid system is on, wheel speed is in excess of 20 knots, and both left and right brake pedals are more than halfway depressed.

In the event of a complete loss of all hydraulic power to the brakes, a pneumatic system that is controlled by the red PNEUMATIC BRAKE handle on the captain's forward panel is provided to restore some braking capability. Rotating this handle toward INCREASE releases pressurized air from a 2,000 psi bottle into the main wheel-braking system to stop the aircraft.

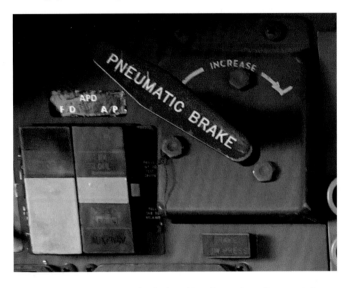

The pneumatic emergency brake handle is located on the captain's instrument panel. *Author's collection*

727-200 Difference
The tail skid is extended and retracted using hydraulic system A pressure.

Power Plant and the Auxiliary Power Unit

The Boeing 727 is powered by three Pratt & Whitney JT8D turbofan engines that can range in thrust levels from 14,000 to 17,400 pounds, depending on the version installed. The engine is of an axial-flow design with two spools, low and high pressure, each featuring a turbine section that drives a compressor component in the forward part of the engine. The low-pressure spool (N1) is composed of a six-stage compressor, of which the first two are substantially larger in diameter. These two stages provide the turbofan effect, both somewhat compressing the air for the following compressor stages, as well as propelling a large quantity of air into the bypass duct. This high-energy air moves quickly around the rest of the engine, supplying additional fuel-efficient thrust while also mixing with the exhaust and significantly decreasing the noise signature. The N1 spool is driven by a three-stage turbine section that transmits power to the compressor section via a direct driveshaft.

The high-pressure (N2) spool uses one turbine stage to drive seven additional compressor stages, 7 through 13, via a hollow shaft. This shaft also incorporates an accessory gear box used to power aircraft generators, hydraulic pumps, and the engine's own fuel control system. Pressurized bleed air is tapped from compressor stages 8 and 13 to provide for cabin pressurization, anti-icing, and hydraulic-reservoir pressurization.

Courtesy of the Boeing Company via Chuck Ballard

Pratt & Whitney JT8D-9 Pressures and Temperatures at Rated Takeoff Thrust (14,500 pounds)

Pressure (psi)	14.7	29	61	233	214	28 (fan air)	30	29
Temperature (F)	59	199	356	785	1766	199 (fan air)	970	591

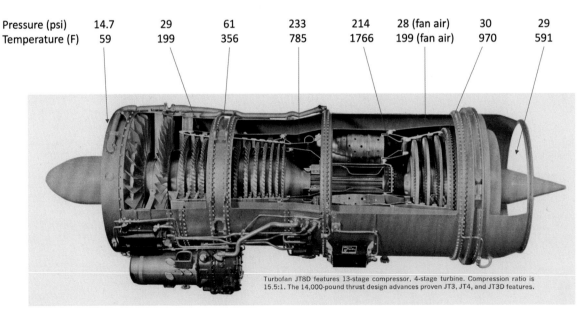

Turbofan JT8D features 13-stage compressor, 4-stage turbine. Compression ratio is 15.5:1. The 14,000-pound thrust design advances proven JT3, JT4, and JT3D features.

Center Engine Installation

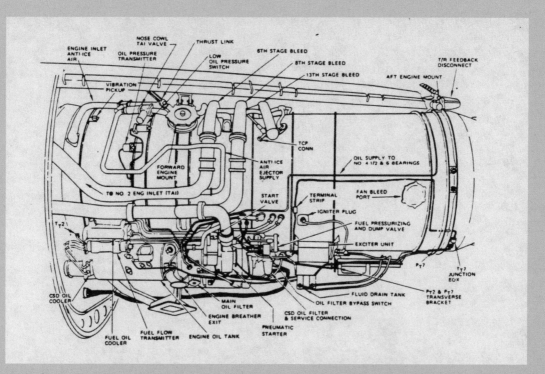

Port Side

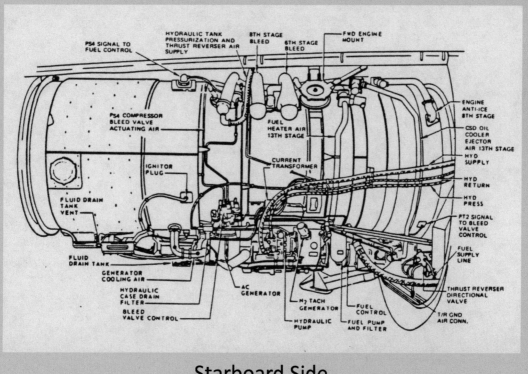

Starboard Side

Courtesy of the Boeing Company

Air that is not bypassed is drawn into the engine's compressors. As this air flows into the compressor, the space available at each stage squeezes the air significantly, thereby increasing its temperature in the process. On a standard day, with a temperature of 59 degrees F, the air enters the first stage at nearly ambient temperature and pressure, but the pressure and temperature increase significantly as the air passes each stage. Provided that the engine is being operated at the JT8D-9's maximum takeoff thrust, the air pressure and temperature measured at the thirteenth stage will reach 233 psi and 785 degrees F. After exiting the last compressor stage, fuel is added that causes combustion and rapid movement while exacting rotational force as it passes through the four turbine stages. These turbines turn the compressors, propagating the chain reaction that will continue until fuel is shut off. A substantial amount of the total energy produced by the engine is used to turn the compressors, run the accessories, and provide bleed air to the aircraft. The energy that is left is expelled out the jet pipe and mixed with the bypass fan air to create forward thrust.

Starting

The JT8D uses a pneumatic starter motor to turn the N2 spool up to a speed that allows ignition. Air pressure for the starter can be supplied from the APU, a ground air cart, or an operating engine via the aircraft's pneumatic system and is controlled by a starter valve.

The electric ignition system is activated in the combustion chambers, and with an N2 speed of 20 percent, fuel is introduced by raising that engine's start lever, located at the base of the throttle quadrant. The starter assists the acceleration until a cutout speed of 40 percent. From there, the combustion reaction steadily accelerates the engine to idle speed. During this time, the pilot monitors the engine's fuel flow and exhaust gas temperature (EGT) gauges carefully, ready to cut fuel if a start malfunction presents itself.

Engine Indications

The JT8D, as well as many other jet engines, uses a metric called engine pressure ratio (EPR) to quantify engine thrust output. EPR, often pronounced "eeper," has a separate gauge in the cockpit for each engine. EPR measures the ratio of pressure between the exhaust and the compressor inlet at the tip of the bullet fairing and divides the two in order to provide an indication of thrust output. A JT8D-9 engine at maximum thrust would have an exhaust pressure of 29 psi and an inlet pressure of 14.7 psi. By dividing the two (29/14.7), we get roughly 1.97 EPR at takeoff thrust. This number could vary on the basis of atmospheric conditions, bleed extraction, and the version of the engine. The desired thrust level must be set carefully, since the JT8D does not have thrust limiters. The engine is actually capable of much-higher thrust settings by pushing the thrust levers full

The engine gauges for all three power plants are arranged into vertical columns for easy interpretation on the instrument panel between the pilots. *Author's collection*

forward in the event of an emergency. This procedure is advisable only during windshear, aerodynamic stalls, or when terrain contact is imminent, because it effectively sacrifices the longevity of the engines to save the aircraft.

On the pilot's center panel, each engine is also supplied with N1 and N2 speed gauges that indicate a percentage of a determined maximum. Exhaust temperatures are provided in degrees centigrade, with fuel flow measured in increments of 1,000 pounds/hour. Green arcs indicate normal operating ranges, while yellow arcs denote operation in a cautionary or time-limited range. Red radials indicate absolute engine limits. Below the landing gear handle, to the right of the engine gauges, red LOW OIL PRESSURE lights warn the pilots of a clogged oil filter or a lack of required pressure.

Oil quantity, temperature, and pressure are monitored from the flight engineer's station. *Author's collection*

Additional indications are provided on the flight engineer's panel for continuous monitoring. Oil quantity in US gallons, oil temperature in degrees centigrade, and oil pressure in pounds per square inch are indicated. Electrical power to the panel pictured above has been removed. Observing the gauges on a depowered

aircraft can tell something about the electrical system. Gauges that show zero, or absolute low indications, are DC powered, while AC-powered gauges show the indication at the moment electrical power was removed. The adage "DC dies and AC lies" is displayed here. In the event of contamination of an engine's oil system, a filter for each is provided along with a bypass valve, which allows unfiltered oil to continue to flow to the engine components in the event of a clogged filter. Amber OIL FILTER BYPASS lights are provided, which indicate a clogged oil filter, and on early -100 airplanes indicate low oil pressure or a clogged filter.

Each engine employs an oil cooler that cools oil by using fuel arriving for use by the engine. This heat exchanger also provides necessary heating for the fuel. Because of the need of fuel flow for oil cooling, oil temperatures tend to be higher during times of low engine thrust and are kept cooler by high fuel flow at maximum thrust settings.

Thrust Control

Each engine employs a jet fuel control unit that is driven by the N2 spool accessory drive. This controls engine thrust settings by sensing thrust lever angle, start lever position, compressor inlet temperature and diffuser pressure, and engine rpm. Using these inputs, the jet fuel control unit schedules fuel appropriately.

Surge Control

During slam acceleration of the engine, the pressures between the compressors become mismatched and can lead to engine surges. To prevent this unwanted characteristic, automatic surge bleed valves are installed on the N1 compressors to balance the pressures. As the engine rpm accelerates above 53, the surge bleed valves close to allow normal engine operation, without further loss of efficiency.

Thrust Reversers

This is an example of an early-style thrust reverser in the deployed position. *Courtesy of the Boeing Company*

Note the differences with the later-model thrust reverser. The blocker doors are completely internal, actuating behind the grilles, which help direct airflow while in reverse thrust. *Author's collection*

Each engine is equipped with a thrust reverser system to aid in slowing the aircraft after landing or during a rejected takeoff. The thrust reverser could also be used under some circumstances to move the aircraft backward—a procedure called "power back." Each reverser is controlled by a reverse-thrust lever located forward of the thrust levers. With the engine thrust levers retarded to idle and when the reverse-thrust levers are raised to detent 1, the reverser buckets deploy by using pneumatic power from the associated engine's thirteenth-stage bleed air system. This action illuminates the respective amber REVERSER OPERATING light. Continuing to pull up and aft on the reverse-thrust levers toward detents 2 and 3 increases engine thrust. This jet thrust is deflected forward by the reverser buckets to assist in slowing the aircraft.

Auxiliary Power Unit (APU)

Because the 727 was designed to be as independent as possible from airport equipment, a small gas turbine engine, the Garrett GTC86 98/C/CK, is installed in the main landing gear well, across the keel beam. The APU, which turns at 41,600 rpm, is intended only for ground operation and provides 115-volt AC power and pressurized air at 47 psi for air-conditioning and engine starting. Fuel for the APU is normally fed by gravity from fuel tank #2, or from the fuel feed manifold for engine #2 on late-model airplanes. For safety, the APU is encased in a stainless-steel shroud with an air intake in the left wheel well area, and an exhaust on the top of the right wing, near the wing root. Early 727 models had an exhaust door that would close when the APU was not in use. These proved to be problematic in operation, often remaining open and eventually parting ways with the aircraft after takeoff. Later-model and retrofitted airplanes were equipped with a louvered exhaust, which was much more dependable.

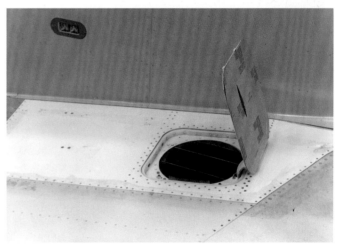

The early auxiliary power unit (APU) exhaust featured a door that closed when not in use. This door proved troublesome in operation, with the door occasionally parting ways with the aircraft. *Courtesy of the Boeing Company*

Fire Detection and Protection

The 727 employs fire detection capability for all three engines, the APU, and wheel wells. Fire-extinguishing provisions are installed for the engines and APU. Overheat detection for identifying a bleed air leak is also included as part of the warning system. All detection systems are equipped with a test feature to allow preflight system checks.

Engines

Fire detection for all three engines is provided through the use of two detector loops for each engine. One surrounds the engine, while the other is concentrated near the strut on the pod engines and the upper firewall on the center engine. Each loop consists of a sealed metal tube filled with inert gas and a pressure switch. As the temperature of the loop reaches a threshold temperature, the gas in the loop expands, increases pressure, and then trips the switch, which provides a fire warning to the cockpit crew. A fire handle for each engine is located on the pilots' glare shield. When a fire is sensed, the respective handle illuminates and the fire bell sounds.

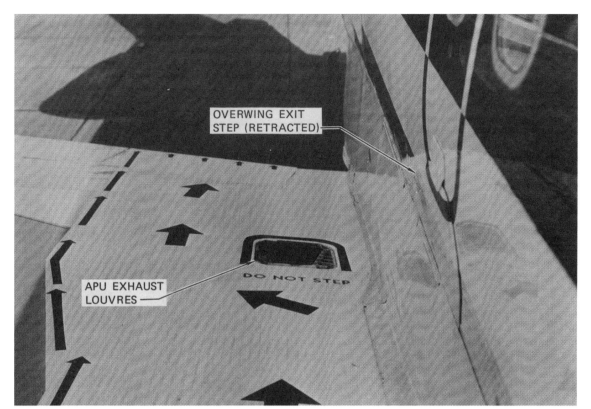

This 727-200 features the newer APU exhaust, with the door replaced with a grille. One often-overlooked difference between the 727-100 and the 727-200 is the addition of a step below the aft overwing exit. When the exit was opened, the small step would automatically deploy. *Courtesy of the Boeing Company*

OVERWING EXIT
STEP (RETRACTED)

APU EXHAUST
LOUVRES

DO NOT STEP

On most 727s, the fire control panel is located on the pilots' glare shield. *Author's collection*

Pulling the lit fire handle begins the fire protection process. Doing so isolates the engine by closing the engine fuel shutoff valve, the engine bleed valve, the engine anti-ice valves, and the hydraulic supply valve (but only for engines 1 and 2), while tripping the generator relay and disarming the respective hydraulic LOW PRESSURE light.

With the engine isolated, the fire-extinguishing system can be employed. The system consists of two 640 psi halon fire bottles located in the ventral stairwell, along with a manifold system that allows either bottle to be discharged into any engine. The bottle, left or right, can be selected with the BOTTLE TRANSFER switch, then the respective engine DISCH switch is depressed, which opens the appropriate engine extinguisher valve and fires a squib. The squib punctures the bottle to allow the flow of halon to the offending engine.

APU

Like the engines, the APU is provided with a fire loop that operates in a similar manner. If a fire is detected, a red FIRE light illuminates on the flight engineer's APU control panel, along with activation of the fire bell. The APU will automatically shut down provided the AUTO FIRE SHUTDOWN switch is in the guarded ARMED position. This switch allows a warning-system test during APU operation, while preventing an auto shutdown.

An APU fire can be managed either from the APU control panel in the cockpit or from the left main landing gear well if the pilot / flight engineer is outside the aircraft. Both locations feature a T handle, which when pulled closes the APU fuel valve, trips the APU generator, and arms the fire bottle. Pushing the BOTTLE DISCHARGE button at either location fires a squib into the APU fire bottle, allowing halon pressurized to 400 psi to flow into the APU shroud.

The APU control panel is located on the aft bulkhead at the flight engineer's station. *Courtesy of the Boeing Company*

Overheat Detection

The bleed air overheat lights are located on the flight engineer's upper panel. *Author's collection*

Bleed air that is extremely hot is extracted from each engine for the purposes of providing cabin pressurization and anti-icing. A leak in one of these ducts could potentially cause severe damage to nearby components and structures if undetected. To mitigate this hazard, the pod engine struts are equipped with sensors that, if tripped, will illuminate the appropriate amber ENG STRUT 1 or ENG STRUT 3 light on the flight engineer's panel. If an overheat is sensed in the ventral stairwell, aft cargo compartment, or keel beam areas, the amber LOWER AFT BODY light will illuminate. This differentiation is important because it will direct which bleed valve(s) need to be closed by the flight engineer, with reference to the non-normal checklist.

Wheel Wells

The inboard main landing gear wells and nose gear well are each equipped with a detector loop in case of a wheel brake or hydraulic fire. If any one of the loops detects a fire, the red glare-shield-mounted WHEEL WELL light will illuminate, along with the sounding of the fire bell. There is no fire protection for the wheel wells because the non-normal checklist will direct the extension of the landing gears to effectively blow the fire out.

727-200 Difference
Engine fire detection consists of two colocated A and B fire loops. If one is found to be faulty during a preflight test, the operating loop can be selected, allowing dispatch under the provisions of the Minimum Equipment List (MEL).

727-200 Advanced Difference
Some aircraft have the engine fire handles relocated from the glare shield to the aft overhead panel, above the pilots.

Later Modification
In the wake of cargo fire accidents such as ValuJet 592 and pursuant to recommendations by the NTSB, air carrier aircraft were required to be retrofitted with cargo fire detection and protection systems.

Fuel System

The fuel system on the 727 is composed of three fuel tanks, which can be filled with jet fuel (a wide-cut type of kerosene). The approved fuel types for the 727 are Jet A, Jet A1, Jet B, JP-1, JP-4, and JP-5 (the JP designations are military-grade fuels) and can be used and mixed without limitation.

The sealed volume between the forward and aft wing spars inside the left and right wings define the fuel storage for tanks 1 and 3, respectively. The center section, between the wings and beneath the cabin floor, as well as a small portion of the inboard wing root section, provides space for the center 2 fuel tank. While the wing tanks, 1 and 3, are integral sealed compartments, the center 2 tank retains its fuel volume by use of two (later aircraft have three) sealed bladders, which are interconnected. During normal cruise flight operations, each tank (1, 2, and 3) is intended to supply its respective engine (1, 2, and 3) with fuel through the use of AC-driven boost pumps. This configuration is known as "tank-to-engine" feed. Although this is the normal configuration, as required for fuel balancing or during non-normal operations with an engine shut down, any engine can be fed by any tank by means of a selectable crossfeed system. To allow further redundancy, in the absence of all electrical power, each engine can be suction fed, but only on a tank-to-engine basis. If suction feeding is required, adequate fuel flow may not be available for full-thrust settings, particularly at altitudes above 25,000 feet.

Wing Tanks (1 and 3)

Each wing tank has a capacity of 12,020 pounds of fuel and employs two AC-powered electric boost pumps to supply positive-pressure feed to the fuel system. These pumps are each powered by different electrical buses, so that a single electrical failure cannot compromise fuel flow. Each boost pump is equipped with a check valve (to prevent

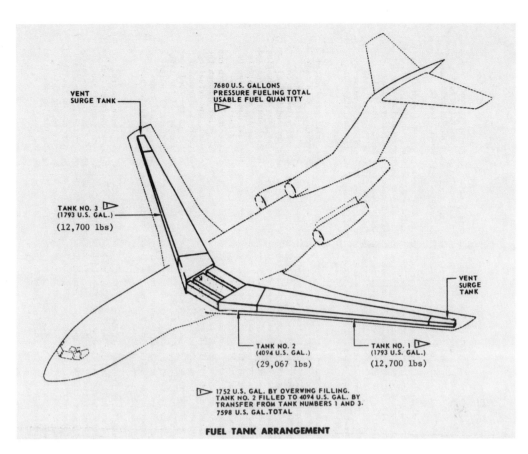

FUEL TANK ARRANGEMENT

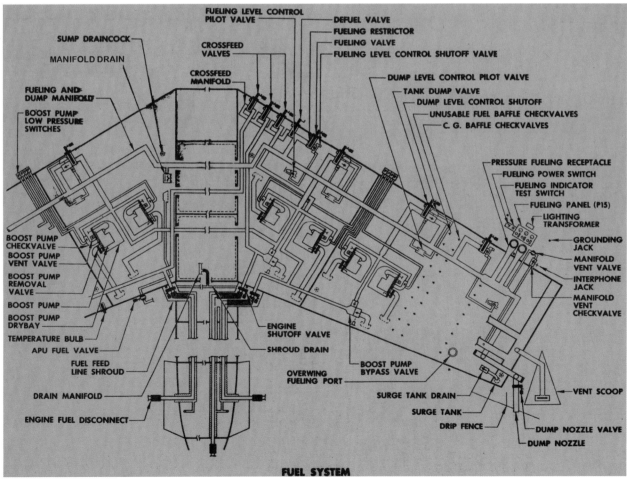

FUEL SYSTEM

reverse fuel flow) and a low-pressure sensor, which if tripped (i.e., less than 5 psi differential) will illuminate a respective amber LOW PRESSURE light on the flight engineer's panel. Each wing tank is equipped with a heat exchanger that uses relatively cold fuel to cool the hydraulic fluid for the A and B systems. Tank 1 has the least-cooling load because it cools A-system fluid, which uses pumps that are engine driven and produce less heat. Conversely, tank 3 cools the electric-pump-driven B-system fluid, which, because the electric pumps are cooled by the fluid they pressurize, tends to be warmer, creating a slightly higher tank temperature. Of the three tanks, tank 2 has the highest temperature because it has less surface area and is radiantly warmed by the passenger cabin directly above it. Because keeping the fuel above the freezing point (−40°F for Jet-A) is important on long, high-altitude flights, a temperature sensor is installed in tank 1, with an associated gauge on the flight engineer's panel.

Center Tank (Tank 2)

Tank 2 has a larger volumetric capacity than tanks 1 or 3 and is plumbed to feed the number 2 engine when the fuel system is set up for tank-to-engine feed. This tank is also used to provide fuel for the APU while the aircraft is on the ground. Tank 2 has a usable fuel capacity of 24,040 pounds of jet fuel, which can be fed using the four AC-powered electric boost pumps. Two of these pumps have pickups in the aft portion of the tank, while the other two scavenge fuel from the forward section of the tank. This allows for positive fuel feed

even with low quantities during extreme pitch and yaw angles. Each boost pump employs a check valve and associated LOW PRESSURE warning light on the flight engineer's panel. In order to ensure operational fuel pumps in the event of multiple electrical failures, two of these boost pumps are powered by the essential buses, directly from any operational generator selected by the flight engineer.

Fuel Crossfeed

In order to allow any engine, or all of them, to feed from any selected fuel tank, the 727 fuel system incorporates a crossfeed system. This feature is used for non-normal operations, such as flight with an inoperative engine or to correct a fuel imbalance between tanks 1 and 3, since they must be kept within 1,000 pounds differential per aircraft limitations. The crossfeed system is also used during normal in-flight procedures, when tank 2 contains more fuel than tanks 1 or 3. Under this normal condition, in order to reduce wing bending moment, all three engines are fed by tank 2 through the crossfeed system until all three tanks contain roughly the same amount of fuel. Once this quantity balance has been achieved, the engines are returned to the standard tank-to-engine feed configuration.

Each fuel tank has an AC motor-powered crossfeed valve, directly controlled by the CROSSFEED rotary switches located on the flight engineer's panel. These valves employ a blue IN TRANSIT light, which indicates that the valve is either in motion or disagrees with the switch position. Opening this valve, provided that there is positive

The flight engineer monitors and controls the fuel system. The three blue gauges are the later digital type and are blank, with electrical power removed from the aircraft. Each gauge shows fuel in pounds remaining for each tank. *Author's collection*

boost pump pressure from the tank being used, will cause fuel to flow into the common crossfeed manifold, making it available to feed any other selected engine. The procedure is quite simple in concept, just requiring positive pressure from the tank in use and an open pathway to the desired engine. For example, if the flight engineer wishes to feed engine 3 with fuel from fuel tank 1, the following procedure is required:

1. Ensure that the tank 1 boost pumps are selected ON and providing pressure (amber LOW PRESSURE lights extinguished).
2. Open the tank 1 crossfeed valve and verify that the blue TRANSIT light has extinguished.
3. Open the tank 3 crossfeed valve and verify that the blue TRANSIT light has extinguished.
4. Turn off the boost pumps in tank 3, ensuring that both amber LOW PRESSURE lights are illuminated.

It is important to note that the crossfeed system cannot be used to transfer fuel from one tank to another while in flight. Also, because the crossfeed system requires positive boost pressure, engines cannot suction-feed through the crossfeed manifold, but only from their respective tanks.

Fueling

Not to be confused with the crossfeed system, a separate manifold is connected to all three fuel tanks. Most commonly, this system is used to fuel the airplane through the use of the attached single-point refueling station. The refueling station is located under the leading edge of the right wing, just aft of slat 5. This compartment contains hookups for two high-pressure refueling hoses with gauges to indicate the fuel quantity in each tank, allowing complete refueling in under twelve minutes, at a rate of 600 gallons per minute. Each tank has an electrically activated refueling valve to control the fueling process, with an associated control switch and valve position status light to allow for precise and fast fueling. For this system to be used, electrical power must be available from either the APU or connected external power. To prevent accidental overfilling of the fuel tanks, likely causing serious damage to the airframe, mechanical float-operated shutoff valves are installed as a backup to cut fuel flow into the tank when it is full.

In the absence of electrical power, or during a mechanical issue with the pressure-refueling system, tanks 1 and 3 are equipped with gravity-fueling ports on the top of each wing. While these can be used to refuel the airplane, notice that tank 2 does not have this ability because of its location in the center section of the airplane. Thus, fuel must be added either to tank 1 or 3 and transferred into tank 2 by use of the defueling valve located just inboard of the refueling station under the right wing. Like with crossfeed operation, fuel transfer and defueling just requires positive boost pressure from the tank being drawn from, and an open pathway to the tank being filled. If the crew desires the transfer of fuel, for example, from tank 1 to tank 2, the following procedure, which requires electrical power, should be accomplished:

1. Turn on all boost pumps for the supply tank (tank 1).
2. Open the CROSSFEED valve for the supply tank and verify that the blue TRANSIT light has extinguished.

3. Open the defueling valve under the right wing.
4. At the refueling panel, open the refueling switch for the tank to be serviced (tank 2).
5. Monitor with the fuel gauges at the fuel station.
6. When complete, close the defueling valve.

Notice that both the defueling valve and the refueling valves are located outside the cockpit, thus making this operation an only-on-the-ground procedure. If required, this system can also be used to pump fuel back into the truck by using the aircraft's boost pumps.

In-Flight Fuel Dumping

The 727 can jettison fuel through one nozzle on each wingtip.
Courtesy of the Boeing Company

The 727 is also equipped with in-flight fuel-dumping ability in the event that an expeditious emergency landing is required early on in the flight, when the airplane is still above maximum landing gross weight. To allow this, four fuel-dumping valves are provided that are connected to the refueling manifold, one for tanks 1 and 3, and two for tank 2. Each end of the refueling manifold is also connected to a dump nozzle and nozzle valve located in each wingtip. Using all tank boost pumps to provide pressure, fuel can be rapidly dumped overboard by opening all four dump valves and the two nozzle valves. If all boost pumps are operational, fuel can be expelled at a rate of 2,300 pounds a minute. Boeing designers, ever aware of crew workload, realized that if fuel dumping is required, there may be many distractions that might temporarily remove the crew's attention from the dumping process. An automatic dump shutoff feature was incorporated that terminates dumping when each tank level approaches 3,500 pounds of fuel, leaving the aircraft with roughly forty-five to sixty minutes of fuel remaining.

727-200 Differences
Tanks 1 and 3 have a total capacity ranging from 11,806 to 12,020 pounds, depending on aircraft serial number.

Tank 2 standard capacities range from 27,430 to 29,560 pounds, depending on aircraft serial number. On later-model aircraft, the center fuel tank bladders were removed and the compartment was integrally sealed. The absence of the bladders allowed for an additional 1,901 pounds of fuel capacity in tank 2.

727-200 Advanced Differences

The tank 2 fuel boost pumps operate at a higher pressure than the boost pumps for tanks 1 and 3. This modification ensures positive fuel feed from this tank to all engines if the appropriate crossfeed valves are properly selected to the OPEN position during takeoff.

The APU, which is normally fed from tank 2, can also be supplied from the source that is supplying engine 2.

Pneumatics

On the 727, the pneumatic system is used for cabin pressurization, air-conditioning, engine starting, thermal anti-ice, hydraulic reservoir pressurization, and thrust reverser actuation.

Bleed Air Sources

The Pratt & Whitney JT8D engines used on the 727 employ a tap on the eighth-stage compressor to provide moderate temperature and pressure "bleed" air to power the aircraft's pneumatic system. Engines 1 and 3 can also augment the eighth-stage bleed air with higher-pressure thirteenth-stage air if necessary. While in flight, the primary source of bleed air is obtained by the eighth-stage bleed, which supplies adequate pressure and volume under most in-flight conditions to operate the aircraft systems. However, when the engines are being operated at very low power settings, such as during descent or while taxiing, the pneumatic load is automatically shifted to the thirteenth-stage bleed ports to maintain the required airflow in the system.

For the purposes of supplying the air-conditioning packs, described later in this section, bleed air from the pod-mounted engines 1 and 3 is typically used. Engine 1 normally feeds the left pack, while engine 3 feeds the right pack. The hot bleed air extracted from these engines is routed through a bleed shutoff valve and a precooler, utilizing passing fan air in the engine's bypass duct to cool the air before it continues on into the system. Once this cooling has occurred, the air passes through a temperature sensor, which ensures that the bleed temperature from that engine is within limits, at this point 490°F. If this temperature is exceeded, the associated amber bleed TRIP OFF light will illuminate and the respective engine's bleed valve will automatically close to protect the system from damage. Next, the air travels through an inertial air filter assembly, which is active on the ground and in flight with flaps extended, to eliminate foreign-object contamination being introduced into the system.

Engine 2 can also supply bleed air to the system but is limited to providing only eighth-stage bleed air to the pneumatic system. Because it is using the somewhat cooler low-pressure stage for bleed extraction, this engine does not use a precooler. While it does employ a temperature switch and associated amber HIGH TEMP light, though, no automatic valve movement is provided. The engine 2 system is equipped with two isolation valves, which, as their name suggests, isolate the bleed source from the left and right sides of the pneumatic distribution system. Normally, the bleed air from engine 2 is isolated from the system and is used as a backup if there is a failure of the bleed sources from engines 1 or 3. This design allows continued use of both air-conditioning packs after an engine bleed failure.

While the APU is usable only for ground operations, it can be used as a source of bleed air for operation of an air-conditioning pack when the engines are not operating or for powering the engines' pneumatic starters. The APU bleed air is fed into the thermal anti-ice manifold and then on to the center-engine bleed air ducting through a check valve. By selectively opening one of the engine 2 bleed valves,

The flight engineer's air-conditioning and pressurization panel. This aircraft features the later-model (737 type) pressurization controller in the lower right corner. *Author's collection*

the APU can supply pressurized air to an air-conditioning pack. In order to use APU bleed air to start engines, the respective engine bleed switches must be selected to the OPEN position.

In the event of an inoperative APU, pressurized air for engine starting can be supplied to the system with the use of an external air cart, commonly known as a "huffer cart," connected to the aircraft's pneumatic system through a port just to the right of the tail skid. Limited to 60 psi, the huffer cart can also be used to obtain the high-pressure air required to operate an air-conditioning pack while the plane is at the gate.

Air-Conditioning Packs

The 727 has two air cycle machines, typically referred to as "packs." The purpose of each pack is to provide temperature-controlled air for cabin pressurization. The left pack is ducted in such a way as to be the primary air-conditioning source for the cockpit and a portion of the passenger cabin. The right pack normally supplies additional conditioned air to the passenger cabin.

Each pack employs an A/C PACK switch, which permits hot, pressurized air to flow from the aircraft's pneumatic system when selected to OPEN. These valves can also be closed automatically to prevent damage to the system if an overheating of the pack is sensed. This condition will also illuminate the respective amber A/C PACK TRIP OFF light to alert the flight engineer of the malfunction and is resettable with the use of the RESET switch, once the pack cools sufficiently.

After the hot bleed air has passed through the pack valve, it is split into two separate pathways: one that will be used to cool a large quantity of the air, while the other will later be used to provide warm air to be introduced for temperature control. On the cold side of the pack, the hot air is first routed through the primary heat exchanger,

which uses outside air to provide cooling. From there, this partially cooled air is passed through a compressor, significantly increasing the pressure and the temperature of the air. A secondary heat exchanger is used to cool this high-pressure air prior to its traveling through a turbine. This turbine provides the power to mechanically drive the compressor, and as the air passes through, the pressure is greatly reduced, and through expansion, the air temperature becomes very cold. This supercooled air then passes through a water separator to remove any condensation before finally being mixed with the hot air and distributed through the air-distribution ducting. The desired mixture of hot and cold air is controlled by modulated valves, which can be controlled either automatically or manually by way of the rotary temperature selectors labeled CONTROL CABIN (left pack) and PASSENGER CABIN (right pack). The air mix valve indicators are located between the temperature selectors to provide mix valve status for the flight engineer.

To allow greater amounts of cooling air through the primary and secondary heat exchangers, the NACA-type inlet is located under the fuselage on the forward portion of the wing-to-body fairing and employs variable-geometry openings. These are controllable directly through the use of the left and right COOLING DOORS switches on the flight engineer's panel, used in conjunction with the colocated PACK TEMP and COOLING DOORS position indicators. During times when less cooling is required, such as high-altitude cruise flight, the flight engineer may wish to close these doors to reduce aerodynamic drag. On some 727 aircraft, these doors can also be controlled automatically.

Upstream of the air-conditioning packs, the air-conditioning duct manifold carries the air to the various registers throughout the cabin and cockpit. A small amount of air from the right pack's cold-air supply is fed to the overhead, passenger-adjustable vents, accelerated

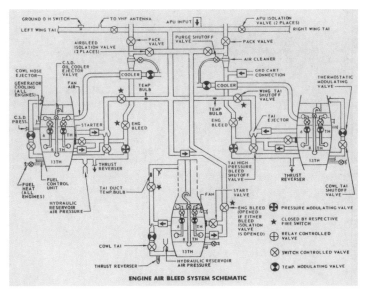

Courtesy of the Boeing Company

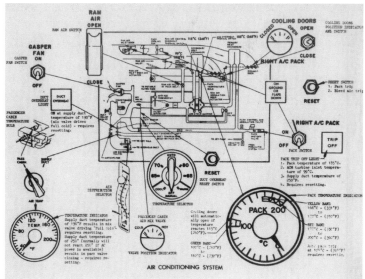

Courtesy of the Boeing Company

Early Pressurization Controller

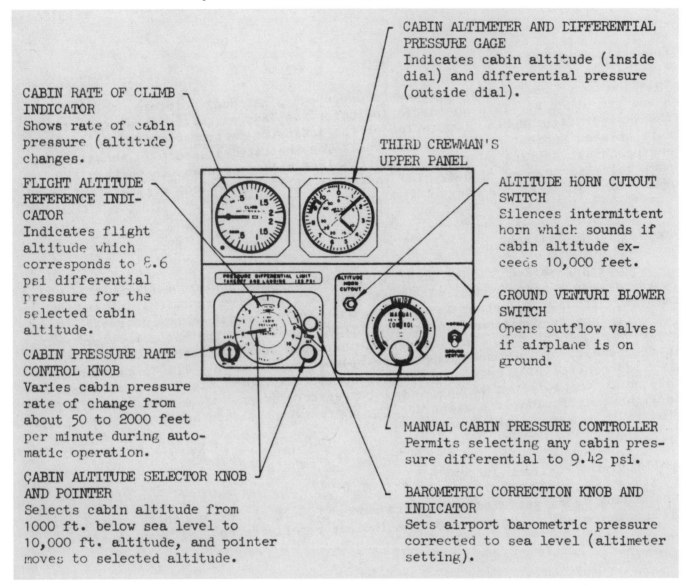

CABIN RATE OF CLIMB INDICATOR
Shows rate of cabin pressure (altitude) changes.

FLIGHT ALTITUDE REFERENCE INDICATOR
Indicates flight altitude which corresponds to 8.6 psi differential pressure for the selected cabin altitude.

CABIN PRESSURE RATE CONTROL KNOB
Varies cabin pressure rate of change from about 50 to 2000 feet per minute during automatic operation.

CABIN ALTITUDE SELECTOR KNOB AND POINTER
Selects cabin altitude from 1000 ft. below sea level to 10,000 ft. altitude, and pointer moves to selected altitude.

CABIN ALTIMETER AND DIFFERENTIAL PRESSURE GAGE
Indicates cabin altitude (inside dial) and differential pressure (outside dial).

THIRD CREWMAN'S UPPER PANEL

ALTITUDE HORN CUTOUT SWITCH
Silences intermittent horn which sounds if cabin altitude exceeds 10,000 feet.

GROUND VENTURI BLOWER SWITCH
Opens outflow valves if airplane is on ground.

MANUAL CABIN PRESSURE CONTROLLER
Permits selecting any cabin pressure differential to 9.42 psi.

BAROMETRIC CORRECTION KNOB AND INDICATOR
Sets airport barometric pressure corrected to sea level (altimeter setting).

Courtesy of the Boeing Company

by an electrically powered gasper fan for passenger comfort. To safeguard against a malfunctioning pack operating outside temperature limits, temperature switches are installed. If the 190°F limit is exceeded, the amber DUCT OVERHEAT light will illuminate, and the pack temperature control valves will drive toward the full cold position. If the overheat progresses to the second, 250°F limit, the associated pack valve will close and shut down the system to prevent damage.

In the event of a failure of both pack systems, flight with an unpressurized cabin will soon be required. If this highly non-normal event were to occur, some aircraft are equipped with a RAM AIR switch that, when activated, will allow some measure of outside air into the air-conditioning distribution manifold directly from the pack heat-exchanger cooling duct.

Pressurization Control

Large quantities of conditioned air are provided by the pneumatic system, through the air-conditioning packs. The volume of airflow is not static and varies with pack usage, temperature selection, and bleed air supply volume. In order to maintain a controlled cabin pressure, a pneumatically controlled outflow valve, located immediately forward of the tail skid on the bottom of the fuselage, modulates open and closed. In effect, this controls the leak rate at which the air is allowed to exit the airplane. By exacting precise control of this "leak," the appropriate cabin pressure can be maintained by the system.

727-200 Differences
A later version of the pressurization control panel developed for the Boeing 737 was adapted to the 727 and allows the flight engineer to set the system up for the entire flight before leaving the gate. Once

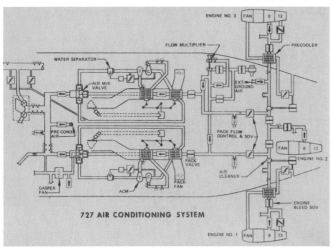

727 AIR CONDITIONING SYSTEM

Courtesy of the Boeing Company

The late-model pressurization controller was standard equipment on the 727-200. *Author's collection*

On the 727-200 series, the pressurization outflow valve, located just above and to the right of the ramp agent's head, is electrically controlled and actuated. *Courtesy of Southwest Airlines*

set, the system is entirely automatic. Even if the aircraft returns to the departure airport because of a non-normal condition, provided the airplane did not reach cruise altitude, pressurization is scheduled without needing to be reset. The amber OFF SCHED DESCENT light will illuminate to alert the crew that the system is set to land back at the departure airport, requiring no action on the part of the crew. In the event of an automatic-controller malfunction, the outflow valve can also be controlled manually by setting the system to MANUAL and utilizing the MANUAL VALVE switch to modulate the valve as required. To prevent the possibility of a malfunction causing an overpressurization and possible damage to the pressure vessel, overpressure relief valves are also installed just forward of the tail skid. The outflow valve is rectangular in shape and is relocated 4 feet above and forward of the tail skid, on the right side of the fuselage.

The APU can be used to supply both air-conditioning packs through the use of a flow multiplier pump, which draws in additional outside air via an APU bleed-driven compressor. This increases the air supply volume sufficiently to allow dual pack operation.

The air-conditioning pack shutoff valves have been moved from the aft stairwell to the pack bays in the wing-to-body fairing. This eliminates the use of the thermal anti-ice ducts for the distribution of APU bleed air.

Due to the higher bleed air demands of the longer fuselage on the 727-200, an autopack trip-off system is incorporated to shut off bleed air from the remaining engines in the event of an engine failure. This allows higher thrust levels by shutting off the air-conditioning systems, thus greatly reducing the need for bleed air extraction. A green AUTO PACK TRIP ARMED light is illuminated when the following conditions cause the system to arm:

1. The aircraft is on the ground
2. Wing flaps are extended
3. The AUTO PACK TRIP switch is in the NORMAL position
4. Engine power is advanced above 1.5 EPR

Some 727-200 series aircraft have a zone temperature control system to allow more-precise temperature control throughout the cabin.

Ice and Rain Protection

On the Boeing 727, components that are considered to be sensitive to ice accumulation are thermally protected, either electrically or through the use of hot bleed air.

Airframe and VHF 1 Antenna Anti-ice

In order to allow the 727 to retain its lifting efficiency, even in the most-adverse weather conditions, most of the wing leading edge surfaces are thermally anti-iced using hot engine bleed air from the anti-ice manifold portion of the pneumatic system. Very early 727-100 series aircraft also were equipped with an anti-icing system for the empennage, which was later found to be unnecessary and thus was not installed on later production aircraft.

Warm air for wing anti-icing is intended to be supplied by the pod-mounted engines. Engines 1 and 3 each employ a wing anti-ice switch that opens two valves per engine, and proper valve operation is indicated by a green VALVE POS light. When the WING anti-ice switch is set to ON, the wing anti-ice valves will open only if the aircraft is airborne. A GRD TEST position of the switch allows momentary ground testing of the system, during which the system is automatically protected by a 93°C temperature sensor. Similarly, in flight a 255C switch will close the wing anti-ice valve and illuminate the amber anti-ice DUCT OVERHEAT light on the overhead panel, alerting the crew. A DUCT TEMP gauge is included and is selectable to anti-ice bleed sensors for all three engines.

When wing anti-ice is selected, hot high-pressure air leaves the engine, and, through the use of an ejector nozzle, the air pressure is reduced. The air, which is still quite warm, is collected by the main wing anti-ice valve near the aft airstair and then sent forward via a common anti-ice duct. From there it is distributed to each wing through a manifold. Through using telescopic tubes, all eight leading edge slats are injected with the warm air. The inboard pair of Krueger

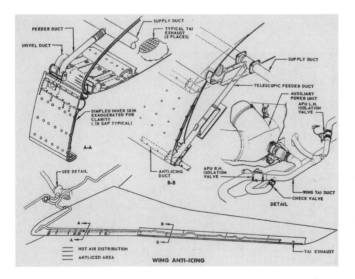

This diagram details the wing leading edge anti-icing system. *Courtesy of the Boeing Company*

The anti-ice-system panel is located over the first officer's head on the overhead panel. *Author's collection*

The Boeing 727 Anti-Ice System

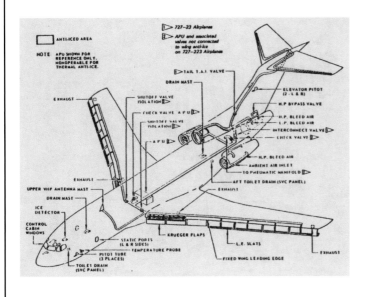

Early Version

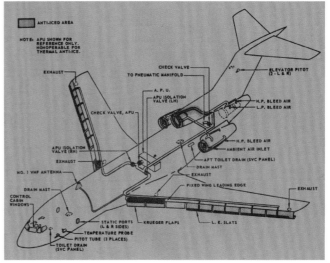

Later Version

Early- and late-model 727 anti-ice-system schematics are shown here. The tailplane anti-ice ducts were removed on later models, since ice buildup in these areas did not present a problem for the 727. The no. 1 VHF antenna and the inboard pair of Krueger flaps are thermally heated to prevent ice from forming and later being ingested by the engines. *Courtesy of the Boeing Company*

flaps (panels 2, 3, 4, and 5) are also heated in a similar manner, using a swivel attachment to deliver the hot air to these surfaces. This action quickly heats the skin surface to remove any collected ice and can be used continuously in severe conditions. Once the anti-ice air has passed through the leading edge devices, it is exhausted overboard via two ports located under the leading edge of each wing.

A small tap from the wing anti-ice ducting is used to supply a limited volume of warm air to the #1 VHF communications antenna, located on the top of the fuselage, when wing anti-ice is selected ON. This prevents ice from collecting on the antenna, which could be shed and ingested by the #2 engine inlet, possibly damaging the engine's S-duct inlet and compressors.

Because the 727 uses wing anti-ice ducting that is largely contained within the fuselage pressure vessel, a ruptured duct could potentially cause a rapid cabin overpressure situation due to the large volume of air involved. In order to mitigate this hazard, a wing anti-ice "autotrip" system is installed. If an increase in cabin pressure exceeds the equivalent of 10,000 feet per minute, the system will automatically close all of the wing anti-ice valves. Aircraft equipped with this safeguard have a small test panel for the system, located at the flight engineer's station for preflight testing.

Engine Anti-ice

If ice accumulation occurs on the engine inlets, guide vanes, or nose dome, it could potentially cause grievous damage to the engine. Additionally, the unobstructed PT2 pressure sensor port is essential for the accurate measurement of engine pressure ratio (EPR), which is the primary means of quantifying engine thrust on the JT8D. In order to prevent ice accumulation on these critical areas, hot engine

bleed air is used to heat the surfaces. On each engine, bleed air from the eighth stage is used to heat the inlet guide vanes, nose dome, and PT2 port. The inlet cowls on the pod-mounted engines are heated using a separate valve supplying thirteenth-stage bleed air mixed with ambient air via an ejector nozzle. For engine 2, with its elaborate S-duct, cowl, and associated vortex generators, anti-icing is provided by mixed eighth- and thirteenth-stage bleed air to provide the additional air volume required for the much-larger surface area.

All the anti-icing valve functions for each engine are controlled by single associated switches labeled ENG 1, ENG 2, and ENG 3. The position of each AC electrically driven valve can be ascertained by selecting the appropriate valve on the rotary VALVE POS selector and observing the illumination of a green VALVE POS light for that engine.

Cockpit Windows

Cockpit Window Layout

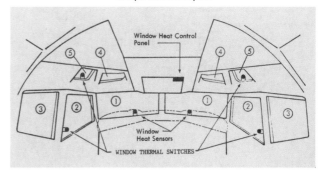

Courtesy of the Boeing Company

The cockpit windows are multilayered and designed for fail-safe operation under the most-demanding conditions. Windows 1, 2, and 5 are composed of two layers of glass, with a vinyl layer between. The innermost layer of glass is designed to carry the pressurization loads, with the inner vinyl layer acting as a backup. The number 4 windows are similar, with an additional Plexiglas layer for further protection. The number 3 windows consist of two Plexiglas layers, separated by a small air space to prevent window fogging.

All the cockpit windows on the 727, with the exception of the number 3 windows, are electrically heated by a transparent element impregnated inside the window pane. On the pilot's overhead panel, two WINDOW HEAT switches allow control of heat operation. The LEFT switch controls the captain's side windows 1, 4, and 5, along with the first officer's window 2. Similarly, the RIGHT switch activates the first officer's windows 1, 4, and 5 in addition to the captain's window 2. This is done so that a single power source failure will still leave at least one heated window operational for each pilot. The temperature of these windows is thermostatically maintained, and heat is always selected ON during normal flight operations for anti-icing. Green ON lights indicate proper operation of the respective window heaters. The use of window heat also significantly increases the ability of the windows to withstand high-speed bird strikes. In the event of a window overheat, the appropriate amber OVERHEAT light will illuminate and the system automatically removes power from the window.

During operations with high outside temperatures at the gate, the windshield temperatures may exceed the thermostat temperature, which will normally remove electrical power to the affected window and extinguish the green ON light. To allow a preflight test of the system, a switch labeled POWER ON TEST / OVERHEAT TEST is provided. In the POWER-ON TEST position, the thermostats are momentarily overridden, allowing a check of the heating system and illuminating the green ON lights. The OVERHEAT TEST position tests the system's overheat circuits, illuminating the amber OVERHEAT lights.

Windshield Wipers and Rain Repellent

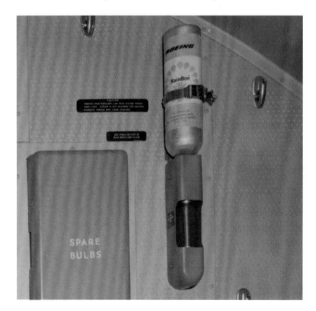

The rain repellent bottle is located on the aft bulkhead of the cockpit, behind the observer seat. *Courtesy of the Boeing Company*

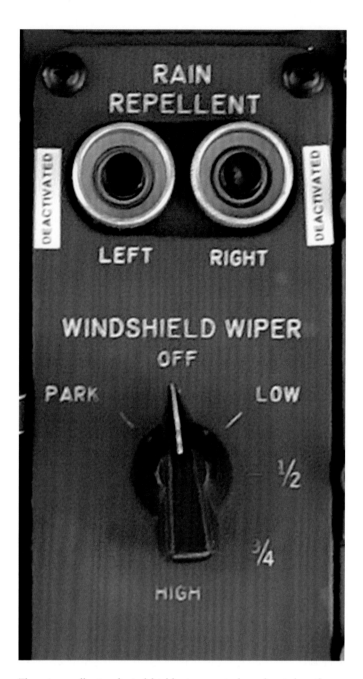

The rain repellent and windshield wiper controls are located on the pilots' overhead panel. *Author's collection*

Both forward windows, L1 and R1, are supplied with an independently operated windshield wiper, controlled by a single switch located on the pilot's overhead panel. These are powered through the normal DC electrical buses.

In keeping with the 727's all-weather capabilities, takeoff and landing through very heavy precipitation are fairly routine. To aid in clearing the windscreens of water, a rain repellent system is provided. A small pressurized bottle of RainBoe, a Boeing-developed rain repellent, is mounted to a dispensing system on the left, aft wall of the cockpit. To warn of a repellent leak in the cockpit, the solution is mixed with a strong citrus scent.

Two RAIN REPELLENT buttons, labeled LEFT and RIGHT, are located toward the center of the pilot's overhead panel. Depressing these buttons will dispense a metered amount of repellent, which should be used only with a wet windshield.

On the pilot's overhead panel, two PITOT STATIC HEAT switches are installed. The system provides electric heat to the pitot tubes and static ports to allow for reliable airspeed and air pressure information, even in extreme icing conditions. The elevator-feel pitot tubes, one on each side of the vertical stabilizer, are also heated through the system, along with the total air temperature probes. Ammeters are provided to allow the observation of current flow to each item, and amber PITOT OFF lights illuminate when power is removed from the associated system.

Late-Model Differences

Some aircraft delivered after February 1969 (c/n 20048, l/n 679) do not have the wing anti-ice autotrip system.

Many 727 airplanes that are still being operated have the #4 and #5 "eyebrow" windows deleted, along with the associated window heaters.

The 727-200 Advanced incorporates WINDOW HEAT switches labeled L-1, L-2, R-1, and R-2. L-1 and R-1 control the respective #1 window heater, while L-2 and R-2 control the on-side window 2. The selection of either switch, L-1 or L-2 and R-1 or R-2, will supply heat to the respective eyebrow windows.

Some airplanes have had the rain repellent system deactivated.

Boeing 727 Walk-Around

The preflight inspection of the Boeing 727 begins with the cockpit preparation duties. At most airlines, the flight engineer is responsible for cockpit setup and preflight systems testing of many items per standard operating procedures. Once complete, the flight engineer begins the exterior preflight inspection, beginning at the nose landing gear and proceeding clockwise around the aircraft, as viewed from above.

The nose landing gear is inspected, paying special attention to the condition of the tires. Note that the correct nose gear tire installation for the 727 has chines on the outboard sides for water deflection away from the engine intakes. The landing gear well is checked for fluid leaks, and the landing gear antiretraction pin is removed. Note

Author's collection

Author's collection

the landing gear viewer window located on the left side of the well, which employs a mirrored sight glass to provide a secondary confirmation that the landing gear is down and locked during non-normal procedures. This round porthole is visible behind the pneumatic brake pressure indicator in the center of the photograph.

Author's collection

Just forward of the nose landing gear well is an access to the forward electronics and equipment (EE) compartment. A similar hatch is located behind the nose landing gear well. The handle must be flush, confirming that the door is secured closed. If these hatches are not completely secure, the aircraft will not pressurize in flight.

These labeled images give a view of the aft EE compartment, normally seen only by maintenance technicians. Electronic modules for multiple aircraft systems reside in this busy compartment.

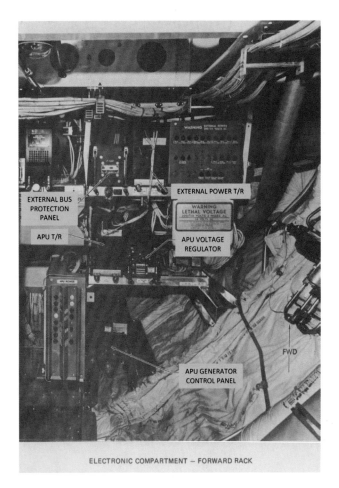

ELECTRONIC COMPARTMENT – FORWARD RACK

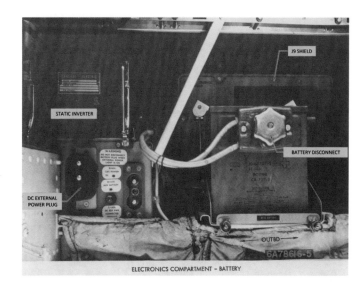

ELECTRONICS COMPARTMENT – BATTERY

ELECTRONIC COMPARTMENT – CENTER FORWARD RACK

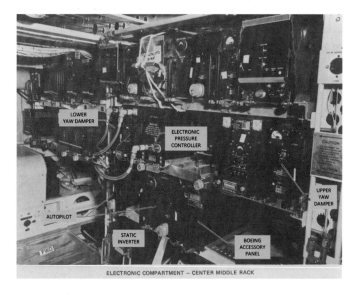

ELECTRONIC COMPARTMENT – CENTER MIDDLE RACK

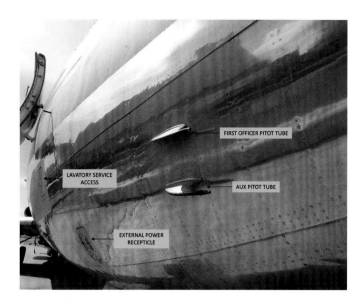

Moving down the right side of the aircraft, the first officer (*upper*) and auxiliary (*lower*) electrically heated pitot tubes are visible. These are used to measure ram air pressure for cockpit airspeed indications. Just behind and slightly below these is the external power receptacle access. The lavatory servicing door is located just forward of and below the open galley (R1) door.

This view of the external power access reveals the 115-volt, 400-cycle receptacle for applying external electrical power to the aircraft. Also included are the communications jacks, a pilot call button, and external power status lights.

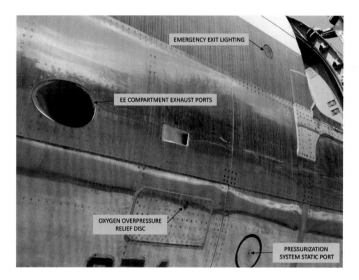

On the forward, right side of the fuselage, the EE compartment exhaust ports and emergency evacuation lighting are installed. Pressurization system static ports are provided on both sides of the fuselage. The oxygen overpressure relief system functions if the passenger or crew oxygen bottles become overpressurized, perhaps because of an EE compartment fire. This causes a relief valve to open, which blows out the green disk and allows the bottles to depressurize by venting overboard in a controlled manner. All three bottles are located on the right side of the EE compartment.

Moving aft along the fuselage, additional static ports for the captain, first officer, and auxiliary instrumentation are surrounded by a red oval outline. The forward baggage compartment door detail is seen in this photograph. The two oval-shaped panels on the baggage door are the pressure relief doors, which open to relieve any unwanted cabin pressure before operating the door.

These are the air-conditioning-pack cooling intakes, photographed looking aft. Note that there are two sides with independent, variable-geometry scoops, separated by a center divider. The intake on the port side cools the left pack, and the starboard inlet cools the right.

Four louvered pack exhaust outlets are provided behind the pack cooling inlets on the lower surface of the wing-to-body fairing, two for each pack. Each pack has a secondary heat-exchanger exhaust installed forward of the respective primary heat-exchanger exhaust.

In the leading edge of the wing root, the inboard landing light and the smaller turnoff light reside. The turnoff light shines to the side at a 45-degree angle to give the pilot a good view when exiting the runway and when necessary during taxi operations.

The right-side main landing gear is seen from behind, with the side strut extending up into the landing gear well. A gravel deflector in installed between the tires to protect the flaps and engines from foreign-object damage. The piping extending up the landing gear strut supplies pressure to the brake assemblies.

Taking a close look at the mounting arrangement of the main landing gear, one can see that the rear pivot point is canted up. This allows the gear to be swept aft when extended, but it retracts inboard and slightly forward into the inboard landing gear well. This is necessary to have proper balance on the landing gear due to the highly swept wing and large trailing edge flap system. The red handle allows the inboard landing gear doors to be opened while on the ground, when pulled down as shown.

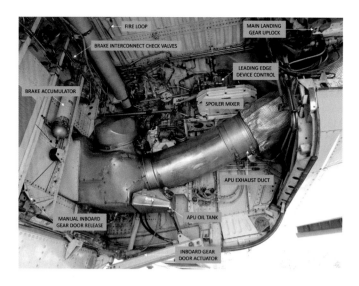

This is a view of the inboard right main landing gear well, looking forward. The spoiler mixer optimizes lateral control by synchronizing spoiler deflection with aileron inputs. The APU exhaust duct extends across the compartment and vents to the top of the right wing, near the fuselage. Note that the fire sensor loop that runs along the compartment ceiling is designed to sense a wheel well fire. The APU has its own independent fire loop inside the stainless-steel shroud.

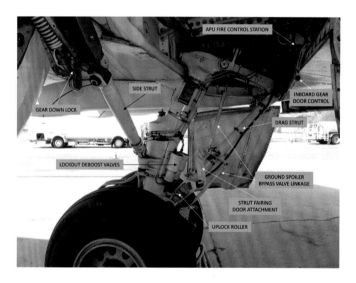

Crossing under the fuselage to the left main landing gear well, looking forward, the APU and associated intake manifolds are visible protruding through the keel beam. The use of the APU while in flight is prohibited on the 727. Additional hydraulic components and the outboard flap drive motor and shafts are installed in this area.

This side view of the main landing gear shows how the main landing gear is swept back. Even with this provision, an empty 727, particularly the -200 series, tends to be very tail heavy.

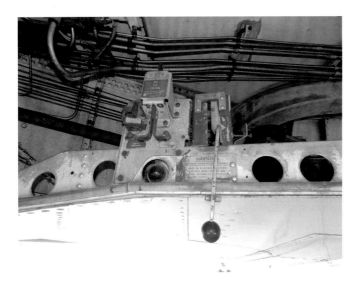

In the event of an APU fire during the flight engineer's walk-around, indicated by the illumination of the red light and warning horn, the issue can be dealt with at ramp level. In the forward left main landing gear well, a station is installed to allow for the shutdown of the APU and subsequent fire extinguishing. The red handle, protruding down as shown, releases the locks on the inboard landing gear doors for maintenance.

Looking at the tail section of this 727, one notices that the late-model cascade-type thrust reversers are installed. Additionally, the longer jet pipes indicate that this aircraft has received the FedEx Stage 3 hush kit modification. Note the row of vortex generators extending up the vertical stabilizer, just behind the red spire marking. These are installed on both sides of the stabilizer to assist in airflow adhesion.

Aft Baggage Doors

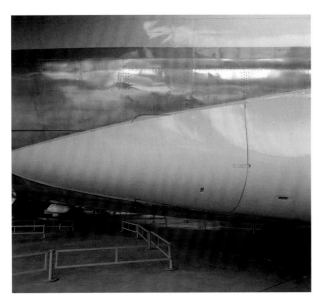

727-100 Series

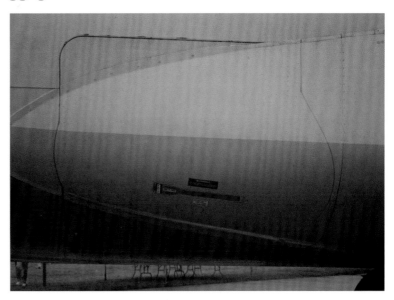

727-200 Series

One significant difference between the 727-100- and -200-series aircraft is the design of the baggage compartment doors. The -100 doors open inward, creating a problem with the bulky wing-to-body fairing. To eliminate issues with the large fairing blocking the compartment opening, the entire aft portion of the fairing is unlocked and translated aft on tracks, prior to opening the door. The baggage doors on the -200 open outward, which allows the fairing to be integral with the door itself, making access a simple, one-step process. Notice the difference in the contour of the aft wing-to-body fairing between the two versions.

Author's collection

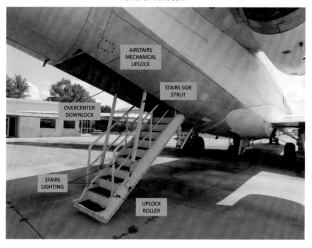

AIRSTAIRS MECHANICAL UPLOCK

STAIRS SIDE STRUT

OVERCENTER DOWNLOCK

STAIRS LIGHTING

UPLOCK ROLLER

Courtesy of Jonathan Jenkins, Middle Tennessee State University

This photograph shows in detail the late-model cascade-type reverser with the non-hush-kit jet pipe. This aircraft is an ex–American Airlines aircraft equipped with the Raisbeck Quiet modification, which allows noise reduction without hush kits for the midweight 727s (see "Raisbeck Quiet" on page 158).

The extended ventral airstair provides expeditious passenger boarding and egress, as well as being designed as a fully structural tail stand to prevent the typically tail-happy 727 from rotating onto its aft fuselage, likely damaging the aircraft and ground equipment.

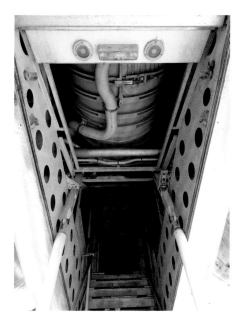

Author's collection

Author's collection

When one is standing at the base of the ventral airstair, looking up and forward, the lower portion of the engine's S-duct can be seen, along with the maintenance access in the upper right-hand corner. The L-shaped duct next to the access door is the CSD cooling duct. The intake for this is located under the number 2 engine inlet. In normal operation, the airstair well walls and ceiling are protected with covers, which are not present on this particular aircraft.

Viewed from the cabin bulkhead door at the top of the ventral stairway facing aft, the S-duct can be seen in detail. The red flight data recorder is seen on the starboard side. The metallic-colored pipe under the S-duct is the wing anti-ice duct from the number 3 engine. On the port side, ducts from engines 2 and 1 join into the system.

Port Side Ventral Airstair Area (Sidewall Covering Removed)

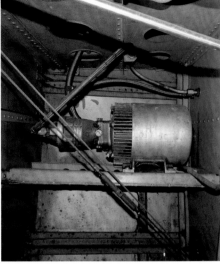

Author's collection

The port ventral airstair area is home to the bulk of the system A and standby system hydraulic components. Shown from left to right are the system A hydraulic reservoir, the standby system electric hydraulic pump, and the standby system reservoir.

Tail Skids

727-100 (Electrically Deployed)   **727-200 (Hydraulically Deployed)**

Author's collection

All 727s are equipped with a retractable tail skid, located immediately forward of the ventral airstair. Early airplanes used an electrically operated system, while the later-model examples use system B hydraulics for extension. Both systems automatically deploy in concert with normal landing gear extension.

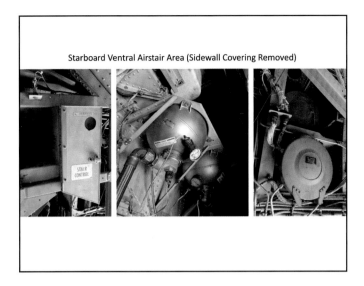

Starboard Ventral Airstair Area (Sidewall Covering Removed)

Author's collection

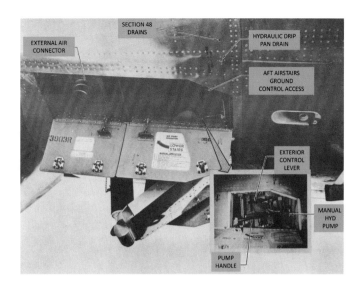

Courtesy of the Boeing Company

Starting forward and moving aft, the starboard ventral airstair area houses the STAIR CONTROL lever and the engine fire suppression bottles. Farther aft, the flight data recorder (*lower*) and cockpit voice recorder (*upper*) are installed. Often referred to as "black boxes," in reality they are normally red or orange to make them readily identifiable in the event of an accident.

The airstair control compartment is colocated with the external air connection port. By using this port, high-pressure air up to 60 psi from a ground cart can be provided to start engines in the absence of an operable APU. To allow coordination with the cockpit, headset jacks enable direct communication with the pilot through the flight interphone system. One of the two overpressure relief valves is seen to the right of the hatch in the photo. An identical valve is installed in the same position on the other side of the rear fuselage.

Author's collection

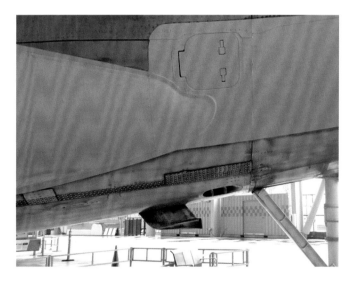

Author's collection

The late-model 727-200F cargo aircraft are equipped with a purposed tail stand in addition to the ventral airstair, to ensure that the aircraft remains in a proper three-point stance.

Immediately behind the portside wing-to-body fairing, the hatch for servicing the aft lavatories gives access both to the waste drain and the filling port for the toilet fluid tank. Protruding under the fuselage, just forward of the tail skid, is the lavatory and toilet drain mast. The mast is heated to prevent ice from forming on the drain opening.

The 727 employs a powerful high-lift system with triple-slotted trailing edge flaps. Here, the flaps are deployed to position 5, which is a common takeoff setting for the 727.

This is a close-up view of one of the jackscrew drives and track assemblies that allow the high-lift flap system to extend and retract.

The wingtip has multiple static wicks, which look like thin wires extending aft of the trailing edge to dissipate static electricity, primarily for enhancing radio reception. The wingtip navigation lights are installed behind the clear fairing just outboard of and behind the extended slat. The white taillight extends from the trailing edge, as does the fuel dump vent, which is slightly inboard. The dark-colored, triangular NACA scoop is for fuel tank venting.

The leading edge slats deploy at a very large angle to the chord line of the wing on a standard 727, as shown. This creates very high lift and also substantial induced drag, necessitating fairly high thrust and attendant noise levels on approach. The Raisbeck Quiet modification mitigates this by using modified actuators, which limit slat extension for better lift-to-drag ratios, thus significantly reducing noise. Note the position of the stall fence on slat 4. During flight testing, different positions and fence sizes were tested until the best configuration was adopted.

A view of the underside of the extended slats shows the curved tracks on which the panels extend forward and down. The hydraulic actuators and deice telescoping ducts are clearly visible.

Here is a detailed view of the stall fence added to the inboard slat on each wing, used to reduce the deep stall tendency of the 727.

Like the slats, the Krueger flaps are heated with engine bleed air during flight in icing conditions to prevent ice from forming, breaking away, and being ingested by the pod engines. Additional landing lights are usable with the Krueger flaps extended. The potable water service access is located directly below the point where the wing leading edge meets the fuselage.

This view shows the backside of the left-wing Krueger flaps, facing outboard. The tubular deice duct that runs just below the hinge line is visible.

Center Engine Inlet Designs

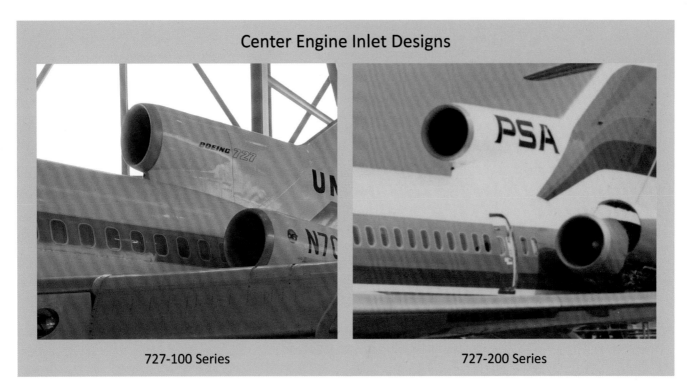

727-100 Series

727-200 Series

Courtesy of the Boeing Company

Notice the slight difference in the center inlet design between the 727-100- and -200-series aircraft. The -100 features an oval-shaped inlet, while the inlet on the -200 is completely round and slightly larger. Below the inlet, the small cooling port for engine 2's constant-speed drive is visible on both aircraft.

Author's collection

This view of the leading edge slats is seen through the galley door (R1) on this 727-100.

Conclusion

While the 727 did retain some built-in similarity with the 707, it offered many additional features that increased versatility and efficiency. High-lift systems that were pioneered on the 727, combined with gravel runway capability, made the airplane immediately popular, both in the United States and abroad. The aircraft handling was crisp and sporty thanks to the fully powered flight control system, while it was comparatively easy to handle during an engine failure because of the rear-engine design. The addition of an auxiliary power unit, single-point refueling, and integral airstairs significantly reduced the required ground equipment. Because of the fail-safe design of the aircraft systems, single points of failure were eliminated while providing multiple backup systems to increase safety and reliability. The culmination of these features on the 727 made it the most numerous jetliner, a record held by the aircraft until March 1990, when it was eclipsed by the Boeing 737.

Boeing 727-100 Series (Typical)

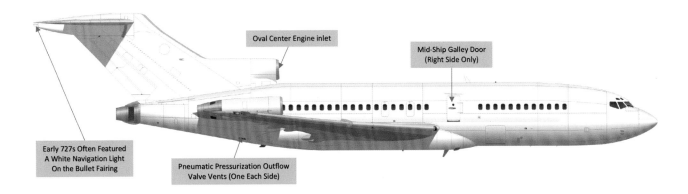

Oval Center Engine inlet

Mid-Ship Galley Door
(Right Side Only)

Early 727s Often Featured
A White Navigation Light
On the Bullet Fairing

Pneumatic Pressurization Outflow
Valve Vents (One Each Side)

Boeing 727-200 Series

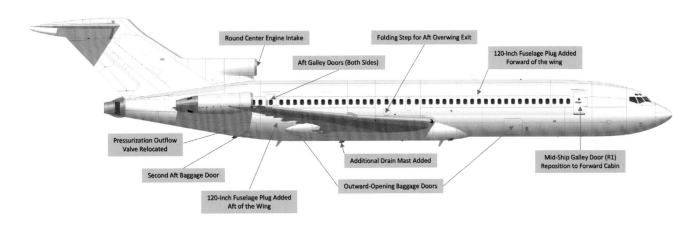

Round Center Engine Intake

Folding Step for Aft Overwing Exit

Aft Galley Doors (Both Sides)

120-Inch Fuselage Plug Added
Forward of the wing

Pressurization Outflow
Valve Relocated

Additional Drain Mast Added

Mid-Ship Galley Door (R1)
Reposition to Forward Cabin

Second Aft Baggage Door

Outward-Opening Baggage Doors

120-Inch Fuselage Plug Added
Aft of the Wing

Courtesy of Jennings Heilig

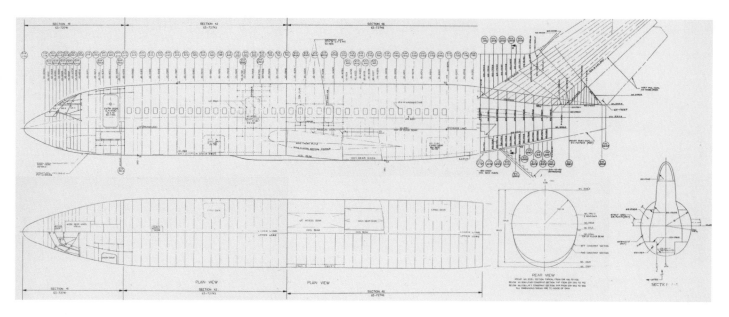

Courtesy of the Boeing Company

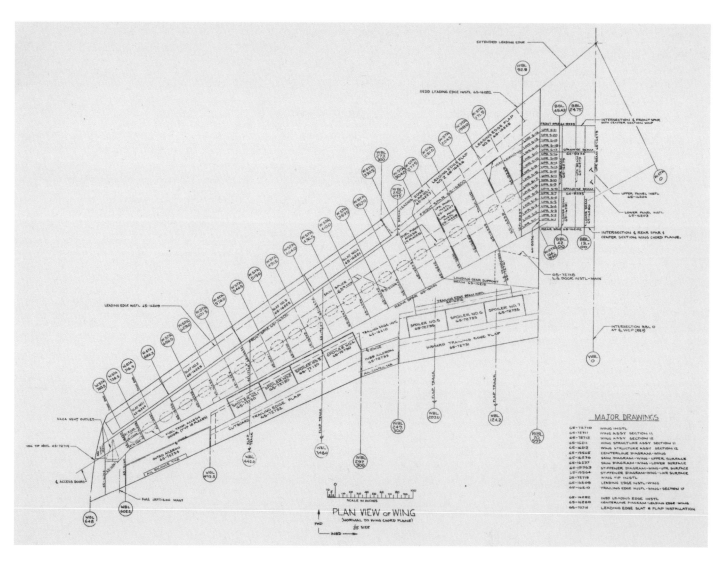

Courtesy of the Boeing Company

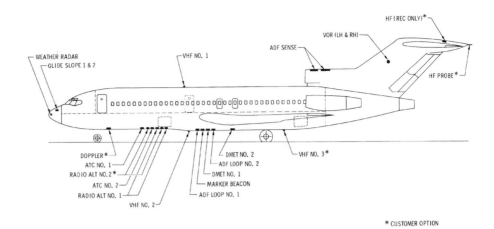

*Courtesy of the
Boeing Company*

* CUSTOMER OPTION

Boeing 727 Specifications

	727-100	727-100C	727-200 (Early)	727-200 Advanced Gross Weight Option 1	727-200 Advanced Gross Weight Option 2	727-200 Advanced Gross Weight Option 3
Length	133" 2"	133' 2"	153' 2"	153' 2"	153' 2"	153' 2"
Wingspan	108' 2"	108' 2"	108' 2"	108' 2"	108' 2"	108' 2"
Height	34'	34'	34'	34'	34'	34'
Max Takeoff Weight - Pounds	142,000 (Optional up to 160,000)	169,000	169,000 (Optional up to 172,000)	190,500	197,000	209,500
Max Landing Weight - Pounds	135,000 (Optional up to 142,500)	142,500	150,000	154,500	154,500	161,000
Max Standard Fuel Capacity -US Gallons	7,174	7,680	7,174 (Optional up to 7,680)	8,090	9,760 (With 1,670 Aux Fuel)	10,585 (With 2,480 Aux Fuel)
Powerplant ICAO Limits (Takeoff Thrust in Pounds)	Pratt & Whitney JT8D-1, -1A, -1B, -7, -7A, -7B (14,000) JT8D-9, -9A (14,500)	Pratt & Whitney JT8D-1, -1A, -1B, -7, -7A, -7B (14,000) JT8D-9, -9A (14,500)	Pratt & Whitney JT8D-9A (14,500) JT8D-15 (15,500) JT8D-17 (16,000) JT8D-17R (17,400)	Pratt & Whitney JT8D-15 (15,500) JT8D-17 (16,000) JT8D-17R (17,400)	Pratt & Whitney JT8D-15 (15,500) JT8D-17 (16,000) JT8D-17R (17,400)	Pratt & Whitney JT8D-15 (15,500) JT8D-17 (16,000) JT8D-17R (17,400)
Vmo (Knots)/Mmo	390/ Mach .90	390/ Mach .90	390/ Mach .90	390/ Mach .90 (Mode B: 350/ Mach .88)	390/ Mach .90 (Mode B: 350/ Mach .88)	390/ Mach .90 (Mode B: 350/ Mach .88)
Approximate Range at Long Range Cruise with Alternate + Reserves- Nautical Miles	2,200	2,700	2,300	2,500	3,000	3,200
Max Certified Altitude	42,000	42,000	42,000	42,000	42,000	42,000
Seating Capacity- FAA Limit	119	119	189	189	189	189
Baggage Compartment Capacity- Cubic Feet	900	900	1,450	1,450	1,130	810

Author's collection

Modeling the Boeing 727

The Basic Build: Airfix's 1/144 Scale Boeing 727

Model building is a relaxing and rewarding hobby, particularly for those of us who enjoy studying aircraft and aviation history. Even better, in today's market the modeler has many kit and scale options from which to choose. In this chapter, we will explore three different builds, ranging from a beginner's first build project to a top-of-the-line model kit using more-exotic equipment, paints, and techniques.

All photos in this chapter are from the author's collection.

The Airfix Boeing 727 kit, released in 1982, still occasionally cycles into production. While the latest release of this kit comes with decals both for Air Canada and Alitalia liveries, I am working with the older kit version, equipped with Lufthansa and Pan Am markings. In general, this kit is reasonably good, and the price point lends itself nicely for a first model-building experience. This 727-200 kit will be built using basic materials and supplies that can be easily acquired. I will be setting aside my trusty airbrush and instead focusing on basic painting techniques using quality aerosol and liquid products. The model will be finished in the attractive Alitalia livery, using aftermarket decals by 26decals of Great Britain.

Airfix Boeing 727-200 #03183
26decals 1/144 Alitalia 727-200 decal #144-271 (www.26decals.com)
Authentic Airliner Decals 1/144 727-200 Cockpit and Cabin
    Windows (www.authentic-airliner-decals.com)
Nazca-Decals 1/144 B727-200 Detail Set (www.nazca-decals.com)

Supplies

AeroMaster RLM 22 Black
Dymo Labeling Tape (optional)
Maxi-Cure Extra-Thick CA Cyanoacrylate
Insta-Set Cyanoacrylate Accelerator
Model Master 1929 Gloss Gull Grey
Model Master 1949 Flat Black
Model Master 2937 Grey Primer
Plastruct Bondene
Pledge Revive It Floor Gloss
Tamiya TS-30 Spray Silver Leaf
Tamiya Masking Tape
Tamiya Masking Tape for Curves
Tamiya Modeling Scriber (optional)
Tamiya X-32 Titanium Silver
Tamiya XF-69 NATO Black
Testors 1245 Spray Gloss White

The classic Airfix 727-200 kit builds into a nice representation of its iconic subject. However, it does have a few minor shape and fit issues that I will either correct or mitigate as much as feasible within the scope of this basic build.

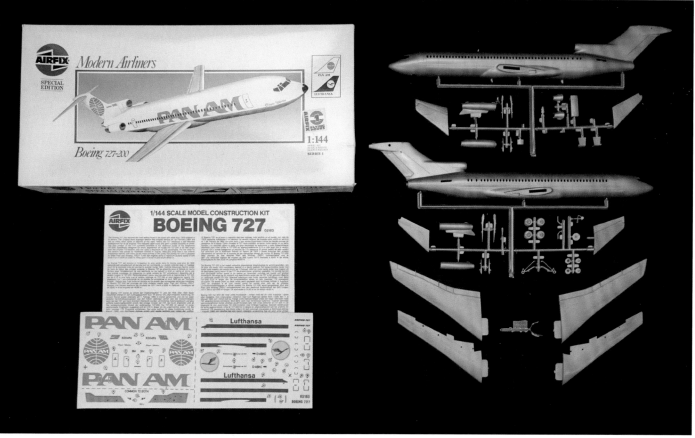

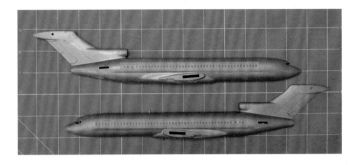

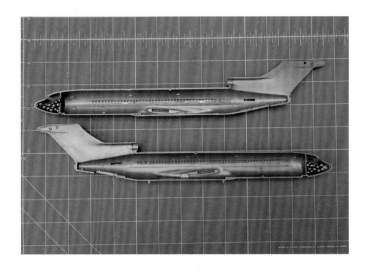

The directions are straight forward and logically call for the fuselage assembly as a first step. As is quite typical for the Airfix airliner series, the cabin windows are open, with no provision for the installation of clear plastic to represent the window panes. A small styrene punch is included for the modeler to open up the windows in the kit's cheat line decal, if so desired. Instead, I have chosen to use window decals to replicate both the cabin and cockpit transparencies and therefore will fill in the windows. The easiest way to accomplish this is to apply a high-quality masking tape to the outside of the window line, then, from the inside, apply cyanoacrylate glue, commonly referred to as CA glue, to fill in the window openings. Be sure to keep the fuselage level and give the glue several hours to cure. While CA accelerators such as Insta-Set can be used in many situations to cause CA glues to cure instantly, the process can occasionally cause bubbles to form in the glue. In this situation, because we are filling the windows, it is best to let it cure naturally. Just like the real airplane, ballast is required to prevent the model from becoming a tail-sitter. Using BBs to provide this weight works well, provided that they are positively secured to the inside of the fuselage with CA glue.

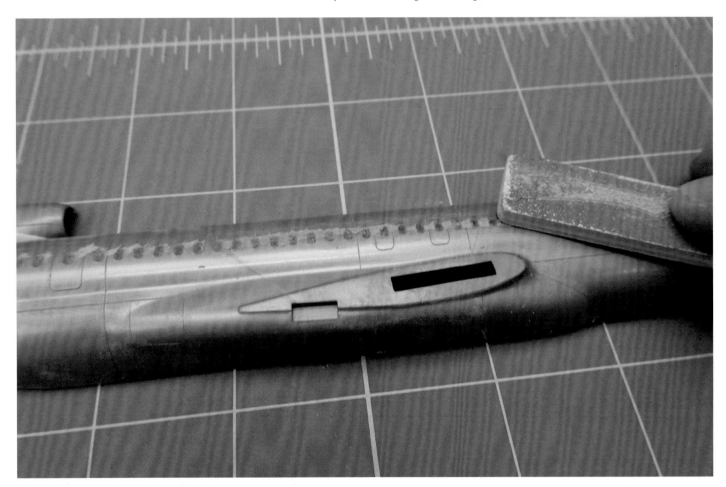

After allowing the CA glue to cure overnight, I removed the masking tape from the windows and used a medium-grit sanding stick to smooth any unevenness.

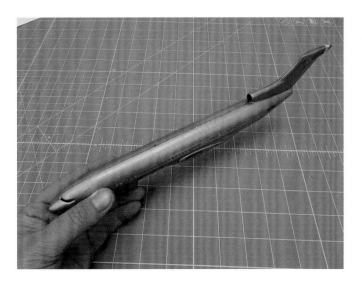

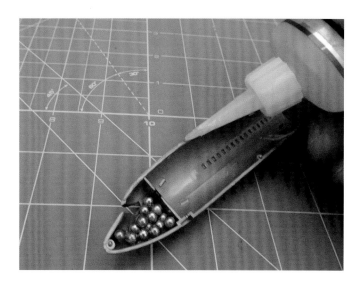

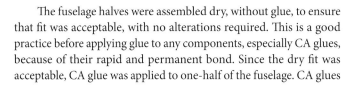

The fuselage halves were assembled dry, without glue, to ensure that fit was acceptable, with no alterations required. This is a good practice before applying glue to any components, especially CA glues, because of their rapid and permanent bond. Since the dry fit was acceptable, CA glue was applied to one-half of the fuselage. CA glues are perfect for large assemblies such as this because of their structural strength. Using these glues also prevents seam splitting, especially later on while removing masking tape during the painting process. Smaller, nonstructural parts such as engine nacelles can be assembled with plastic solvents such as Plastruct Bondene.

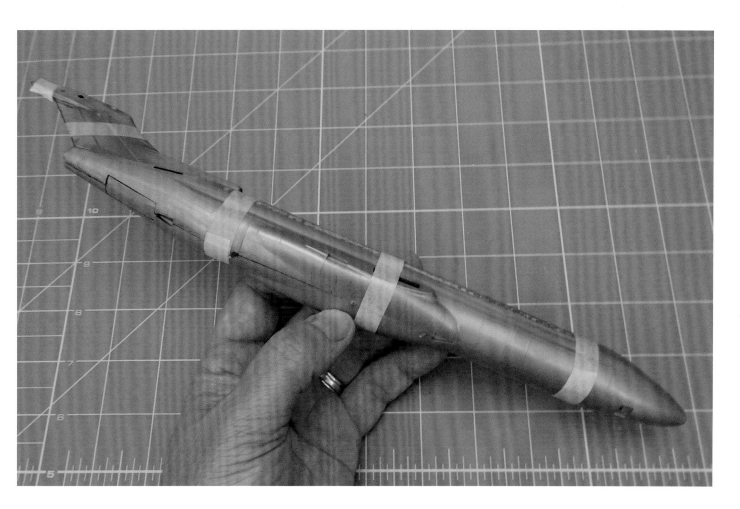

Once the CA glue was applied and good alignment achieved, the two fuselage halves were taped together. Generally, a spacing of every 3–4 inches is adequate, but it is important to look for any gaps. Apply additional tape as necessary to close up gaps to the maximum extent possible.

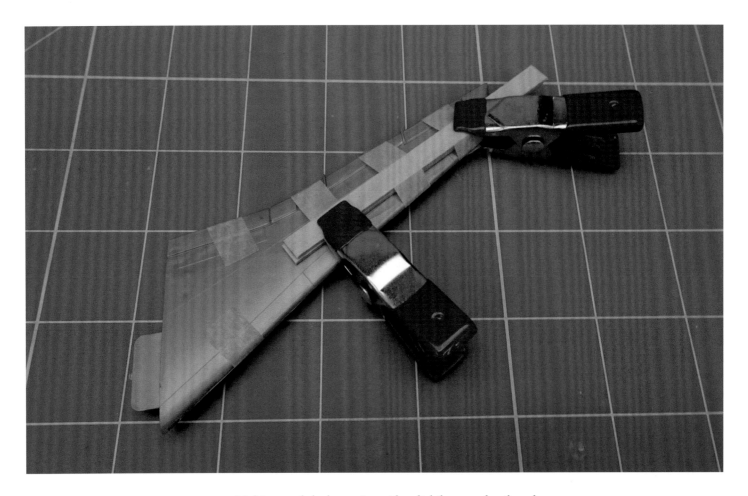

My kit example had one wing with a slightly warped outboard section. I corrected the warping by first applying CA glue and assembling the two halves of the wing, then taping and clamping a rigid piece of scrap wood to the wing as the glue cured. The end result was a nicely straightened wing.

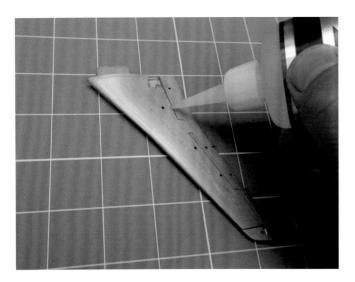

Filling gaps is certainly optional but, when done correctly, will definitely enhance the finished model. Although the wing seams are contained on the lower surfaces, the gaps are too large to be believable as panel lines for the flaps. So, I filled these with extra-thick CA glue before using a medium-grit sanding stick to complete the smoothing process.

Another optional endeavor is to scribe the panel lines of the trailing edge flaps. Using Dymo labeling tape and a scriber (the one shown here is from Tamiya), I set down the tape as a guide and slid the scriber along it, which leaves a fine trench in the plastic. After three light passes, the recessed line to delineate a trailing edge flap is created, significantly adding to realism of the finished model.

Parts are best removed from the sprues with either a sharp hobby knife or high-quality set of snips. A clean break from the sprue will save time later in obtaining adequate parts fitment and preparing the model for painting.

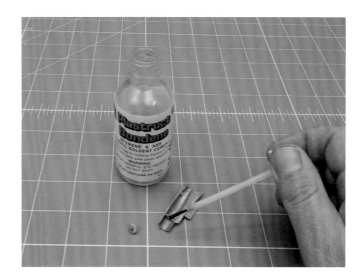

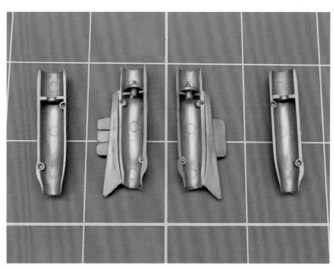

On smaller parts, I prefer to use Plastruct Bondene, which uses a chemical reaction with the plastic to melt the mating surfaces together. Note that Airfix hasn't just intelligently given each engine alignment pins but has also provided each with a unique tongue-and-groove fitting. This makes it clear which engine should be installed on each side of the fuselage, eliminating the possibility of an error on the part of the modeler.

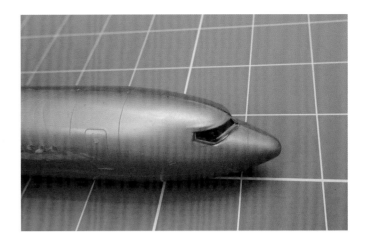

Prior to final assembly, I cleaned up the seams on each component by filling and sanding them with a medium-grit sanding stick as necessary. The cockpit windshield was also added at this point, and while there were some gaps around the transparency, these were also filled with CA glue and sanded since I was planning to use window decals. The Airfix windshield is a bit rounded in shape, so some additional sanding of the front windshields was needed to make them as flat as they are on the real aircraft.

With all of this accomplished, a light dusting of primer was applied to the wings and fuselage. Oftentimes, especially with silver plastic, it is difficult to see if the gaps have been completely eliminated. The primer coat will accentuate any issues that still need to be addressed. During this phase, I discovered that there was still a gap on the center engine inlet. CA glue was applied to the gap, and light sanding solved the problem.

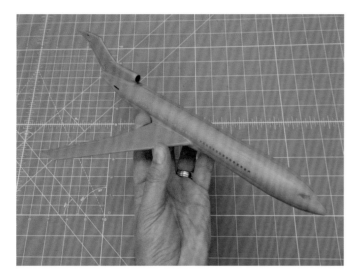

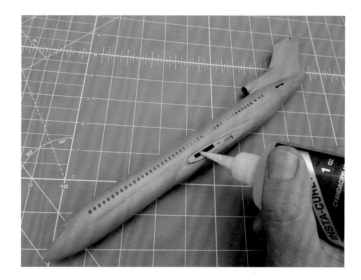

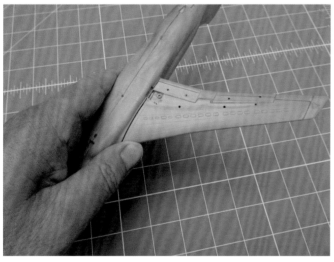

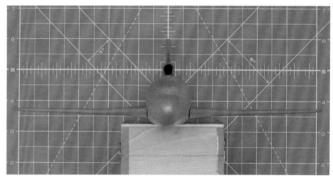

A quick fit check showed that without filling, the gaps where the wings mount to the fuselage would be unacceptably large and unsightly. At this point, I decided to conduct final assembly prior to painting the model, so that the gaps could be effectively filled.

The wings were added to the fuselage by using a sparingly small amount of CA glue. The idea here is to add just enough glue to hold the wing in position. This allowed some minor dihedral adjustment before the glue cured, and, using a gridded hobby mat, I verified that proper dihedral was symmetrically achieved. Once this was ensured, CA glue was added to the gaps, which also provided considerable structural strength to the model.

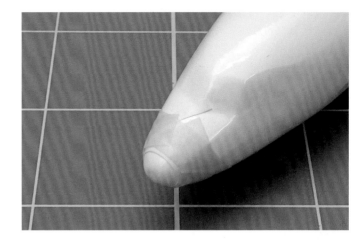

Masking tape was used to protect the surface detail on the wings and stabilizers while the gaps were filled with CA glue and sanded. Since the gaps were fairly sizable, more than one addition of CA glue was required to eliminate the gaps, and this was a case in which CA accelerator could be used to significantly expedite the process.

With the gaps filled and sanded, the entire model was lightly sanded with 1500-grit sandpaper to give a smooth surface that the paint would adhere to solidly. Testors Gloss White spray paint was used and applied in swift coats to avoid an overly heavy application that can lead to paint runs. The can should be held 10–12 inches away from the model, and the spray cone should pass from the nose to the tail in roughly half a second. The model was rotated using a wire hanger specially bent for this purpose, inserted into the nose landing gear well. The first coat should be speckled, with some of the primer still showing through. This will give the next heavier coats something to cling to, thereby preventing paint runs later. Two more coats were applied for full-color coverage and to create as glossy of a finish as possible. One of the difficulties encountered when using spray paints is getting an even finish across the entire model without having some amount or orange peel texture in the paint. This will be corrected after the gloss coats are complete, prior to the Coroguard and metal finishes.

Begin by masking the demarcation lines between the white and the rest of the other colors to be applied later, and then add masking tape to cover all the white areas on the model. Choosing the right masking tape for the job is essential. The black antierosion coating on the nose was masked with Tamiya Masking Tape for Curves, which is nearly the same color as the white finish it is protecting, and allows small-radius arcs to be masked. This is ideal for masking areas such as radomes and engine inlets, which have compound curves that make conventional tapes difficult to use. It is thicker, however, and does not overlap well. Applying a small piece of standard yellow masking tape along the line where the white tape will overlap first will prevent any overspray from making its way under the overlap. The yellow tape shown behind the white tape is Tamiya Masking Tape, which comes in a variety of widths. It is resistant to paint "submarining" underneath it and creates large-radius curves with relative ease. Best of all, it is fairly low tack, so it is unlikely to damage the surface during unmasking.

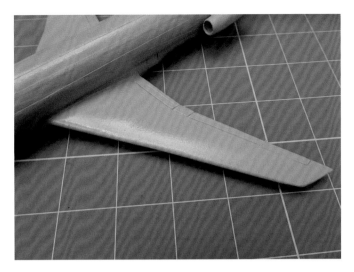

Given the situation with the orange-peel effect generated by the aerosol Gloss Grey and White paints, I elected to remask the model after smoothing both finishes with sanding and the Pledge Revive It Floor Gloss treatment. The primer was sprayed next, which can be used to replicate the Coroguard wing interspar areas. After allowing them twenty-four hours to dry, the interspar areas were masked, leaving only the bare-metal leading edges and engine pod surfaces. Several misting coats of Tamiya Silver Leaf were added from roughly 14 inches away. As aerosol silver paints go, I felt that the finish was convincing.

After painting the Gloss Gull Grey color, it was apparent that there was far too much orange-peel texture on the finish for my liking. After allowing the paint to dry for forty-eight hours, I used 1500-grit sandpaper and water to gently wet-sand the surfaces to level out the finish. Once completed, the model was smooth, but the gray paint was dulled quite a bit by the process. I filled a mist sprayer with Pledge Revive It Floor Gloss and lightly misted the model from about 24 inches away. This did the trick, and the model had the shiny finish that I wanted to achieve.

The removal of the masking tape is an operation to be conducted slowly and carefully. If at all possible, try to pull the tape away from the surface at a 45-degree angle, as shown. This not only prevents the paint underneath from being pulled up with the tape, but it also helps retain a sharp line between colors.

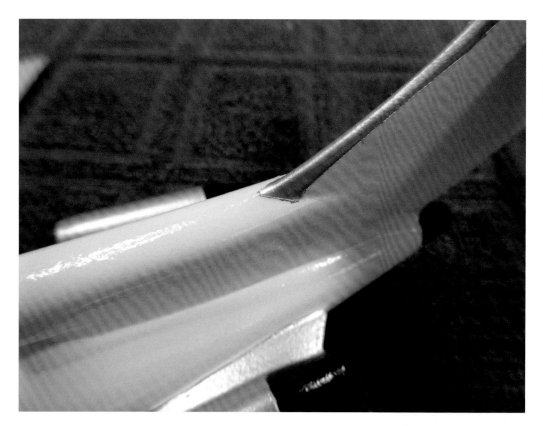

Upon removing the masking tape, I found that there was a small area at the bottom of the silver stabilizer leading edge where paint had transitioned under the tape. Fortunately, this is an easy fix.

To ensure a perfect paint match, a small amount of the aerosol Gloss White paint was decanted into a small paint jar. A fine brush was then employed to repair the paint seepage.

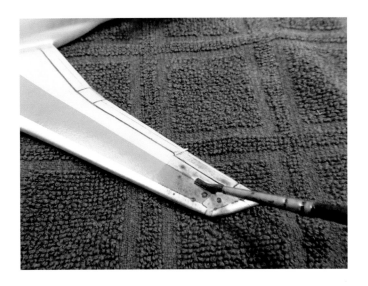

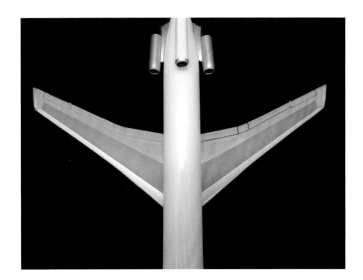

A wash of 20 percent AeroMaster Black and 80 percent water mixed with a dash of dish soap was brushed onto the wing surface and quickly wiped away with a cloth in the direction of airflow. This brings out the recessed flight control detail while leaving subtle streaks, which adds to the realism of the model. The difference can be seen between the washed wing on the right, and the untreated wing on the left side of the photo.

With the model fully painted and the wash applied to the wings and stabilizers, it is time to begin the application of decals.

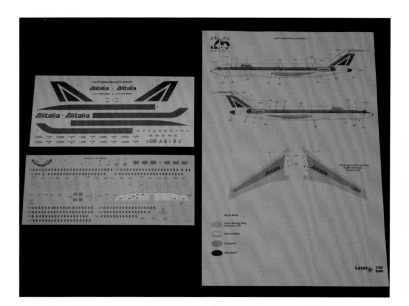

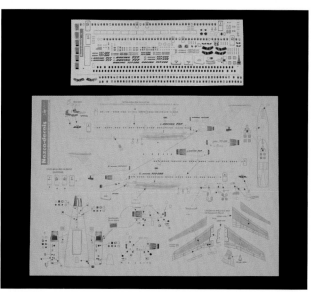

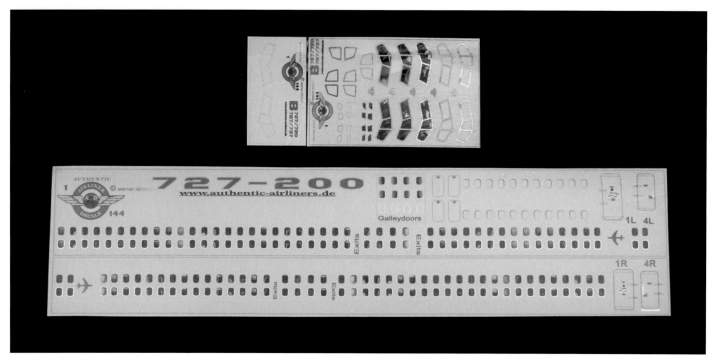

I have chosen the attractive Alitalia livery from 26decals and will be enhancing the finished model with window decals from Authentic Airliner Decals, along with airframe details from Nazca-Decals. The combination of the wash already applied and the details added here will produce a strikingly detailed model. It is important to make a photocopy of the Alitalia decal because of the engine pylon interface with the cheat line on the rear fuselage. We will use it later to get a perfect fit for our decal.

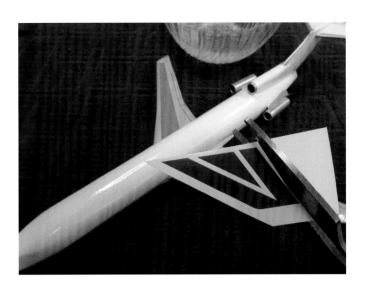

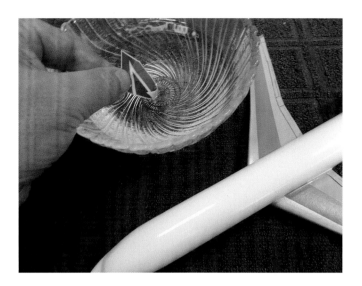

Many decals come on a continuous plastic film, as is the case with all the decals used on this model. This means that the decal must be cut close to the marking to eliminate excess clear carrier film on the model. Be sure to take your time. Once the decal is cut away from the sheet, place it in lukewarm water until it moves freely on the sheet. Place the decal with the paper backing in the position that it should sit on the model. Hold the decal in position with one hand while sliding the backing out from under it with the other. Once this is complete, gently wipe away any excess water and push out any air bubbles under the decal with a paper towel. It may be necessary to hold the decal in place while wiping the decal.

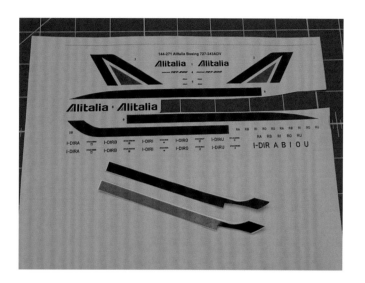

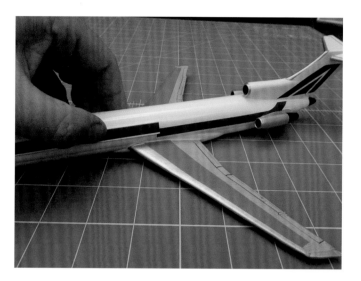

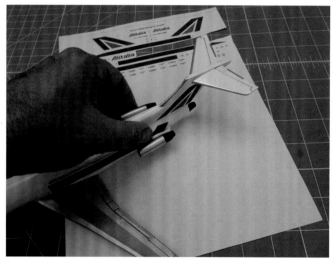

In many cases, aftermarket decals have some amount of extra stripe to make the set fit the different model kits available on the market. Because the decals are somewhat transparent, the overlapping portion must be carefully removed. Overlapped decals will present a section of the stripe that will be too dark.

Because the engines were attached to the fuselage prior to painting and decaling, it was necessary to trim the areas on the cheat line where the engine pylons interface. Using the photocopy of the decal sheet, I carefully trimmed away material until the fit was correct. After this was done, I used the photocopy as a template to get the cutout perfect on the actual decal.

After the livery decals were allowed to dry, I added the Authentic Airliner Decals cockpit and cabin windows. Once this was complete, the cabin doors and overwing exit outlines can be added. This order ensures that they are perfectly aligned with the window frames.

The landing gear legs and side struts were carefully attached to the inside of the kit box with Tamiya Tape to prevent them from moving during painting. They were then given a coat of aerosol gloss white. After drying overnight, the parts were turned over and resprayed.

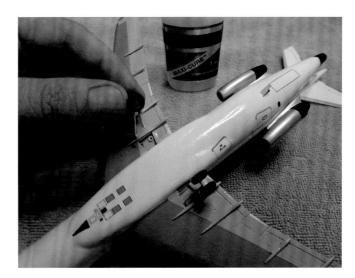

To ease the tire-painting procedure, each wheel was attached to a toothpick. Using a fine brush, each wheel was carefully painted with NATO Black while slowly rotating the toothpick. The landing gears were then assembled and glued to the model, using CA glue.

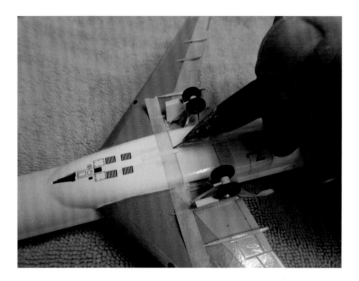

Using masking tape as a guide, a fine drafting pencil was used to replicate the outlines of the main landing gear wells. This area of the aircraft is typically somewhat dirty, so the use of colored pencils is effective at creating a streaked appearance. Prior to the nearly universal prohibition on smoking aboard airliners, the outflow valve typically had a brown streak behind it as well. The outflow valve on the 727-200 is just forward of and above the ventral airstair on the right side of the fuselage, outlined in red on the model. A wash was added to the landing gears and blotted lightly with Q-tips.

Even using basic supplies and aerosol paints, a nice rendition can be achieved with a few special techniques. That being said, this type of finish presents some challenges, as we have seen. In the following builds, we will explore painting with an airbrush to produce a slightly smoother and more controlled finish. As you continue modeling, a good-quality airbrush will be an excellent investment that can bring even more enjoyment to your hobby.

The Intermediate Build: Hasegawa's 1/200 Scale Boeing 727-200

The esteemed Japanese model kit manufacturer Hasegawa first released their Boeing 727-200 kit in 1982. This kit is accurately scaled to 1/200 scale, which is perfect for those who have limited shelf space. For those who would like to model many other airliner subjects in scale, Hasegawa has a wide variety of kits from which to choose. Although this kit is typical of the period in offering mostly raised panel detail versus the more modern recessed lines, the kit parts fit extremely well, even by modern standards. The shape of the model is quite convincing and, in this author's opinion, is still one of the best kits of the 727. While construction of this kit is nearly a "shake the box and it falls together" experience, I have deemed this to be an intermediate build. This is because the selected early American Airlines bare-metal paint scheme offers a challenging modeling experience that requires extensive airbrush use.

Kit and Decals

Hasegawa 1/200 Boeing 727-200 (51911)
Vintage Flyer Decals American Airlines 727-100/-200 #VFD200-105 (www.vintageflyerdecals.com)

Supplies

Alclad II ALC 107 Chrome
Alclad II ALC-304 Gloss Black Base
Alclad II ALC-105 Polished Aluminum
Alclad II ALC-116 Semi-Matte Aluminum
Alclad II ALC-102 Duraluminium
Insta-Cure Super Gold Foam Safe Cyanoacrylate
Insta-Set Cyanoacrylate Accelerator
Maxi-Cure Extra Thick Cyanoacrylate
Model Master 1731 Aircraft Gray
Model Master 2737 Primer
Model Master 2720 Classic White
Plastruct Bondine Plastic Solvent
Pledge Revive It Floor Gloss
Tamiya X-32 Titanium Silver
Testors 8824 Airbrush Thinner

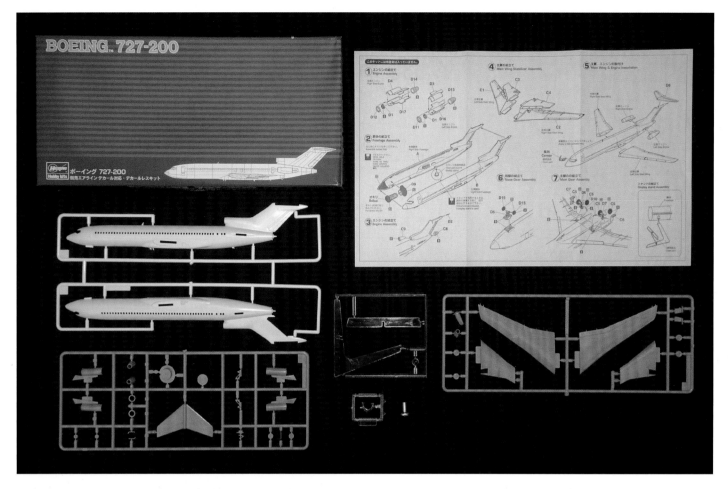

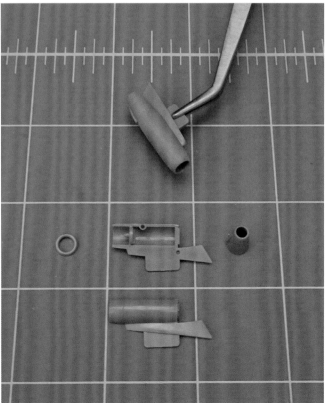

The assembly of the kit begins with the pod-mounted engines. On smaller models, such as this, I generally prefer to use a liquid cement such as Plastruct Bondene, because it leaves very little residue. Unlike the fuselage, the engines do offer some recessed detail, but with their proximity to the seams between the top and bottom nacelle halves, even light sanding will likely obliterate it. Fortunately, the fit of the nacelles to the fuselage is impeccable and will require very little, if any, filling and sanding.

Using a high-quality pair of sprue snips, the wing halves are removed from the runner. The lower inboard portion of the wing fits snugly in position, so removing all trace of the sprue connection is a must. If done correctly, the two pieces will fit together with little to no gap remaining.

The use of sprue snips is also demonstrated with the removal of the fuselage halves from the runners. Resist the urge to simply break them off, since this usually leaves an uneven break, likely creating additional work and fit issues later.

As with the Airfix kit, the passenger windows are open and were filled with CA glue by using the same technique as before. This kit is builder friendly in many ways, among which is the inclusion of a galvanized screw that was installed into the cockpit bulkhead to provide proper three-point balance. The directions call for everything inside the cockpit to be painted black, but since decals will be used, I deemed this step to be unnecessary.

I utilized CA glue to join the fuselage sections together but used Plastruct Bondene to glue the vertical stabilizer due to its tighter tolerances.

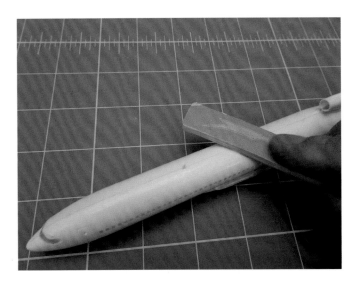

After using accelerator to expedite the curing of the CA glue, the fuselage seams were sanded. A small amount of CA glue was applied to the cockpit windshield to fill the small gaps, allowing me to sand it smooth using a medium-grit sanding stick. A major advantage of the Hasegawa kit is that it accurately captures the complex nose shape of the 727.

With all the gaps filled and their seams sanded smooth, the parts were hung in the paint booth in such a way that the surfaces will not have to be touched at all during the painting process. A small wood scrap covered with tape was inserted through the wing-mounting holes in the fuselage to allow handling throughout the process. This will be particularly important when using the Alclad II lacquers later. A 50/50 mixture of enamel thinner and primer was airbrushed onto the model. Thin coats expedite drying and will be less likely to cover the finer details, particularly on the wings. The primer coat serves two purposes: the first is that it will encourage paint adhesion, and the second is that it will make any gaps or seams that are not perfect immediately obvious to the modeler.

Inevitably, there were a few seams that still needed further attention. I used 400-grit sandpaper dipped in water to wet-sand the upper fuselage seam. Once satisfied that it had been adequately eliminated, I used very fine, 1500-grit sandpaper to polish the area until it was smooth. With this accomplished, another light primer coat was applied to confirm the results.

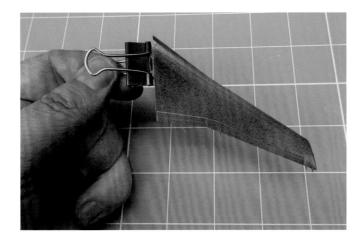

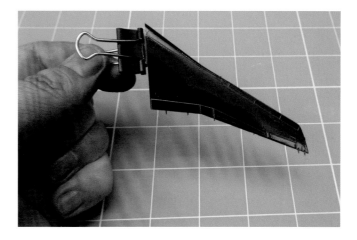

Using bare-metal paints can cause fear for many modelers, but with a little knowledge and proper procedures, it is reasonably easy to create a convincing metal finish. The early American Airlines scheme is almost entirely bare metal, so this will be an important step. I used Alclad II Lacquers to replicate the various metallic shades on the model. The fuselage, wings, and engines were all airbrushed with three coats of Gloss Black Base. The first coat should be more

of a dusting coat, with the second coat achieving good color coverage. The third coat should be slightly heavier to ensure a shiny black finish. The parts were then allowed to dry overnight. It is important to note that when using Alclad II lacquers, once the Black Base coat is applied, the painted surfaces must not be touched with bare hands until the process is completed, since fingerprints will appear when the subsequent metallic colors are applied.

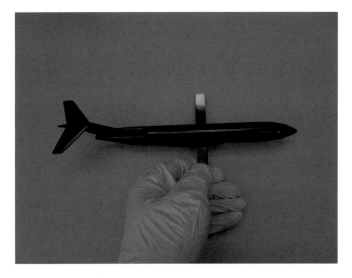

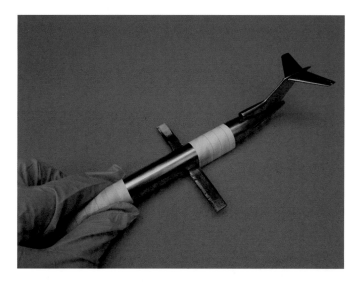

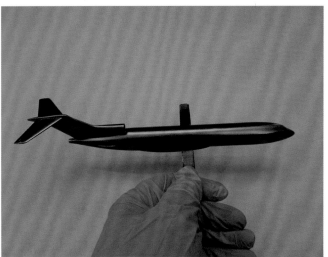

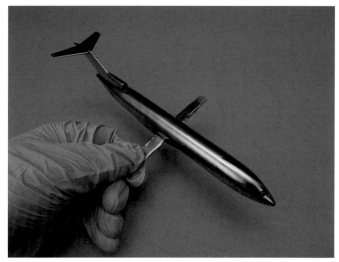

The fuselage was painted with Alclad II Chrome to give it a highly polished look. Eight to ten VERY light coats were applied, transforming the fuselage from gloss black to a shiny, metallic finish. A light flow rate was set, with approximately 20 psi applied to the airbrush. Always test the spray pattern with a scrap piece of cardboard or plastic prior to operating it on the model. If the chrome is applied too heavily, it will dry with a cloudy appearance. If this occurs, simply recoating the model, or the offending portion, with Gloss Black Base will reset the process, allowing a "redo" if necessary.

After getting the entire fuselage to a point where it was a realistic shade, Post-it notes were used to mask and single out panels and fuselage body sections. With the masks in place, I applied two more light coats of Chrome, which provides a subtle but noticeable panel variation. If it is desired to have more-obvious tone differences, simply applying more coats will achieve this effect. One or two light coats is perfect in this case because the color of the metals used on 727 fuselages was fairly consistent. Once the panel effect was to my liking, the model was sprayed with a coat of Pledge Revive It Floor Gloss to protect the finish prior to further masking. Even using a high-quality, low-tack masking tape, I have found that metallic colors can often be lifted off the model, so this is a highly recommended step.

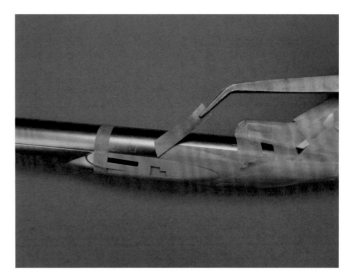

The masking tape was removed from the fuselage one piece at a time. Pulling off the tape at an angle away from the painted area is advisable to ensure the crispest line possible, while minimizing the possibility of any paint lifting up from the surface.

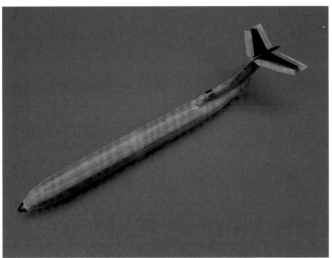

With the metal shades complete and sealed, I turned my attention to the areas that should be painted gray on the airplane. This includes the wing-to-body fairing, portions of the vertical and horizontal stabilizer, and the nose cone. While you are masking the wing-to-body fairing, due to the small scale of the model, even Tamiya's Masking Tape for Curves couldn't make the corner on the aft section. Masking here was accomplished by using several small pieces of Tamiya Masking Tape around the corner. Make sure that the tape is completely burnished down to the surface. Two coats of a 70/30 mixture of Aircraft Grey to thinner was applied and given twenty-four hours to dry.

The engines were painted using the same techniques employed on the fuselage. Alclad II Gloss Base Coat, followed by several light coats of Alclad II Chrome, was applied as the base color. Pledge Revive It Floor Gloss was sprayed to seal this, and, once dry, the inlet and exhaust areas were masked and the exposed areas were airbrushed with Black Base Coat. The inlets were painted with Alclad II Semi-Matte Aluminum, which replicates the unpolished surfaces on the 727 well, particularly on smaller-scale models such as this. The exhaust and thrust reverser sections were treated with two coats of Alclad II Duraluminium. In this photo, I have conducted a test fit of the pod engines, and the fit was excellent. The inlet for the number 2 engine has not yet been installed.

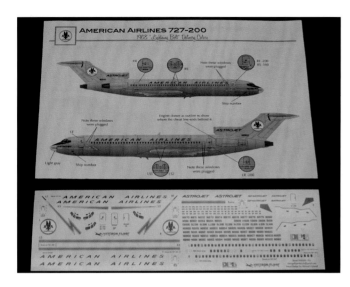

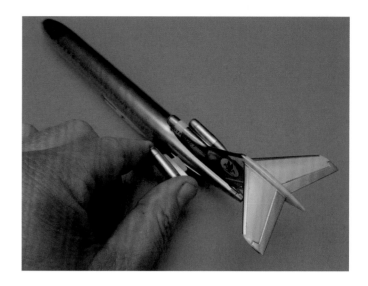

The decal set I am using for the early American Airlines livery comes from Vintage Flyer Decals and is available in several scales. These are particularly nice because they also include a full set of cabin and cockpit windows, and the set is adaptable to either a 727-100- or a -200-series airplane.

The engines were permanently installed with Super-Gold Foam Safe CA glue. Add only a thin film glue to the mounting tab. This glue is ideal for the final assembly of prefinished parts because it will not fog the surrounding areas like most CA-type glues.

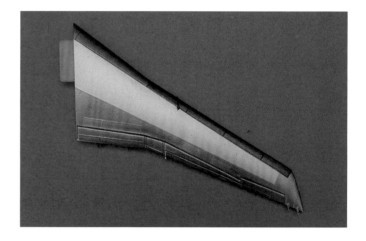

Similar to the Alitalia decals used on the basic build, these are also printed on a continuous decal sheet and need to be carefully trimmed prior to application. After a short soak in lukewarm water, the decal is ready for application. The ability to add the engines and wings later on this kit is a real bonus and makes the application of decals straightforward. The window and windshield decals were added first, followed by the cheat lines. Water can be reintroduced as necessary until the positioning is perfect.

The wings were painted using the Alclad II system. I chose Polished Aluminum for the wing upper surfaces and singled out the flight spoilers and sundry other panels for additional coats to provide some measure of color variation. The leading edges were painted with Semi-Matte Aluminum, and then the inboard sections were given a dusting of Polished Aluminum to finish the effect. The inspar, or center, sections of the wings on the real aircraft were painted with Coroguard, an epoxy that was impregnated with metal flakes and used as an anticorrosion measure on early jetliners. It had the interesting effect of appearing to be lighter or darker depending on how light was reflected off its surface. This leaves the modeler with some latitude in choosing the color. I think the closest color that replicates it well in scale is Tamiya Titanium Silver. After sealing the Alclad colors with Pledge Revive It Floor Gloss, the inspar sections were masked off and two light coats of Titanium Silver were applied. Once this dried, additional masking was carried out to paint the flap track fairings and Krueger flaps with Aircraft Grey.

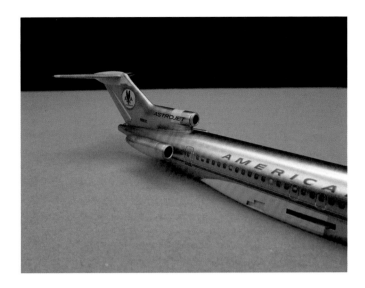

The center engine inlet was painted with Semi-Matte Aluminum and added to the model. It fits well enough to be added after painting, which saved me the difficult task of masking the inlet lip. Once inserted, the part has enough depth to be convincing without the need for replicating the entire S-duct.

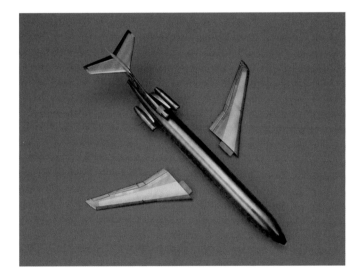

Once dried, the wings were joined to the fuselage with a sparing amount of Super-Gold CA glue. It is important to view the model from the front and back to ensure that the wings have the correct dihedral before the glue becomes fully cured. I found that one wing fit snugly at the perfect angle, while the other needed a bit of encouragement to get it just right.

The landing gear components are quite small in this scale, so the biggest hazard is either losing one of them or having them blown off the cardboard during painting. I elected to tape them to the inside of the kit box to adequately mitigate the issue. These were painted with a mixture of 80 percent Classic White and 20 percent Aircraft Grey, mixed with a small amount of thinner to help it flow through the airbrush. The landing gear components are a bit thick looking because of the scale, but Hasegawa struck a good balance between scale looks and adequate strength to withstand a hard landing or two on the shelf.

The wheels were added to the main landing gear legs and installed using Insta-Cure Super Gold Foam Safe CA glue. The landing gears are handed and fit into the mountings such that they cannot be installed incorrectly—a nice engineering touch.

A wash of 20 percent Aero Master Tire Black and 80 percent water and dish soap solution was added and wiped away in the direction of airflow over the airframe. This accentuated the flap and panel detail and adds shadowing to such components as the landing gears. Light streaking is typical of even fairly new jetliners, so wiping the wash off in the direction of airflow nicely replicates this effect.

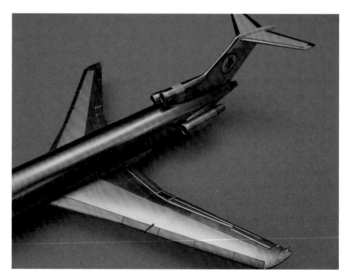

One of the only flaws of this kit, albeit a minor one, presented itself while adding the main landing gear doors, since they won't physically fit between the landing gear leg and the flap track fairing. This caused me to cut ¹⁄₁₆ inch off the top of the door, which allowed me to install it at the proper angle.

The Hasegawa kit represents a great value, especially for those with limited display space. It is accurate in shape and has stood the test of time, even by today's standards. The build sequence is simple and requires minimal filling and sanding.

The Advanced Build: Authentic Airliners 1/72 Scale 727-100

I have chosen to use Authentic Airliners' beautiful 1/72 scale Boeing 727-100 for the advanced build. The kit builds easily, as we will see, but is quite large and will allow us to add a lot of extra detail. Additionally, it is a solid resin kit, which requires some minor changes to the standard techniques. N7001U is a key player in this book and was also a participant in one of the most remarkable and celebrated last flights of any aircraft. During my research for this book, I spent hours with this particular machine at the Museum of Flight, learning of the many adventures she had in her long life. Because of this, I chose to paint this model in the United Airlines delivery paint scheme, along with the FedEx hush kits, which this great airplane currently sports in the museum.

Kit and decals

Authentic Airliners 1/72 Boeing 727-100 (available at www.authentic-airliners.de)

Authentic Airliner Decals 1/72 Boeing 727 Cockpit and Cabin Window Decals (www.authentic-airliner-decals.com)

Nazca-Decals 1/72 B727-100 Detail Set (www.nazca-decals.com)

Vintage Flyer Decals 1/72 United Airlines Boeing 727-100 #VFD072-252 (www. vintageflyerdecals.com)

Supplies

Maxi-Cure Extra Thick CA Cyanoacrylate
Insta-Cure Super Gold Foam Safe Cyanoacrylate
Insta-Set Cyanoacrylate Accelerator
Alclad II Gloss Black Base #ALC 305
Aero Master 1004 Tire Black
Alclad II ALC 105 Polished Aluminum
Alclad II ALC 112 Steel
Alclad II ALC 123 Exhaust manifold
Model Master 2737 Primer
Model Master 2720 Classic White
Model Master 1731 Aircraft Grey
Model Master 1709 Radome Tan
Pledge Revive It Floor Gloss
Tamiya 87034 Masking Tape
Tamiya 87177 Masking Tape for Curves
Testors 8824 Airbrush Thinner
Vallejo 73.602 Surface Primer
Vallejo Metal Color 77.707 Chrome
Vallejo Metal Color 77.702 Duraluminium

The first thing that I noticed when opening the Authentic Airliners 1/72 scale 727-100 kit was both its weight and size. The kit is made from solid resin, so for a model this size it is quite hefty. As is typical of Authentic Airliners' products, the shape is outstanding, flawlessly capturing the complex geometry of the 727. Engine inlet detail even faithfully replicates the stator and compressor blades for the pod-mounted engines. The center-engine S-duct, while not replicated down to the compressor face, is deep enough to create the proper effect with some measure of creative paint application.

Author's collection

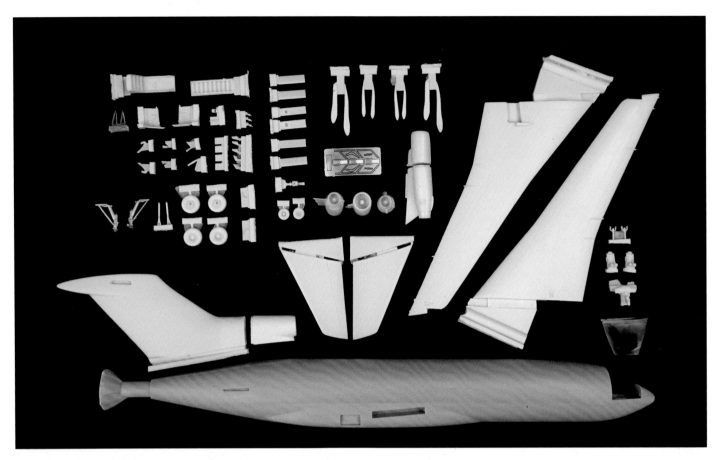

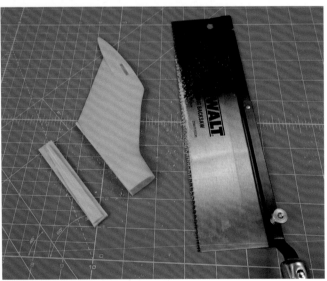

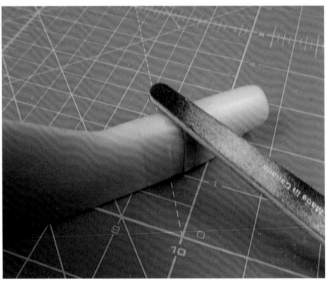

Resin kit components are created by pouring resin into a mold, allowing it to cure, and then removing it. To ensure that there will not be any voids in the part, the mold is overfilled a bit, leaving an extra portion that needs to be removed. On smaller parts, this can sometimes be accomplished with a hobby knife, but large parts such as the 727's vertical stabilizer require the careful use of a razor saw. Proceed slowly and frequently check the alignment of the saw to avoid damaging the part.

Initially, the center inlet was added using just a dab of Medium Insta-Cure CA glue, while I carefully checked its orientation from the side and top. Once this cured and I was content with the alignment, Extra Thin Insta-Cure was added to the joint to seal the small gap and to add strength. After it was thoroughly cured, a medium-grit sanding stick was deployed to eliminate the seam. Tamiya Tape was added to protect the adjacent surface detail, as shown.

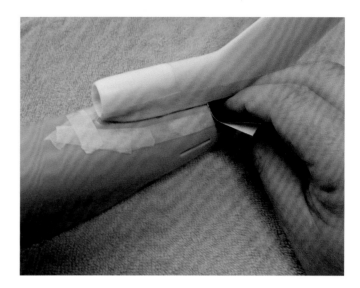

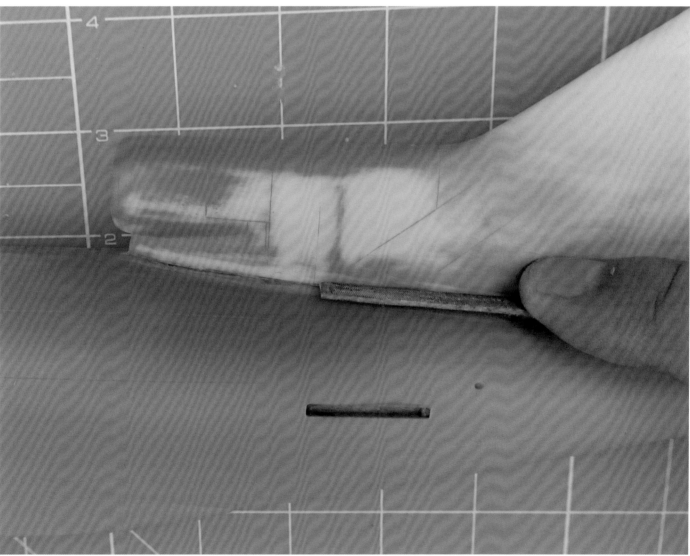

A similar procedure was used to install the vertical stabilizer and center inlet to the fuselage. A small amount of glue was used, and while proper alignment was confirmed, the union did present a small gap that needed to be filled with CA glue. The joint was sanded with 320-grit sandpaper, followed by a fine square file to "square off" the joint between the vertical stabilizer and fuselage.

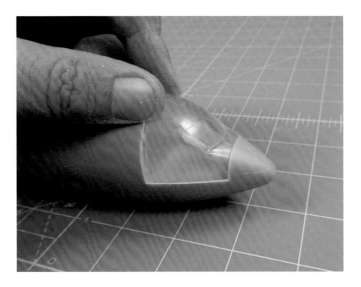

Authentic Airliners designs all its kits to balance properly on the landing gears without the need for ballast. If the modeler prefers, the clear resin cockpit windows can be utilized. A partial cockpit from the #3 cockpit windows forward is included, complete with seats, yokes, and an instrument panel. Instead, I have chosen to use Authentic Airliner Decals' window decals, so I have not built up the cockpit. The resin canopy was carefully fit into place with judicious sanding and secured with CA glue.

Once the canopy was secured into position, the small gaps were filled with CA glue and sanded. The elimination of all gaps here will be extremely important to the appearance of the finished kit. The application of primer will make any discontinuities obvious to aid me in correcting any gaps or irregularities.

  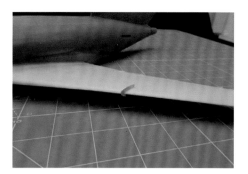

The Authentic Airliners kit is well detailed and contains many small details such as VHF antennas, drain masts, and the stall fences mounted to the #4 and #5 slats. The other details can be added later with ease, but I felt that it would be important to add the stall fences prior to painting the model. The resin parts are quite good, but they are also very delicate. I feared that at some point during the finishing process, there was a good likelihood that they would be damaged, so I elected to use the kit parts as templates to make aluminum replacements. Using tin shears, I carefully cut out the parts and used sanding sticks to perfect the shape. Employing a fine razor saw, a small slot was cut into the wing to allow the installation of the newly manufactured fences.

One really nice feature that Authentic Airliners added to the kit is the inclusion of a completely detailed airstair well. The pressure door and upper portion of the stairway are molded in resin, and the fit is spot on. Once the pressure door assembly is installed, it will be difficult to paint, so I have prepainted it with Tamiya XF-1 Flat White paint. Adding the remainder of the airstair assembly will be the last step prior to completion of the model.

  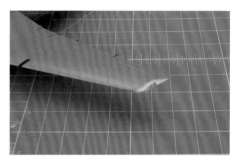

Just prior to applying the finish colors, a light coat of Model Master Primer, mixed 50/50 with enamel thinner, was applied. The primer coat will bring out any gaps or irregularities that may still remain. At this stage, they can be quickly filled, sanded, and reprimed. The gaps left around the navigation light fairings were filled with CA glue and sanded flush with 400-grit sandpaper. This left a cloudy appearance on them, so further sanding with 1500-grit paper, and a coat of Pledge Revive It Floor Gloss, was needed to make the transparent part clear and shiny again.

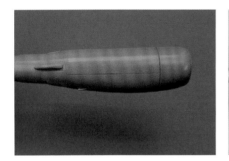  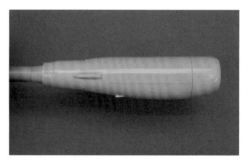

I found that the fit of the engine pylons to the fuselage and the horizontal stabilizers to the empennage was good, leaving virtually no gaps. Because of this, I will leave them off during painting and reunite them with the model after all paint and decals have been applied. In most situations, it makes sense to begin airliners with the fuselage crown color, especially if it is a light shade. Using Model Master Classic White, I begin using a 70/30 percent mix of paint to thinner. Making the first application a light misting coat gives the subsequent coats something to adhere to and prevents paint runs later. Allowing about thirty minutes between coats, I continued with moderate coats until good color coverage was achieved, normally two to three coats for white, and one to two for darker colors. Once this was complete, there was some "orange peel" effect to the surface. One of the major challenges with airliners is replicating the glossy aircraft surfaces. The key to achieving a proper finish comes with implementing one additional, easy step. Add more paint thinner to make the solution a 30/70 mix of paint to thinner. With the majority of this mixture being thinner, the medium will be very thin in viscosity, and the airbrush flow rate will need to be adjusted accordingly. After the adjustment was complete, I applied one more coat—but only just enough to give the desired mirrorlike finish. More is not necessarily better, so be sure not to overdo the effect, since runs can still occur.

The engines were mounted onto a scrap brass tube for painting. Notice the progression from a light-misted first coat, to color coverage, to eventually having the desired high-gloss finish. Gloss paints, especially white, are thick and will dull fine details. To prevent this, the wings and reverser grilles were masked ahead of time.

  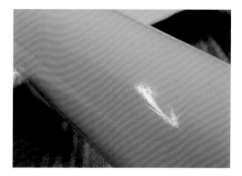

During what was planned to be the last "glossy" coat of white paint, disaster struck. A piece of lint landed on the paint just after the application of the 30/70 paint-to-thinner mixture. While a complete sand-down is certainly an option, I elected to try a simpler course of action first. After allowing the paint to dry for forty-eight hours, I used extremely fine 1500-grit sandpaper and water to lightly wet-sand the affected area. Because there were already white coats beneath the disturbed paint, this eliminated the problem but left a slightly dull appearance. One more light application of the 30/70 mixture made the issue virtually vanish, saving me much time and despair.

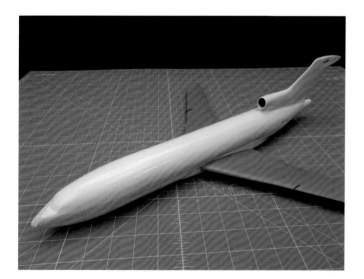 

After the white paint had dried for forty-eight hours, masking for the next coat, Model Master Aircraft Grey, began. The goal is to accurately mask the white areas on the aircraft for further painting, and it is generally best to start with the outlines. This can be a trial-and-error process while cross-checking photo references or, in their absence, the instruction sheets. Oftentimes it can be helpful to look down the side of the fuselage from the front to determine if the line is straight and that both sides appear symmetrical.

Here, I began to mask around the pod engine inlets since it will be painted with an unpolished aluminum color. Choosing the correct type of masking tape for the task is essential, since the inlets present compound curves that only a flexible tape can manage without wrinkles and subsequent paint demarcation issues.

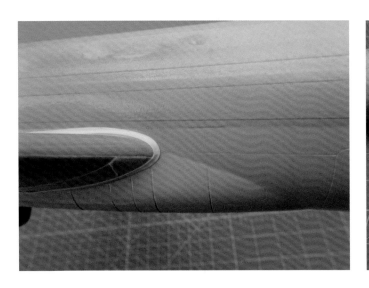

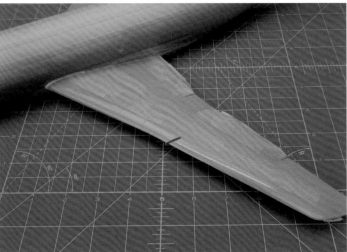

Ship One, as displayed in the Museum of Flight, displays some minor differences in the paint scheme worn on the wings and how it would have been finished in service. When first delivered from Boeing, the center interspar section of the wing would have been finished with a corrosion-inhibiting Coroguard finish, with bare-metal leading and trailing edges. The gray surfaces are more typical of later finishes, but since I wished to make the model true to the configuration as displayed today, the wings will be finished in gray and bare metal.

After allowing the Aircraft Grey paint to dry thoroughly, the surfaces that are intended to remain gray were carefully masked with reference to photos of the actual airplane. Take extra time to ensure that all the tape is burnished down so that lines will be sharp and crisp. The next color application will be using the Alclad II bare-metal paint system.

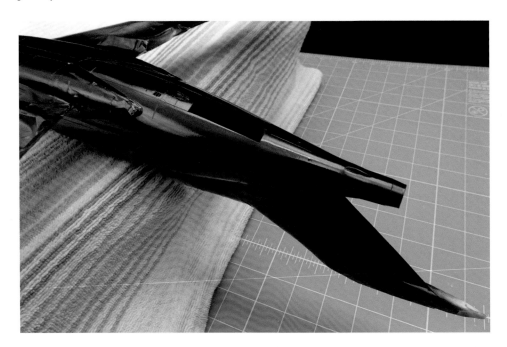

In preparation for this, the Alclad II Gloss Black lacquer undercoat was applied in much the same way as the gloss enamels, except that it was applied unmixed with thinner because it is prethinned for airbrush application. An initial light coat was followed by successive heavier coats until a shiny finish was achieved. Be cautious not to touch the finish until the Alclad II process is complete, because any fingerprints will show through the subsequent coats. Cotton gloves can be used, though, or great care can be taken to mask without allowing hand contact.

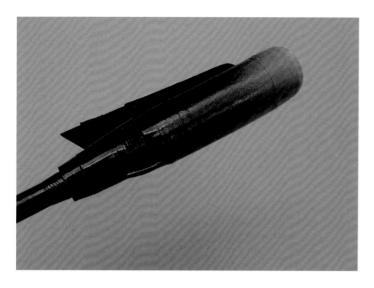
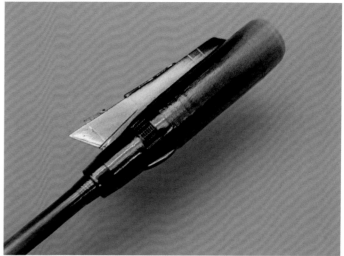

Starting with Alclad II Polished Aluminum, several light dusting coats were applied since even a moderately heavy application can lead to a cloudy finish. Take your time until the surface looks the part of shiny aluminum. Most aircraft, and the 727 is no exception, have some minor metal panel variation on the unpainted surfaces. Using Post-it notes as masks, panels were picked out for an additional light coat or two with the Polished Aluminum paint. Once complete, the Polished Aluminum–painted surfaces were sealed with Pledge Revive It Floor Gloss. This is important, since it allowed further masking without fear of damaging the finish.

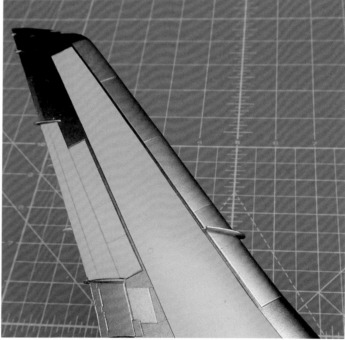

The leading edge slats and engine inlets on the 727 are typically not as highly polished as the fuselage. Because of this, I used Vallejo Metal Color acrylic paints, which I feel better replicate this type of finish on large-scale models. The undercoat is accomplished by airbrushing Vallejo Surface Primer, followed by Vallejo Chrome, which dries shiny and convincing without being mirrorlike. To create a panelized effect, Vallejo Chrome is mixed with Vallejo Duraluminium in proportions of 70/30 and 50/50, respectively. These mixtures created the subtle shade mismatch between the slats.

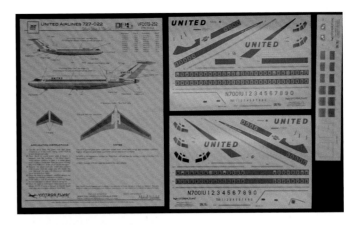

The inlet rim was replicated with Vallejo Chrome. After being sealed with Pledge Revive It Floor Gloss and allowed to thoroughly dry, the intake was masked with pieces of 5 mm Tamiya Tape cut square and carefully placed in the inlet. Each piece of tape needs to be properly aligned with the previous piece so that the result will be a straight line around the inlet. Once the masking was completed and the tape had been burnished down with a toothpick, the inlet was painted with Model Master Radome Tan and masked once more, as shown, for the color application to the compressor face. Alclad II Gloss Black Base was used, followed by several light coats of Alclad II Steel. The thrust reversers and tailpipes were painted with Alclad II Duraluminium for the forward portion and Alclad II Steel for the aft sections.

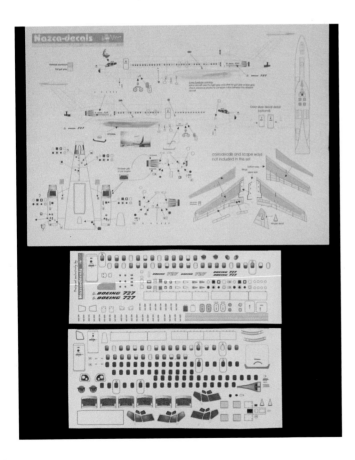

To achieve the greatest level of detail for this advanced build, I am using decal elements from three different sources. The basic paint scheme for N7001U was supplied by Vintage Flyer Decals. This decal is well thought out and encapsulates many fine details, such as the thin silver stripes above and below the blue cheat lines. Additionally, VFD also included optional stripes with and without window shade detail. Cockpit windows are supplied by Authentic Airliner Decals, which represent an occupied cockpit very nicely and fit the model perfectly. The third decal source for this kit comes from Nazca-Decals. While I have elected to use the VFD and Authentic Airliner Decals for the windows, the Nazca set offers many small details such as static ports and placards, which were quite useful.

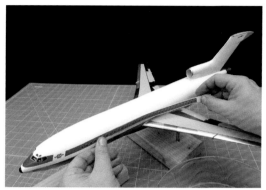

The decals were carefully cut and added one by one. Especially with paint schemes that wrap around the nose, as this one does, it is advisable to add the left and right nose stripe decals first to ensure proper alignment. From there, it is best to move aft. Since the VFD decals are not screen printed, the stripe decals must buttress against one another without overlapping, which can produce a darker-blue overlap due to the slight transparency of these types of decals.

Since the kit is made from solid resin, even setting it down on a soft surface can cause the paint to become slightly marred because of the sheer weight of the model. This is solved when adding decals and weathering by making a stand that supports the model from the wheel wells. A pair of 2-by-4-inch wood sections were cut and drilled, then scrap brass tubing was used to construct the stand. This allowed unrestricted access to the entire model without compromising the finish, and also reduced the possibility of fingerprints causing issues.

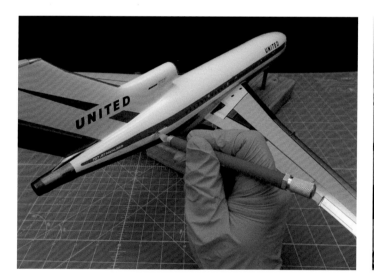
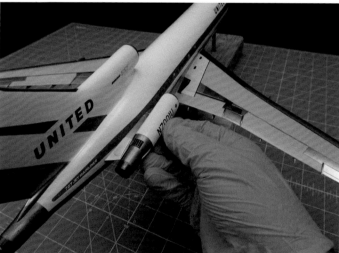

The dry fit of the engines prior to painting previously revealed an exceptionally good fit, as did the horizontal stabilizers. After the cheat line decals were in position and had been allowed to dry (very important!), a hobby knife was used to trim the decal away from the mounting holes for the pod engines. By using Insta-Cure Super Gold Foam Safe CA glue, the engine nacelles were then added. Standard CA glue can emit vapors, which discolor the surrounding areas while it cures. On painted surfaces, the use of Foam Safe CA prevents this unwanted side effect.

The horizontal stabilizers were added and the approximate 2-degree anhedral angle was verified. On my kit, they naturally sat at the correct angle without any fuss. Great engineering!

After completing the addition of the livery decals and windows, I turned my attention to providing some light weathering detail. The airplane as it sits in the museum is quite clean, so this will be fairly minimal. A mixture of 20 percent Aero Master Tire Black acrylic to 80 percent water with a drop of dish soap works well as a wash over the Pledge clear coat. Since Pledge Revive It Floor Gloss is an acrylic coating, the use of anything "hotter" than an acrylic paint as a wash, such as enamels or lacquers, will destroy the paint job, which is a less-than-desirable effect. Apply the wash with a brush and then streak it in the direction of the airflow with a dry napkin or paper towel. If this leaves too much residue, simply dampen the napkin and wipe it off. Do small sections at a time, though, because once it dries, it is difficult to remove.

One way to add panel detail and streaking is to use a pencil and card stock taped around the fuselage. However, be extremely careful not to allow the masking tape to touch the decals. Even with the clear coat added, this will likely pull up the decal and ruin the day.

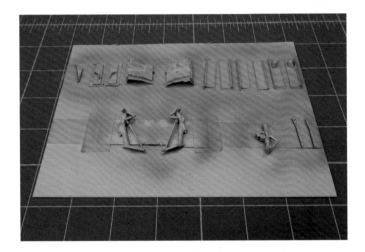

The landing gears and the interior surfaces of the gear well doors and Krueger flaps were painted with a mixture of 80 percent Classic White and 20 percent Aircraft Grey, since this mixture accurately replicates the color Boeing uses on interior structures. It was also mixed with a small amount of enamel thinner to allow it to smoothly flow through the airbrush. The outsides of the doors and Krueger flaps had already been painted Aircraft Grey and masked prior to finishing the interior portions.

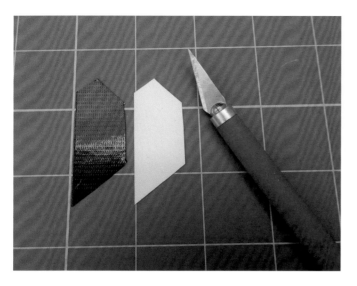

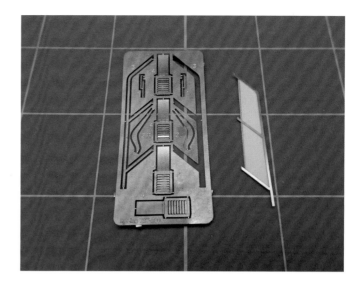

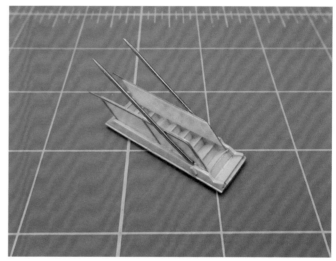

The ventral airstair detail on this kit is a nice touch, but knowing that the sidewalls of the well were lined with a heavy canvas, I elected to provide a bit of additional detail. Using a piece of thin card stock and through some measure of trial and error, the correct shapes of the sidewalls were eventually determined. The card stock shapes were then used as templates to cut out appropriately sized pieces of Gorilla Tape, which has a textured finish. Carefully, these tape pieces were installed in the compartment and then masked off with Post-it notes. The 80/20 mixture of Classic White and Aircraft Grey was then carefully sprayed into the airstair compartment, along with the wheel wells.

Authentic Airliners provided the resin airstair ramp, along with photo-etched railings. Most passenger 727s had a canvas attached to the railing for aesthetic and safety purposes. This has been replicated with cardstock and CA glued to the railings. Large needles were added to replicate the extension system, and the airstair ramp was assembled and painted with the light-gray mixture.

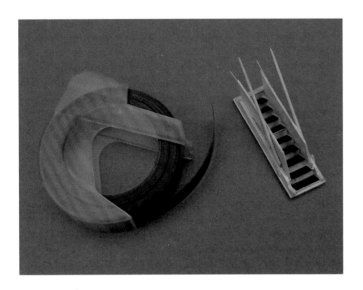

The steps on the ventral airstair were accentuated with the use of carefully cut pieces of Black Dymo labeling tape. I will not be gluing the airstair to the airframe, because it can break off during movement. Instead, I will keep it separate and simply set it into position once the model is placed for display.

For me, the most practical way to paint wheels is to first apply the hub color, which in this case was Alclad II Duraluminium. After this was allowed to dry, each wheel was mounted to a large toothpick and brush-painted with Tamiya NATO Black. The metal main landing gear legs are a necessity, given the weight of the model. I had concerns with the swept-back landing gear design and the mass of the model, but Authentic Airliners provides an extremely ingenious solution. The forward tab of the main landing gear leg slides into a recess, and then the aft portion rests on a mounting cast into the wing. These were secured with Insta-Cure Super Gold Foam Safe Cyanoacrylate glue, and the main gears are quite strong. The resin nose gear does not have to bear nearly as much weight and is situated vertically, so it is more than adequate, if not somewhat delicate. Once these were allowed to cure, the wheels were installed, ensuring the flat spots were aligned with the surface.

Aircraft tires are never completely round while bearing the weight of the aircraft. To replicate weighted tires with resin wheels, each was sanded down in one position to create the effect. Keep in mind that resin dust can be harmful, so it is advisable to use a mask during the sanding process.

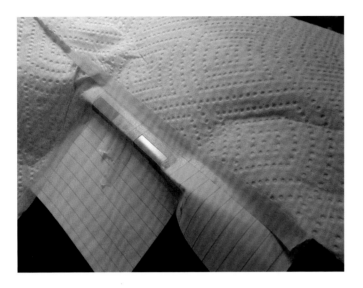

The kit includes all six Krueger flaps, which can be installed to replicate the typical drooping of these surfaces when system A hydraulic power has been removed for a few moments. On the actual aircraft, they tend to slowly extend randomly and asymmetrically. I chose to display the model featuring this trait, with various extension of panels 1, 2, 3, 4, and 6. Since there is no compartment molded into the solid resin wing, I masked the flap outlines and painted the wing surfaces NATO Black, using the airbrush to create the illusion of depth. Each flap was carefully added, using a small amount of foam-safe CA glue.

The Authentic Airliners 727 kit is certainly a high-end model kit and provides the best representation of the subtle details and curves that define the aircraft. The sheer mass and size of the model do create minor challenges, though, particularly with painting and finishing, but the result is certainly worth the effort. Because only one 727-100-series aircraft is known to have used the FedEx hush kits, they are not normally provided with the kit but are available upon request if the modeler wishes to replicate N7001U in its current configuration. An equally nice 727-200-series kit is also available in this scale from Authentic Airliners and includes both the standard and hush-kitted exhausts.

Disclaimer: Please note that this book is not sponsored, endorsed, or otherwise affiliated with any of the companies whose products are represented herein. Most of the products in this book may be covered by various copyrights, trademarks, and logotypes. Their use herein is for identification purposes only. All rights are reserved by their respective owners. The information herein is derived from the author's independent research and experience.

Glossary

aileron: Hinged surfaces attached to the trailing edges of each wing, which work in opposition to each other to effect aircraft roll control

air-conditioning pack: An air cycle machine that cools engine bleed and allows for temperature control and cabin pressurization

airplane flight manual (AFM): A manual used by the pilot to operate an air carrier aircraft

alternating current (AC): An electric current that reverses polarity a certain number of times a second. Aircraft typically use 400-cycle AC, which cycles 400 times a second.

angle of incidence: The angular difference between the chord line of a wing or stabilizer and the reference axis of the fuselage

anhedral: A tilting down toward the tips of the wing or horizontal stabilizer

automatic direction finder (ADF): A navigational instrument that displays the relative bearing of a tuned radio beacon

auxiliary power unit (APU): A small jet engine that can supply compressed air and electrical current to operate aircraft systems while the aircraft's engines are not operational. The 727 APU can also be used as a backup in case of aircraft systems failures while on the ground.

bypass ratio: The volume of air that bypasses a jet engine core compared to the volume that is involved with the combustion process in the engine core

camber: The curvature of a wing surface with relation to the camber line

CAR 4b: The set of regulations pertaining to the certification of American air carrier aircraft prior to 1967

cathode ray tube (CRT): A vacuum tube type of display that produces an image when an electron beam strikes a phosphorescent surface, similar to older-generation computer screens

center of gravity (CG): A calculated balance point of an aircraft, which can change depending on the loading and distribution of weight onboard

checkride: A qualification test for pilots that usually involves a knowledge test and a simulator or aircraft flight evaluation

chord line: A theoretical line extending from the leading edge to the trailing edge of an airfoil

Civil Aviation Authority (CAA): A British government entity responsible for overseeing aviation activities

cockpit voice recorder (CVR): An audio recorder that operates on multiple channels in an aircraft cockpit, used for incident investigation purposes. Normally, the CVR is powered any time normal electrical power is supplied to the aircraft systems.

compressor stall: Sometimes referred to as an engine surge, this condition causes the reversal of airflow in a jet engine, leading to a temporary loss of thrust.

constant-speed drive (CSD): A drive mechanism that rotates an electrical generator at constant RPM, regardless of the input drive speed

cruciform tail: An empennage design where the horizontal stabilizers are mounted to the vertical stabilizer at midsection, above the fuselage

cyanoacrylate glue (CA glue): A fast-acting adhesive used for household, medical, and hobby uses

deep stall (also known as a "locked-in stall" or "super stall"): An aggravated aerodynamic stall where the turbulent airflow over the wings and rear-mounted engines blanks out an aircraft's elevators, which makes recovery difficult, if not impossible

dihedral: An upward angle of a wing from the root to the tip, which provides stability in roll control

direct current (DC): Electrical current that flows in only one direction

drag: An aerodynamic force that resists an object's movement through a fluid (air)

Dutch roll: An alternating rolling and yawing motion typical of swept-wing or short-coupled aircraft.

effectivity number: An alphanumeric code used internally within Boeing to identify a specific aircraft by its build specification. This convention started with the Boeing 727 Prototype, which had Effectivity Number E1.

elevator: Flight control surfaces hinged to the trailing edges of an airplane's horizontal stabilizers, used to effect pitch (nose up and down) control of an aircraft

engine pressure ratio (EPR): The pressure ratio between the exhaust nozzle and inlet of a jet engine, which can be used to quantify engine thrust

explosive decompression: An aircraft cabin depressurization that occurs suddenly and often leads to major structural damage. This can also cause lung damage and other physiological trauma to an aircraft's occupants.

flap asymmetry: A condition where the trailing edge flaps on a wing are not deployed to the same position as the other, creating a rolling and yawing moment

flap, leading edge "Krueger": A small flap that deploys forward from underneath the leading edge of the wing and is used to increase lift at low airspeeds

flap, trailing edge "Fowler": A type of trailing edge flap that slides rearward and down, increasing lift by expanding the effective wing area and increasing camber

flight data recorder (FDR): A device that records aircraft parameters for research and incident investigations

flutter: An aerodynamic vibration that can cause structural damage and is most commonly experienced at very high airspeeds

Fowler flap: A trailing edge flap design that extends both aft and down to increase wing area when deployed

fuse plug: A small plug on an aircraft's wheel assembly that melts at very high temperatures, as with extremely hot brake assemblies. When melted, the fuse plug allows a tire to deflate in a rapid but controlled manner, thus preventing the tire from exploding.

fuselage: The main body of an aircraft, which is used to carry passengers, cargo, and sometimes fuel

glide slope: A final-approach descent path, normally defined by a radio beam signal

head-up display (HUD) and **head-up guidance system** (HGS): A glass surface located between the pilot's eyes and the windshield, upon which flight instrument data is projected

HF (high frequency): A radio that uses frequencies that are usable over very long distances and do not require line of sight for reception

horizontal situation indicator (HSI): An instrument that combines heading and VOR/Localizer/ILS indications into a single unit, typically located below the attitude indicator

horizontal stabilizer: An aerodynamic surface normally mounted horizontally on the rear portion of an aircraft, which creates aircraft stability in pitch (nose up and down)

hydraulic system: A hydromechanical aircraft system commonly used to actuate primary and secondary flight controls as well as landing gear systems

instrument landing system (ILS): A navigation system used for landing that consists of radio beams both for lateral and vertical navigation to the touchdown point on a runway

instrument meteorological conditions (IMC): Weather conditions limiting visibility to the point where the aircraft must be controlled by the use of instrumentation instead of visually with outside references

Krueger flap: *See* flap, leading edge "Krueger"

localizer: A radio beam that aligns an aircraft with the final-approach course to a specific runway

LORAN (long-range navigation): Widely used for long distance navigation prior to the advent of GPS

Mach number: The ratio of an aircraft's velocity to the speed of sound. For example, Mach 0.79 would represent 79 percent of the speed of sound.

master caution system: A system designed to warn pilots of non-normal conditions and situations

mean aerodynamic chord (MAC): A measurement of the average length of the aerodynamic lifting surface, expressed as a percentage for weight and balance purposes

minimum equipment list (MEL): A document approved by the administrator that allows flight with certain inoperative equipment

Mmo: Maximum certified Mach number

mode control panel (MCP): An interface between the pilot and the aircraft's autopilots and flight directors, allowing the selection of different modes of operation

nondirectional beacon (NDB): A low-to-medium-frequency (190 to 1750 kHz) transmitter used for navigation in conjunction with an automatic direction finder (ADF)

P-static: A static-electricity buildup on an airframe due to the effects of precipitation

parasite drag: Aerodynamic resistance not associated with the generation of lift

pitch: The up or down movement of the nose of an aircraft while in flight

pitot-static system: An aircraft system that provides airspeed and altitude information by sampling ram air pressure and static air pressure for use with cockpit instrumentation and onboard aircraft systems

power plant: An aircraft engine used for the generation of thrust

precession (gyro): A change in the orientation of the axis of a gyroscope, such as an aircraft-heading indicator (directional gyro) over time. Slowly, gyros that are not slaved to a compass will eventually become inaccurate over long periods of time unless corrected periodically.

primary flight display (PFD): A modern flight instrument arrangement that combines all major fight instruments into a single EFIS-based display

rejected takeoff (RTO): A maneuver in which a takeoff is terminated and the aircraft brought to a complete stop on the runway.

roll: The motion of the aircraft tilting from side to side, also known as "banking." Airplanes use roll control to make directional changes to the flight path.

rudder: A control surface attached to the vertical stabilizer of an airplane, which controls the "yaw" (or nose side-to-side motion) of an aircraft

runway visual range (RVR): Horizontal visibility along a specific runway, expressed in feet or meters

slat, leading edge: A high-lift device that extends from the top of the leading edge of a wing and allows the aircraft to be operated at much-slower airspeeds, typically used for takeoff and landing

spoiler: A panel located on the upper surface of a wing that, when deployed, "spoils" the airflow, thus reducing lift and increasing aerodynamic drag

stall (aerodynamic): A condition where the angle between the chord line of a wing and the passing air (angle of attack) becomes excessive, resulting in a turbulent airflow pattern on the wing and an attendant loss of lift

stall characteristic: A term that describes the handling tendencies of an aircraft during an aerodynamic stall

T-tail: A popular tail design that employs a horizontal stabilizer mounted on the upper tip of the vertical stabilizer

tau: A concept that allows the calculation of slant range between two aircraft, divided by the closure rate

thrust: Jet engine power, normally measured in pounds-force or kilonewtons

thrust reverser: A device that deflects jet engine thrust or fan air forward to aid in slowing an aircraft during landing or a rejected takeoff

transformer-rectifier: An electrical component that converts alternating current (AC) into direct current (DC) power

transonic: A range of speed close to the speed of sound

turbine: The section of a jet engine that converts energy from exhaust gases into rotational force to drive the engine's compressors, fan section, and accessory drives

turbofan engine (or fan jet): A subset of jet engines in which some of the air pulled into the intake bypasses the engine's core and is used for thrust

turbojet: A turbine engine that develops thrust solely from jet exhaust, without the use of a propeller or fan air bypass

turboprop: A type of power plant that uses a turbine engine to drive a propeller

type certificate data sheet: A specification that the FAA uses as a basis for the certification of an aircraft

type inspection authorization (TIA): An authorization granted once an aircraft manufacturer has demonstrated an aircraft type's compliance with regulations, allowing progression toward aircraft certification

V1: A calculated takeoff performance speed that is sometimes referred to as "decision speed" and is a speed below which a takeoff can be safely rejected, and above which it can be safely continued with an engine failure. This speed must be between Vmcg and Vbe.

Vbe: The maximum speed at which the aircraft can be stopped without exceeding brake energy limits

Vd: Maximum design speed, which is well in excess of Vmo

vertical stabilizer: The vertical component of an aircraft's tail that stabilizes the aircraft in "yaw" (or nose side to side) and incorporates the aircraft's rudder, hinged to the trailing edge of the surface

Vmcg: Minimum directional control speed on the ground with a critical engine failed, with the remaining engine(s) at full power

Vmo: The maximum airspeed at which an aircraft is certified to be flown during normal flight

Vmu: The minimum airspeed at which an aircraft can lift off. This speed is substantially less than the normal takeoff speed for a given set of conditions.

vortex generator: A small aerodynamic vane used to energize the boundary layer on aircraft surfaces. On the Boeing 727, vortex generators are used on the vertical stabilizer and the center engine inlet to stabilize airflow.

Vr: The airspeed at which the nose is raised during a normal takeoff

Vs: Aerodynamic stall speed

water injection: Water that is injected into the jet pipe of a jet engine will turn to steam, expand rapidly, and create additional thrust. This was commonly used on first-generation turbojet engines for takeoff and initial climb.

whirl mode: A phenomenon in which the aircraft's natural aerodynamic frequency comes into phase with that of an aircraft's propellers, leading to aircraft structural damage

yaw: A nose side-to-side motion of an aircraft

Bibliography

Books

Andrade, Martin, Jr., and Martin Andrade Sr. *Finding D. B. Cooper: Chasing the Last Lead in America's only Unsolved Skyjacking.* Scotts Valley, CA: CreateSpace, 2016.

Ballantine, Colin. *Tupolev Tu-154.* Shrewsbury, UK: Airlife, 1995.

Barbier, Doug. *World's Fastest Single-Engine Jet Aircraft: The Story of Convair's F-106 Delta Dart Interceptor.* Forest Lake, MN: Specialty Press, 2017.

Boeing Airplane Company. *Boeing 727C General Description.* Seattle, WA: Boeing, 1965

Boeing Airplane Company. *Boeing 727 Operations Manual.* Seattle, WA: Boeing, 1975.

Boeing Airplane Company. *Boeing 727 QC Operations Manual.* Seattle, WA: Boeing, 1965.

Boeing Airplane Company. *Boeing 737-300/-400/-500 Advance Maintenance Manual.* Seattle, WA: Boeing, 1989.

Boeing Airplane Company. *Continental Airlines Boeing 727 Flight Manual.* Seattle, WA: Boeing, 1982.

Boeing Airplane Company. *Servicing the Boeing 727 Aircraft: Maintenance and Engineering Training (TWA).* Seattle, WA: Boeing, 1984.

British European Airways. *Hawker Siddeley Trident (1C) Operations Manual.* London: British European Airways, 1964.

Cearley, George, Jr. *Boeing 707 and 720: A Pictorial History.* Dallas: Cearley, 1993.

Convair Aircraft Company. *Convair 880 Airframe and Powerplant Handbook.* San Diego, CA: Convair, 1960.

Convair Aircraft Company. *Convair 880 Operations Manual.* San Diego, CA: Convair, 1961.

Darling, Kev. *De Havilland Comet.* Wiltshire, UK: Crowood, 2005.

Dornseif, Dan. *Boeing 737: The World's Jetliner.* Atglen, PA: Schiffer, 2017.

Duffy, Paul, and Andrei Kandalov. *Tupolev: The Man and His Aircraft.* Warrendale, PA: SAE International, 1996.

Germain, Scott E. *Lockheed Constellation and Super Constellation.* North Branch, MN: Specialty Press, 1999

Gordon, Yefim, Dmitriy Komissarov, and Sergey Komissarov. *OKB Yakovlev: A History of the Design Bureau and Its Aircraft.* Hinckley, UK: Midland, 2005

Green, William, Gordon Swanborough, and John Mowinski. *Modern Commercial Aircraft.* New York: Portland House, 1987.

Habermehl, C. Mike, and Robert S. Hopkins III. *Boeing B-47 Stratojet: Strategic Air Command's Transitional Bomber.* Manchester, UK: Crecy, 2018.

Hassan II. *The Challenge: The Memoirs of King Hassan II of Morocco.* London: Macmillan, 1977.

Henely, Steve. *The Avionics Handbook.* Boca Raton, FL: CRC, 2001.

Howard, Terris. *United 727 N7001U: The Restoration and Last Flight.* Columbia, SC: Terris Howard, 2019.

Kingsley-Jones, Max. *Classic Civil Aircraft 5: Hawker Siddeley Trident.* Surrey, UK: Ian Allen, 1993.

Komissarov, Dmitriy. *Tupolev Tu-154: The USSR's Medium-Range Jet Airliner.* Hinckley, UK: AeroFax, 2007.

Mansfield, Harold. *Billion Dollar Battle.* New York: David McKay, 1965.

Moktadier, John A. *Boeing 727 Flight Master.* Bloomington, IN: Author House, 2004.

Morgan, Len, and Terry Morgan. *The Boeing 727 Scrapbook.* Fallbrook, CA: Aero, 1978.

Pacific Southwest Airlines. *Boeing 727 Checklists.* San Diego, CA: PSA, 1975.

Pearcy, Arthur. *McDonnell Douglas MD-80 and MD-90.* Osceola, WI: MBI, 1999.

Peeler, Jodie, *Douglas DC-9/MD-80.* Carrollton, TX: Squadron Signal, 2007.

Powers, David G. *Great Airliners, Volume Five: Lockheed 188 Electra.* Miami, FL: World Transport, 1999.

Powers, David G. *Lockheed L-188 Electra.* Miami, FL: World Transport, 1999.

Proctor, Jon. *Convair 880 and 990.* Great Airliners 1. Miami, FL: World Transport, 1996.

Proctor, Jon. *Boeing 720.* Great Airliners 7. Miami, FL: World Transport, 2001.

Rolls-Royce. *Rolls-Royce RB.163 Aero Engines for the de Havilland Trident.* Derby, UK: Rolls-Royce, 1960.

Simons, Graham M. *Comet! The World's First Jetliner.* London: Pen and Sword, 2013.

Skinner, Stephen. *Classic Airliner: The Hawker Siddeley Trident.* Lincolnshire, UK: Key, 2014.

Testrake, John, and David J. Wimbish. *Triumph over Terror on Flight 847.* Old Tappan, NJ: Revell, 1987.

Trans World Airlines. *Boeing 727 Flight Handbook.* Revision 135. Kansas City, MO: Trans World Airlines, 1988.

Wallick, Rebecca. *Growing Up Boeing.* Lynnwood, WA: Maian Meadows, 2014.

Zimmermann, B. Christian. *Hostage in a Hostage World.* St. Louis, MO: Concordia Publishing House, 1985.

Websites

www.aerosavvy.com/ups-727-passenger-flights/
www.aircraftdemolition.com/news/94-3-boeing-727-100-recycled-by-aircraft-demolition-llc
www.airlinercafe.com
www.aviation-safety.net
www.boeing.com
www.boeing.com/commercial/727family/index.html
www.historynet.com/homesick-angel-last-flight-da-nang.htm
www.lessonslearned.faa.gov
www.planelogger.com
www.quietwing.com/winglet/
www.rzjets.net

Unpublished Works

Boeing Aircraft Company. "727 Structures, Design and Structural Test Program." Boeing Archives, 1961.

Boeing Aircraft Company. "Boeing 737-300 Program" (file 2882/10). Boeing Archives, June 1974.

Boeing Aircraft Company. "E001 Test Flight Notes and Post Flight Briefings." Boeing Archives, 1963–64.

Boeing Aircraft Company. "Flight Test Daily Activity Reports." Boeing Archives, 1963–64.

Boeing Aircraft Company. "Flight Test Monthly Summaries." Boeing Archives, 1963–64.

Boeing Aircraft Company. "Model 727-300-S15H & 200B-S58A" (file 2882/1). Boeing Archives, June 1974.

Boeing Aircraft Company. "N7002U (E002) Sales Evaluation Tour and High-Altitude Testing File." Boeing Archives, 1963.

Boeing Airplane Company. "757 & 767 Program Review: PSA." Boeing Archives, March 1980.

Boeing Airplane Company. "Retrofit of Advanced 727 Features." Boeing Archives, February 1971.

Federal Aviation Administration. "Boeing 727 Type Certificate Data Sheet A3WE." Federal Aviation Agency, December 24, 1963.

Steiner, Jack. "History of the 727-200 Long Body Aircraft." Boeing Archives, 1965.

Steiner, Jack. "Managing the Technical Development of the 727." Boeing Archives, 1962.

Steiner, Jack. "Serling/Steiner Interview." Unpublished manuscript, Boeing Archives, 1990.

Steiner, Jack. "Wilson/Steiner Interview." Unpublished manuscript, Boeing Archives, 1988.

Published Articles, Essays, and Reports

Boeing Airplane Company. "727-300 General Description." Boeing Archives, 1969.

Boeing Airplane Company. "727 Jet Liner Drawings & Diagrams." Boeing Archives, ca. 1961.

Boeing Airplane Company. "727 Product Development Program." Boeing Archives, 1971.

Boeing Airplane Company. "727 QC General Description." Boeing Archives, 1965.

Boeing Airplane Company. "727 Structures Design and Structural Test Program." Boeing Archives, October 1961.

Boeing Airplane Company. "Boeing 727-200 General Description." Boeing Archives, April 1966.

Boeing Airplane Company. "Boeing 727-200 General Description D6-24004." Boeing Archives, 1968.

Boeing Airplane Company. "New Interior Program." Boeing Archives, 1969.

Burgess, Malcolm, Dean Davis, Walter Hollister, and John A. Sorensen. "Traffic Alert and Collision Avoidance System (TCAS)—Cockpit Display of Traffic Information (CDTI) Investigation: Phase I Feasibility Study." Federal Aviation Administration, April 1991.

Civil Aeronautics Board. "CAB Aircraft Accident Report: Braniff Airways Lockheed Electra, N9705C." Civil Aeronautics Board, May 5, 1961.

Civil Aeronautics Board. "CAB Aircraft Accident Report: Northwest Airlines Lockheed Electra N121US," Civil Aeronautics Board, April 28, 1961.

Dunsire, Charles. "Maiden Flight of Jetliner Draws Praise." *Seattle Post-Intelligencer*, February 9, 1963.

Federal Aviation Administration. "Active Beacon Collision Avoidance System (BCAS) Conference." FAA, January 1981.

Federal Aviation Administration. "Advisory Circular 00-54." Federal Aviation Administration, November 1988.

Federal Aviation Administration. "Introduction to TCAS II, Version 7.1." FAA, 2011.

Fredrickson, John. "Resurrecting a 727." Independent article, 2016.

Hullett, Alysa. "Kenneth Holtby, Major Designer of Boeing Aircraft, Dies." *Seattle Times*, April 18, 2013.

International Civil Aviation Organization. "Manual on Low Level Windshear—First Edition." ICAO, 2005.

Kanellis, George. "Payload Capability Analysis, Allentown–Chicago, United Airlines 727-300B." Boeing, 1975.

Munoz, Cesar, Anthony Narkawicz, and James Chamberlain. "A TCAS-II Resolution Advisory Detection Algorithm." NASA Langley Research Center, 2013.

National Transportation Safety Board. "Aircraft Accident Report: Trans World Airlines Inc., Boeing 727-31, N840TW." National Transportation Safety Board, 1979.

National Transportation Safety Board. "Aircraft Accident Report NTSB AAR 68 AJ." National Transportation Safety Board, September 5, 1968.

National Transportation Safety Board. "Continental Air Lines Inc., Boeing 727-224, N88777, Stapleton Int'l Airport, Denver, Colorado, August 7, 1975, Aircraft Accident Report." National Transportation Safety Board, May 5, 1976.

National Transportation Safety Board. "LEAP Lockheed Electra Action Program Findings Document," National Transportation Safety Board, September 15, 1960.

National Transportation Safety Board. "National Transportation Safety Board Final Report—Pacific Southwest 182 (AAR-79-05)," National Transportation Safety Board, 1979.

National Transportation Safety Board. "National Transportation Safety Board Final Report—United 663," National Transportation Safety Board, 1984.

Pratt & Whitney. "JT8D Turbofans." Hartford, CT: Pratt & Whitney, 1974.

Rinearson, Peter. "Making It Fly" (parts 1–8). *Seattle Times*, June 19–26, 1983.

Steiner, Jack. "Case Study in Aircraft Design: The Boeing 727." Reston, VA: American Institute of Aeronautics and Astronautics, 1978.

Steiner, Jack. "The 727 Story: Presentation to the American Institute of Aeronautics and Astronautics." Seattle, WA: Boeing, 1963.

Twiss, Robert. "Future of 727-300 Depends on One Airline's Decision." *Seattle Times*, September 15, 1974.

Williams, Ed. "Airborne Collision Avoidance System." Canberra, Australia, n.d.

Media and Videos

King Schools 727 Systems Course. San Diego, CA: King Schools, ca. 1980.

Index